Viz Graphic Novel

OF RECCA™

Vol. 8

Story & Art by Nobuyuki Anzai

Contents

Flame of Recca
Vol. 8
Action Edition

Story and Art by
Nobuyuki Anzai

English Adaptation/Lance Caselman
Translation/Joe Yamazaki
Touch-Up & Lettering/Kelle Han
Graphics & Cover Design/Sean Lee
Editors/Eric Searleman & Yuki Takagaki

Managing Editor/Annette Roman
Editorial Director/Alvin Lu
Production Manager/Noboru Watanabe
Sr. Director of Licensing & Acquisitions/Rika Inouye
Vice President of Sales/Joe Morici
Vice President of Marketing/Liza Coppola
Executive Vice President/Hyoe Narita
Publisher/Seiji Horibuchi

Published by VIZ, LLC
P.O. Box 77064
San Francisco, CA 94107

Action Edition
10 9 8 7 6 5 4 3 2 1
First Published, September 2004

For advertising rates or media kit, e-mail advertising@viz.com

store.viz.com

www.viz.com

ANIMERICA
ANIME & MANGA MONTHLY
www.animerica-mag.com

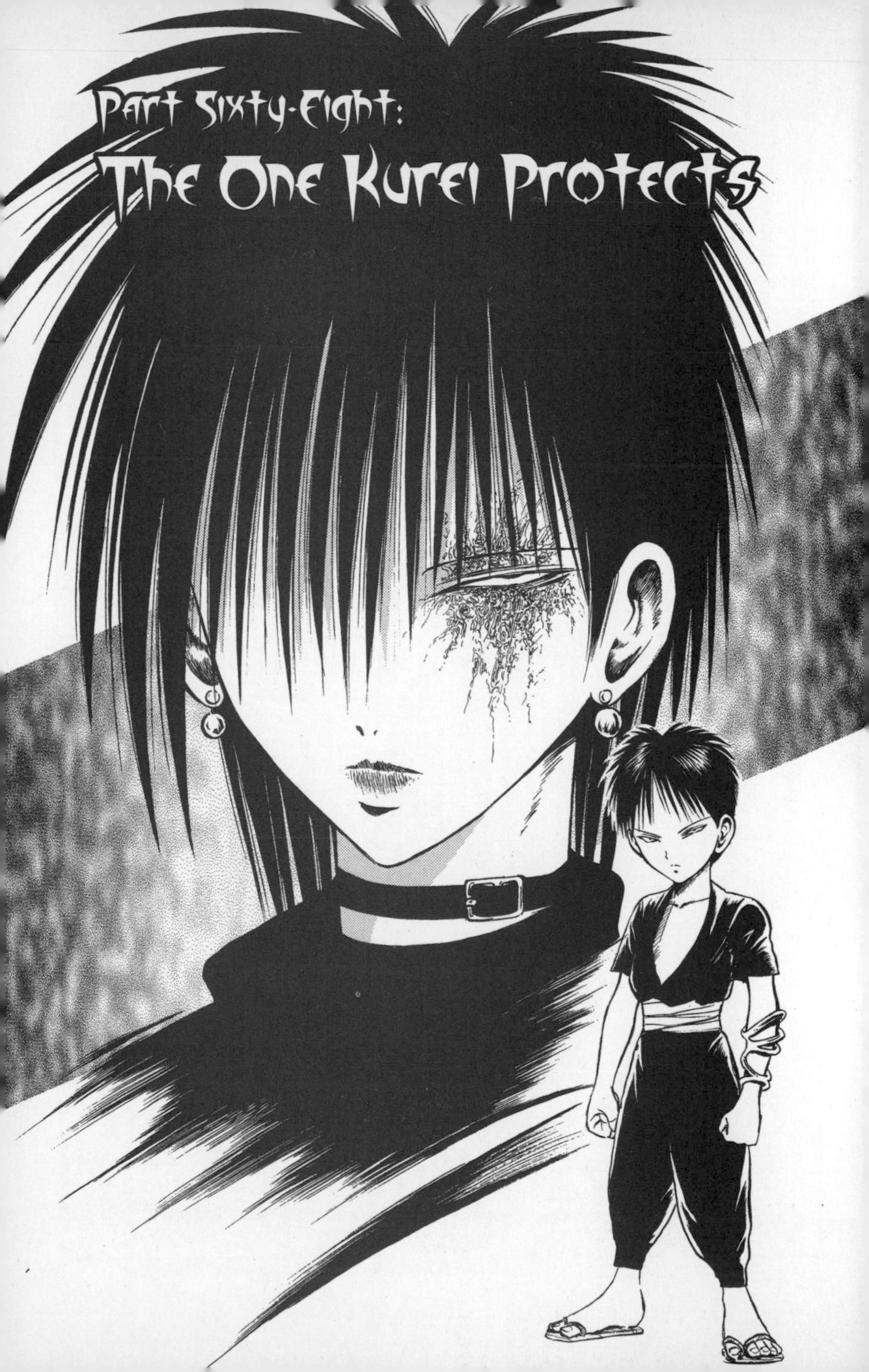
Part Sixty-Eight:
The One Kurei Protects

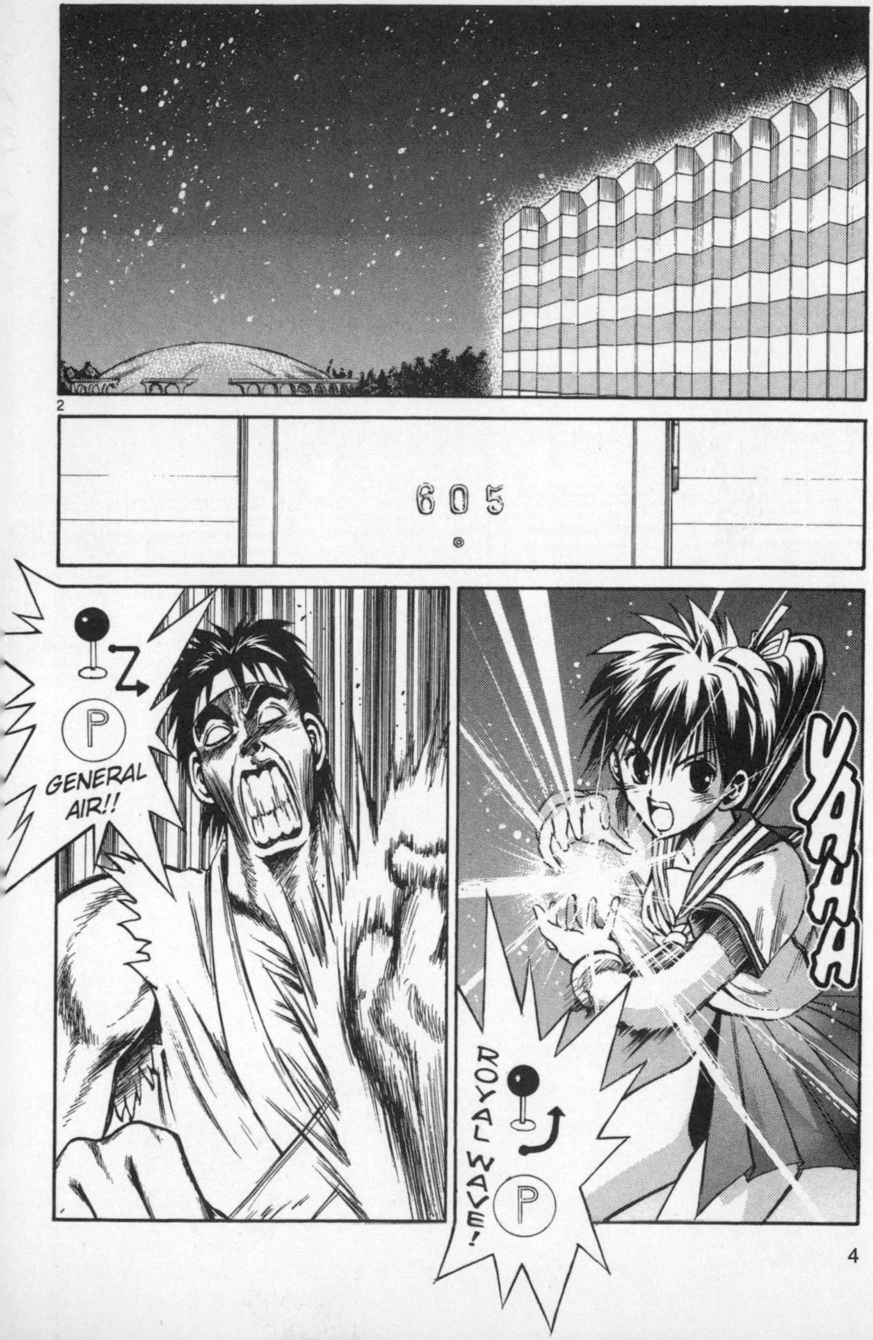
605
YAHHA
P
ROYAL WAVE!
P
GENERAL AIR!!

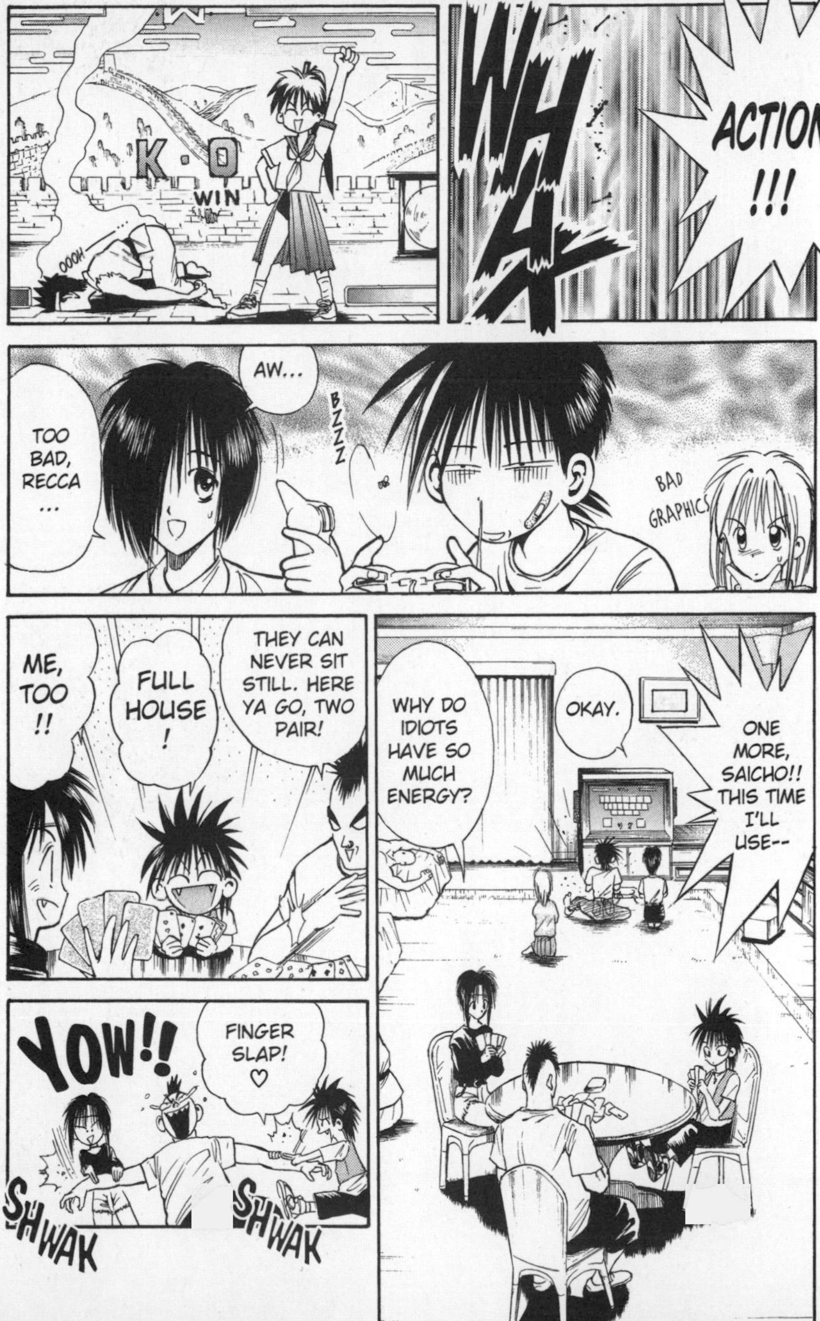
ACTION !!!
WHA
K.O
WIN
OOOH
...
BAD GRAPHICS
BZZZ
AW...
TOO BAD, RECCA ...
ONE MORE, SAICHO!! THIS TIME I'LL USE--
OKAY.
WHY DO IDIOTS HAVE SO MUCH ENERGY?
THEY CAN NEVER SIT STILL. HERE YA GO, TWO PAIR!
FULL HOUSE !
ME, TOO !!
FINGER SLAP! ♡
YOW!!
SHWAK
SHWAK

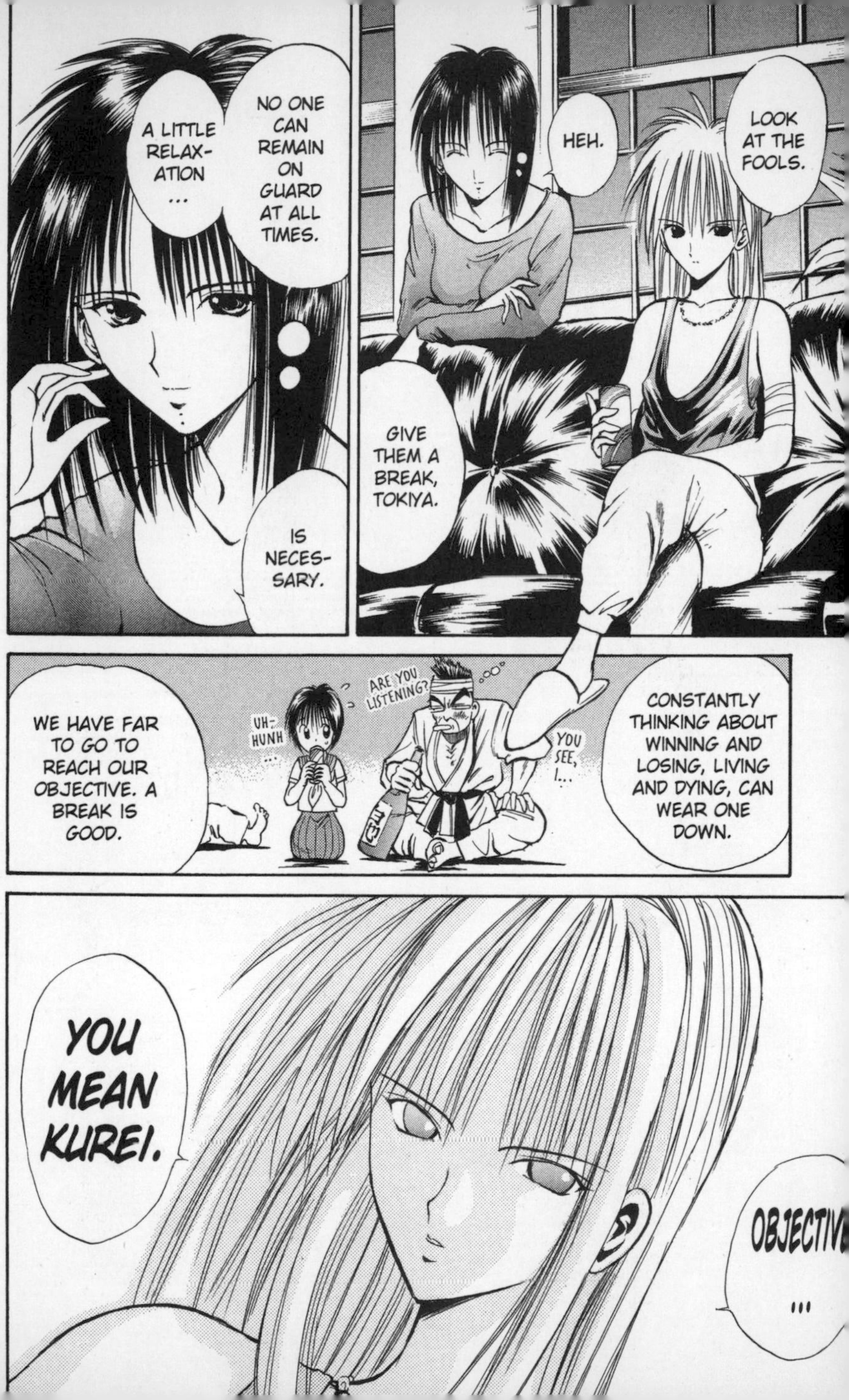
LOOK AT THE FOOLS.
HEH.
GIVE THEM A BREAK, TOKIYA.
NO ONE CAN REMAIN ON GUARD AT ALL TIMES.
A LITTLE RELAXATION ...
IS NECESSARY.
CONSTANTLY THINKING ABOUT WINNING AND LOSING, LIVING AND DYING, CAN WEAR ONE DOWN.
YOU SEE, I...
ARE YOU LISTENING?
UH-HUNH ...
WE HAVE FAR TO GO TO REACH OUR OBJECTIVE. A BREAK IS GOOD.
OBJECTIVE ...
YOU MEAN KUREI.

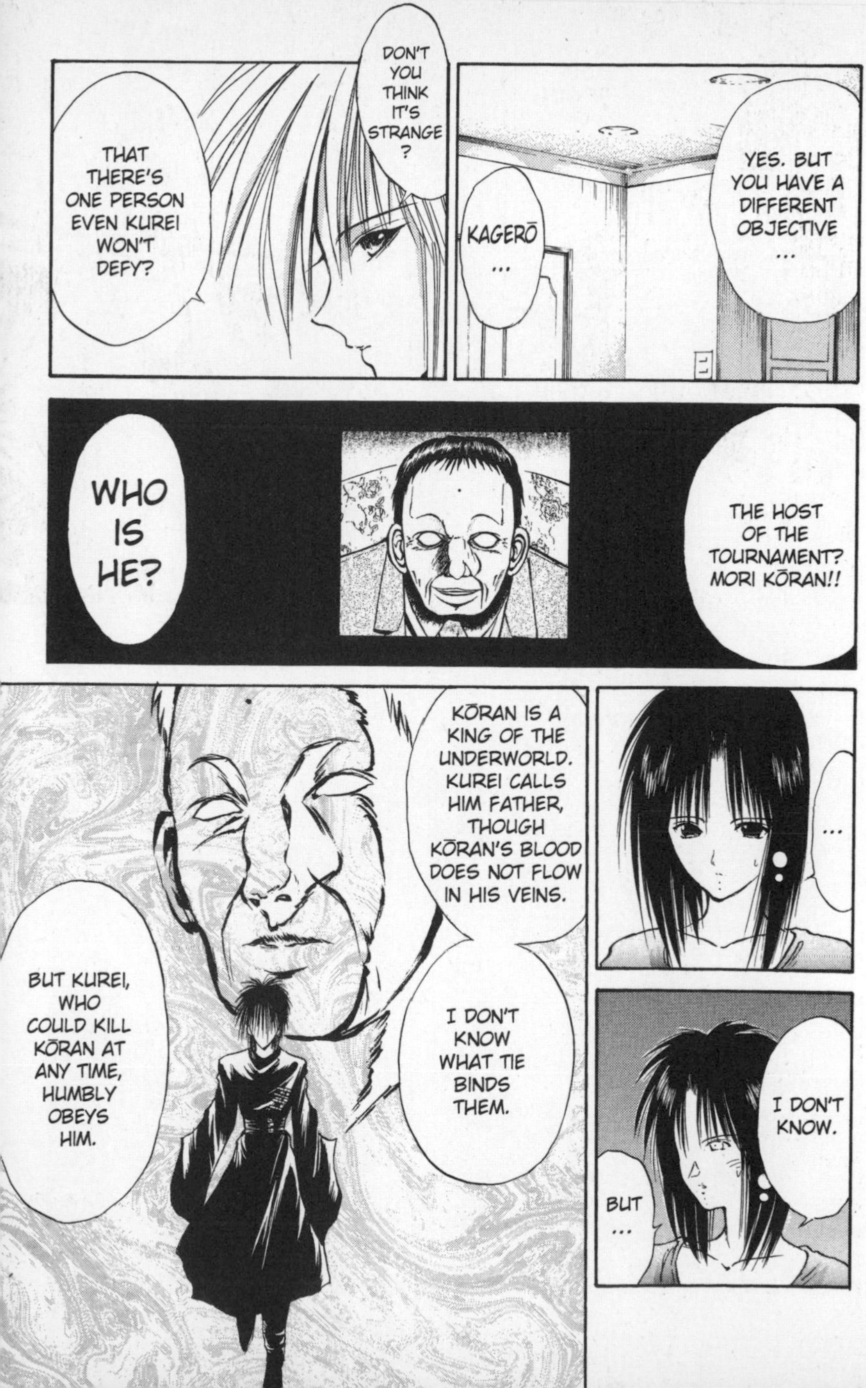
YES. BUT YOU HAVE A DIFFERENT OBJECTIVE ...
KAGERŌ ...
DON'T YOU THINK IT'S STRANGE ?
THAT THERE'S ONE PERSON EVEN KUREI WON'T DEFY?
THE HOST OF THE TOURNAMENT? MORI KŌRAN!!
WHO IS HE?
...
I DON'T KNOW.
BUT ...
KŌRAN IS A KING OF THE UNDERWORLD. KUREI CALLS HIM FATHER, THOUGH KŌRAN'S BLOOD DOES NOT FLOW IN HIS VEINS.
BUT KUREI, WHO COULD KILL KŌRAN AT ANY TIME, HUMBLY OBEYS HIM.
I DON'T KNOW WHAT TIE BINDS THEM.

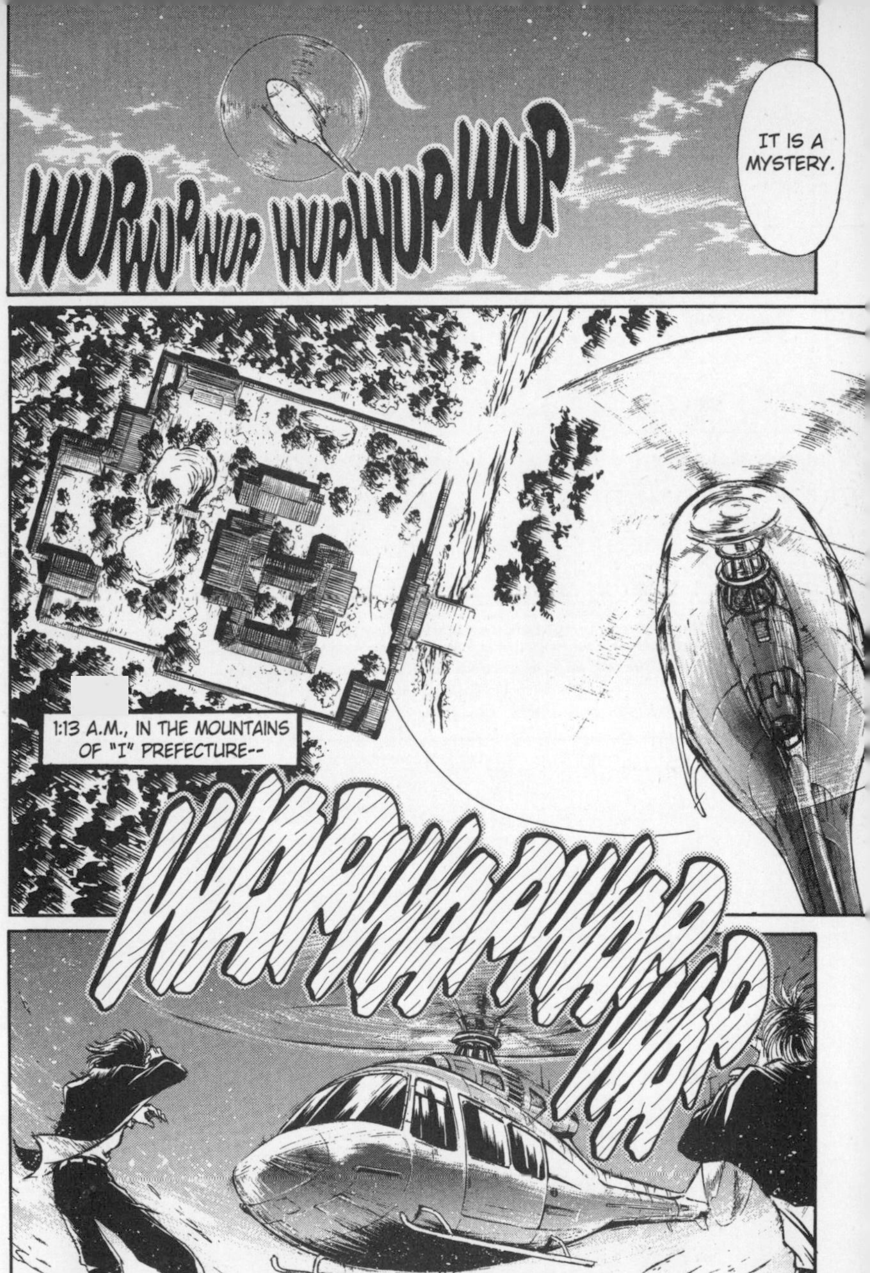
IT IS A MYSTERY.
WUPWUPWUP WUPWUPWUP
1:13 A.M., IN THE MOUNTAINS OF "I" PREFECTURE--

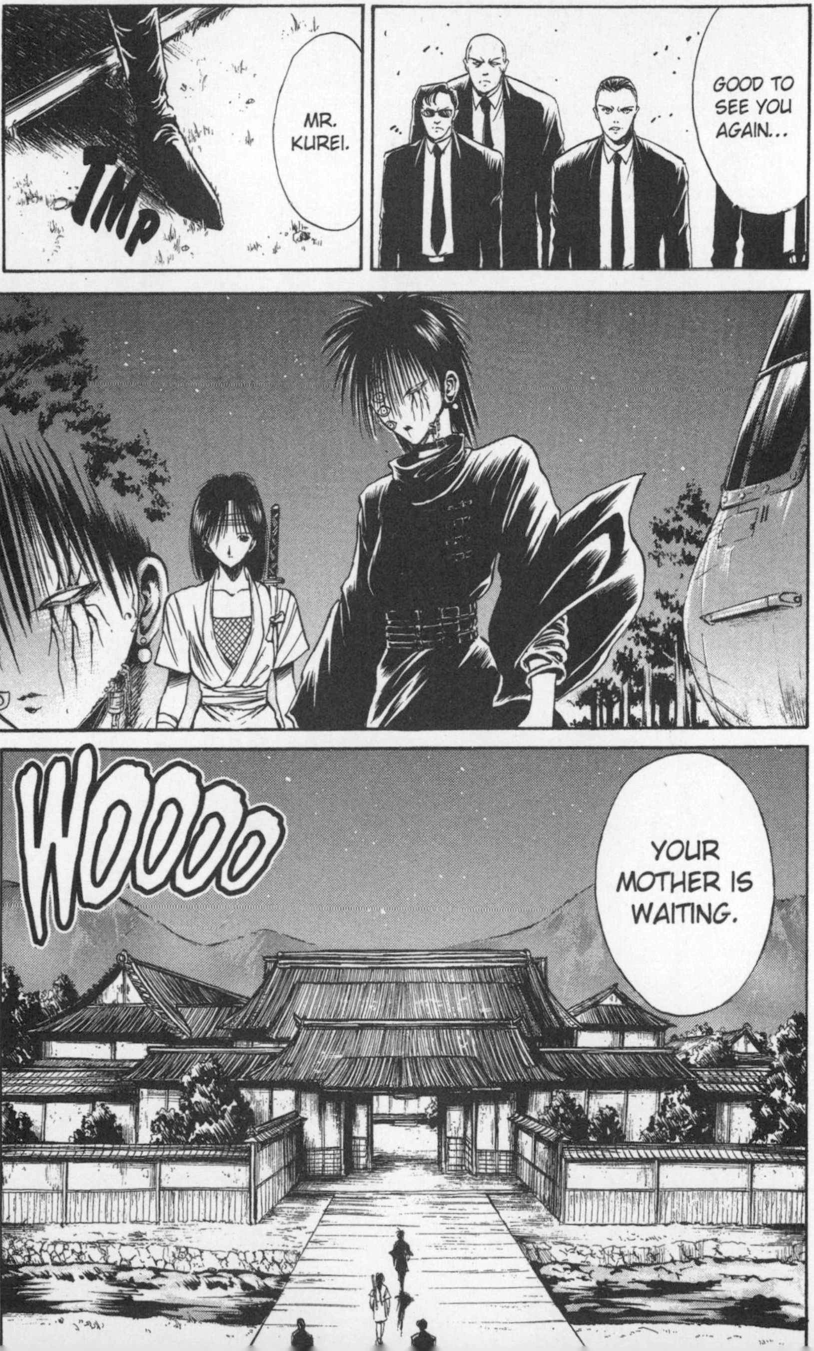
GOOD TO SEE YOU AGAIN...
MR. KUREI.
TMP
YOUR MOTHER IS WAITING.
WOOOO

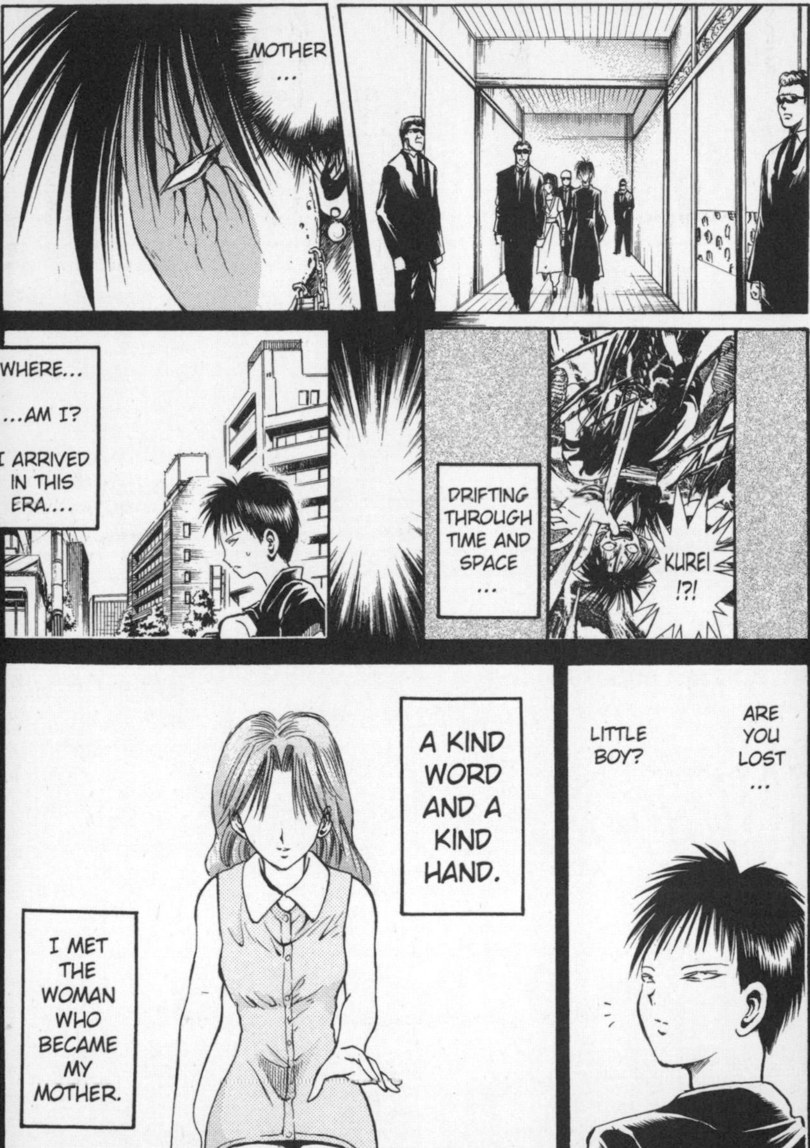
MOTHER ...
KUREI !?!
DRIFTING THROUGH TIME AND SPACE ...
WHERE...
...AM I?
I ARRIVED IN THIS ERA....
ARE YOU LOST ...
LITTLE BOY?
A KIND WORD AND A KIND HAND.
I MET THE WOMAN WHO BECAME MY MOTHER.

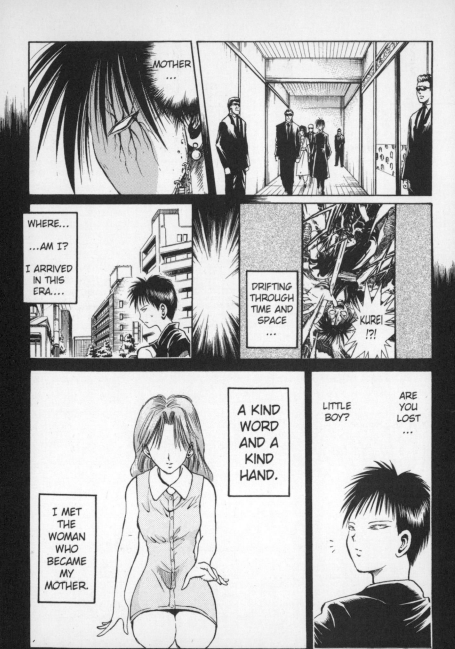

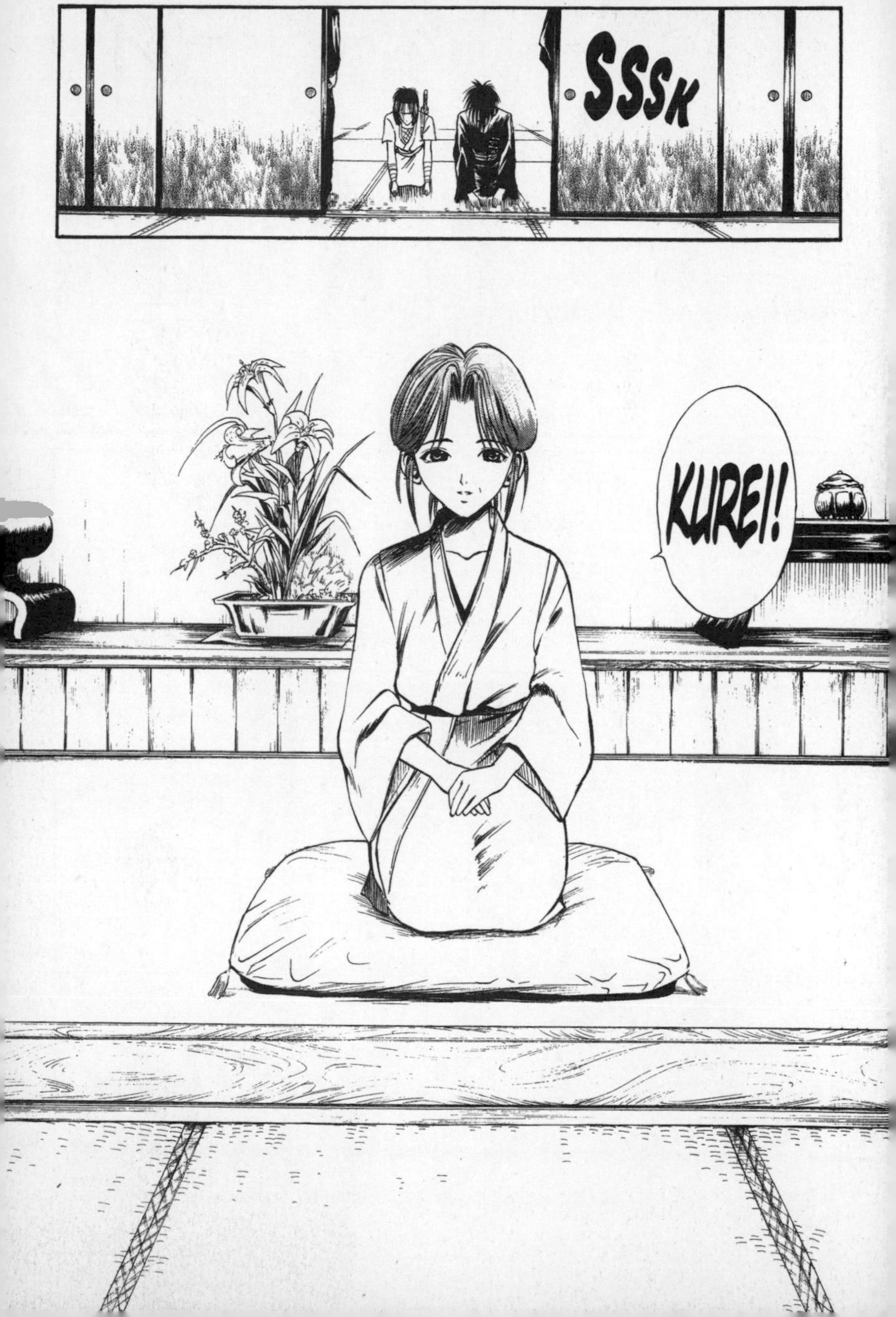
SSSK
KUREI!

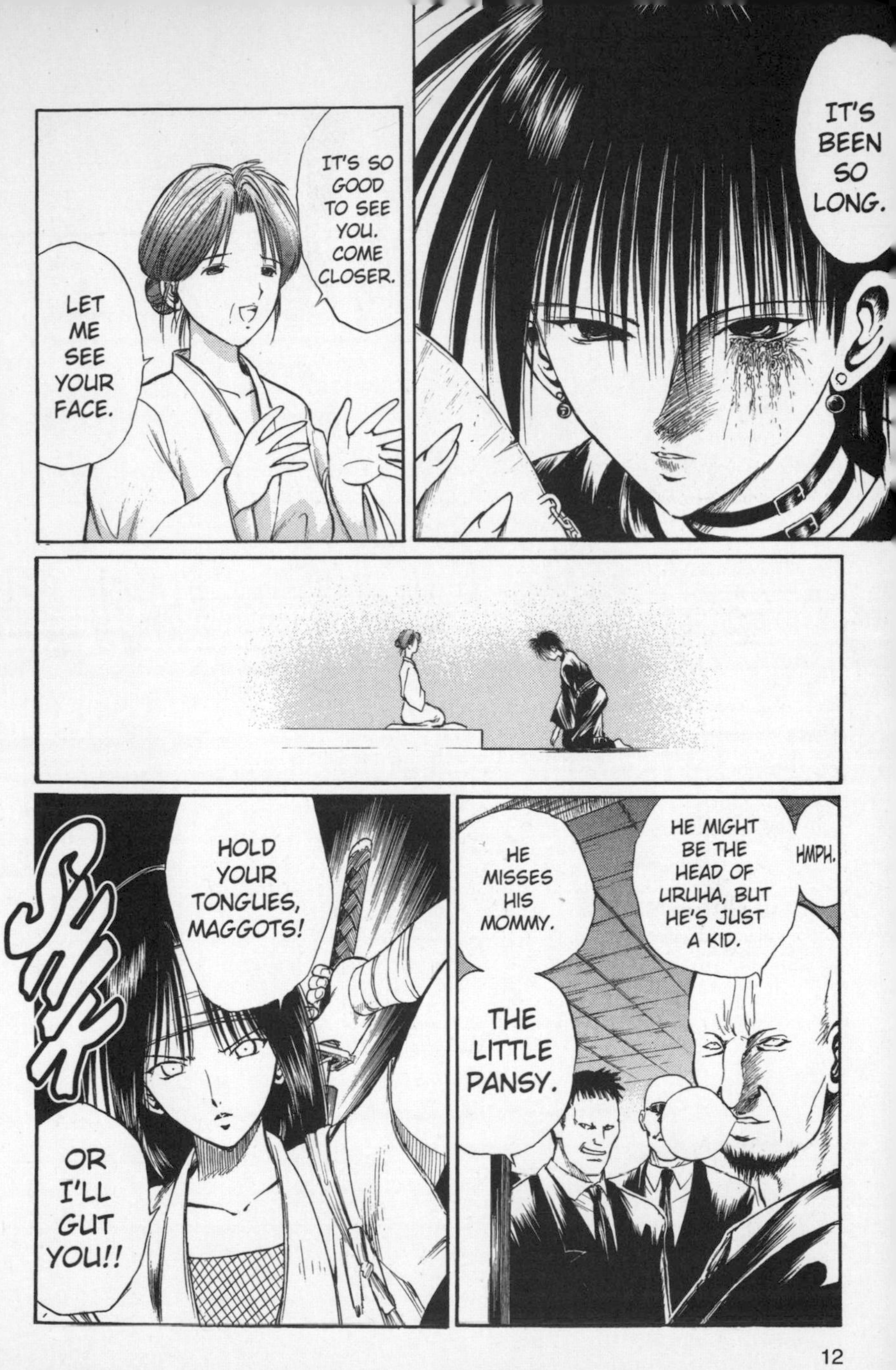
IT'S BEEN SO LONG.
IT'S SO GOOD TO SEE YOU. COME CLOSER.
LET ME SEE YOUR FACE.
HMPH.
HE MIGHT BE THE HEAD OF URUHA, BUT HE'S JUST A KID.
HE MISSES HIS MOMMY.
THE LITTLE PANSY.
HOLD YOUR TONGUES, MAGGOTS!
SHK
OR I'LL GUT YOU!!

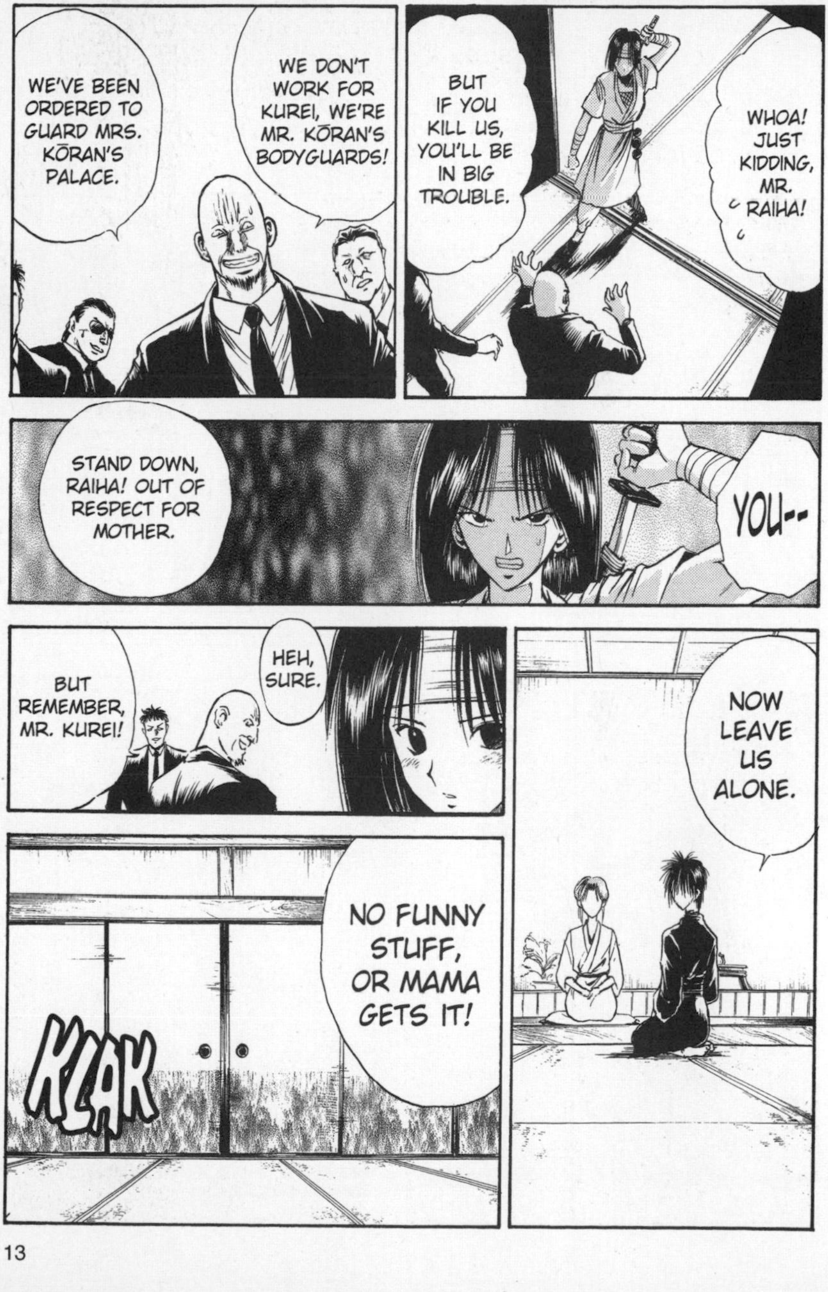
WHOA! JUST KIDDING, MR. RAIHA!
BUT IF YOU KILL US, YOU'LL BE IN BIG TROUBLE.
WE DON'T WORK FOR KUREI, WE'RE MR. KŌRAN'S BODYGUARDS!
WE'VE BEEN ORDERED TO GUARD MRS. KŌRAN'S PALACE.
YOU--
STAND DOWN, RAIHA! OUT OF RESPECT FOR MOTHER.
NOW LEAVE US ALONE.
HEH, SURE.
BUT REMEMBER, MR. KUREI!
NO FUNNY STUFF, OR MAMA GETS IT!
KLAK

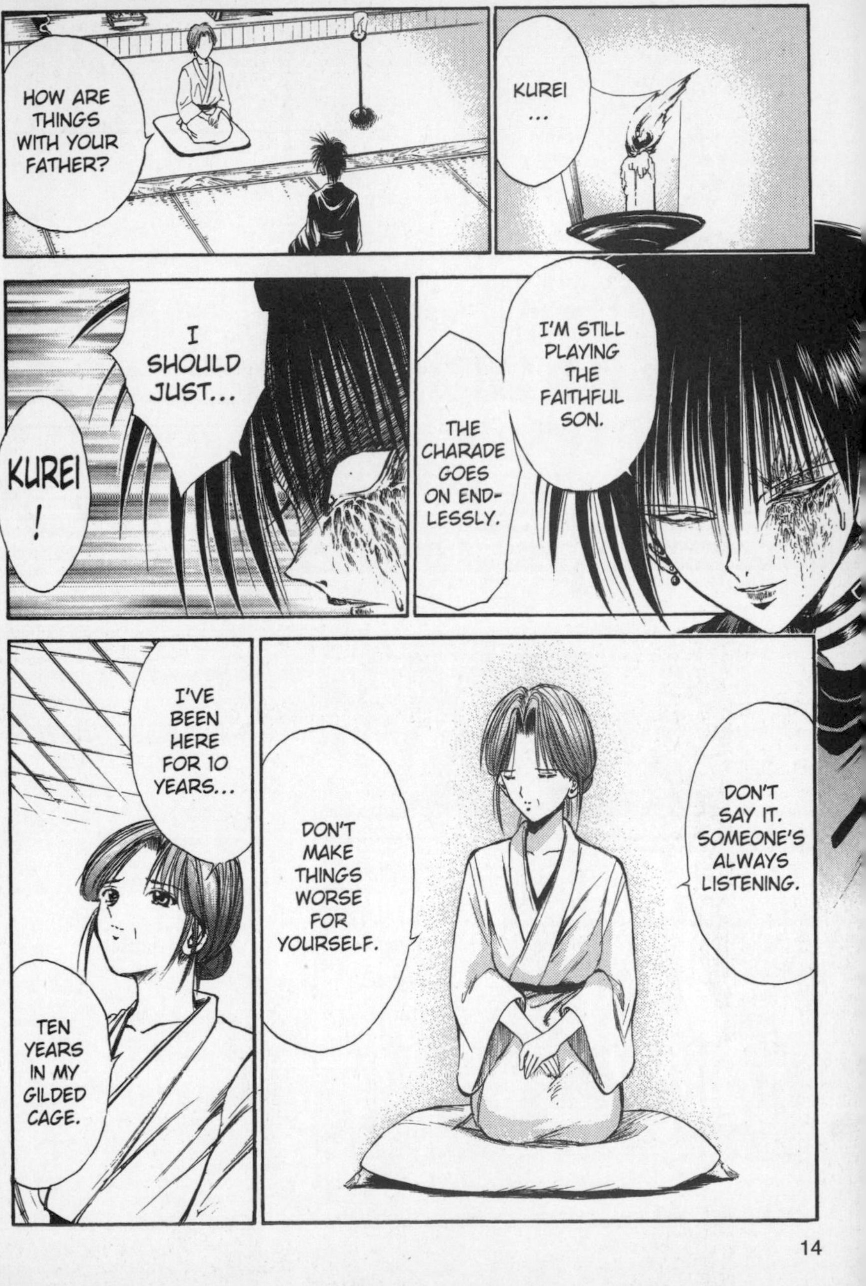
KUREI ...
HOW ARE THINGS WITH YOUR FATHER?
I'M STILL PLAYING THE FAITHFUL SON.
THE CHARADE GOES ON END-LESSLY.
I SHOULD JUST...
KUREI!
DON'T SAY IT. SOMEONE'S ALWAYS LISTENING.
DON'T MAKE THINGS WORSE FOR YOURSELF.
I'VE BEEN HERE FOR 10 YEARS...
TEN YEARS IN MY GILDED CAGE.

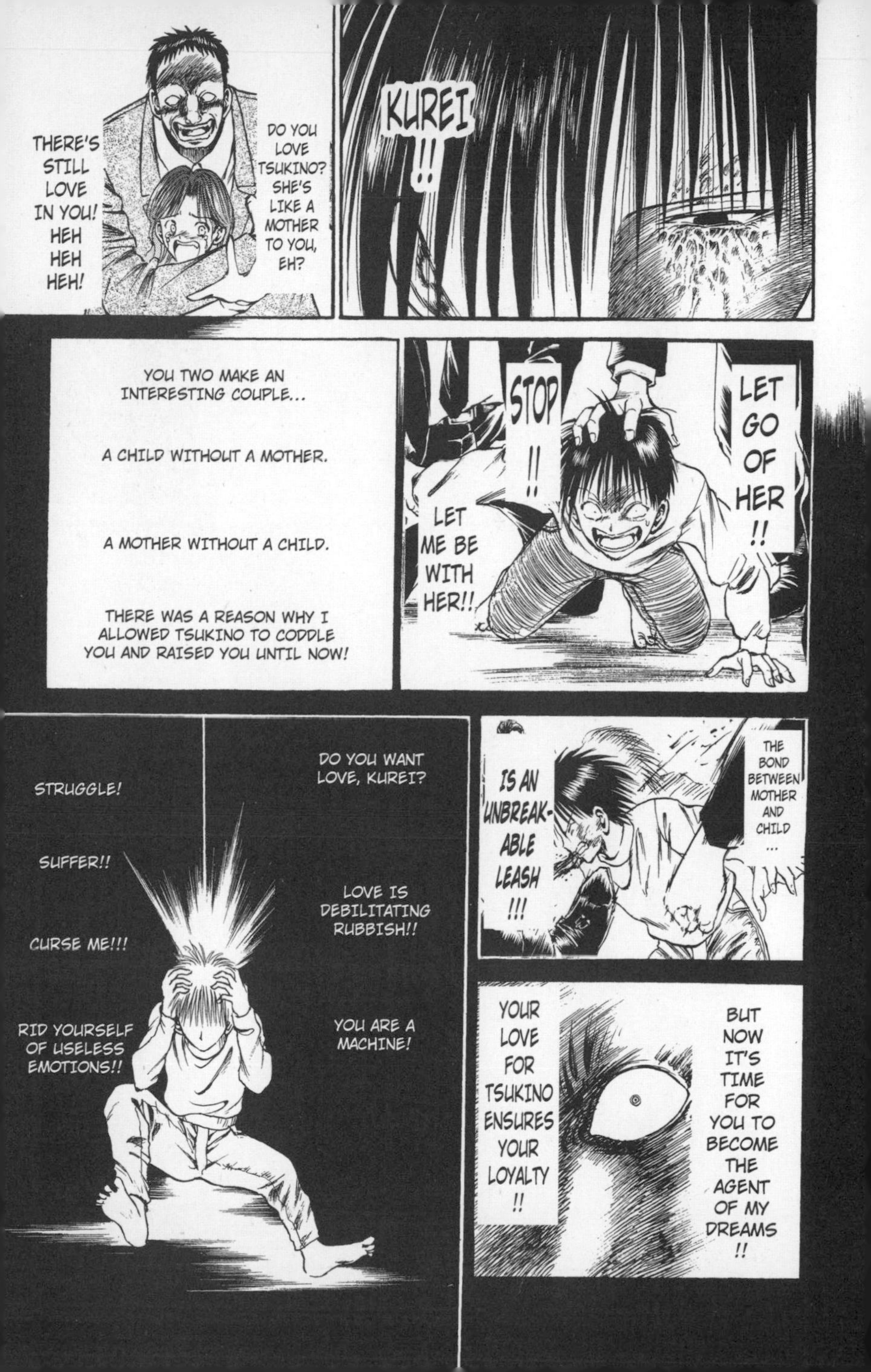
KUREI!!
DO YOU LOVE TSUKINO? SHE'S LIKE A MOTHER TO YOU, EH?
THERE'S STILL LOVE IN YOU! HEH HEH HEH!
LET GO OF HER!!
STOP!!
LET ME BE WITH HER!!
YOU TWO MAKE AN INTERESTING COUPLE...
A CHILD WITHOUT A MOTHER.
A MOTHER WITHOUT A CHILD.
THERE WAS A REASON WHY I ALLOWED TSUKINO TO CODDLE YOU AND RAISED YOU UNTIL NOW!
THE BOND BETWEEN MOTHER AND CHILD...
IS AN UNBREAKABLE LEASH!!!
BUT NOW IT'S TIME FOR YOU TO BECOME THE AGENT OF MY DREAMS!!
YOUR LOVE FOR TSUKINO ENSURES YOUR LOYALTY!!
DO YOU WANT LOVE, KUREI?
LOVE IS DEBILITATING RUBBISH!!
YOU ARE A MACHINE!
STRUGGLE!
SUFFER!!
CURSE ME!!!
RID YOURSELF OF USELESS EMOTIONS!!

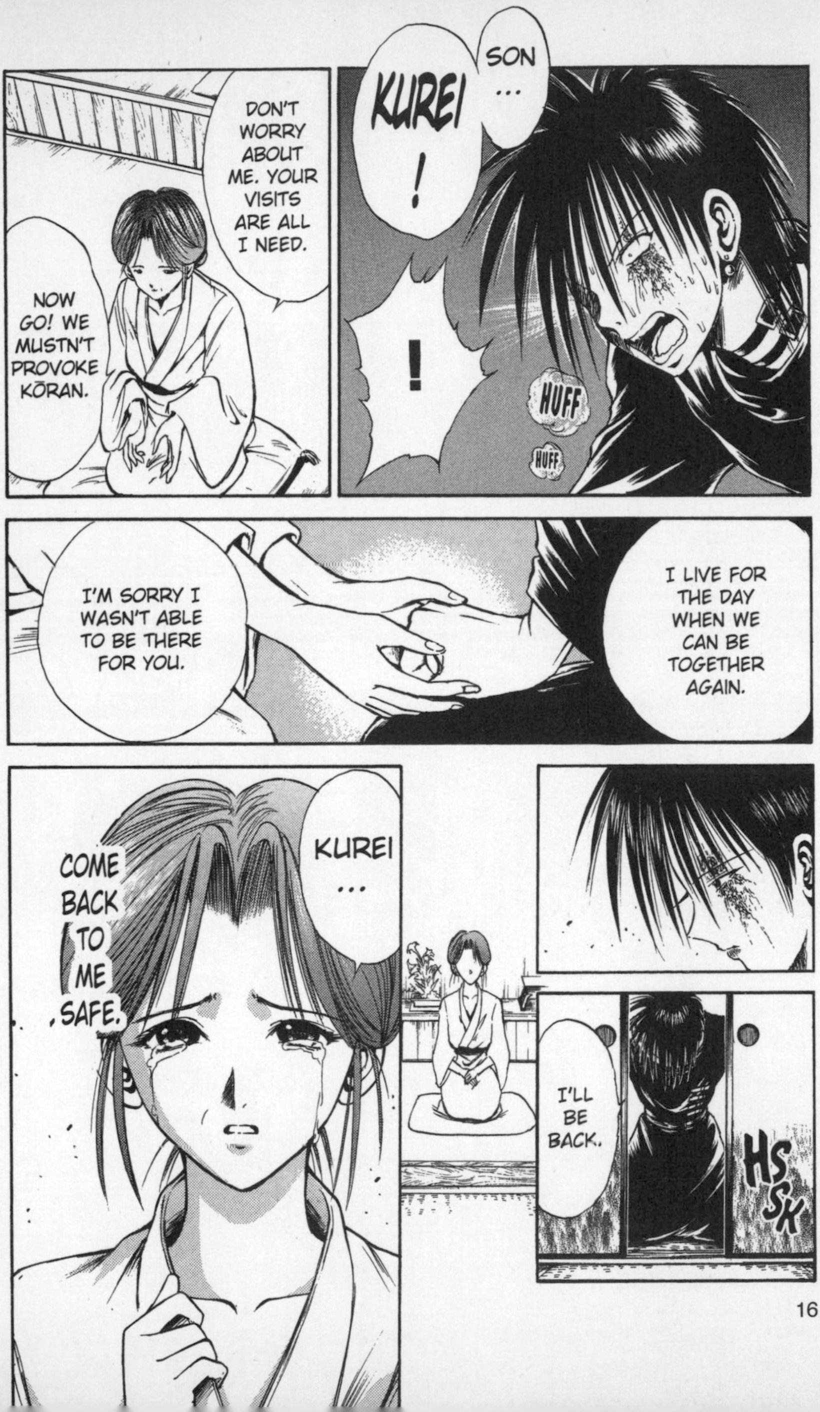
SON ...
KUREI !
!
HUFF
HUFF
DON'T WORRY ABOUT ME. YOUR VISITS ARE ALL I NEED.
NOW GO! WE MUSTN'T PROVOKE KŌRAN.
I LIVE FOR THE DAY WHEN WE CAN BE TOGETHER AGAIN.
I'M SORRY I WASN'T ABLE TO BE THERE FOR YOU.
I'LL BE BACK.
HSSK
KUREI ...
COME BACK TO ME SAFE.

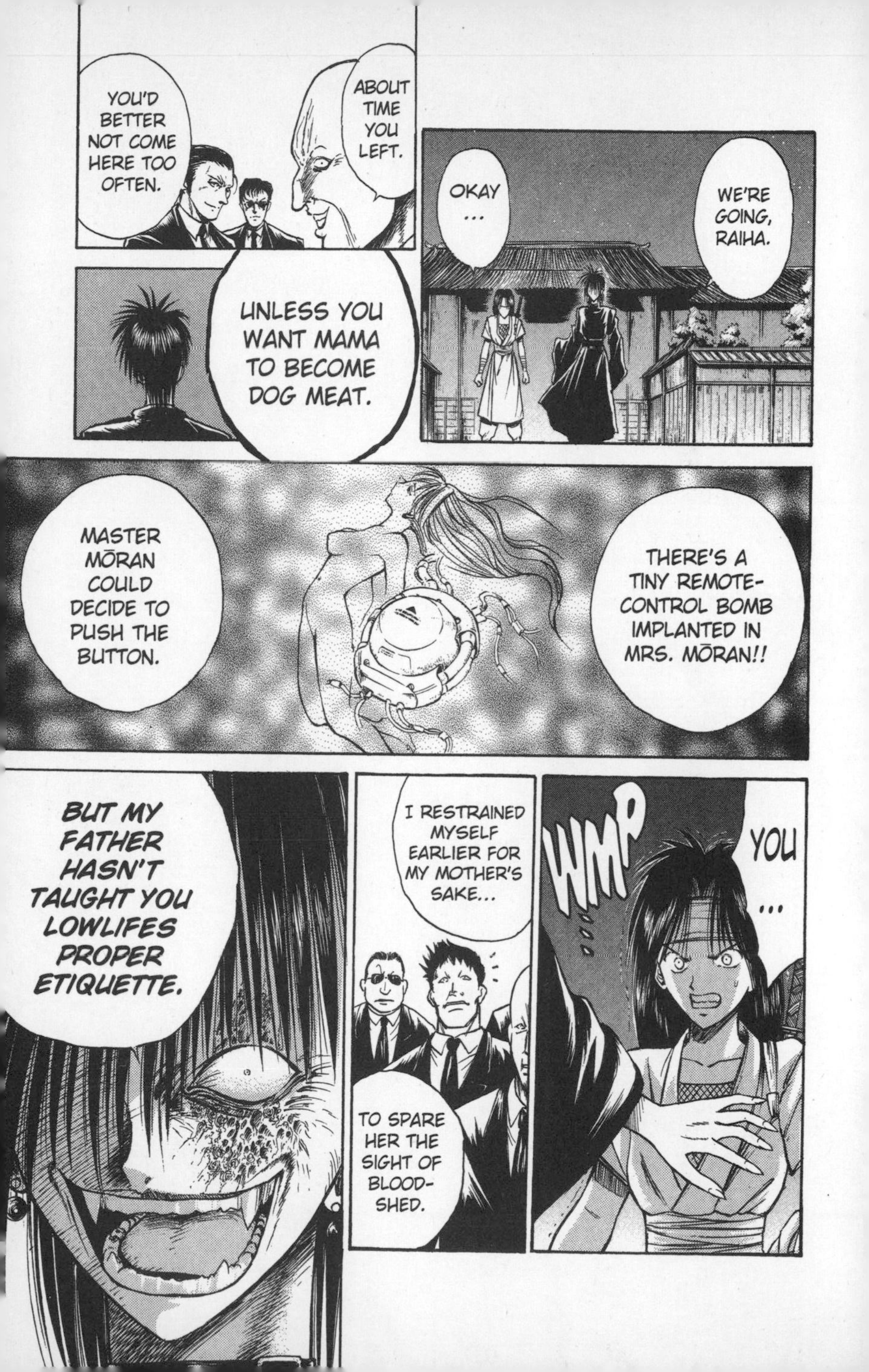
WE'RE GOING, RAIHA.
OKAY ...
ABOUT TIME YOU LEFT.
YOU'D BETTER NOT COME HERE TOO OFTEN.
UNLESS YOU WANT MAMA TO BECOME DOG MEAT.
THERE'S A TINY REMOTE-CONTROL BOMB IMPLANTED IN MRS. MŌRAN!!
MASTER MŌRAN COULD DECIDE TO PUSH THE BUTTON.
YOU ...
WMP
I RESTRAINED MYSELF EARLIER FOR MY MOTHER'S SAKE...
TO SPARE HER THE SIGHT OF BLOOD-SHED.
BUT MY FATHER HASN'T TAUGHT YOU LOWLIFES PROPER ETIQUETTE.

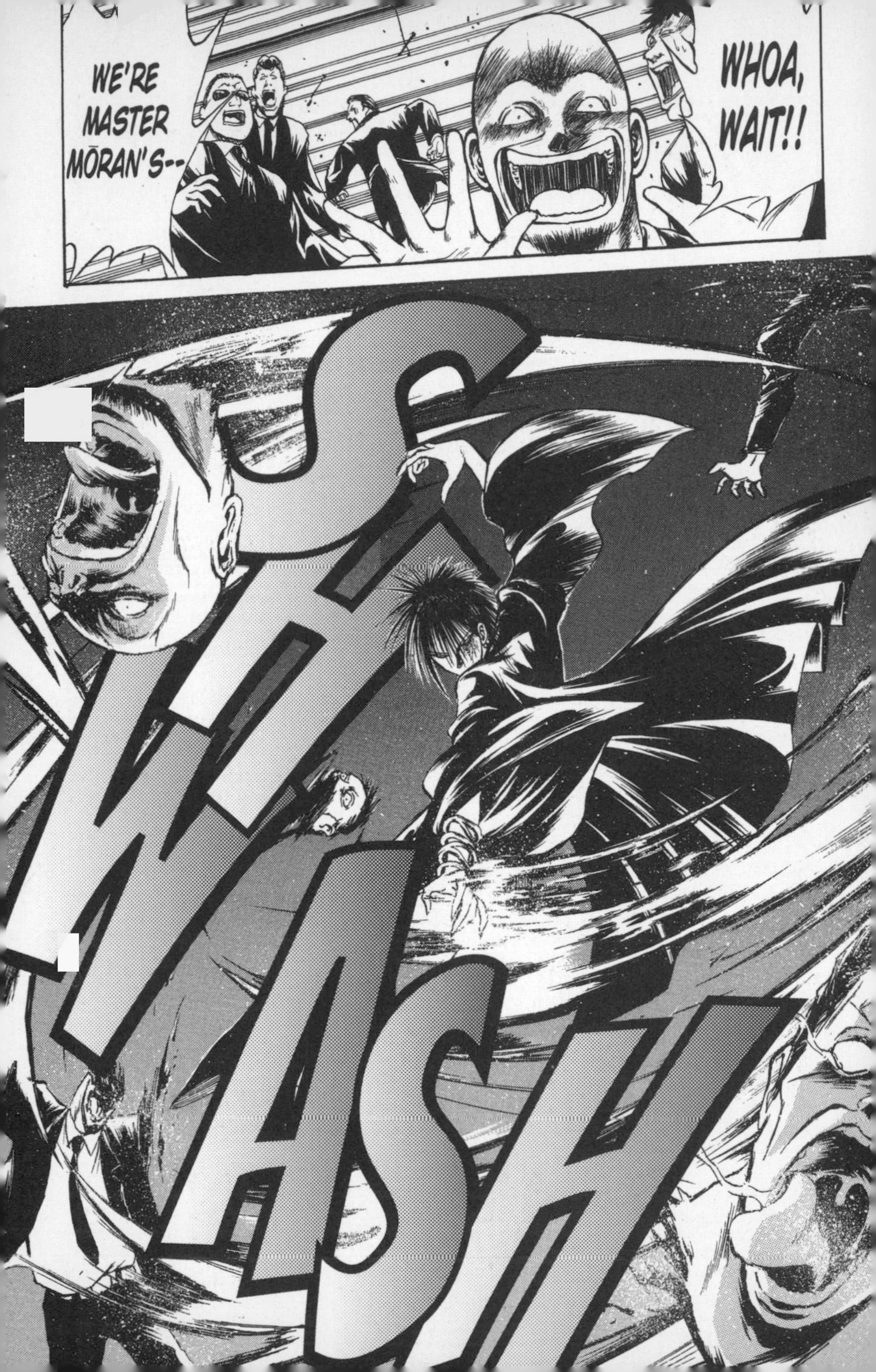
WHOA, WAIT!!
WE'RE MASTER MŌRAN'S--
SWASH

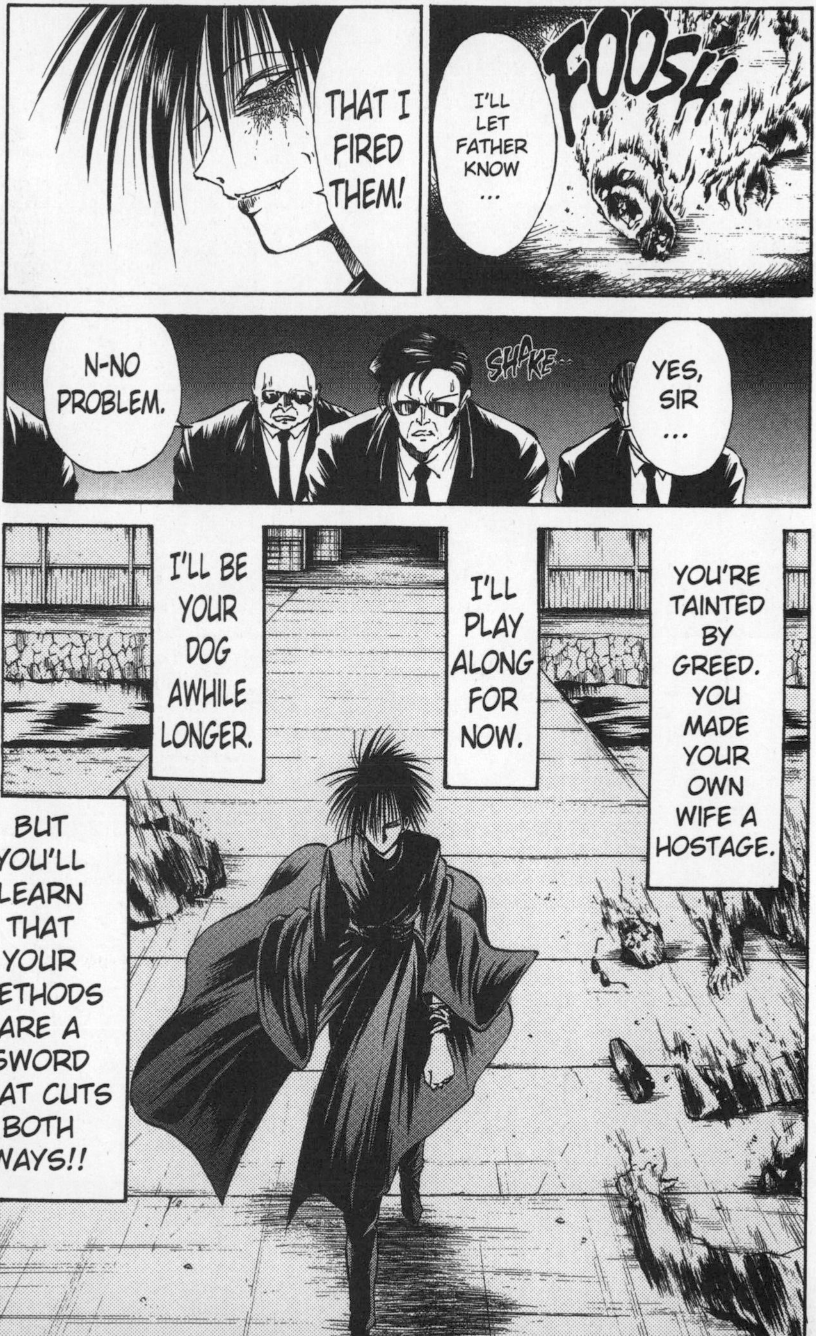
FOOSH
I'LL LET FATHER KNOW ...
THAT I FIRED THEM!
YES, SIR ...
SHAKE...
N-NO PROBLEM.
YOU'RE TAINTED BY GREED. YOU MADE YOUR OWN WIFE A HOSTAGE.
I'LL PLAY ALONG FOR NOW.
I'LL BE YOUR DOG AWHILE LONGER.
BUT YOU'LL LEARN THAT YOUR METHODS ARE A SWORD THAT CUTS BOTH WAYS!!

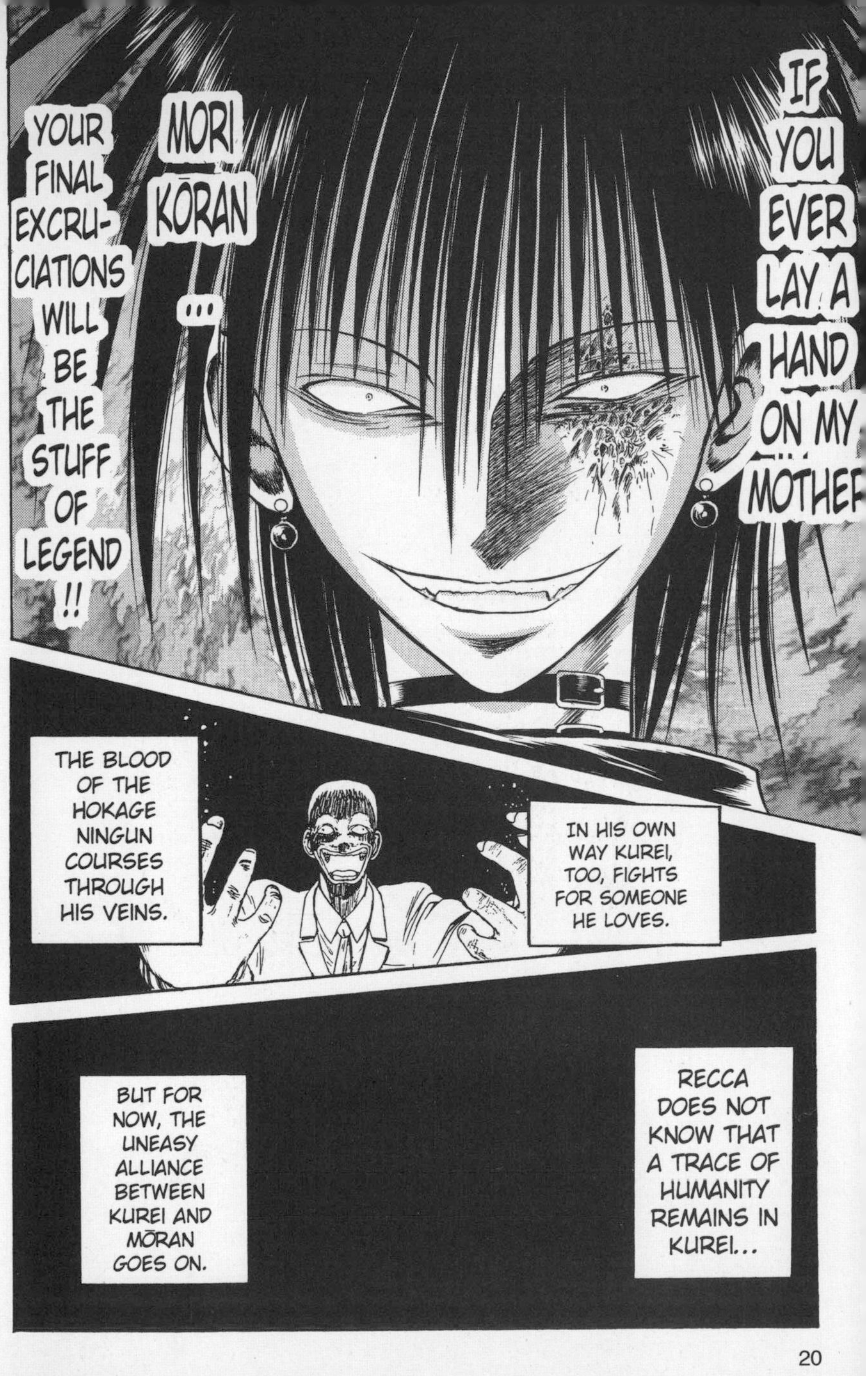
IF YOU EVER LAY A HAND ON MY MOTHER
MORI KŌRAN ...
YOUR FINAL EXCRU-CIATIONS WILL BE THE STUFF OF LEGEND !!
IN HIS OWN WAY KUREI, TOO, FIGHTS FOR SOMEONE HE LOVES.
THE BLOOD OF THE HOKAGE NINGUN COURSES THROUGH HIS VEINS.
RECCA DOES NOT KNOW THAT A TRACE OF HUMANITY REMAINS IN KUREI...
BUT FOR NOW, THE UNEASY ALLIANCE BETWEEN KUREI AND MŌRAN GOES ON.

Part Sixty-Nine:
Live (1) The Night Before

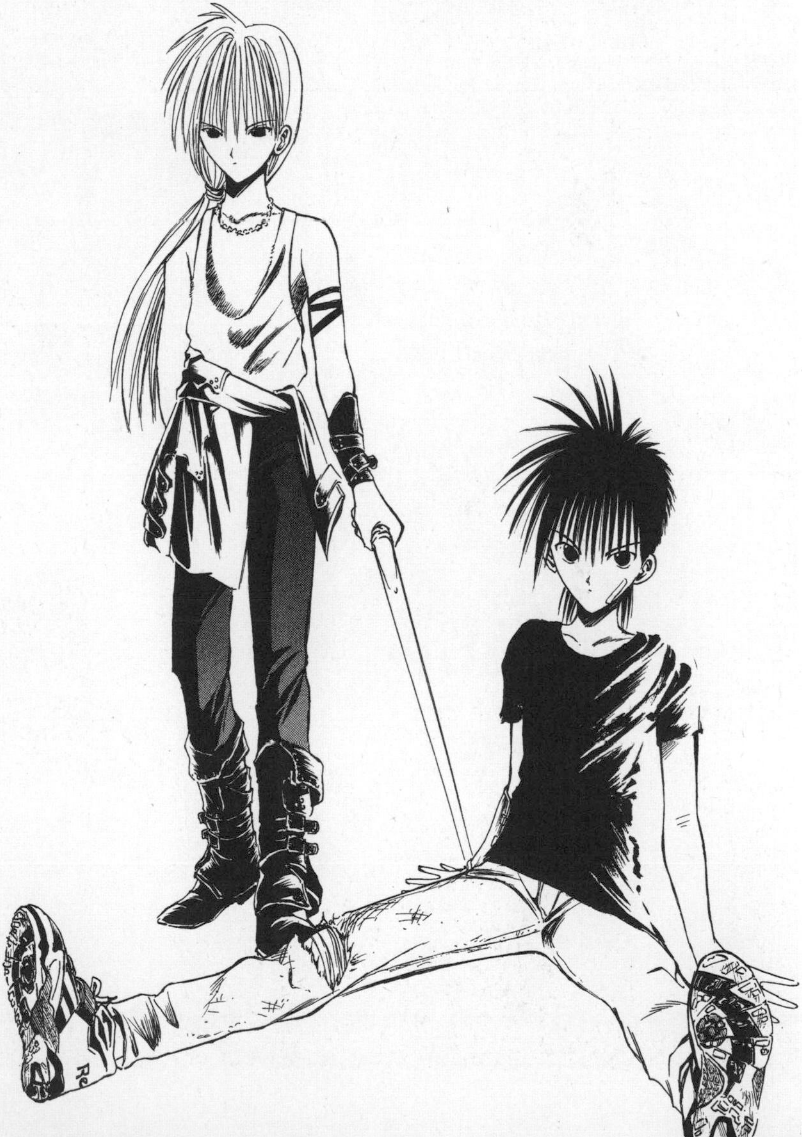

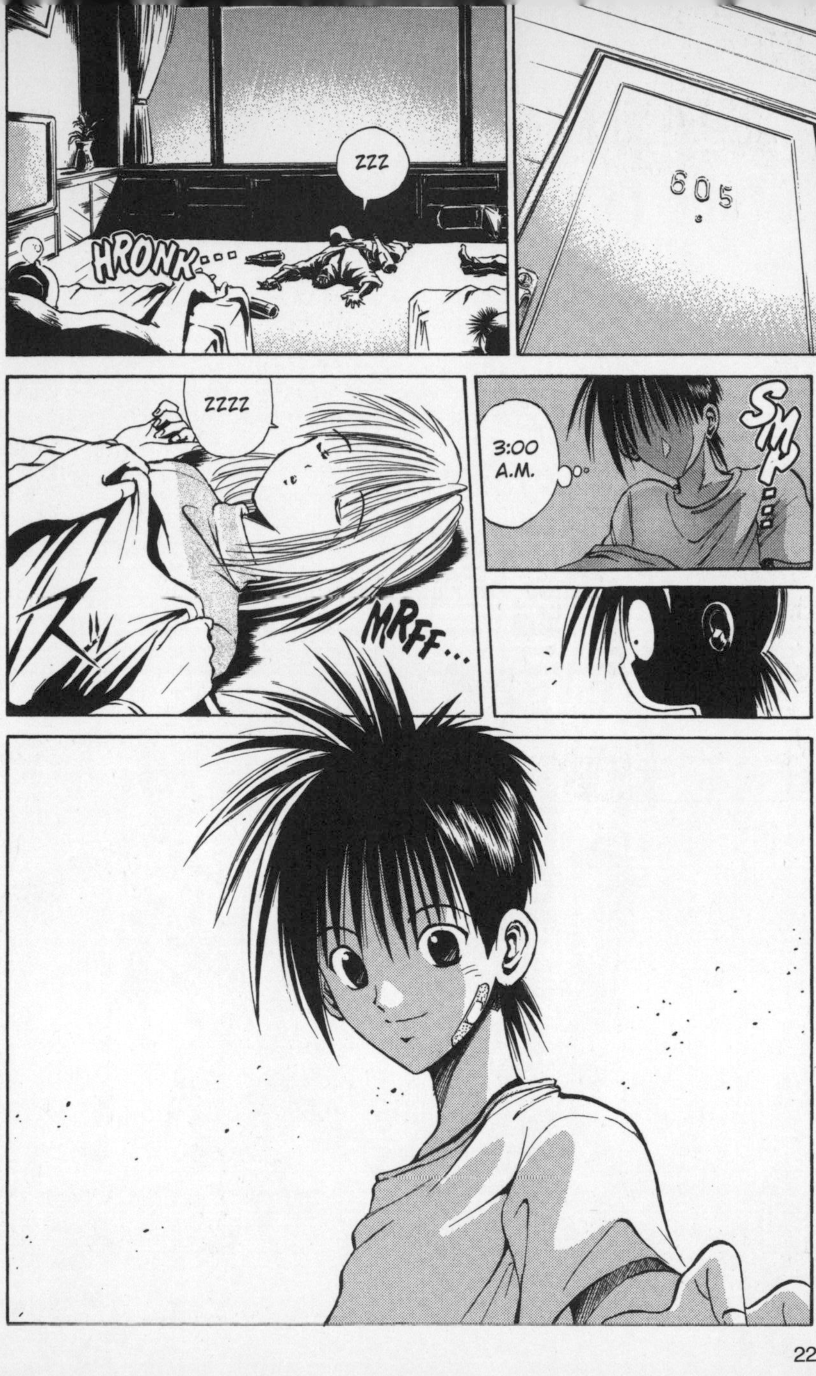
605
ZZZ
HRONK...
3:00 A.M.
SMP...
ZZZZ
MRFF...

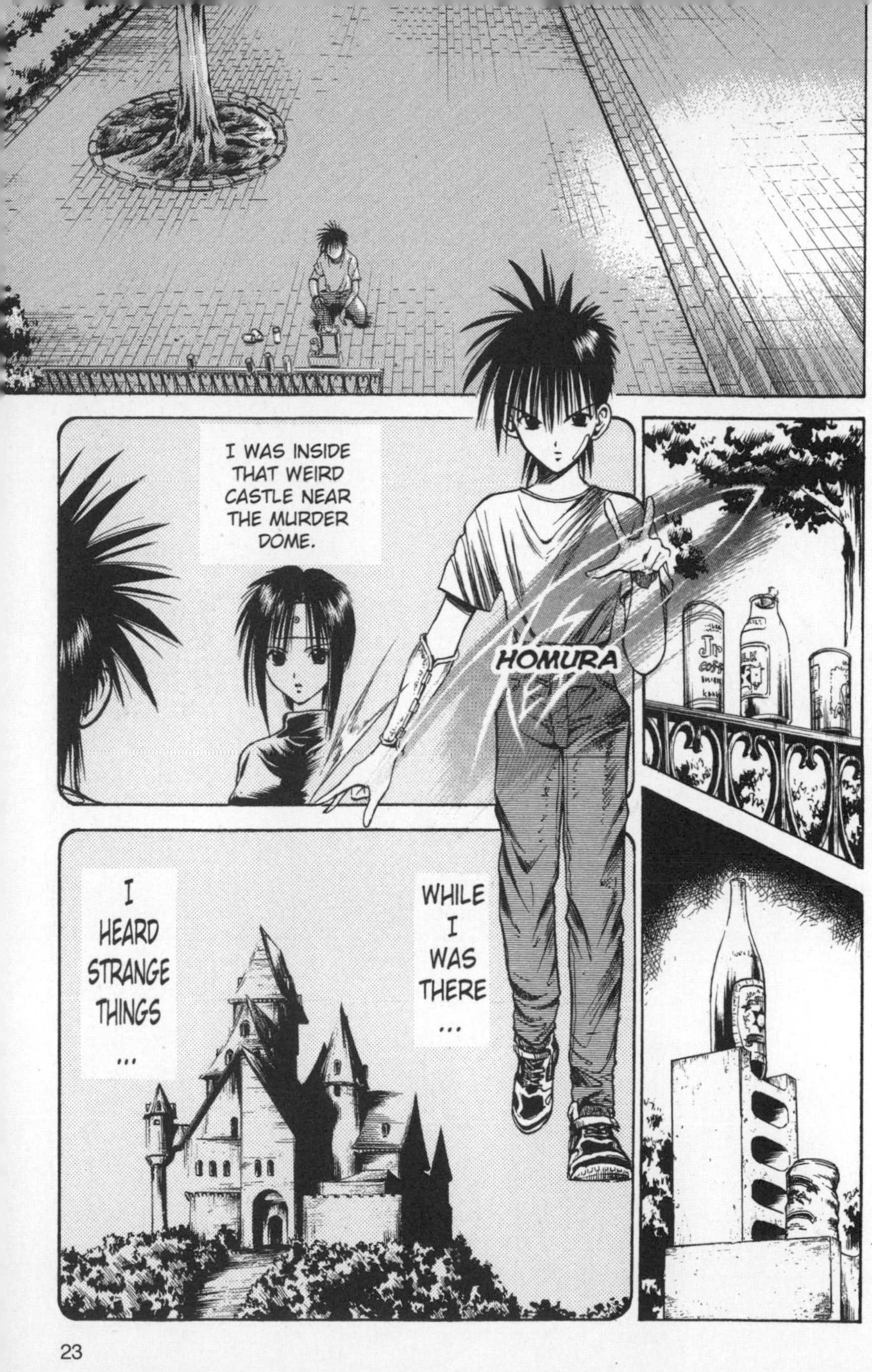
HOMURA
I WAS INSIDE THAT WEIRD CASTLE NEAR THE MURDER DOME.
WHILE I WAS THERE ...
I HEARD STRANGE THINGS ...

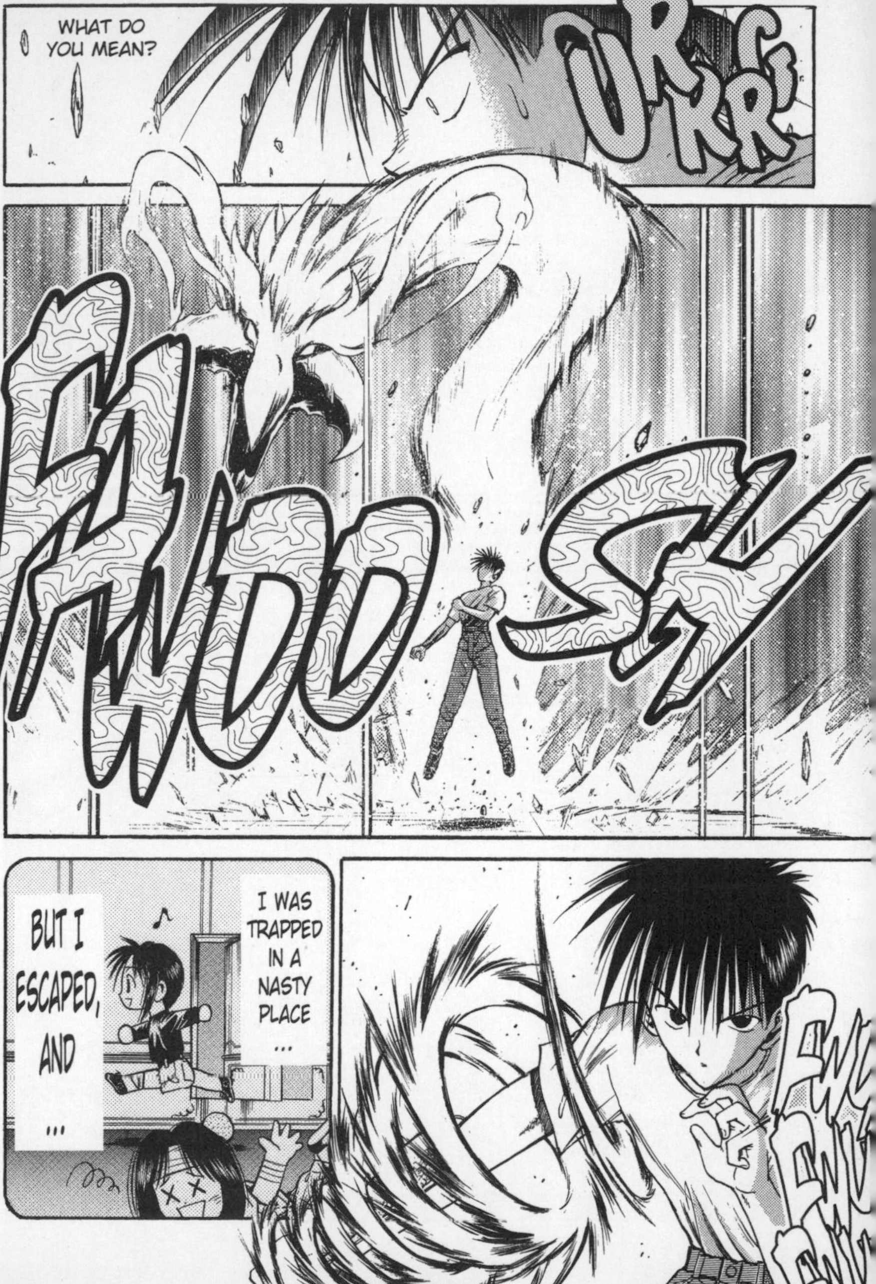
WHAT DO YOU MEAN?
FWOOSH
I WAS TRAPPED IN A NASTY PLACE ...
BUT I ESCAPED, AND ...

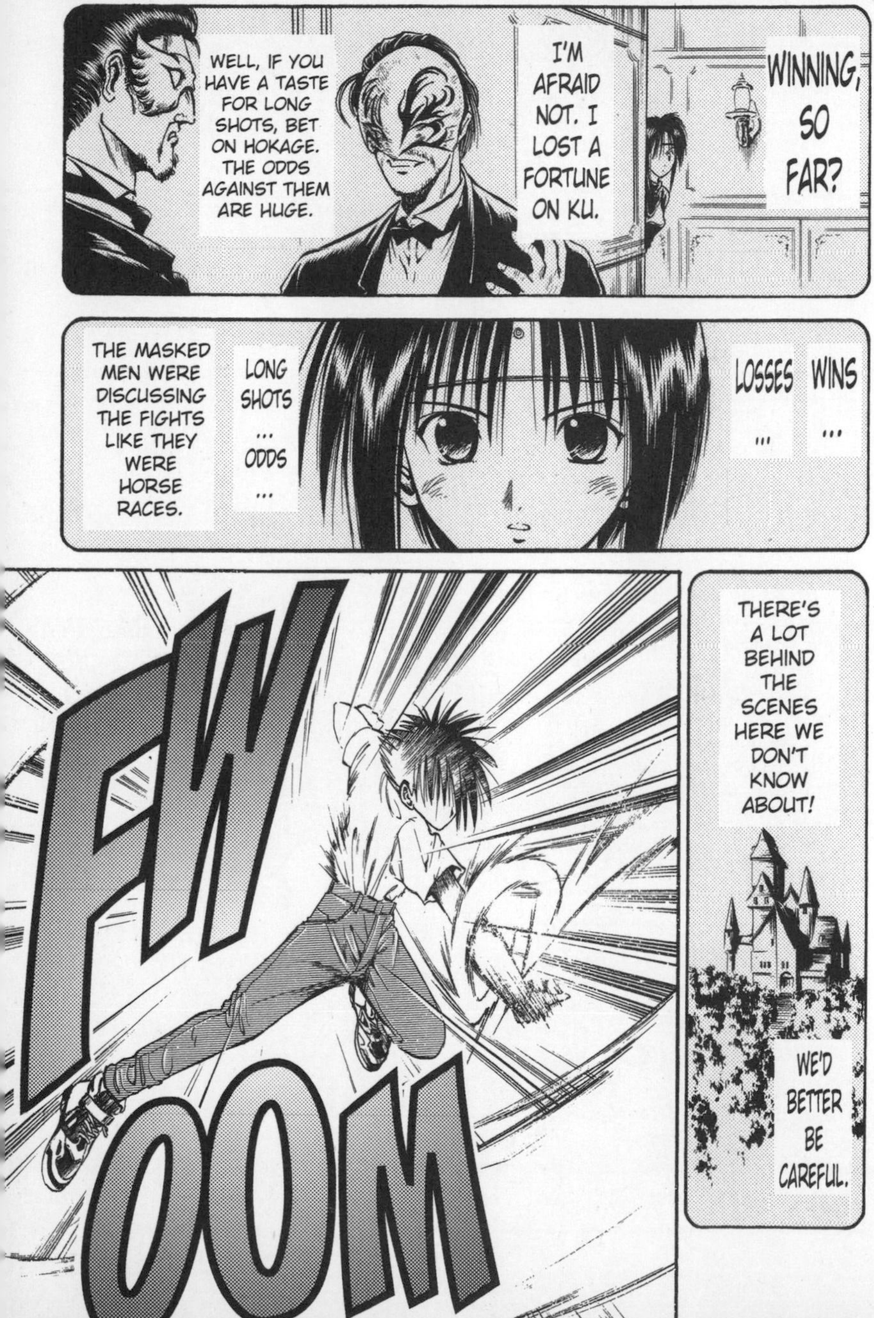
WINNING, SO FAR?
I'M AFRAID NOT. I LOST A FORTUNE ON KU.
WELL, IF YOU HAVE A TASTE FOR LONG SHOTS, BET ON HOKAGE. THE ODDS AGAINST THEM ARE HUGE.
WINS ...
LOSSES ...
LONG SHOTS ... ODDS ...
THE MASKED MEN WERE DISCUSSING THE FIGHTS LIKE THEY WERE HORSE RACES.
THERE'S A LOT BEHIND THE SCENES HERE WE DON'T KNOW ABOUT!
WE'D BETTER BE CAREFUL.
FWOOM

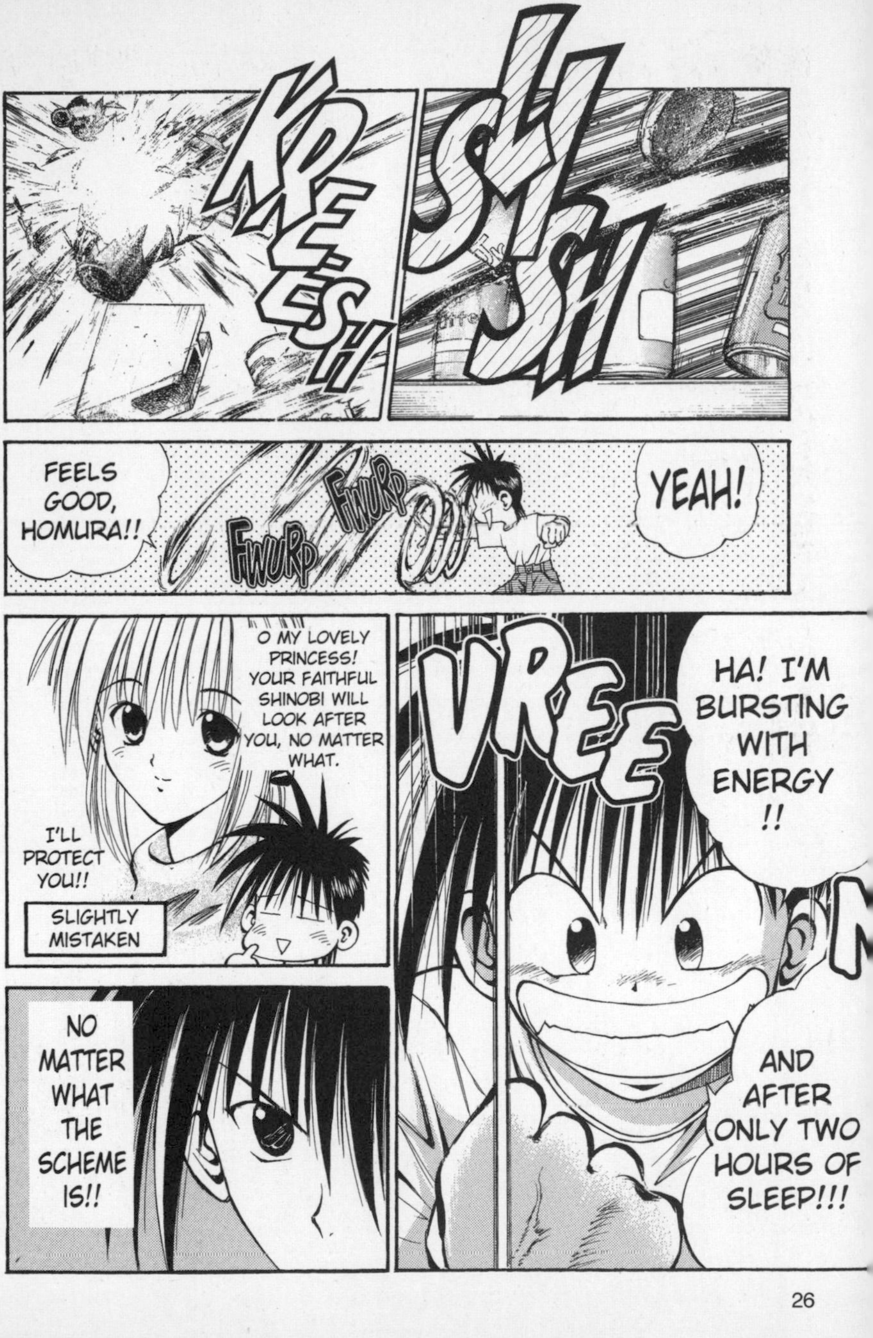
SLISH
KREESH
YEAH!
FWURP
FWURP
FEELS GOOD, HOMURA!!
VREE
HA! I'M BURSTING WITH ENERGY !!
AND AFTER ONLY TWO HOURS OF SLEEP!!!
O MY LOVELY PRINCESS! YOUR FAITHFUL SHINOBI WILL LOOK AFTER YOU, NO MATTER WHAT.
I'LL PROTECT YOU!!
SLIGHTLY MISTAKEN
NO MATTER WHAT THE SCHEME IS!!

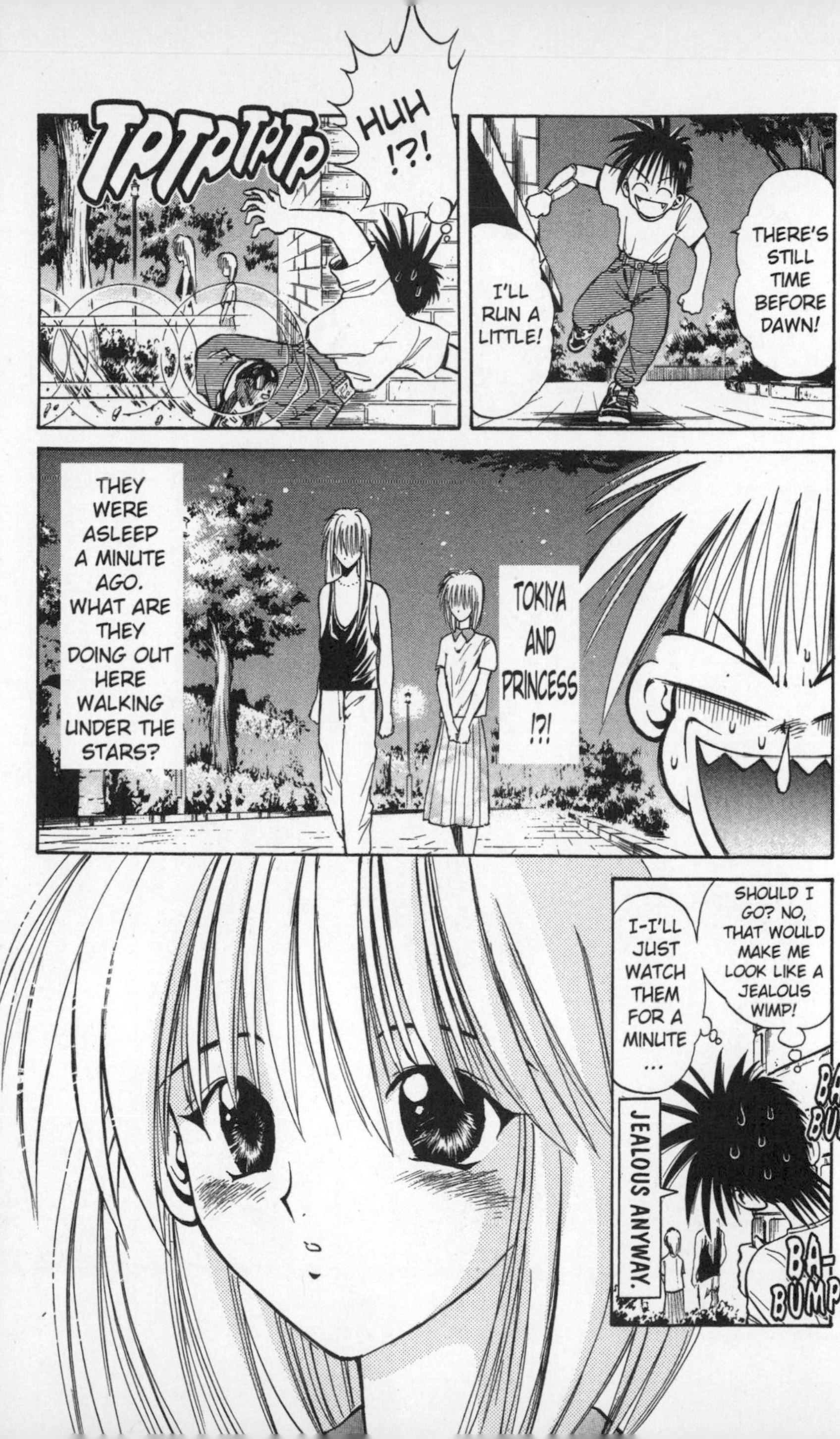
THERE'S STILL TIME BEFORE DAWN!
I'LL RUN A LITTLE!
TPTPTPTPTP
HUH !?!
TOKIYA AND PRINCESS !?!
THEY WERE ASLEEP A MINUTE AGO. WHAT ARE THEY DOING OUT HERE WALKING UNDER THE STARS?
SHOULD I GO? NO, THAT WOULD MAKE ME LOOK LIKE A JEALOUS WIMP!
I-I'LL JUST WATCH THEM FOR A MINUTE ...
JEALOUS ANYWAY.
BA-BUMP
BA-BUMP

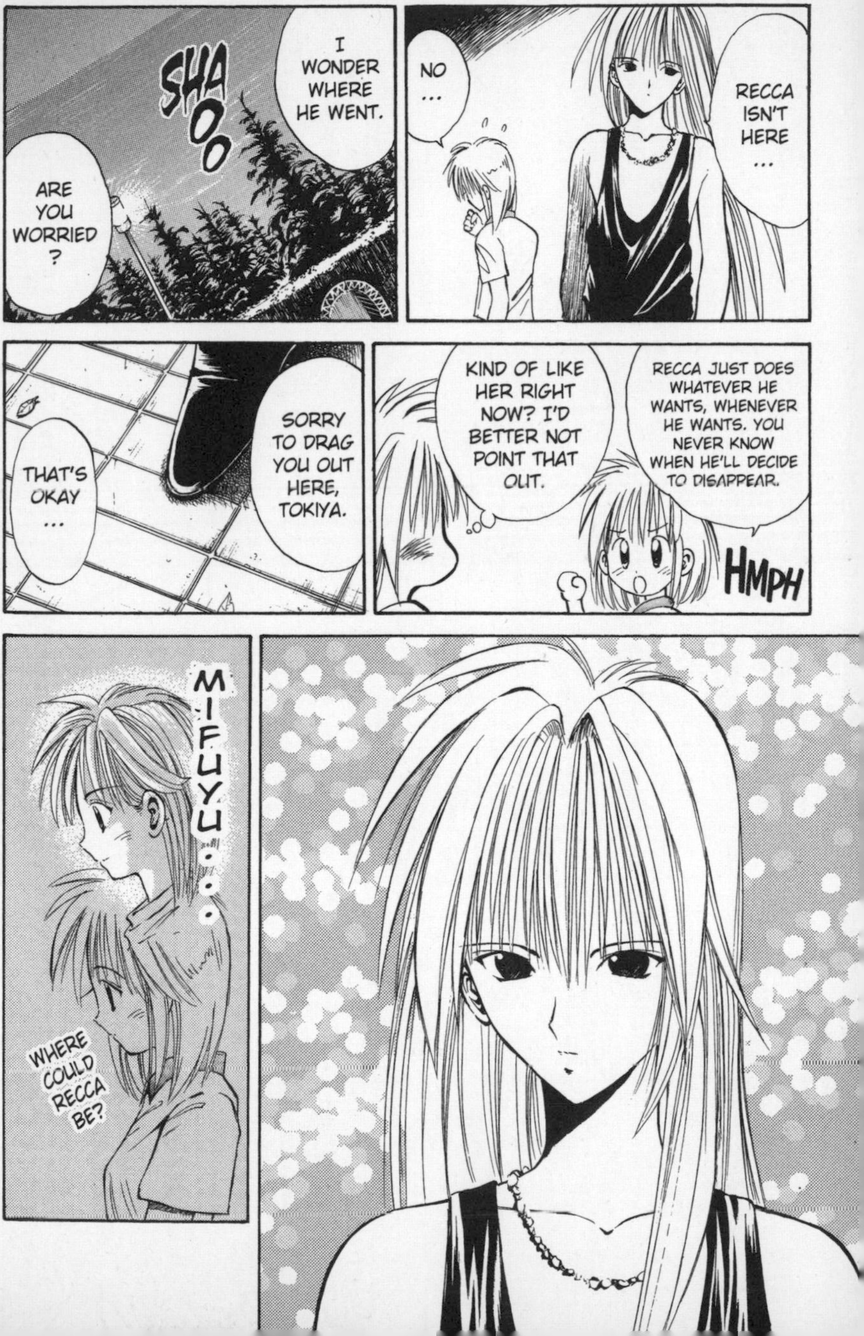
RECCA ISN'T HERE ...
NO ...
I WONDER WHERE HE WENT.
SHAOO
ARE YOU WORRIED ?
RECCA JUST DOES WHATEVER HE WANTS, WHENEVER HE WANTS. YOU NEVER KNOW WHEN HE'LL DECIDE TO DISAPPEAR.
KIND OF LIKE HER RIGHT NOW? I'D BETTER NOT POINT THAT OUT.
HMPH
SORRY TO DRAG YOU OUT HERE, TOKIYA.
THAT'S OKAY ...
MIFUYU...
WHERE COULD RECCA BE?

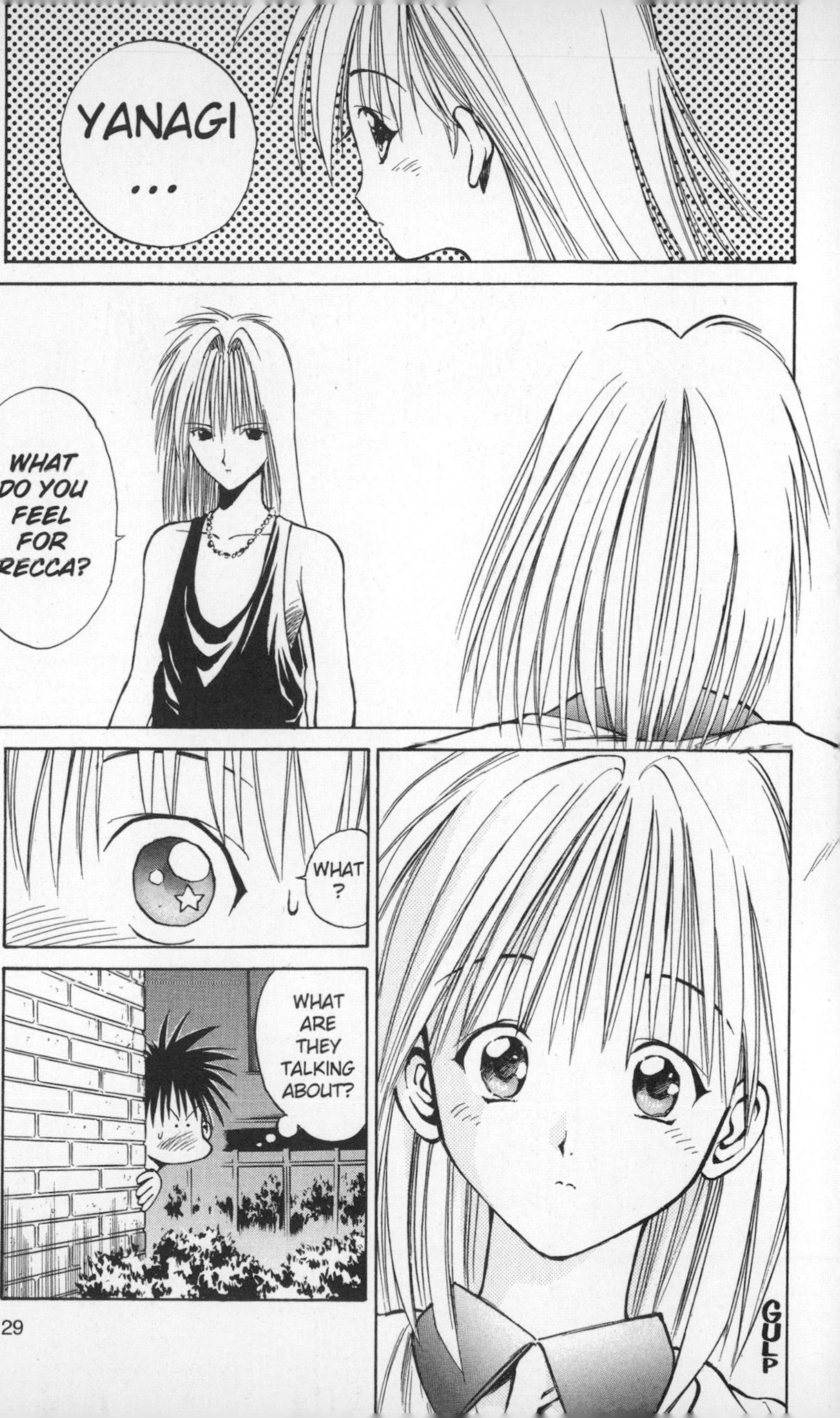
YANAGI ...
WHAT DO YOU FEEL FOR RECCA?
GULP
WHAT ?
WHAT ARE THEY TALKING ABOUT?

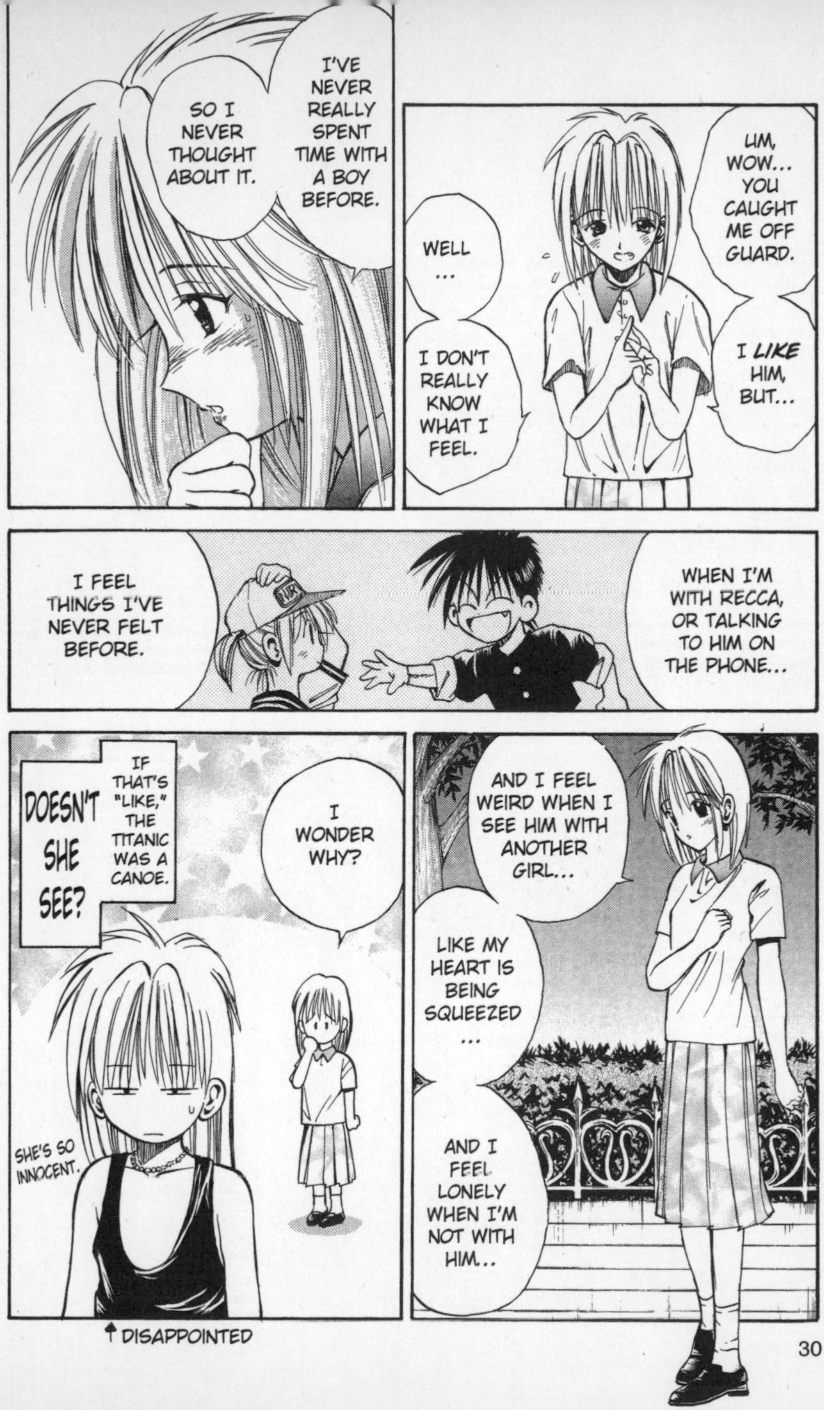
UM, WOW... YOU CAUGHT ME OFF GUARD.
I *LIKE* HIM, BUT...
WELL ...
I DON'T REALLY KNOW WHAT I FEEL.
I'VE NEVER REALLY SPENT TIME WITH A BOY BEFORE.
SO I NEVER THOUGHT ABOUT IT.
WHEN I'M WITH RECCA, OR TALKING TO HIM ON THE PHONE...
I FEEL THINGS I'VE NEVER FELT BEFORE.
AND I FEEL WEIRD WHEN I SEE HIM WITH ANOTHER GIRL...
LIKE MY HEART IS BEING SQUEEZED ...
AND I FEEL LONELY WHEN I'M NOT WITH HIM..
I WONDER WHY?
IF THAT'S "LIKE," THE TITANIC WAS A CANOE.
DOESN'T SHE SEE?
SHE'S SO INNOCENT.
DISAPPOINTED

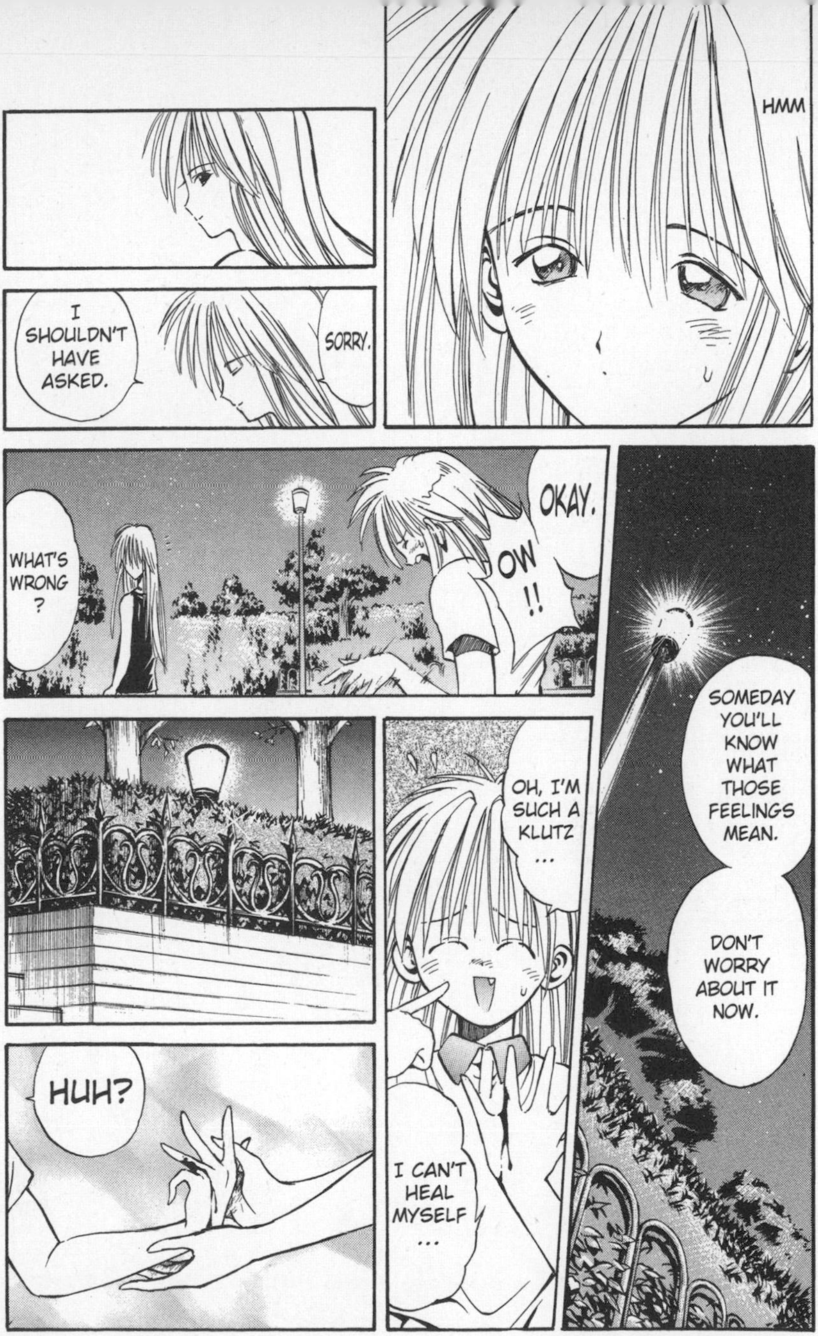
HMM
SORRY.
I SHOULDN'T HAVE ASKED.
SOMEDAY YOU'LL KNOW WHAT THOSE FEELINGS MEAN.
DON'T WORRY ABOUT IT NOW.
OKAY.
OW !!
WHAT'S WRONG ?
OH, I'M SUCH A KLUTZ ...
I CAN'T HEAL MYSELF ...
HUH?

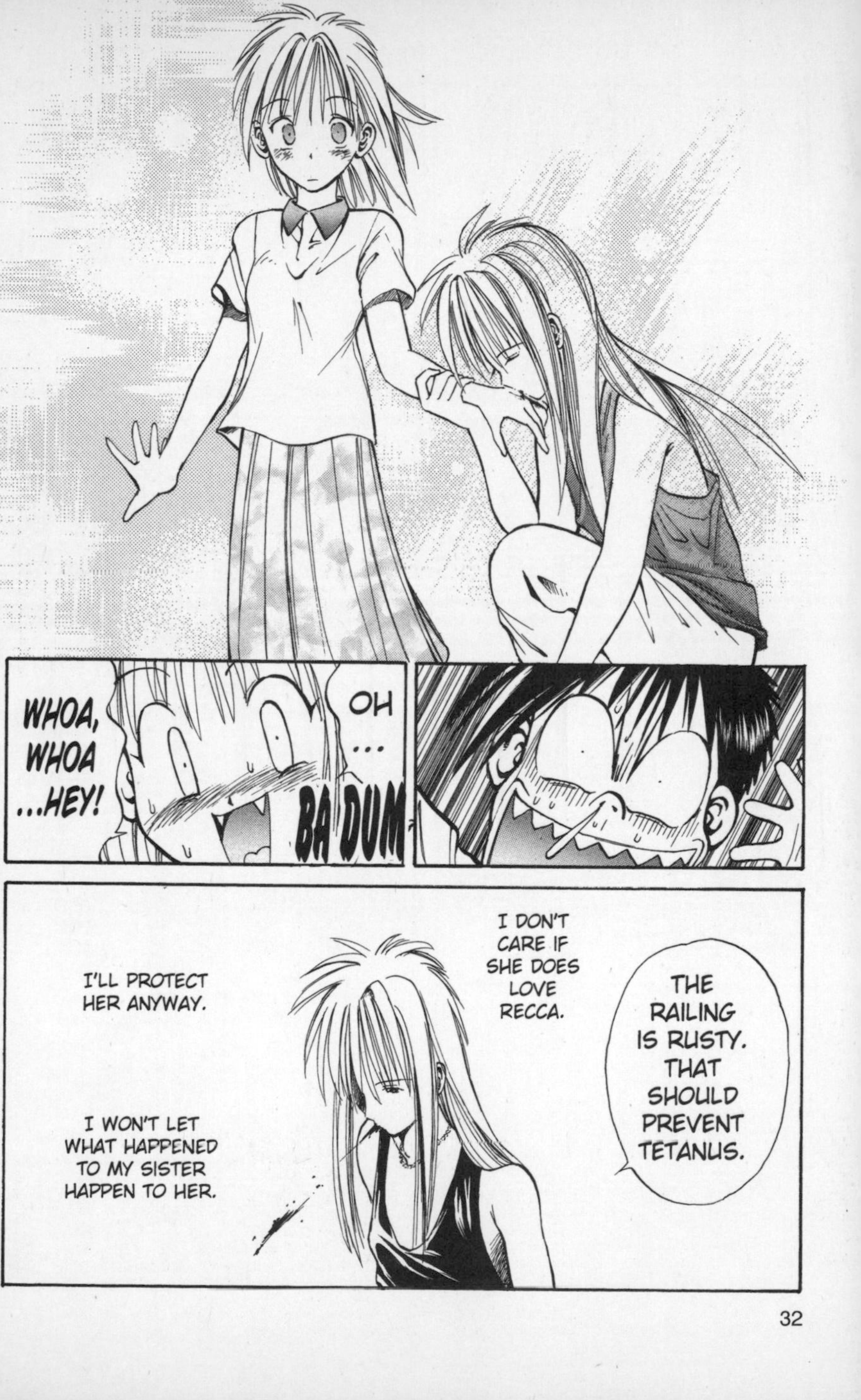
OH ...
WHOA, WHOA ...HEY!
BA DUM
THE RAILING IS RUSTY. THAT SHOULD PREVENT TETANUS.
I DON'T CARE IF SHE DOES LOVE RECCA.
I'LL PROTECT HER ANYWAY.
I WON'T LET WHAT HAPPENED TO MY SISTER HAPPEN TO HER.

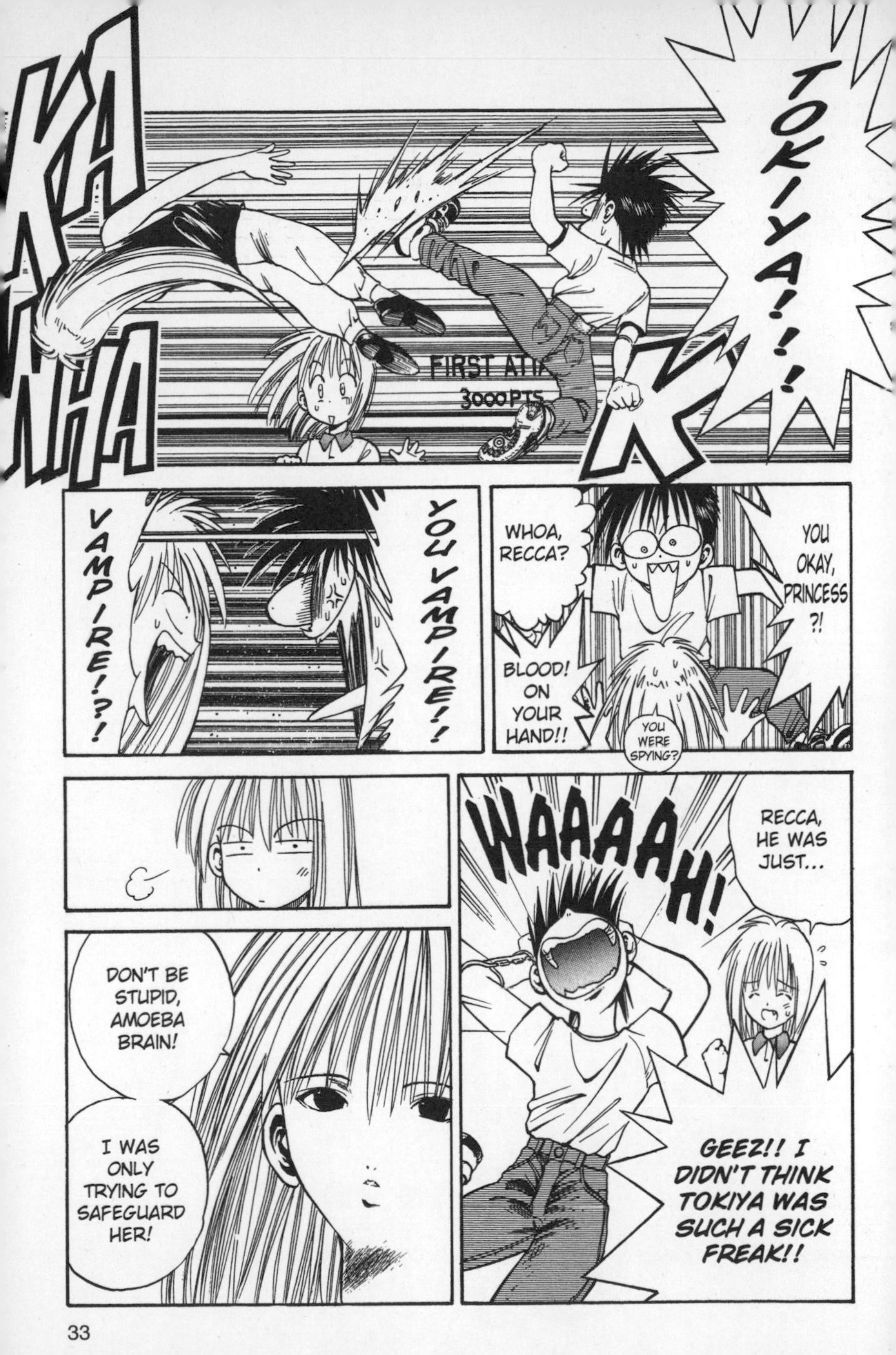
TOKIYA!!!
3000PTS
YOU OKAY, PRINCESS?!
WHOA, RECCA?
BLOOD! ON YOUR HAND!!
YOU WERE SPYING?
YOU VAMPIRE!!
VAMPIRE!?!
RECCA, HE WAS JUST...
WAAAAH!
GEEZ!! I DIDN'T THINK TOKIYA WAS SUCH A SICK FREAK!!
DON'T BE STUPID, AMOEBA BRAIN!
I WAS ONLY TRYING TO SAFEGUARD HER!

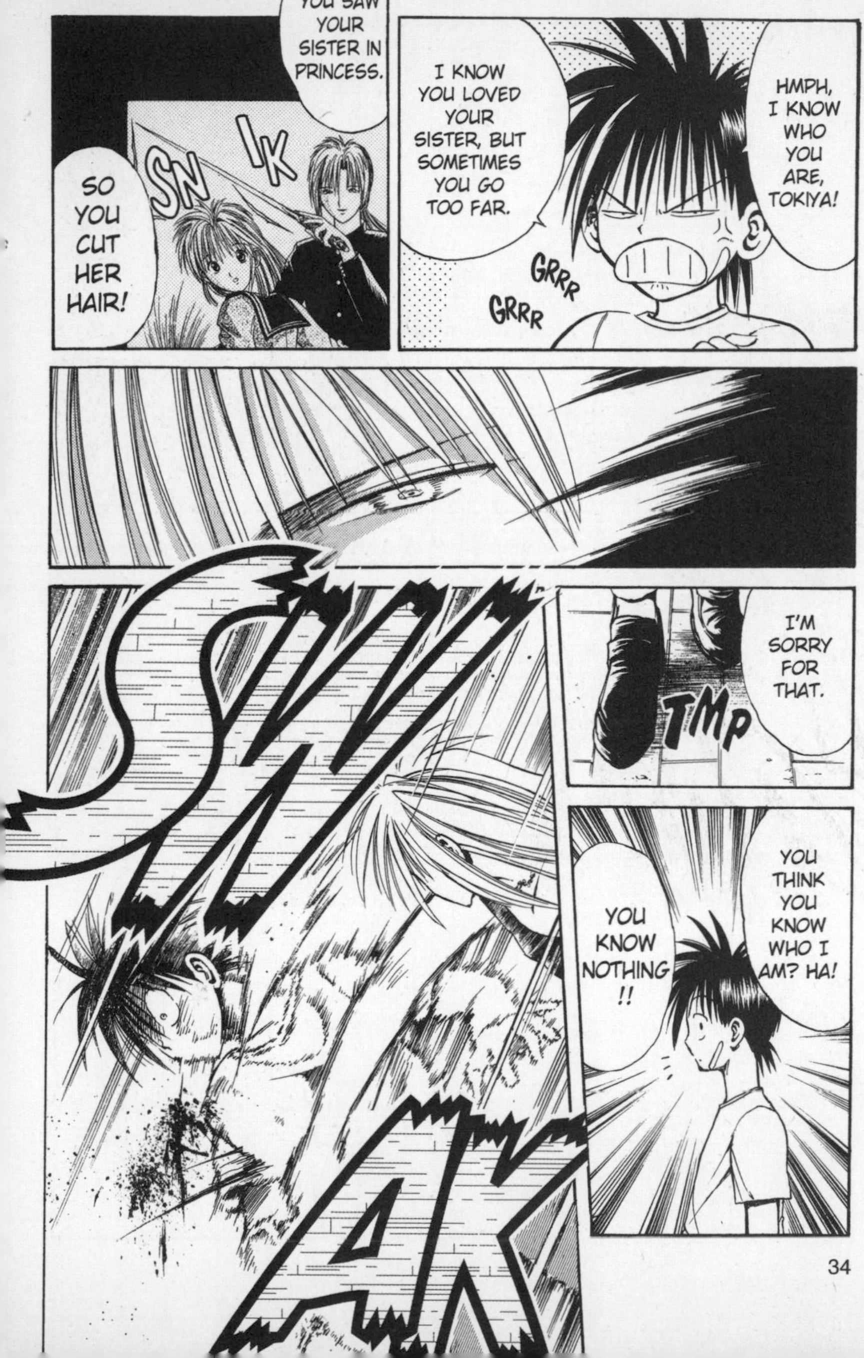
HMPH, I KNOW WHO YOU ARE, TOKIYA!
I KNOW YOU LOVED YOUR SISTER, BUT SOMETIMES YOU GO TOO FAR.
GRRR
GRRR
YOU SAW YOUR SISTER IN PRINCESS.
SNIK
SO YOU CUT HER HAIR!
I'M SORRY FOR THAT.
TMP
YOU THINK YOU KNOW WHO I AM? HA!
YOU KNOW NOTHING !!

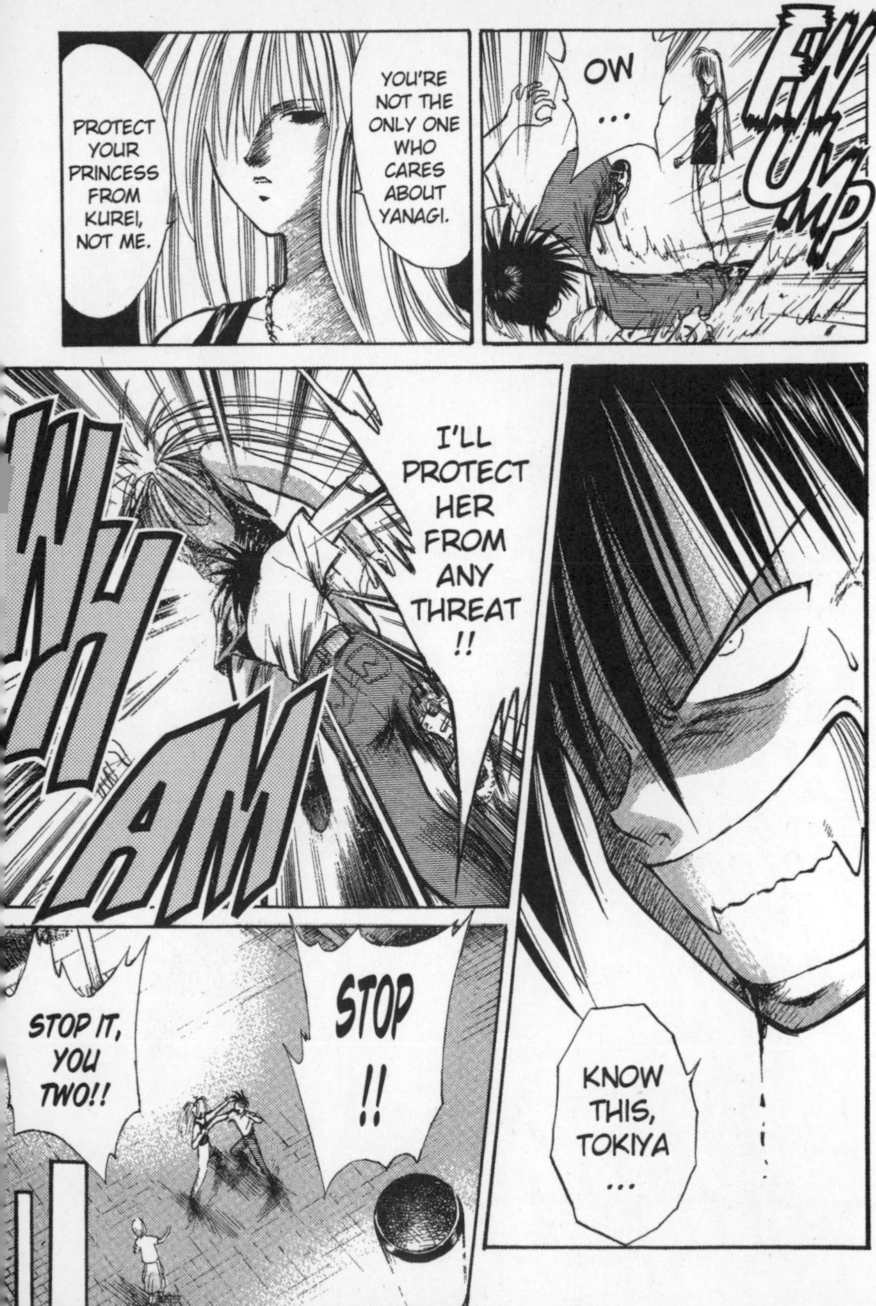
FWUMP
OW ...
YOU'RE NOT THE ONLY ONE WHO CARES ABOUT YANAGI.
PROTECT YOUR PRINCESS FROM KUREI, NOT ME.
KNOW THIS, TOKIYA ...
I'LL PROTECT HER FROM ANY THREAT !!
WHAM
STOP !!
STOP IT, YOU TWO!!

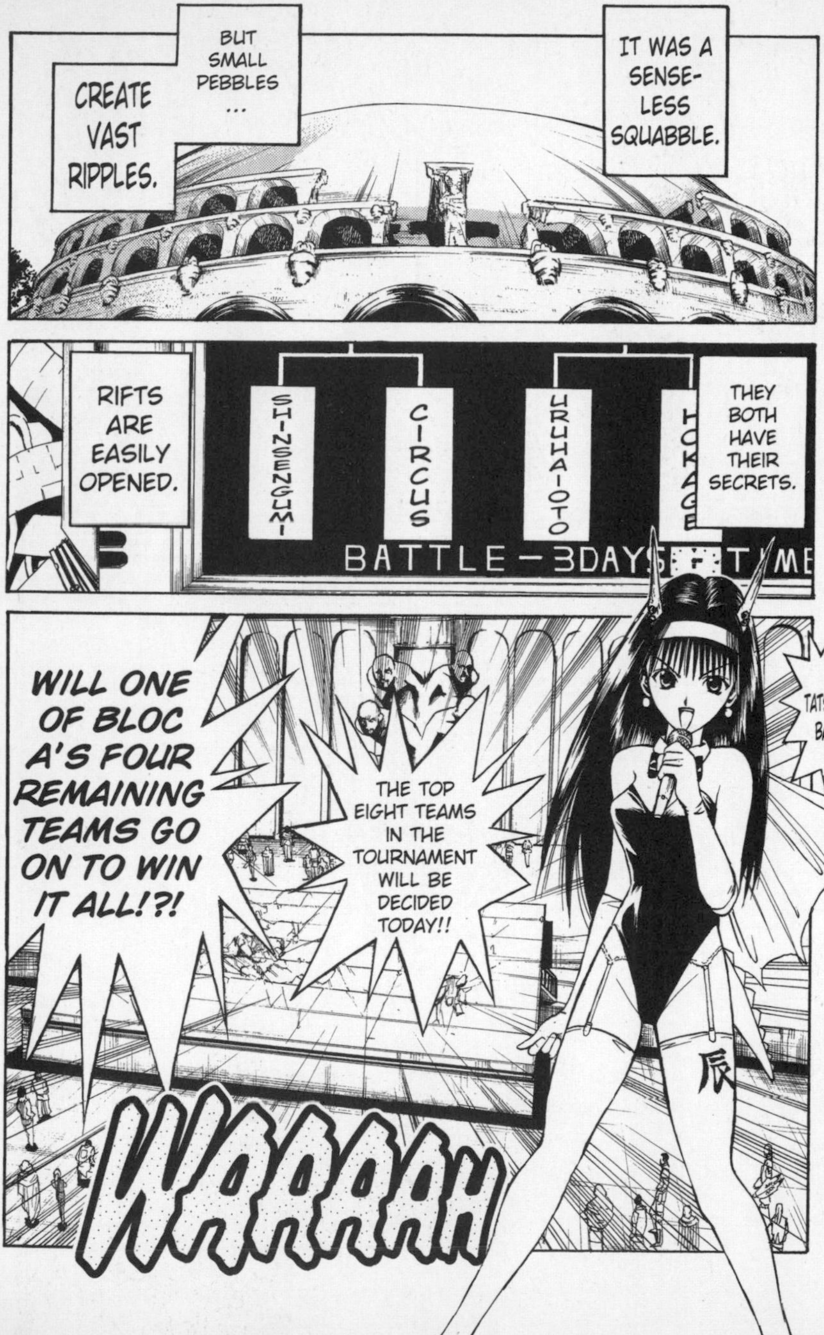
IT WAS A SENSELESS SQUABBLE.
BUT SMALL PEBBLES...
CREATE VAST RIPPLES.
THEY BOTH HAVE THEIR SECRETS.
SHINSENGUMI
CIRCUS
URUHAI-OTO
HOKAGE
BATTLE-3DAYS
TIME
RIFTS ARE EASILY OPENED.
TATSUKO'S BACK!!
THE TOP EIGHT TEAMS IN THE TOURNAMENT WILL BE DECIDED TODAY!!
WILL ONE OF BLOC A'S FOUR REMAINING TEAMS GO ON TO WIN IT ALL!?!
WAAAAH

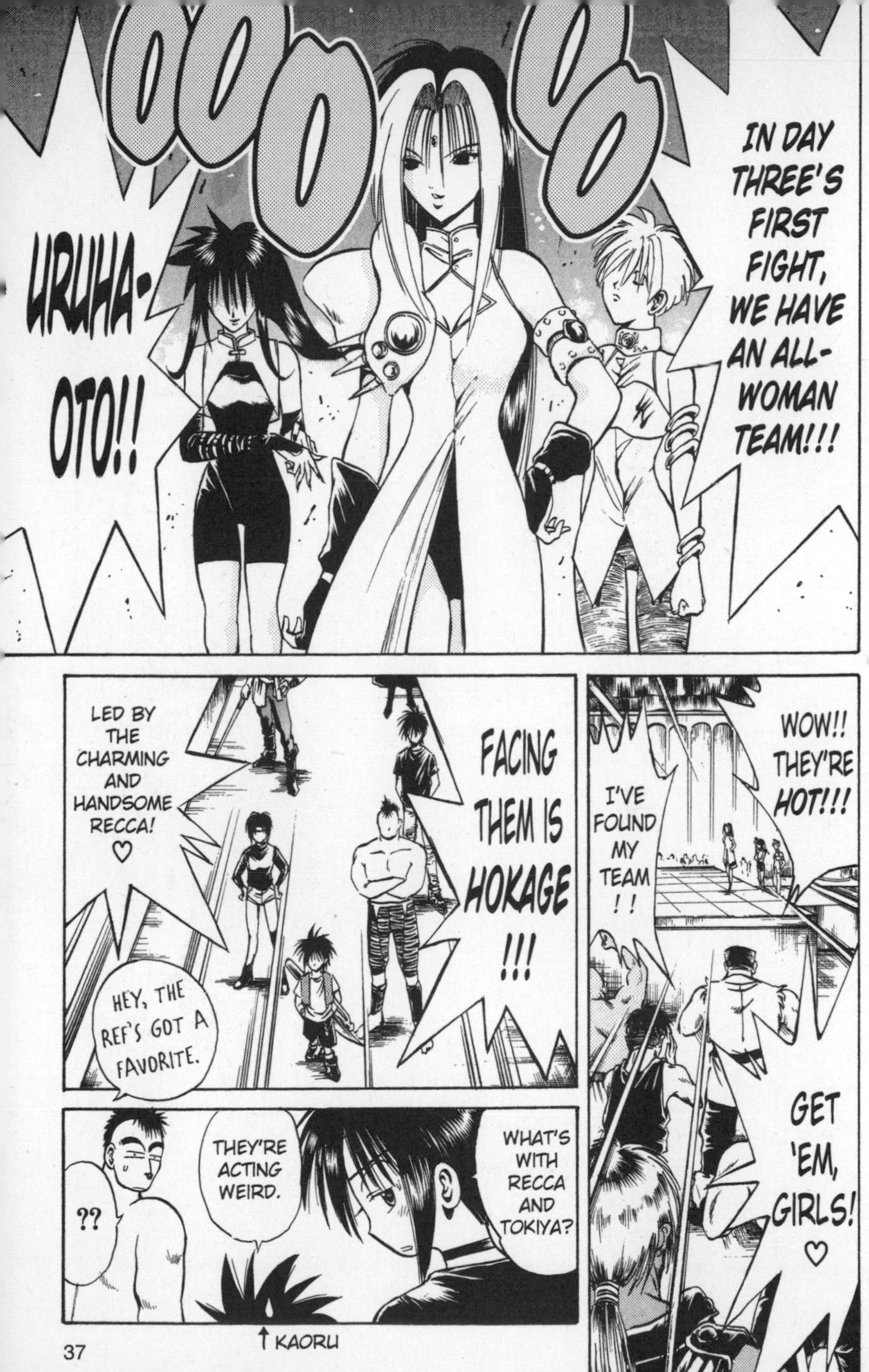
IN DAY THREE'S FIRST FIGHT, WE HAVE AN ALL-WOMAN TEAM!!!
URUHA-OTO!!
WOW!! THEY'RE HOT!!!
I'VE FOUND MY TEAM!!
GET 'EM, GIRLS! ♥
FACING THEM IS HOKAGE!!!
LED BY THE CHARMING AND HANDSOME RECCA! ♥
HEY, THE REF'S GOT A FAVORITE.
WHAT'S WITH RECCA AND TOKIYA?
THEY'RE ACTING WEIRD.
??
↑ KAORU

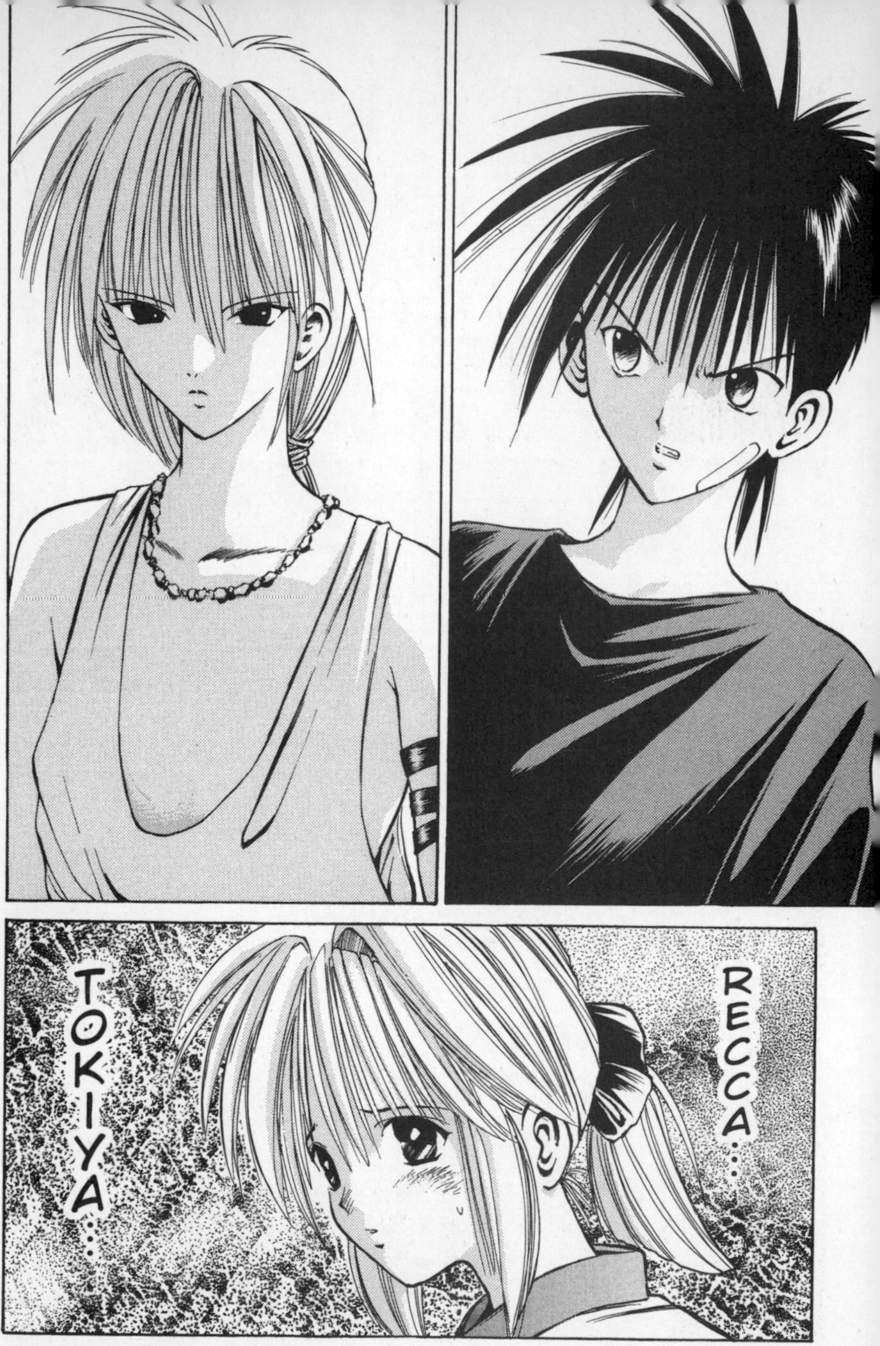
RECCA...
TOKIYA...

Part Seventy: Live (2) The Curtain Rises

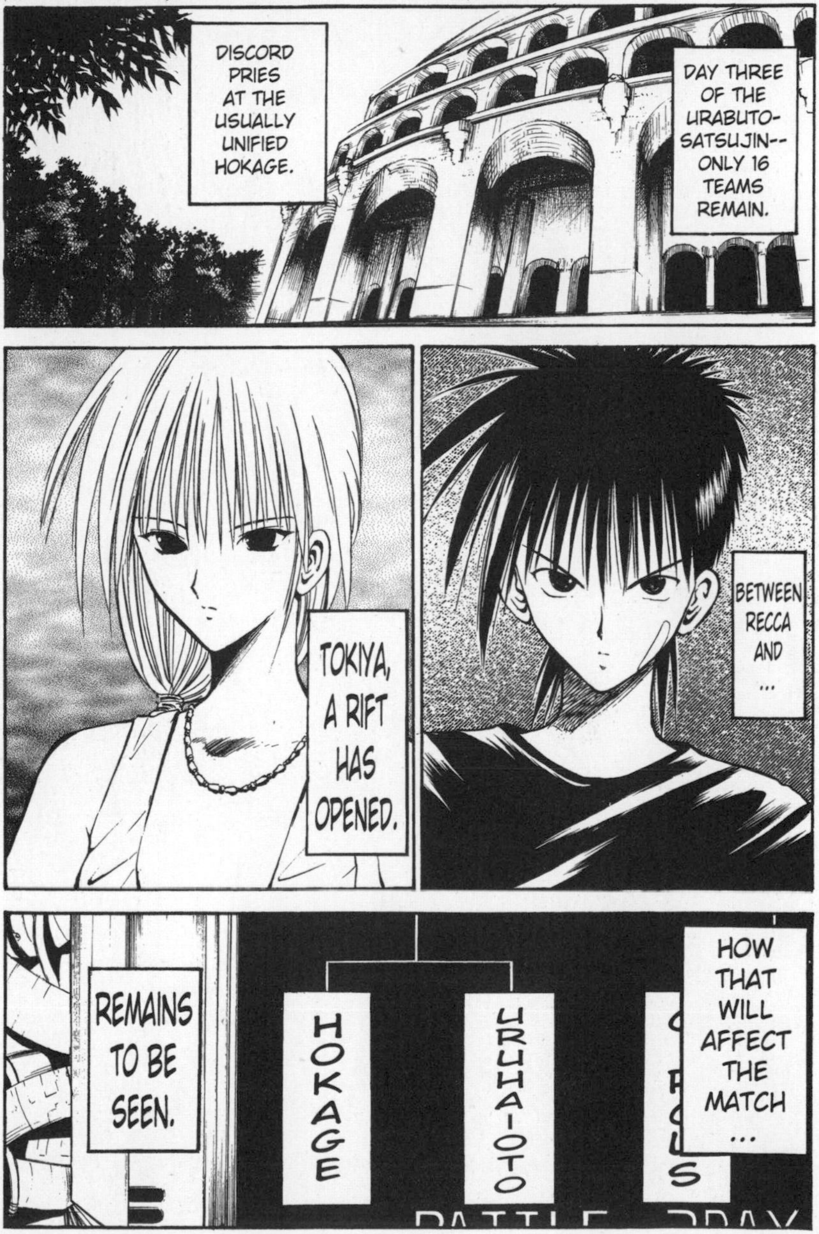

DAY THREE OF THE URABUTO-SATSUJIN--ONLY 16 TEAMS REMAIN.
DISCORD PRIES AT THE USUALLY UNIFIED HOKAGE.
BETWEEN RECCA AND ...
TOKIYA, A RIFT HAS OPENED.
HOW THAT WILL AFFECT THE MATCH ...
URUHAI-OTO
HOKAGE
REMAINS TO BE SEEN.

Part Seventy:
Live (2) The Curtain Rises

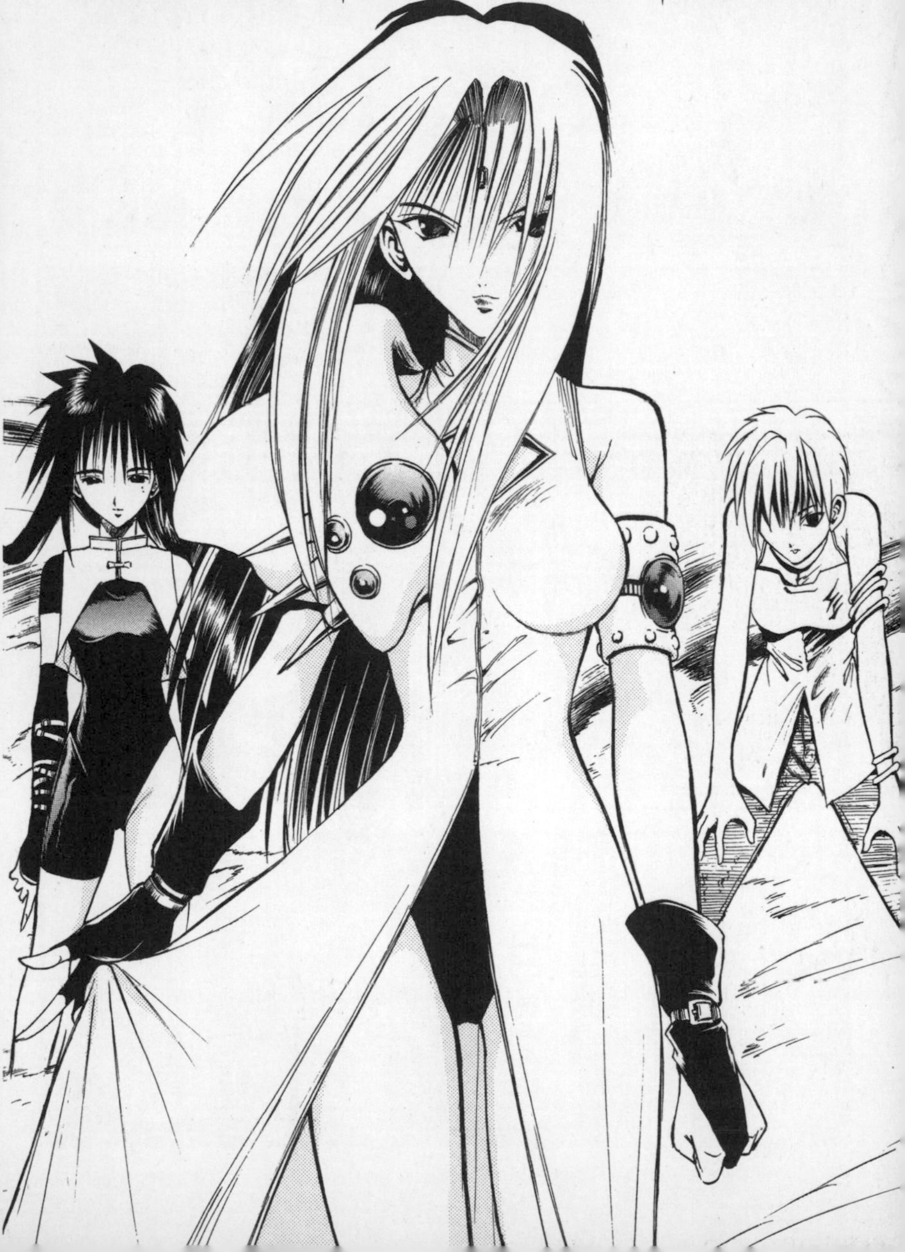

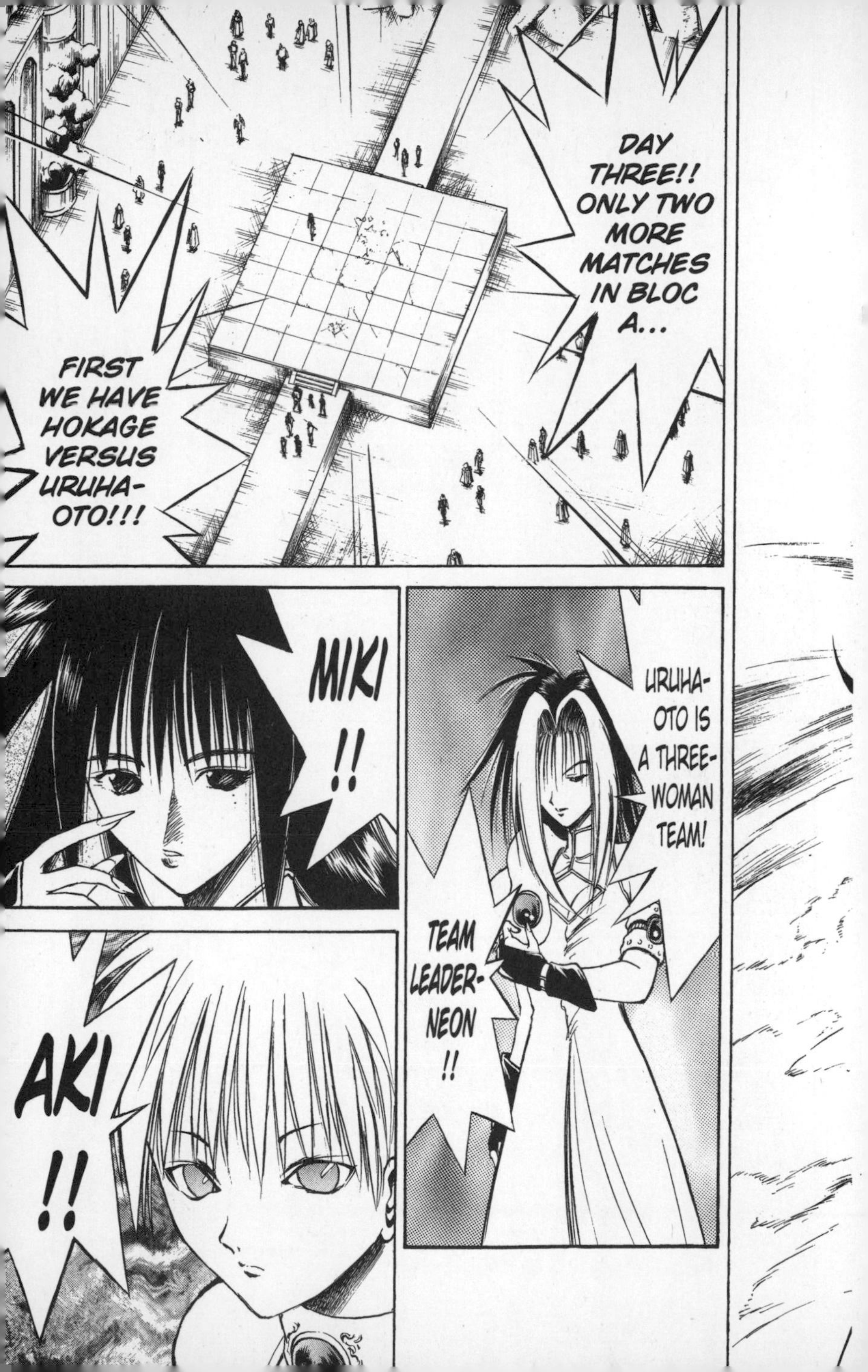
DAY THREE!! ONLY TWO MORE MATCHES IN BLOC A...
FIRST WE HAVE HOKAGE VERSUS URUHA-OTO!!!
URUHA-OTO IS A THREE-WOMAN TEAM!
TEAM LEADER-NEON !!
MIKI !!
AKI !!

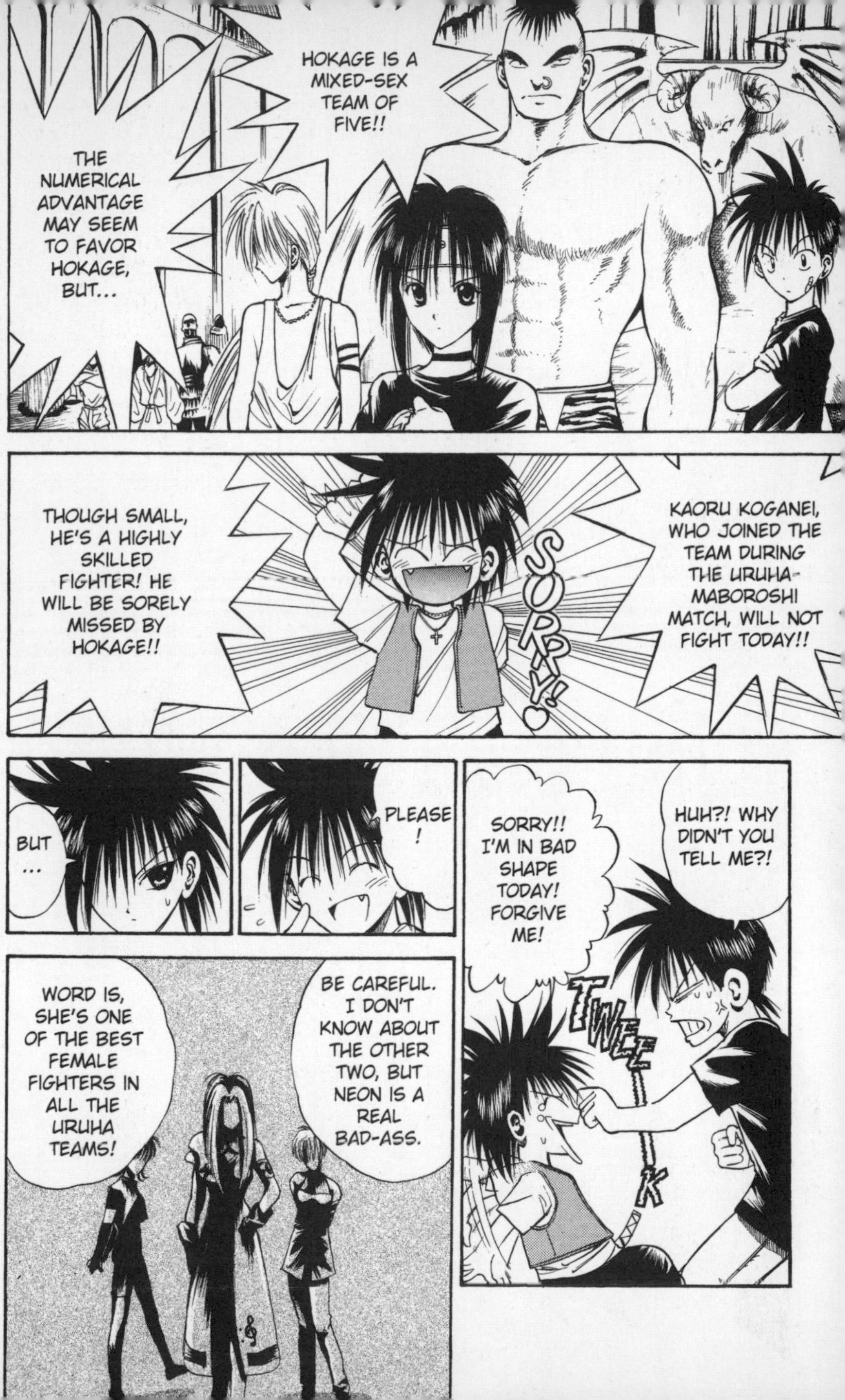
HOKAGE IS A MIXED-SEX TEAM OF FIVE!!
THE NUMERICAL ADVANTAGE MAY SEEM TO FAVOR HOKAGE, BUT...
KAORU KOGANEI, WHO JOINED THE TEAM DURING THE URUHA-MABOROSHI MATCH, WILL NOT FIGHT TODAY!!
SORRY!
THOUGH SMALL, HE'S A HIGHLY SKILLED FIGHTER! HE WILL BE SORELY MISSED BY HOKAGE!!
HUH?! WHY DIDN'T YOU TELL ME?!
SORRY!! I'M IN BAD SHAPE TODAY! FORGIVE ME!
TWEEK
PLEASE!
BUT...
BE CAREFUL. I DON'T KNOW ABOUT THE OTHER TWO, BUT NEON IS A REAL BAD-ASS.
WORD IS, SHE'S ONE OF THE BEST FEMALE FIGHTERS IN ALL THE URUHA TEAMS!

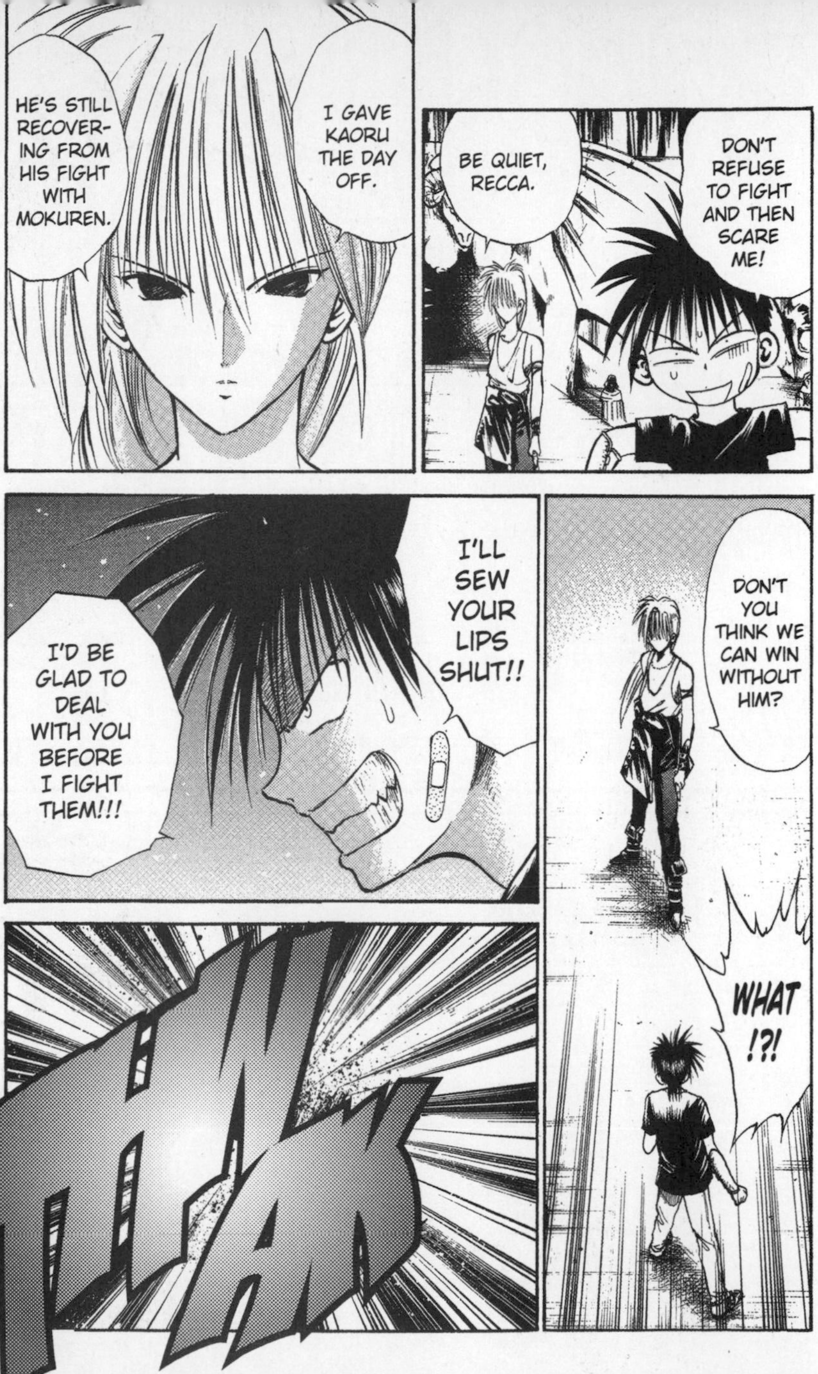
DON'T REFUSE TO FIGHT AND THEN SCARE ME!
BE QUIET, RECCA.
I GAVE KAORU THE DAY OFF.
HE'S STILL RECOVER-ING FROM HIS FIGHT WITH MOKUREN.
DON'T YOU THINK WE CAN WIN WITHOUT HIM?
I'LL SEW YOUR LIPS SHUT!!
I'D BE GLAD TO DEAL WITH YOU BEFORE I FIGHT THEM!!!
WHAT !?!
THWAK

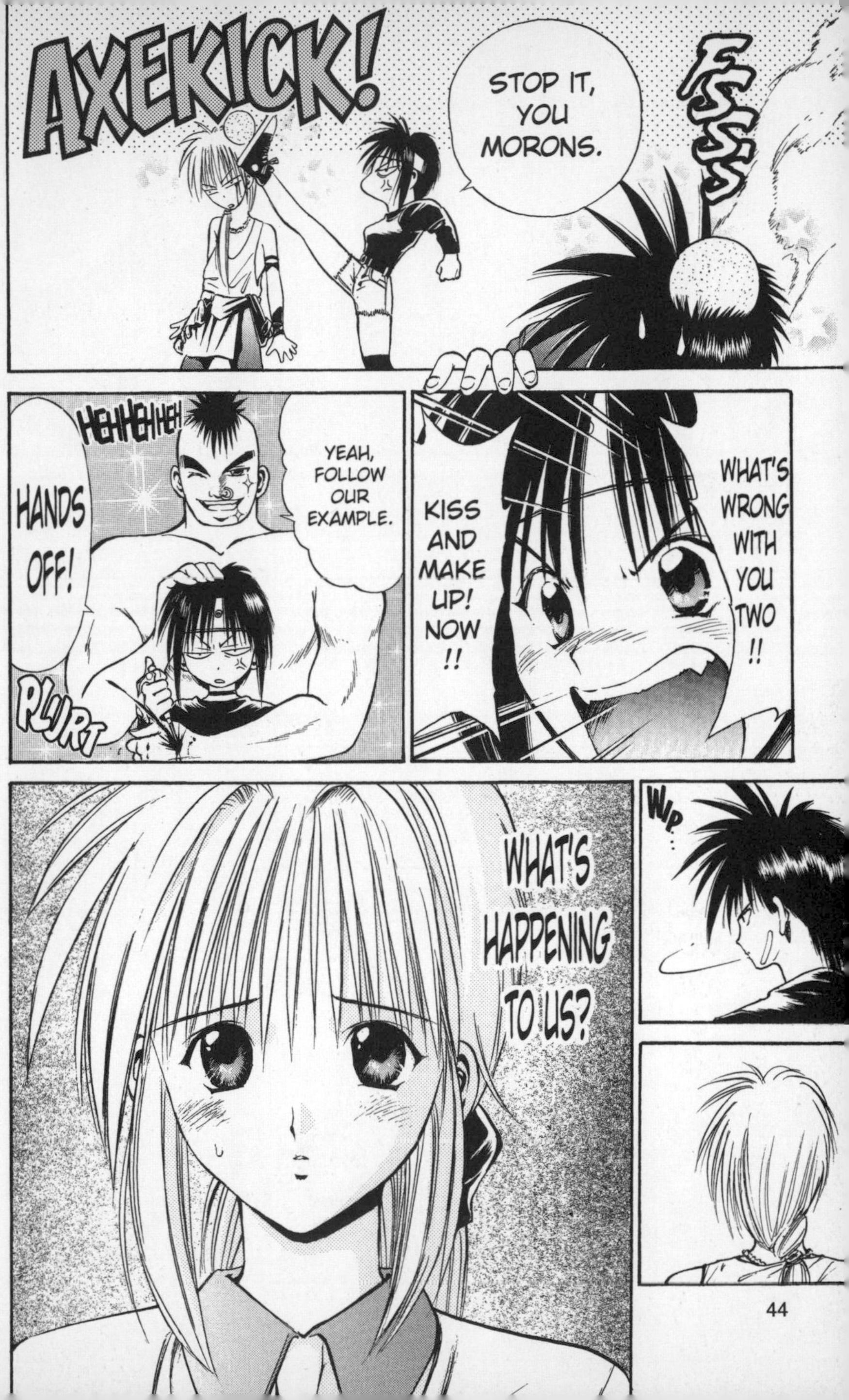
FSSS
STOP IT, YOU MORONS.
AXEKICK!
WHAT'S WRONG WITH YOU TWO !!
KISS AND MAKE UP! NOW !!
YEAH, FOLLOW OUR EXAMPLE.
HEHHEHHEH
HANDS OFF!
PLURT
WIP...
WHAT'S HAPPENING TO US?

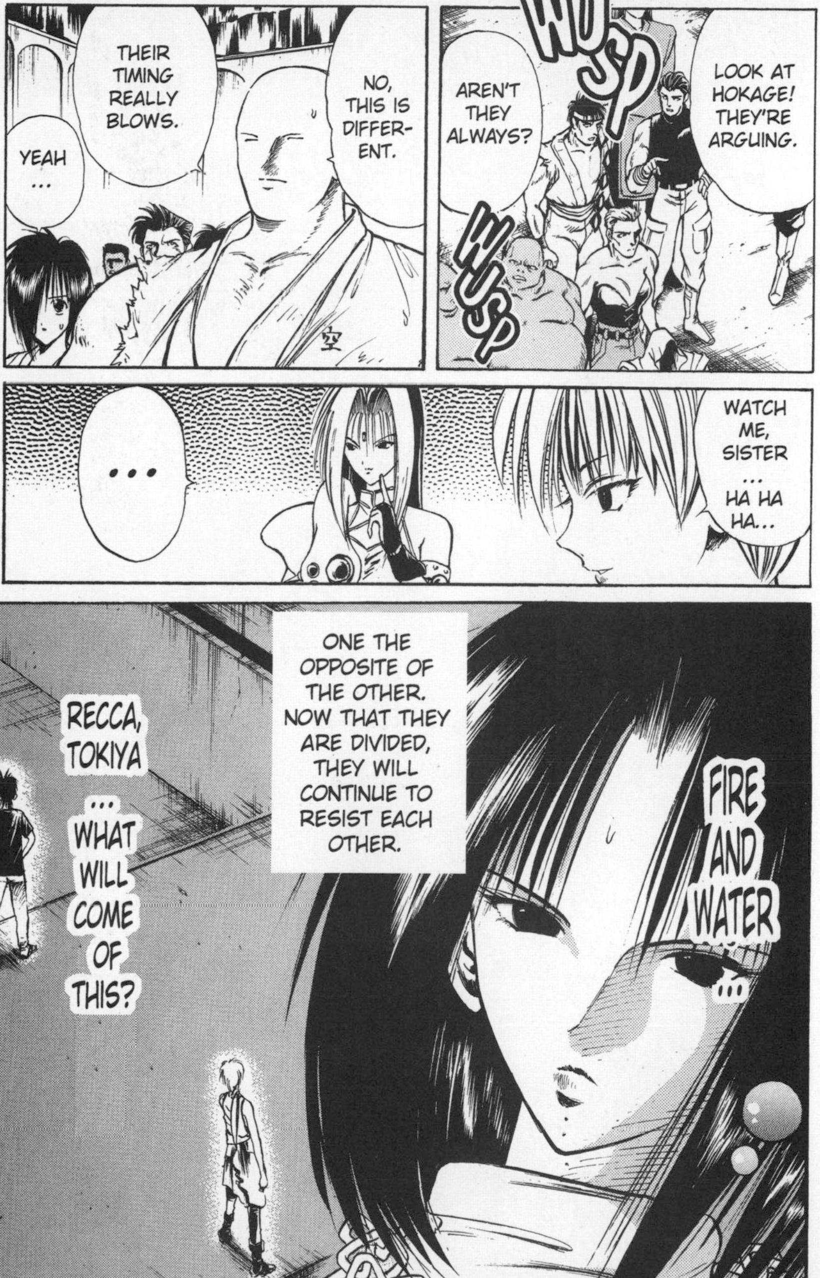
WUSP
LOOK AT HOKAGE! THEY'RE ARGUING.
AREN'T THEY ALWAYS?
WUSP
NO, THIS IS DIFFER-ENT.
THEIR TIMING REALLY BLOWS.
YEAH ...
WATCH ME, SISTER ... HA HA HA...
...
FIRE AND WATER ...
ONE THE OPPOSITE OF THE OTHER. NOW THAT THEY ARE DIVIDED, THEY WILL CONTINUE TO RESIST EACH OTHER.
RECCA, TOKIYA ... WHAT WILL COME OF THIS?

BLOC A SEMI-FINALS ROSTER

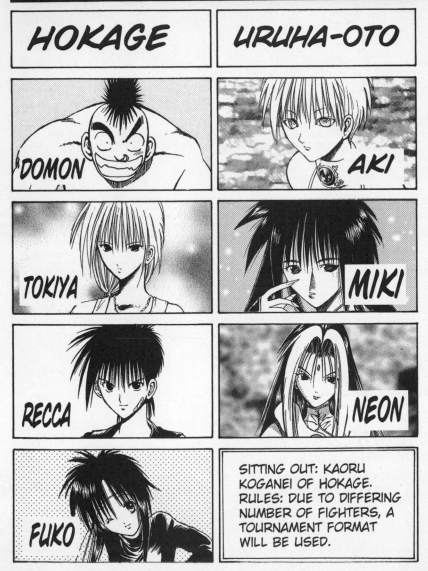

URUHA-OTO

HOKAGE

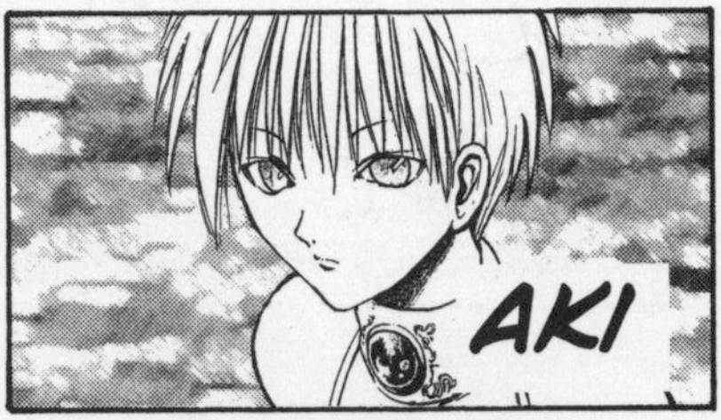
AKI

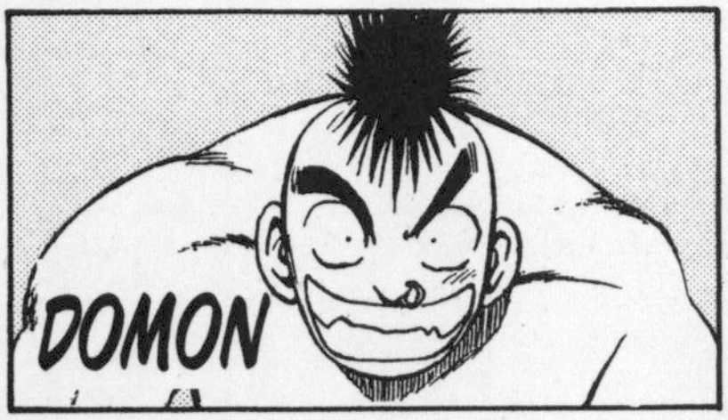
DOMON

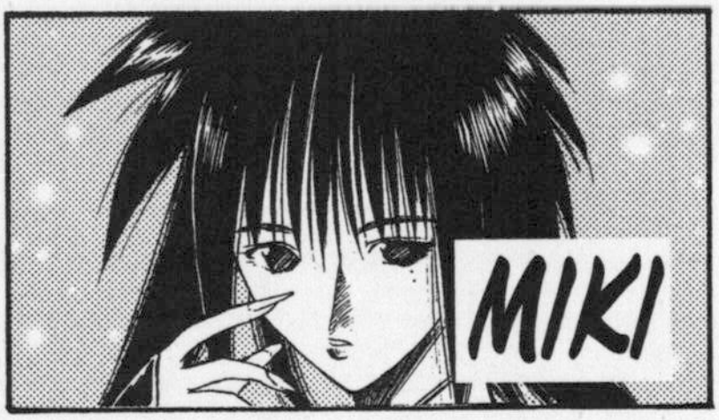
MIKI

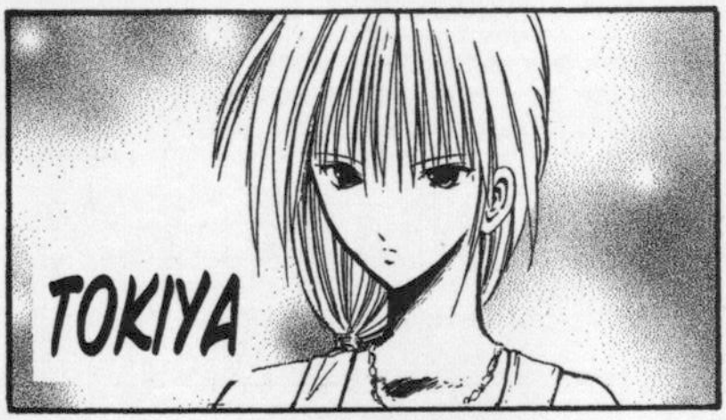
TOKIYA

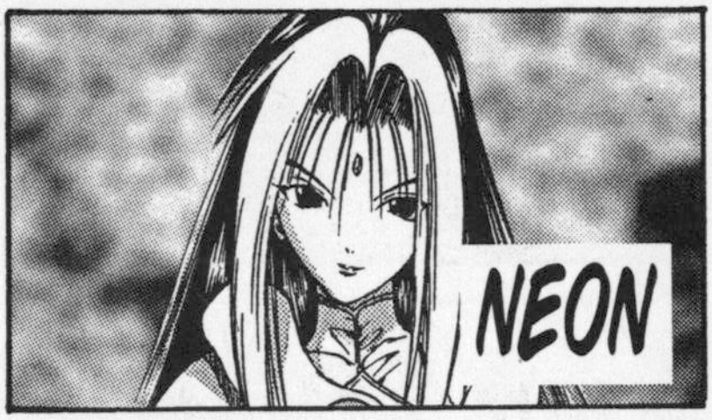
NEON

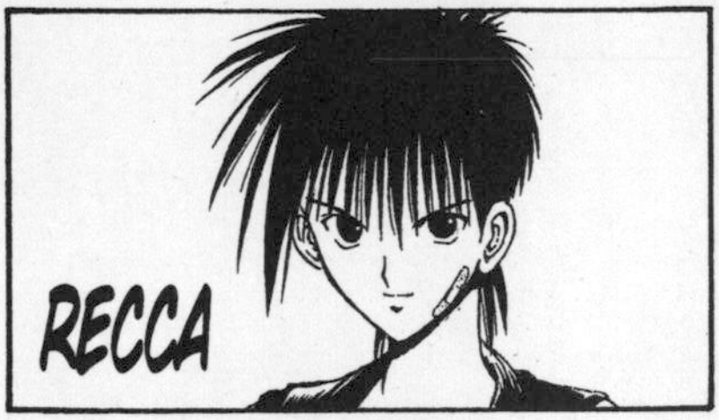
RECCA

SITTING OUT: KAORU KOGANEI OF HOKAGE.
RULES: DUE TO DIFFERING NUMBER OF FIGHTERS, A TOURNAMENT FORMAT WILL BE USED.

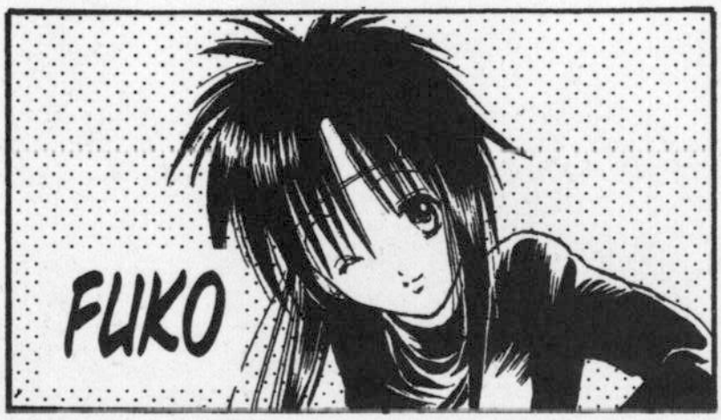
FUKO

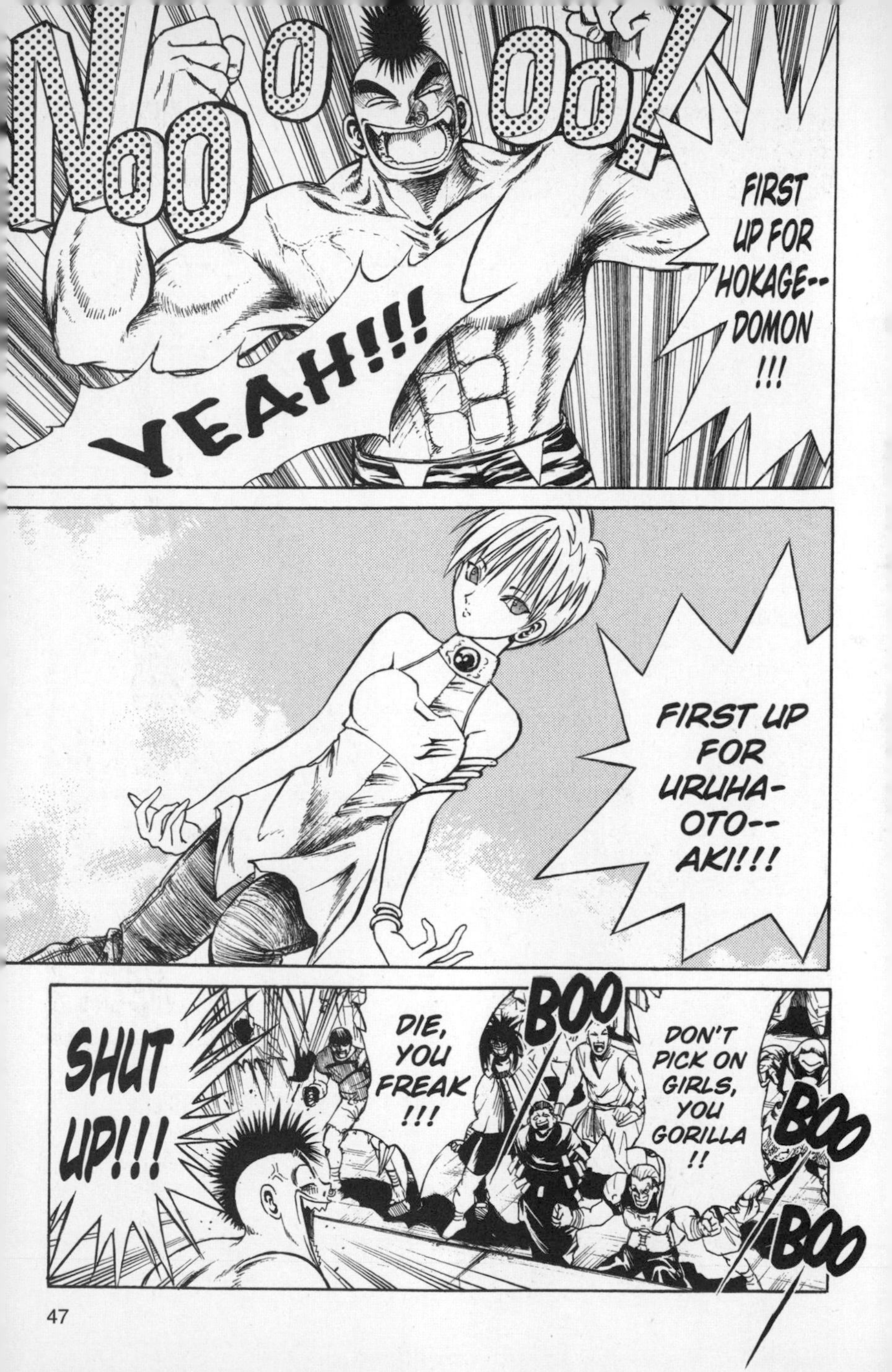
NOOOOOOO!
FIRST UP FOR HOKAGE-- DOMON!!!
YEAH!!!
FIRST UP FOR URUHA-OTO-- AKI!!!
BOO
BOO
BOO
DON'T PICK ON GIRLS, YOU GORILLA!!
DIE, YOU FREAK!!!
SHUT UP!!!

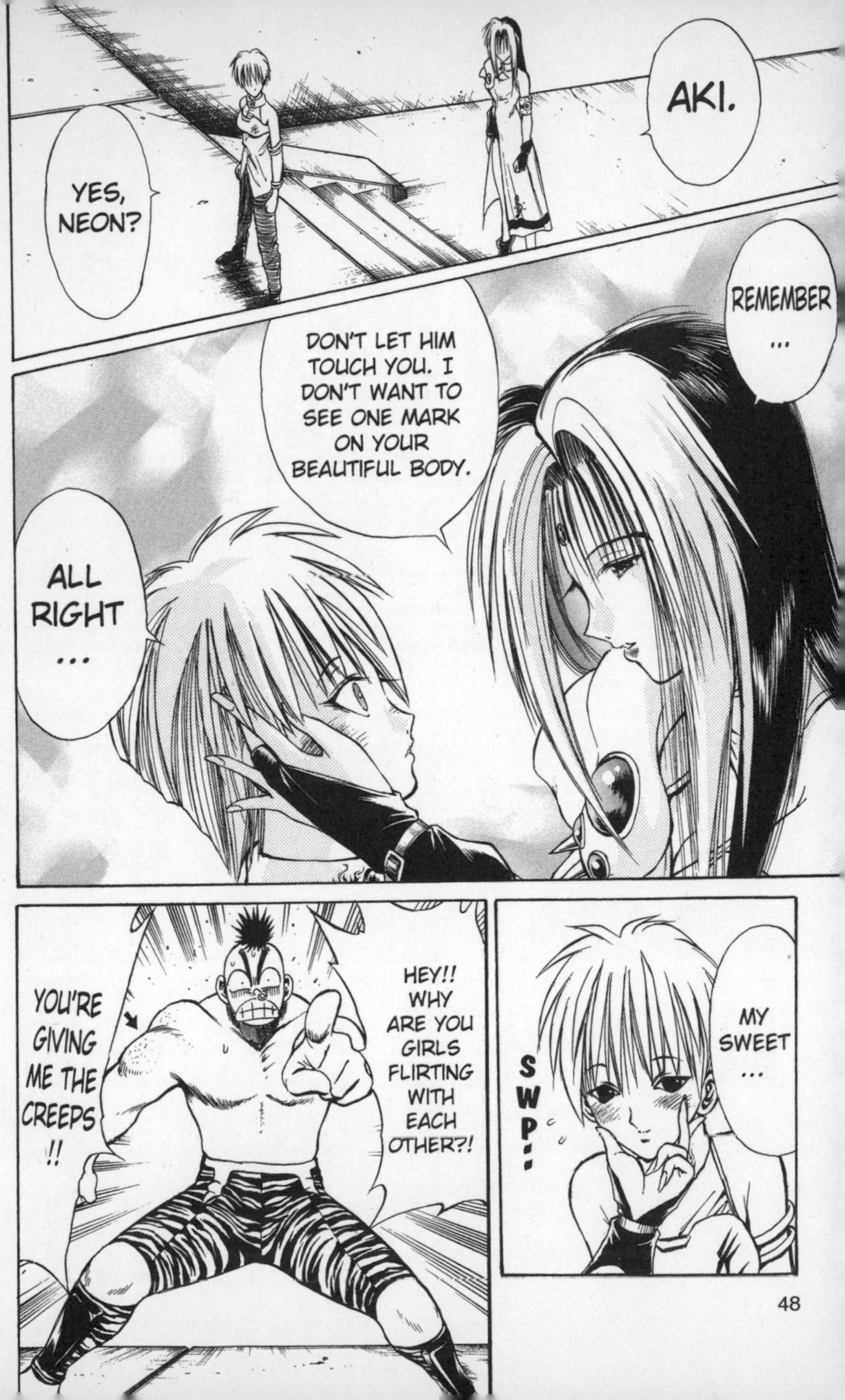
AKI.
YES, NEON?
REMEMBER ...
DON'T LET HIM TOUCH YOU. I DON'T WANT TO SEE ONE MARK ON YOUR BEAUTIFUL BODY.
ALL RIGHT ...
MY SWEET ...
SWP..
HEY!! WHY ARE YOU GIRLS FLIRTING WITH EACH OTHER?!
YOU'RE GIVING ME THE CREEPS!!

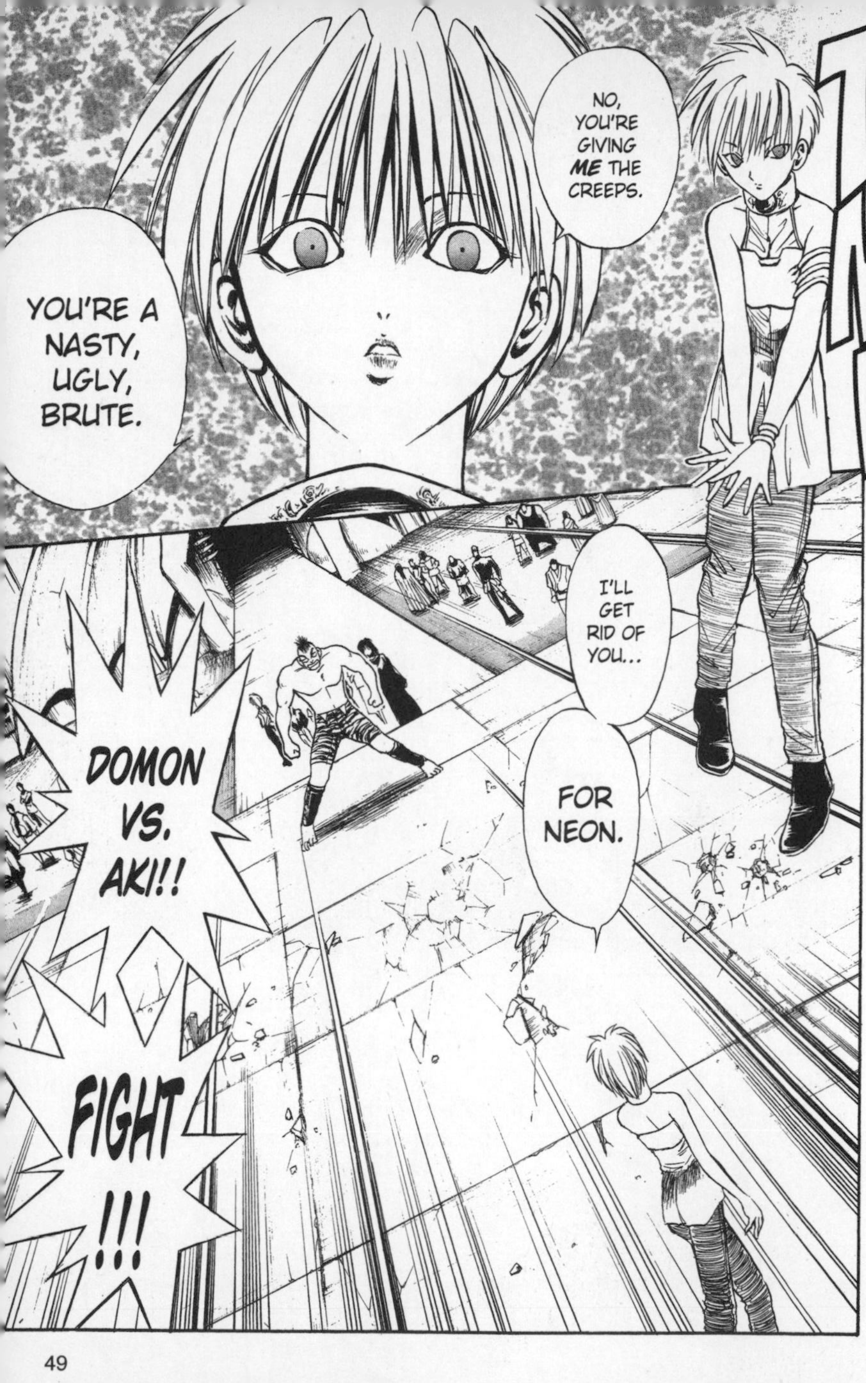
TMP
YOU'RE A NASTY, UGLY, BRUTE.
NO, YOU'RE GIVING *ME* THE CREEPS.
I'LL GET RID OF YOU...
FOR NEON.
DOMON VS. AKI!!
FIGHT!!!

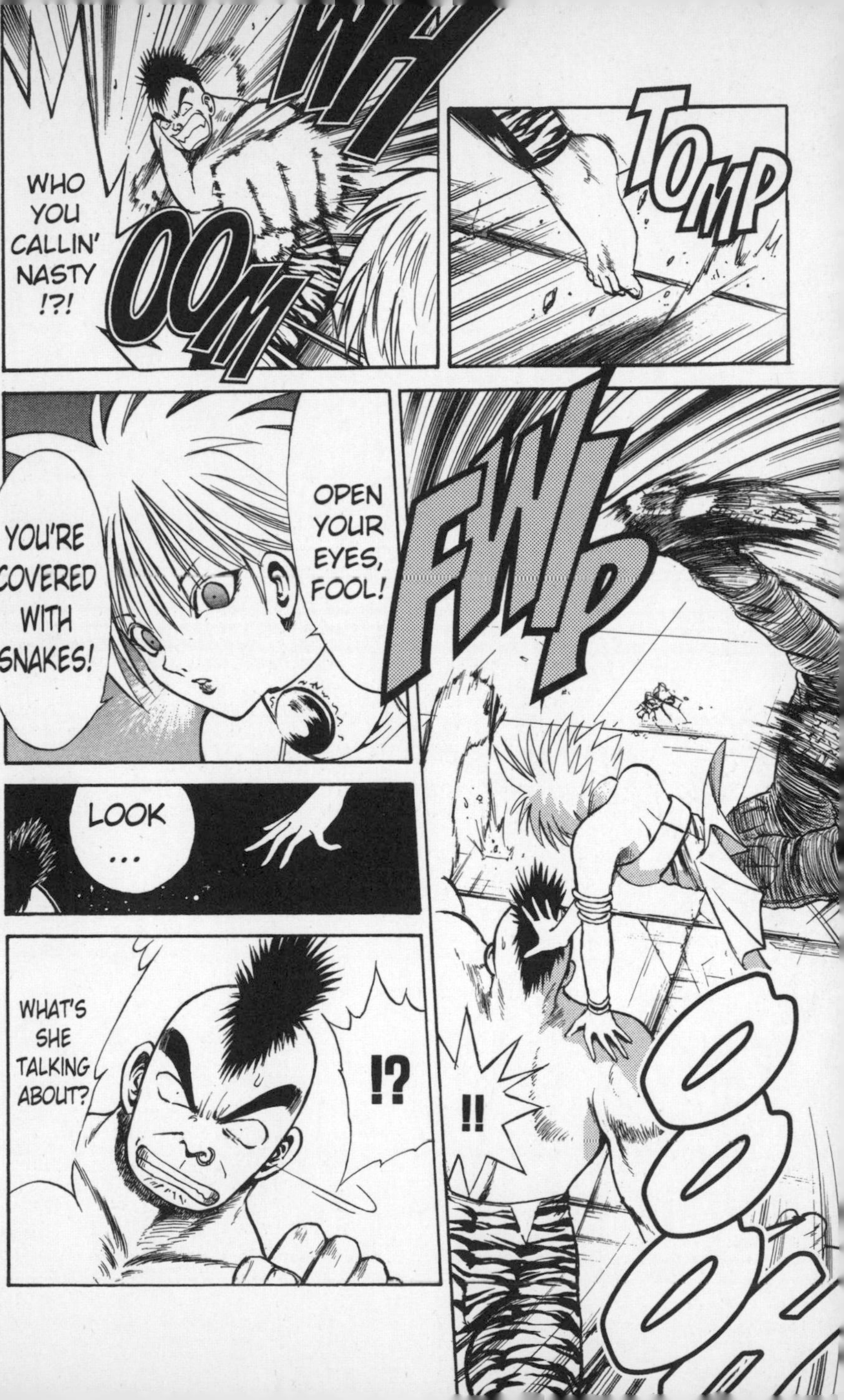
TOMP
WHOOM
WHO YOU CALLIN' NASTY !?!
FWIP
!!
OOOO
OPEN YOUR EYES, FOOL!
YOU'RE COVERED WITH SNAKES!
LOOK ...
!?
WHAT'S SHE TALKING ABOUT?

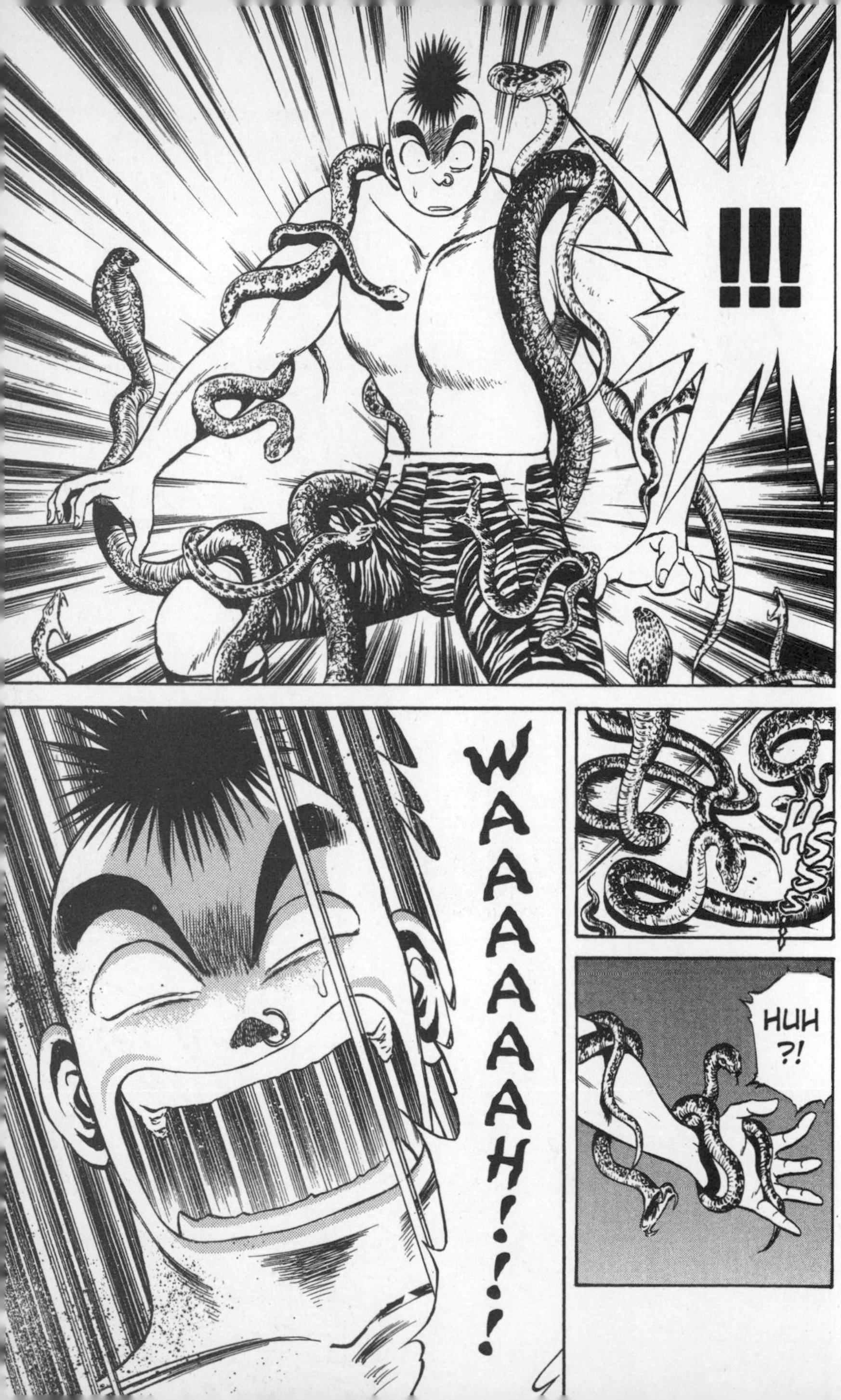
!!!
HSSS
HUH ?!
WAAAAAAH!!!!

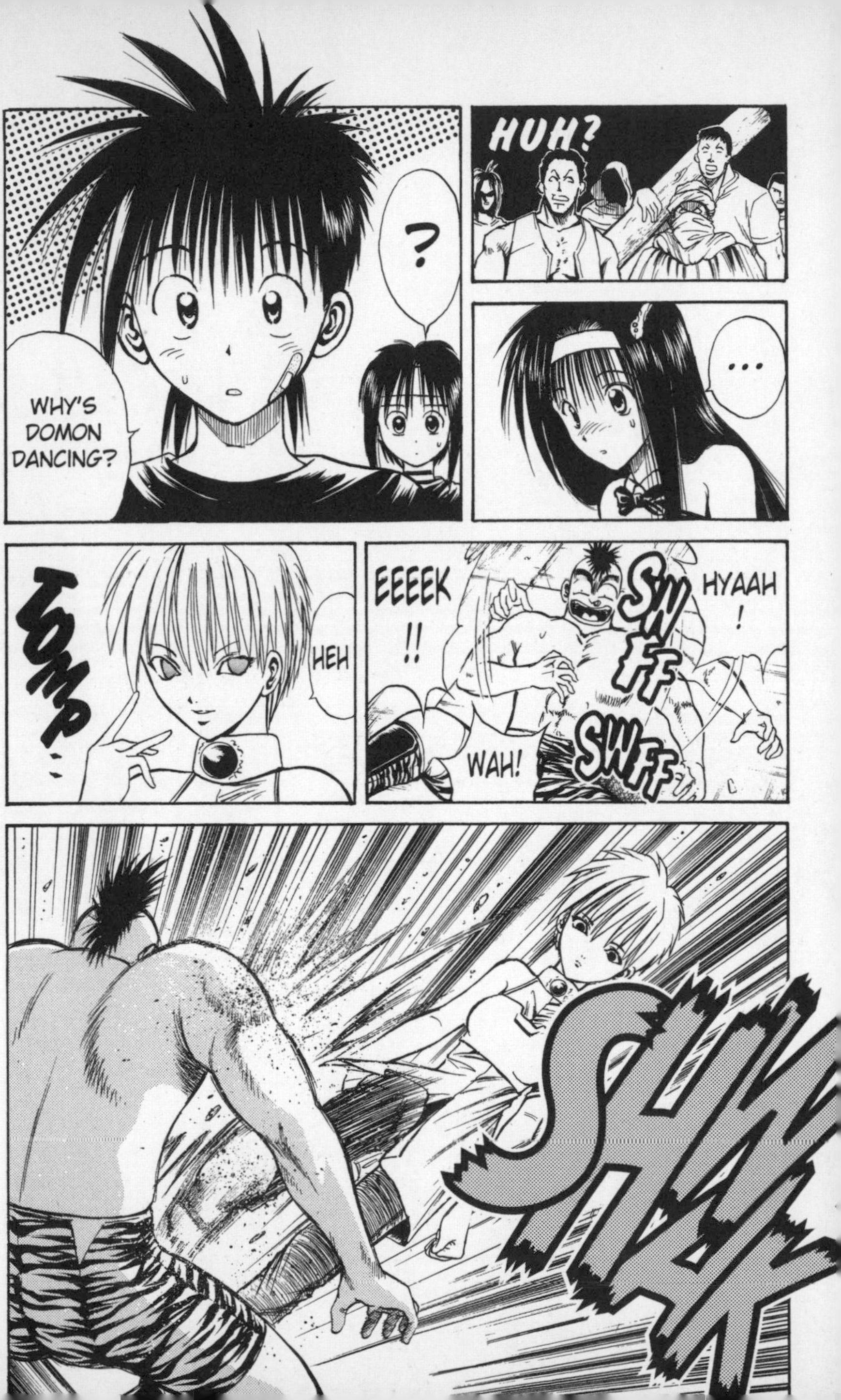
HUH?
...
?
WHY'S DOMON DANCING?
HYAAH !
SNFF
EEEEK !!
SWFF
WAH!
HEH
TOMP

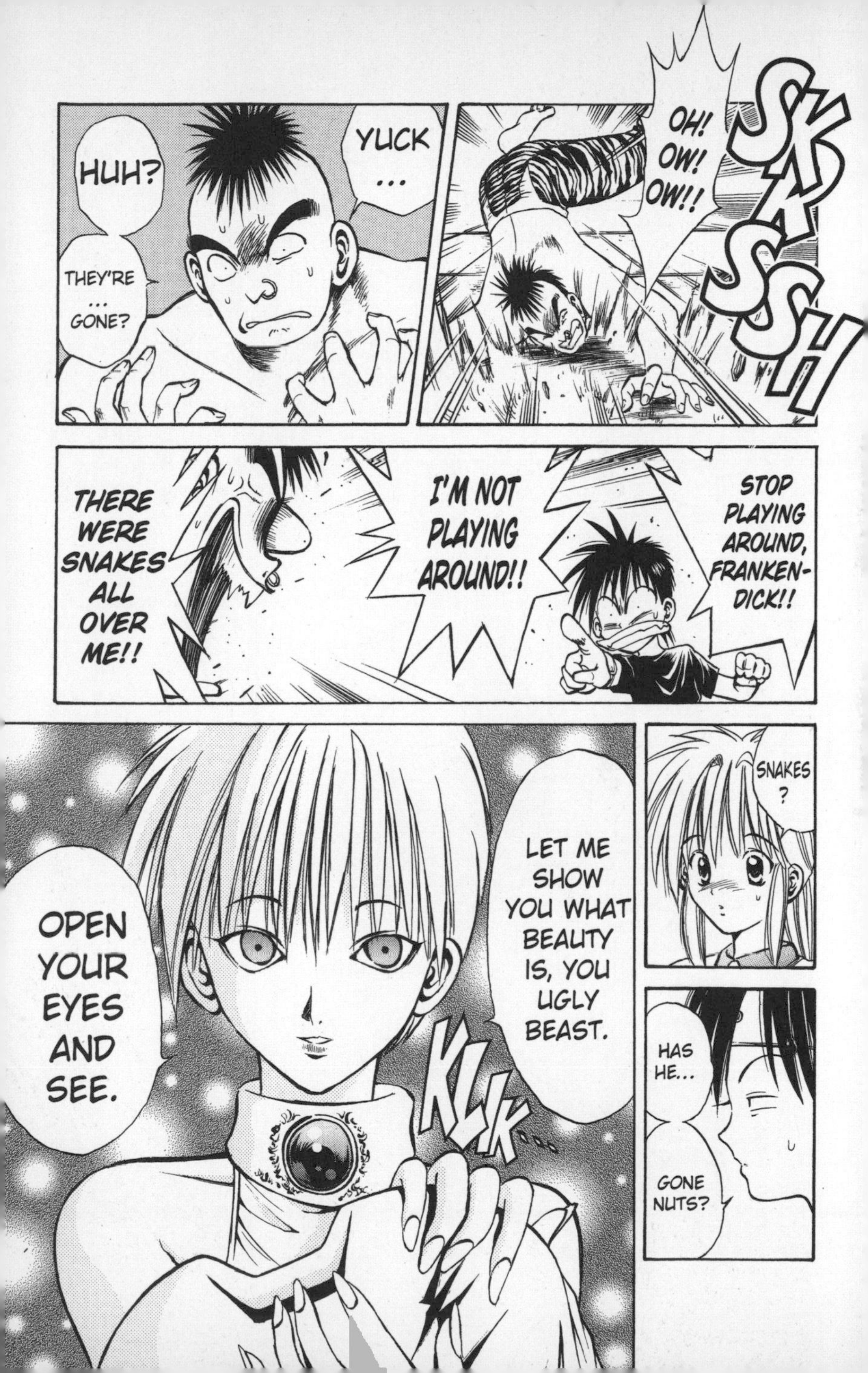
SKSSSH
OH! OW! OW!!
YUCK ...
HUH?
THEY'RE ... GONE?
STOP PLAYING AROUND, FRANKEN-DICK!!
I'M NOT PLAYING AROUND!!
THERE WERE SNAKES ALL OVER ME!!
SNAKES ?
HAS HE...
GONE NUTS?
LET ME SHOW YOU WHAT BEAUTY IS, YOU UGLY BEAST.
KLIK...
OPEN YOUR EYES AND SEE.

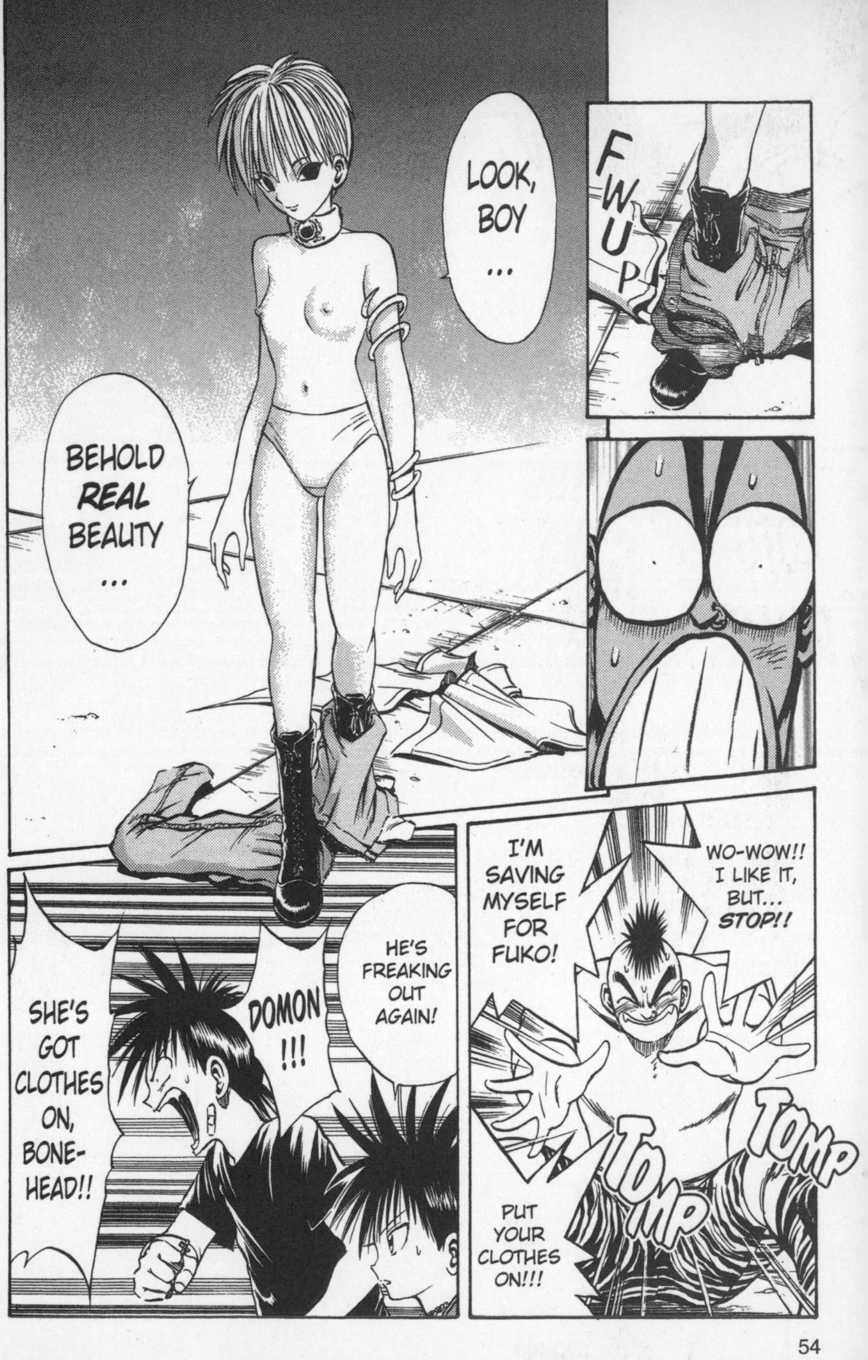
FWUP
LOOK, BOY ...
BEHOLD REAL BEAUTY ...
WO-WOW!! I LIKE IT, BUT... STOP!!
I'M SAVING MYSELF FOR FUKO!
TOMP
TOMP
PUT YOUR CLOTHES ON!!!
HE'S FREAKING OUT AGAIN!
DOMON!!!
SHE'S GOT CLOTHES ON, BONE-HEAD!!

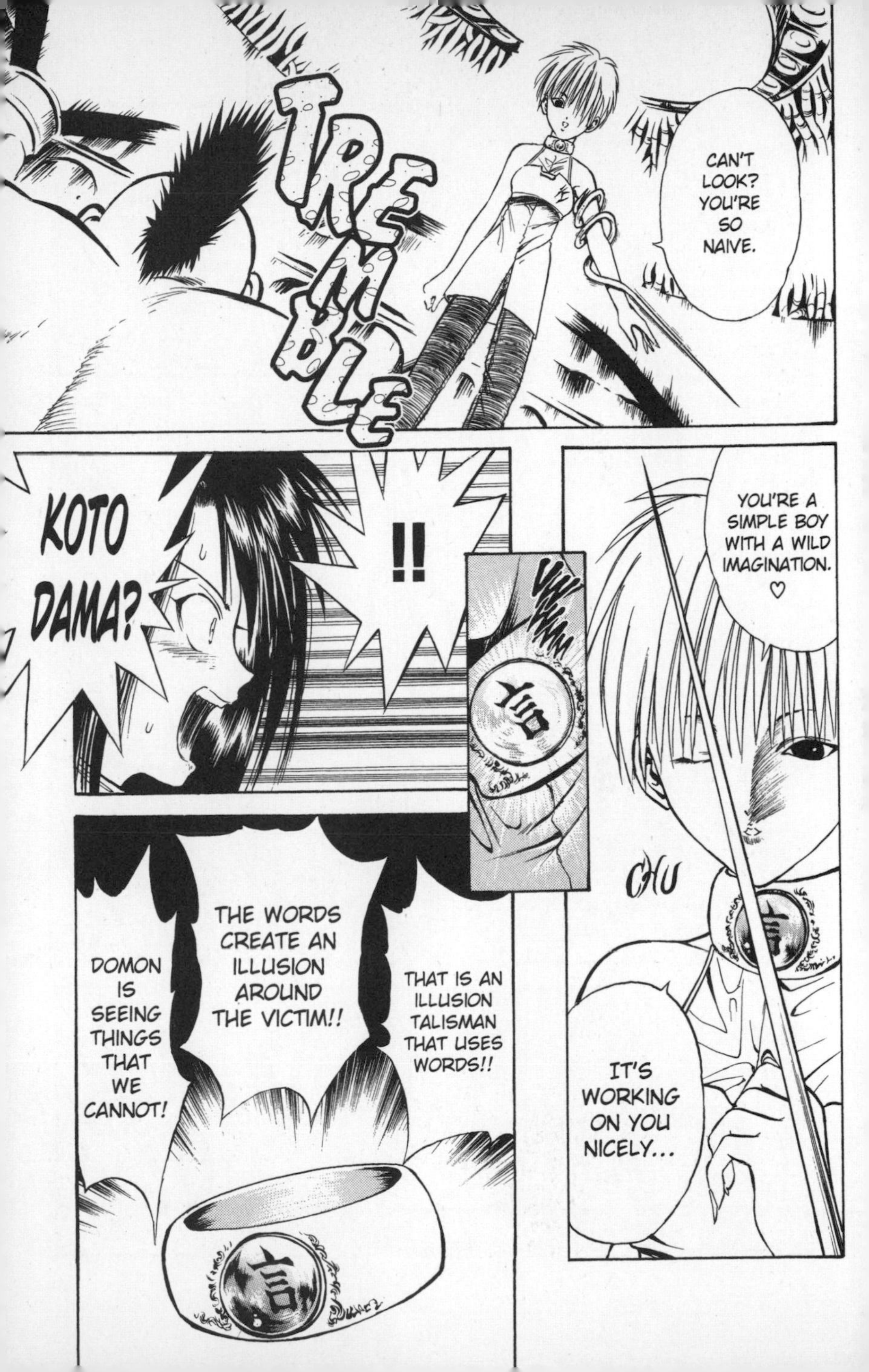
CAN'T LOOK? YOU'RE SO NAIVE.
TREMBLE
YOU'RE A SIMPLE BOY WITH A WILD IMAGINATION. ♡
CHU
IT'S WORKING ON YOU NICELY...
!!
KOTO DAMA?
THAT IS AN ILLUSION TALISMAN THAT USES WORDS!!
THE WORDS CREATE AN ILLUSION AROUND THE VICTIM!!
DOMON IS SEEING THINGS THAT WE CANNOT!

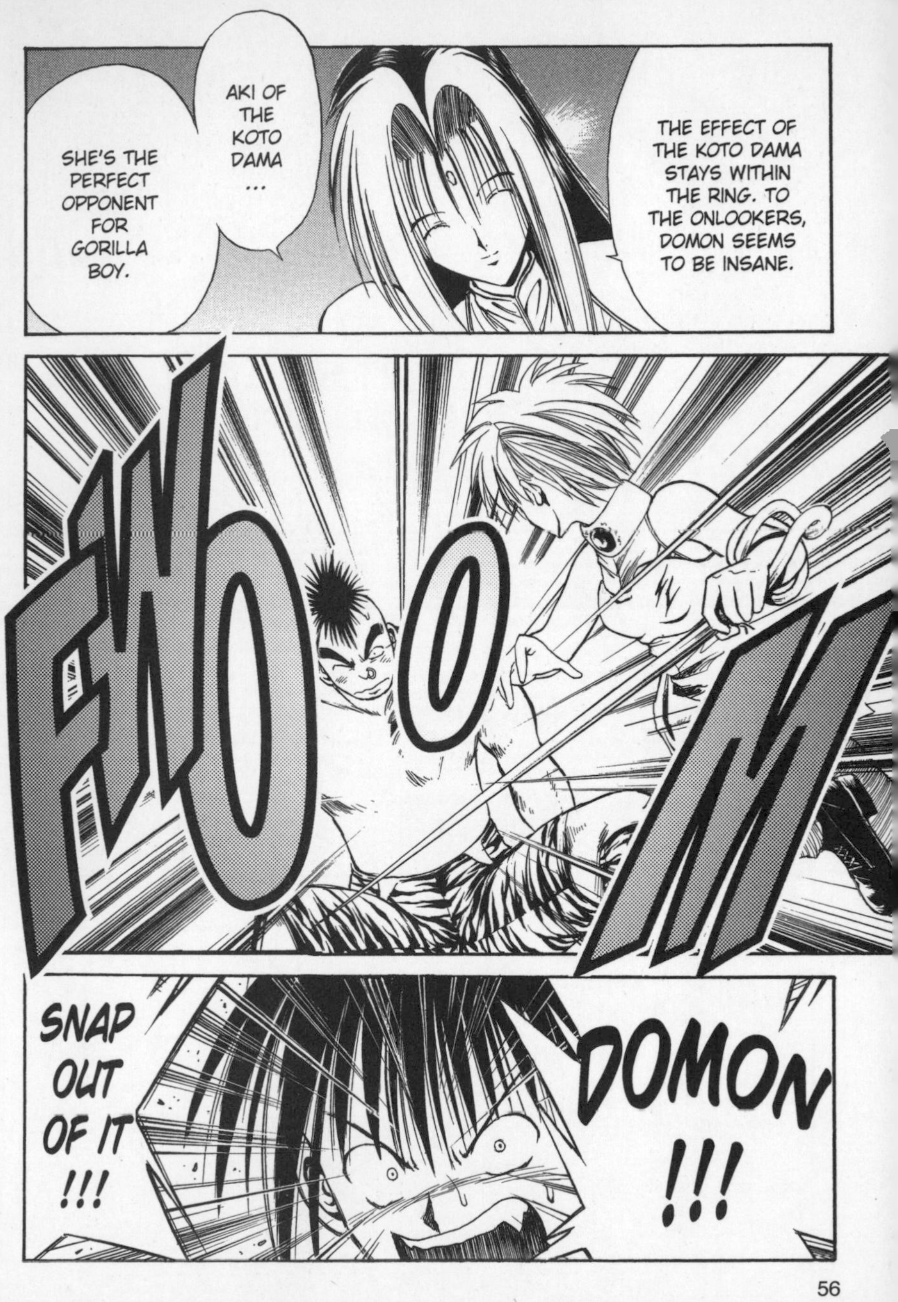
THE EFFECT OF THE KOTO DAMA STAYS WITHIN THE RING. TO THE ONLOOKERS, DOMON SEEMS TO BE INSANE.
AKI OF THE KOTO DAMA ...
SHE'S THE PERFECT OPPONENT FOR GORILLA BOY.
FWOOM
DOMON !!!
SNAP OUT OF IT !!!

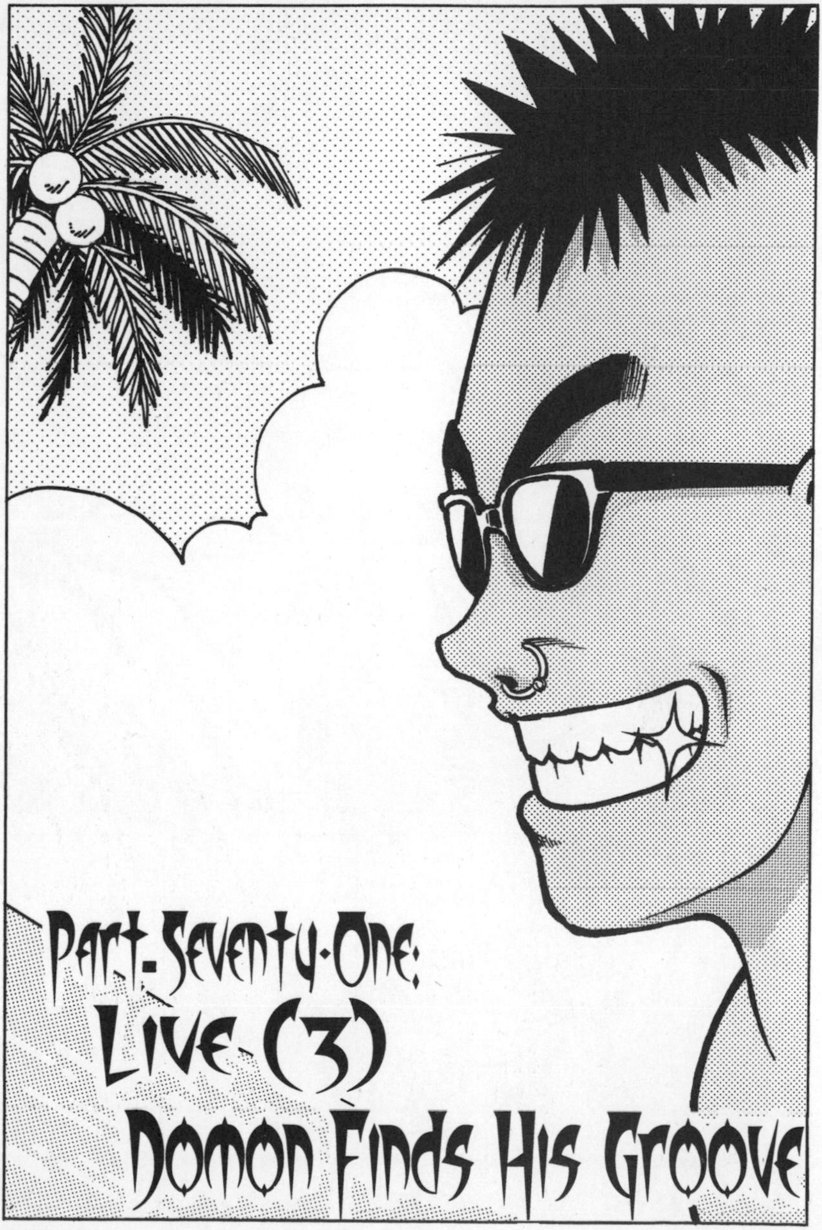
Part Seventy-One:
Live (3)
Domon Finds His Groove

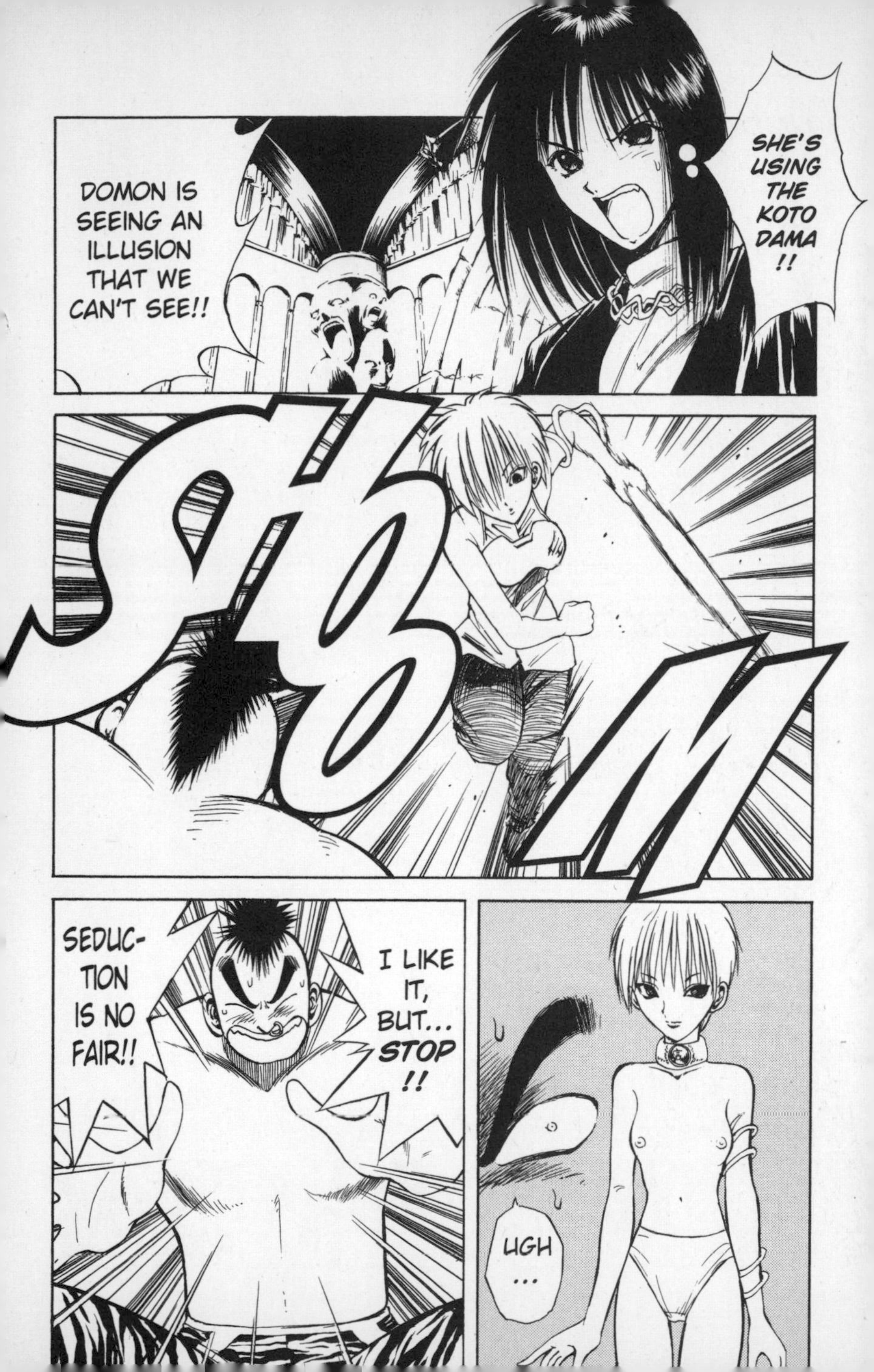
SHE'S USING THE KOTO DAMA!!
DOMON IS SEEING AN ILLUSION THAT WE CAN'T SEE!!
UGH...
I LIKE IT, BUT... STOP!!
SEDUC-TION IS NO FAIR!!

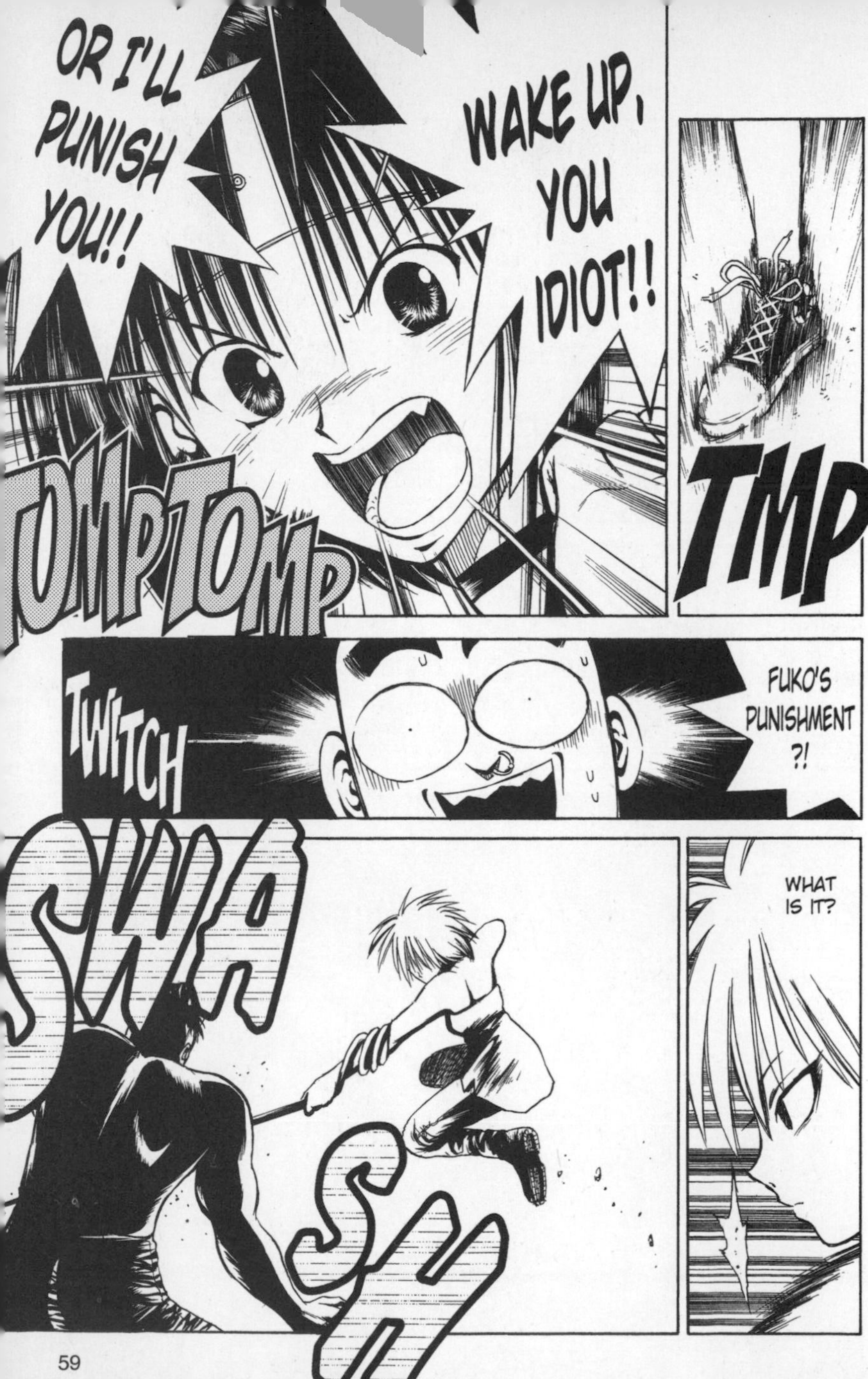
TMP
WAKE UP, YOU IDIOT!!
OR I'LL PUNISH YOU!!
TOMPTOMP
FUKO'S PUNISHMENT ?!
TWITCH
WHAT IS IT?
SWA

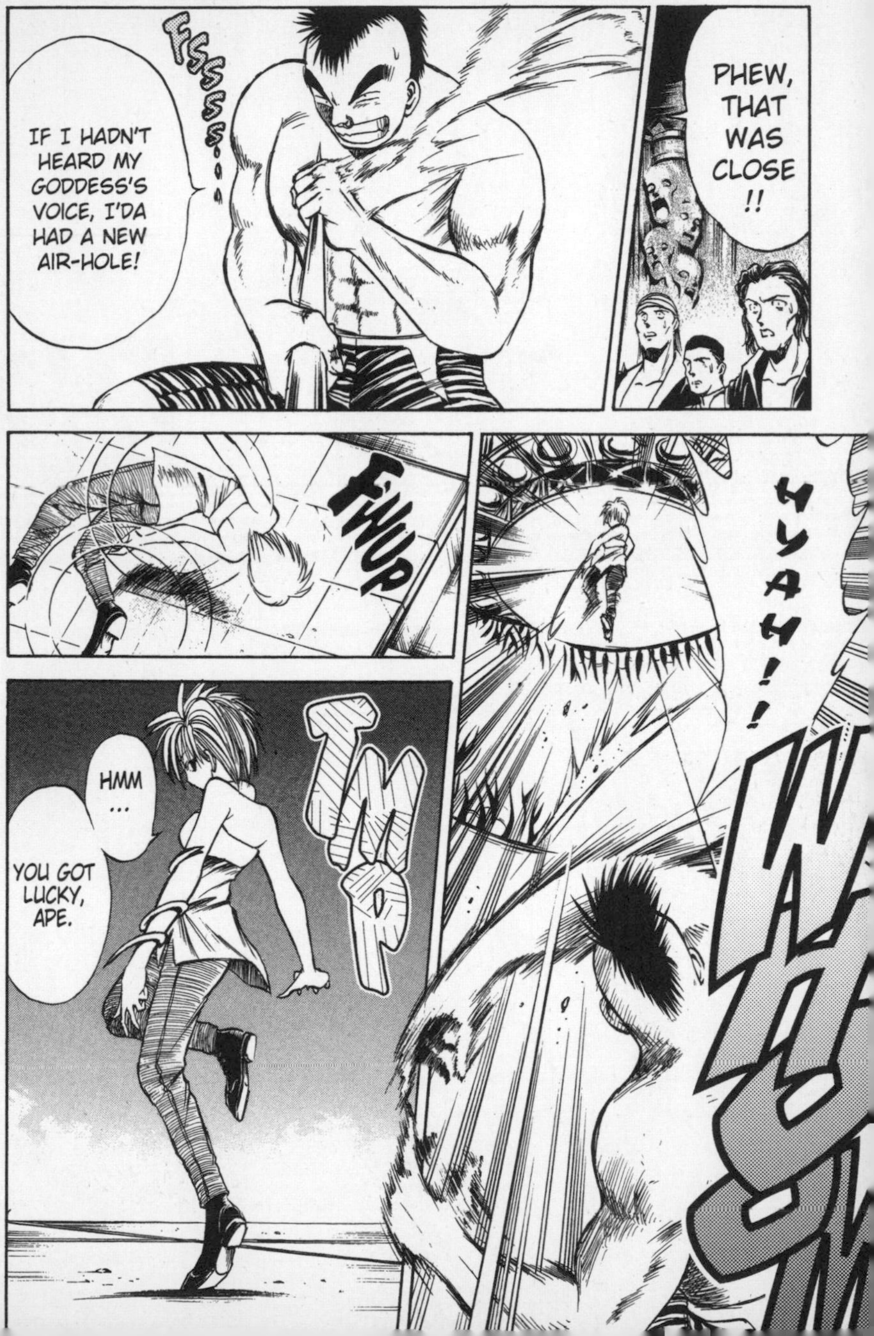
PHEW, THAT WAS CLOSE !!
FSSS
IF I HADN'T HEARD MY GODDESS'S VOICE, I'DA HAD A NEW AIR-HOLE!
HYAH!!!
FWUP
HMM ...
YOU GOT LUCKY, APE.

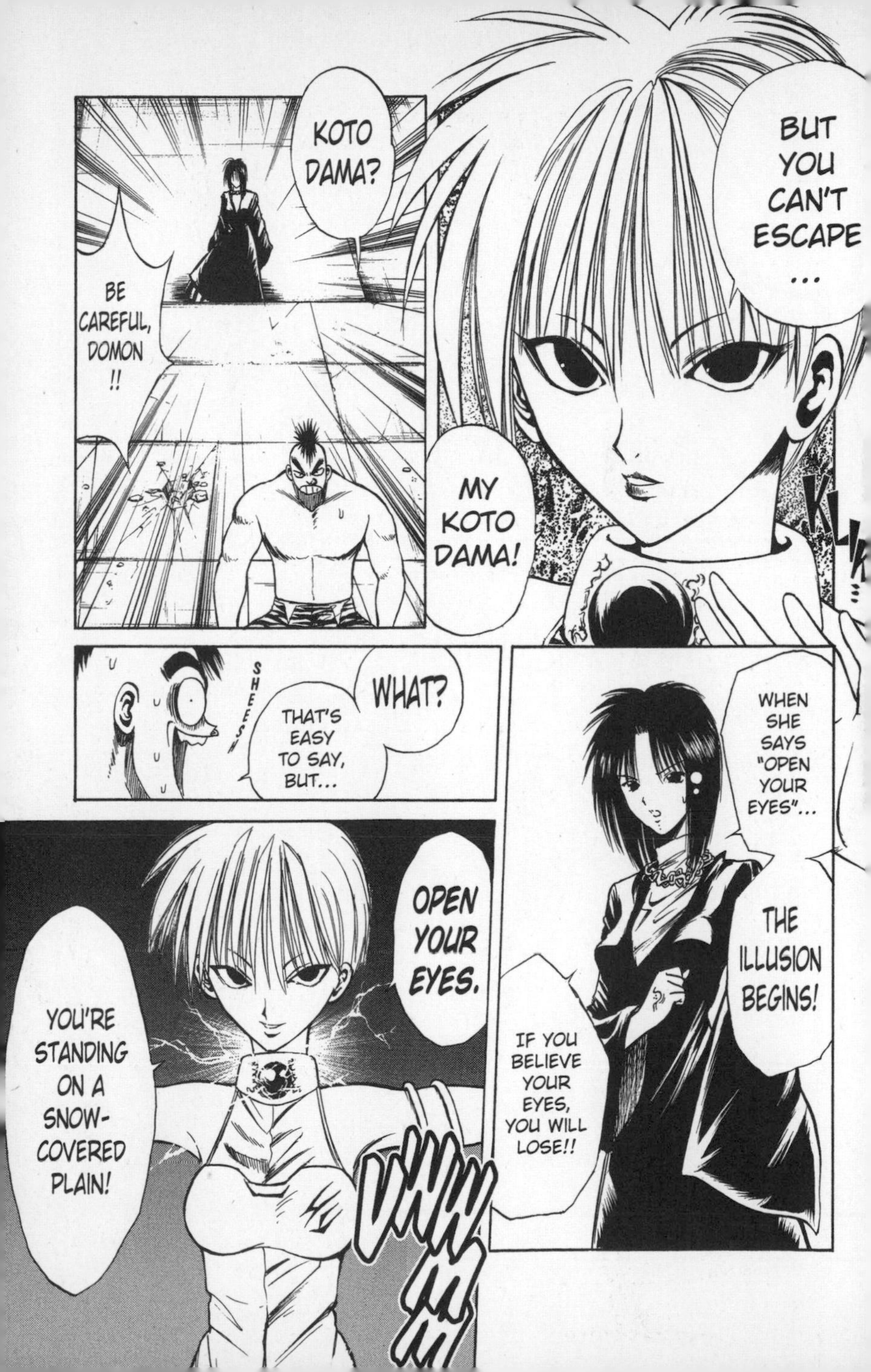
BUT YOU CAN'T ESCAPE ...
MY KOTO DAMA!
KLIK
KOTO DAMA?
BE CAREFUL, DOMON !!
WHEN SHE SAYS "OPEN YOUR EYES"...
THE ILLUSION BEGINS!
IF YOU BELIEVE YOUR EYES, YOU WILL LOSE!!
WHAT?
SHEESH
THAT'S EASY TO SAY, BUT...
OPEN YOUR EYES.
YOU'RE STANDING ON A SNOW-COVERED PLAIN!

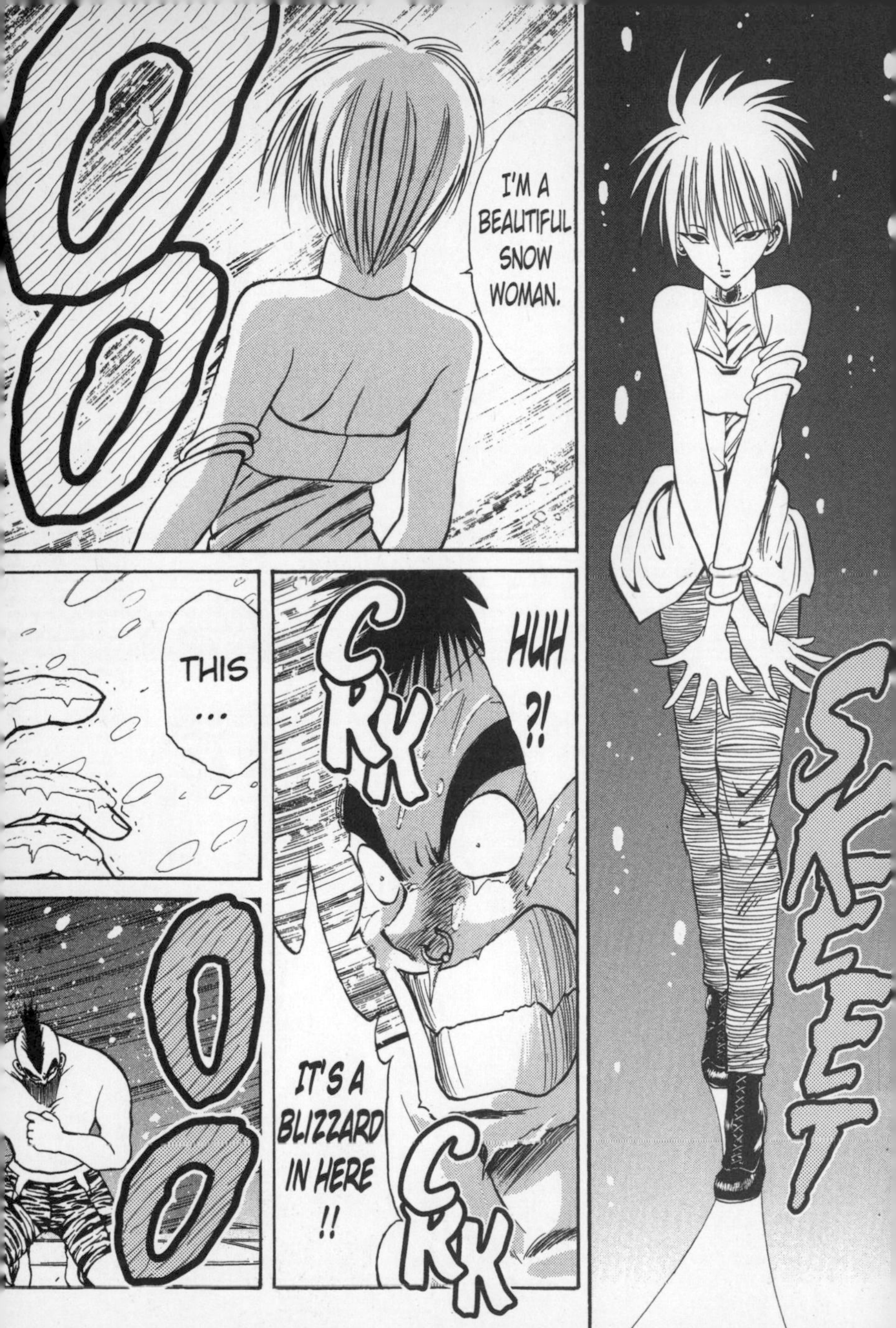
SKEET
OO
I'M A BEAUTIFUL SNOW WOMAN.
CRK
HUH ?!
IT'S A BLIZZARD IN HERE !!
CRK
THIS ...
OO

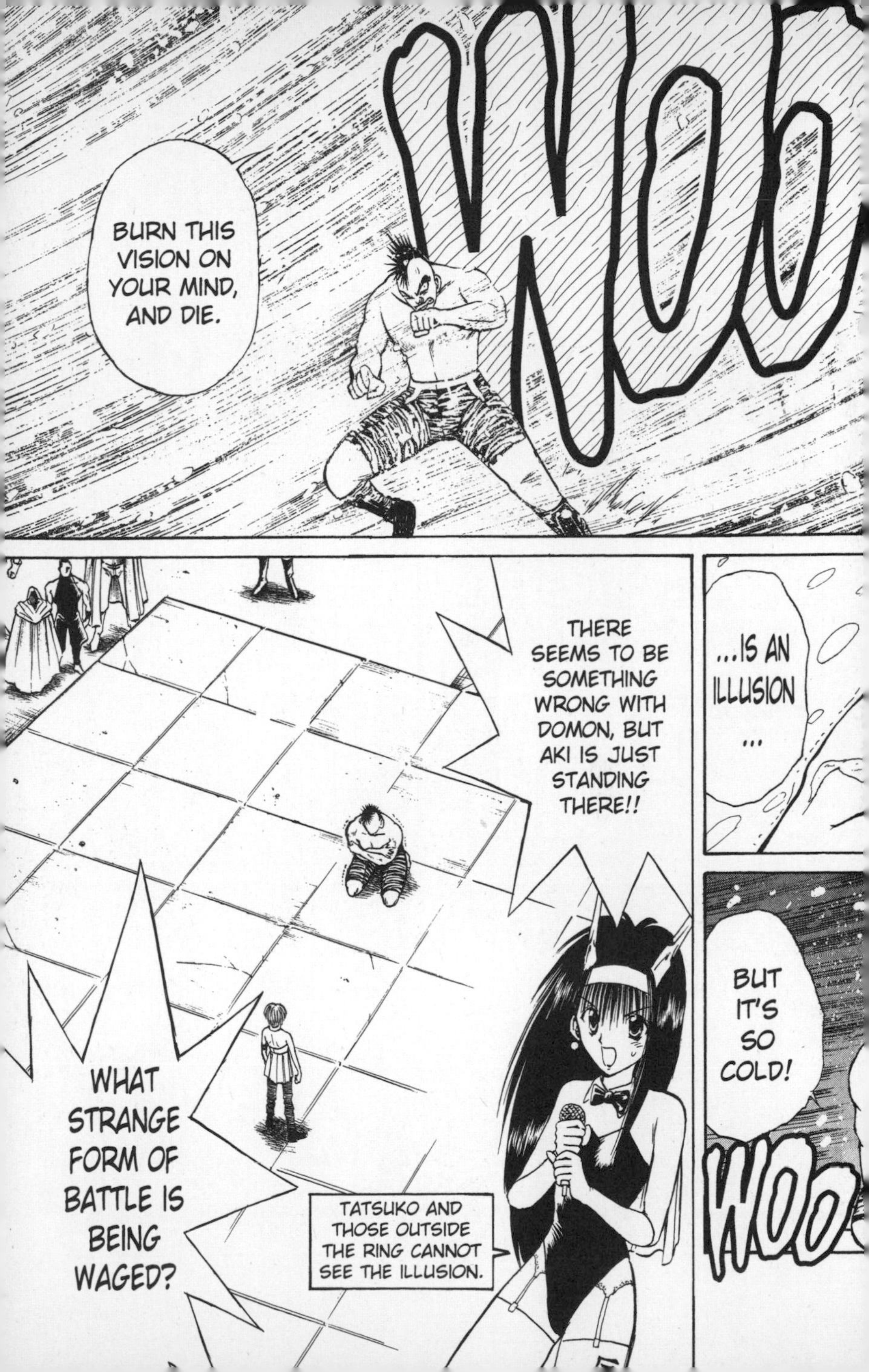
BURN THIS VISION ON YOUR MIND, AND DIE.
...IS AN ILLUSION ...
BUT IT'S SO COLD!
WOO
THERE SEEMS TO BE SOMETHING WRONG WITH DOMON, BUT AKI IS JUST STANDING THERE!!
WHAT STRANGE FORM OF BATTLE IS BEING WAGED?
TATSUKO AND THOSE OUTSIDE THE RING CANNOT SEE THE ILLUSION.

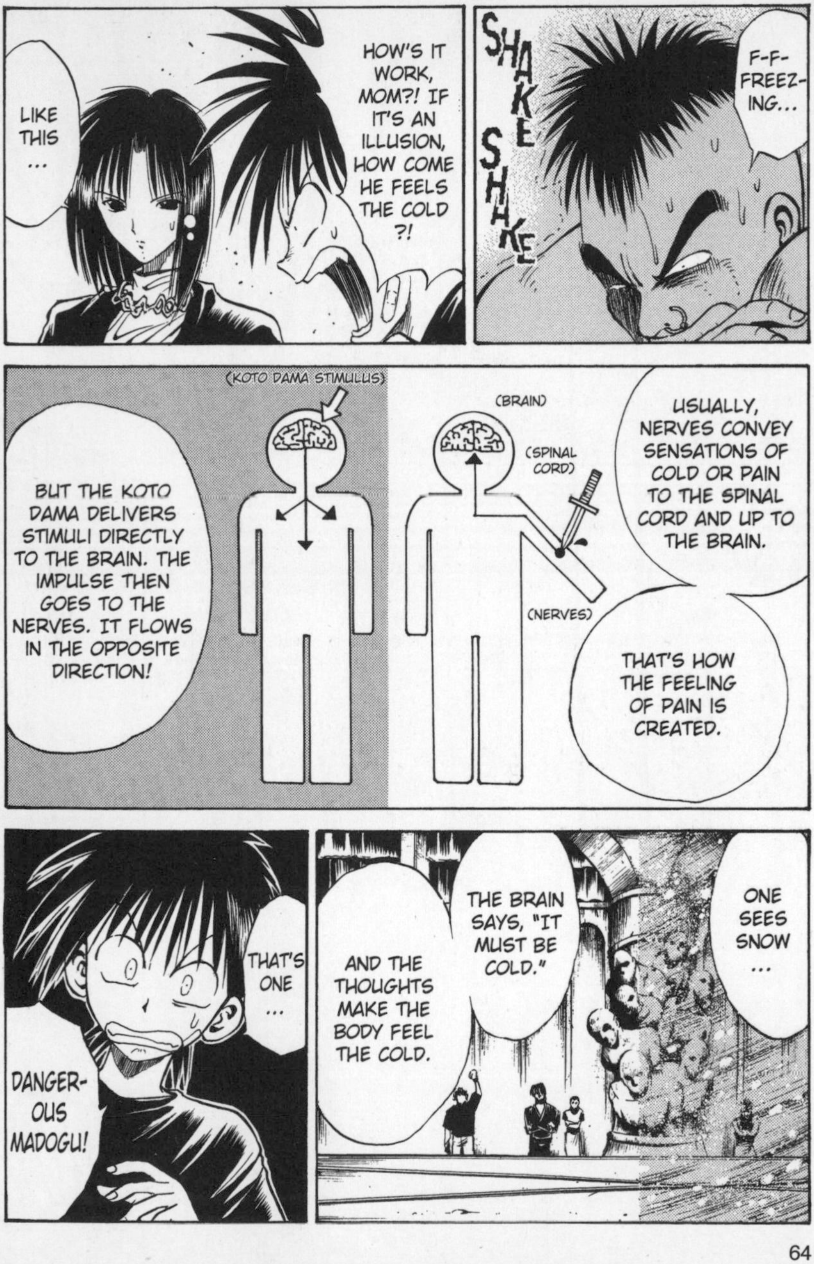
SHAKE SHAKE
F-F-FREEZ-ING...
HOW'S IT WORK, MOM?! IF IT'S AN ILLUSION, HOW COME HE FEELS THE COLD ?!
LIKE THIS ...
USUALLY, NERVES CONVEY SENSATIONS OF COLD OR PAIN TO THE SPINAL CORD AND UP TO THE BRAIN.
THAT'S HOW THE FEELING OF PAIN IS CREATED.
(BRAIN)
(SPINAL CORD)
(NERVES)
(KOTO DAMA STIMULUS)
BUT THE KOTO DAMA DELIVERS STIMULI DIRECTLY TO THE BRAIN. THE IMPULSE THEN GOES TO THE NERVES. IT FLOWS IN THE OPPOSITE DIRECTION!
ONE SEES SNOW ...
THE BRAIN SAYS, "IT MUST BE COLD."
AND THE THOUGHTS MAKE THE BODY FEEL THE COLD.
THAT'S ONE ...
DANGER-OUS MADOGU!

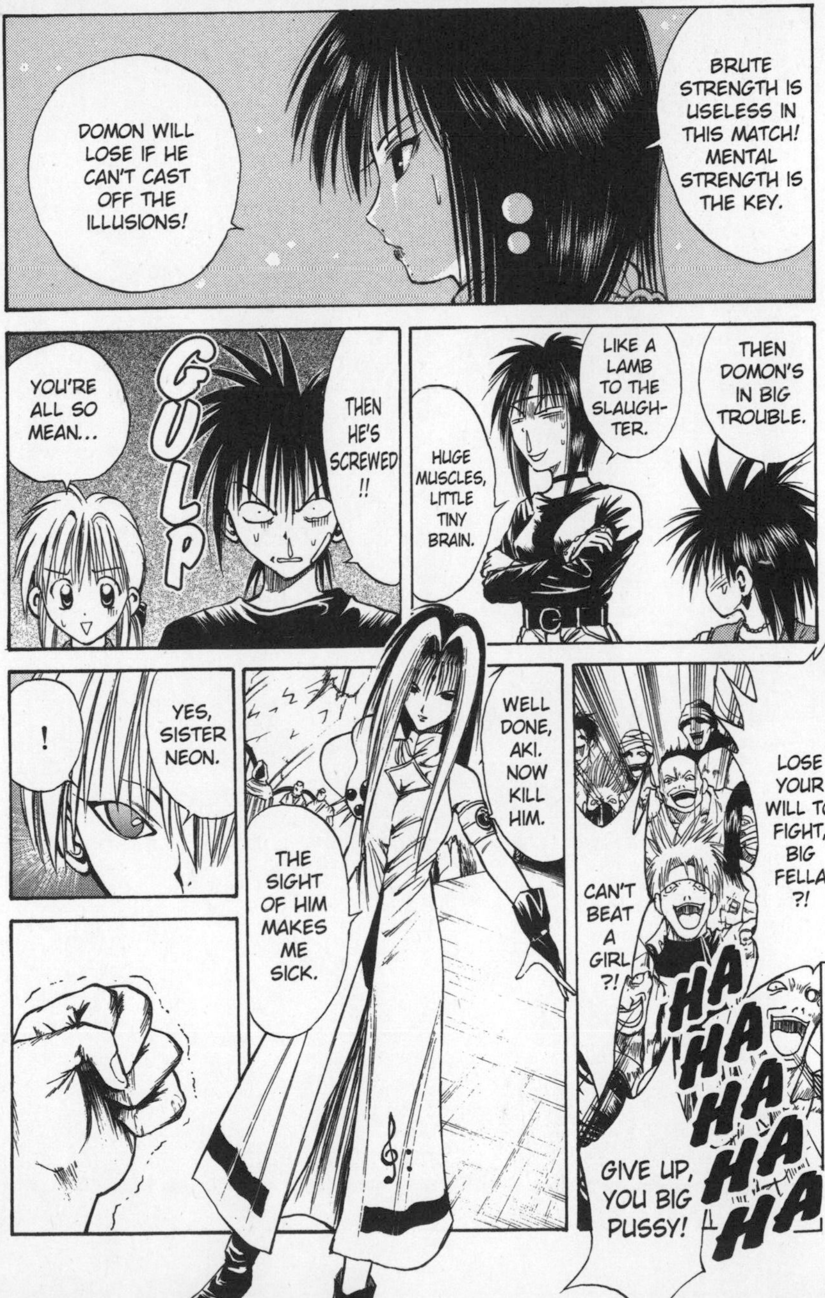
BRUTE STRENGTH IS USELESS IN THIS MATCH! MENTAL STRENGTH IS THE KEY.
DOMON WILL LOSE IF HE CAN'T CAST OFF THE ILLUSIONS!
THEN DOMON'S IN BIG TROUBLE.
LIKE A LAMB TO THE SLAUGHTER.
HUGE MUSCLES, LITTLE TINY BRAIN.
THEN HE'S SCREWED!!
GULP
YOU'RE ALL SO MEAN...
LOSE YOUR WILL TO FIGHT, BIG FELLA?!
CAN'T BEAT A GIRL?!
HA HA HA HA HA HA HA
GIVE UP, YOU BIG PUSSY!
WELL DONE, AKI. NOW KILL HIM.
THE SIGHT OF HIM MAKES ME SICK.
YES, SISTER NEON.
!

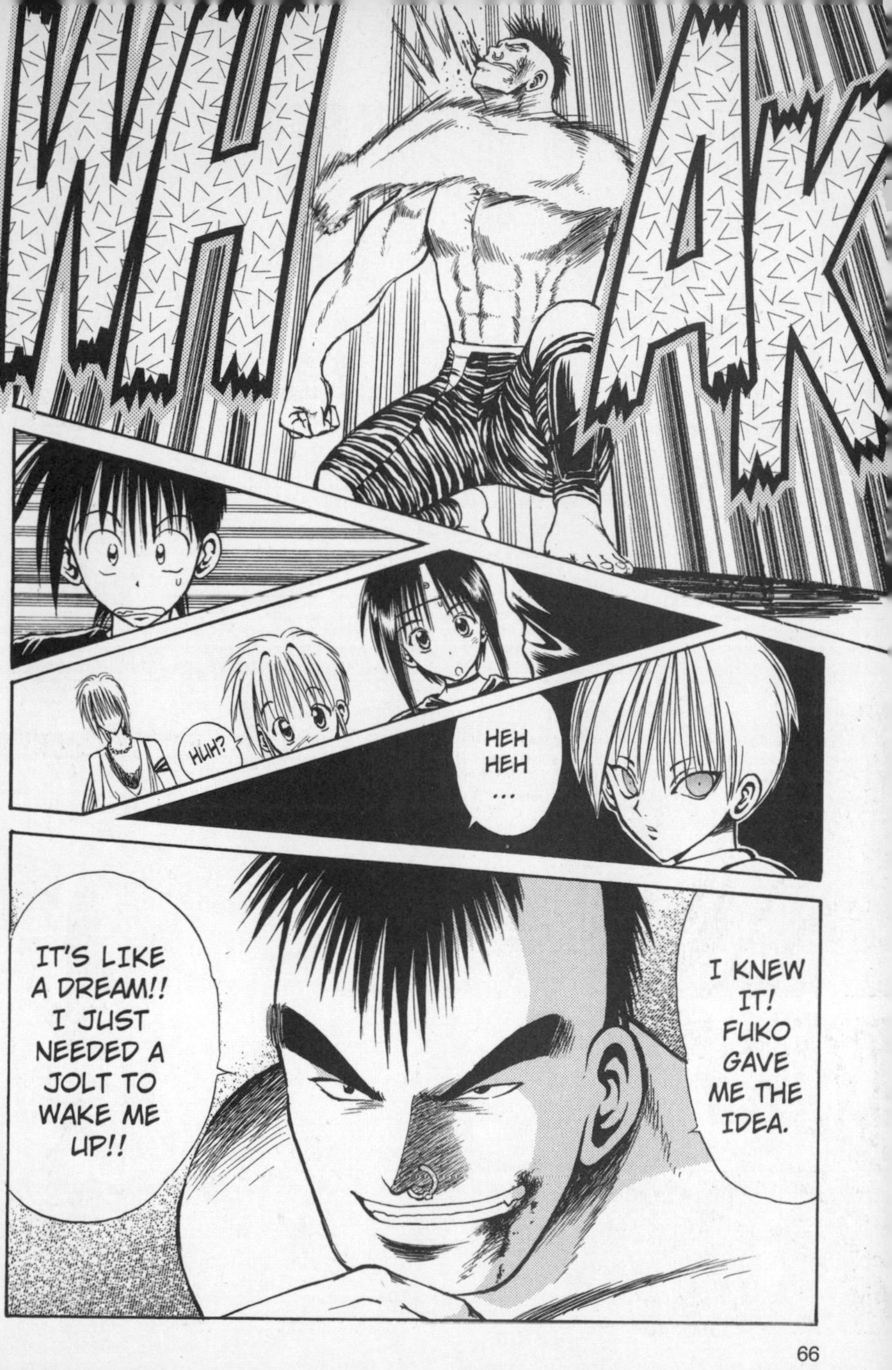
WHAK
HUH?
HEH HEH ...
I KNEW IT! FUKO GAVE ME THE IDEA.
IT'S LIKE A DREAM!! I JUST NEEDED A JOLT TO WAKE ME UP!!

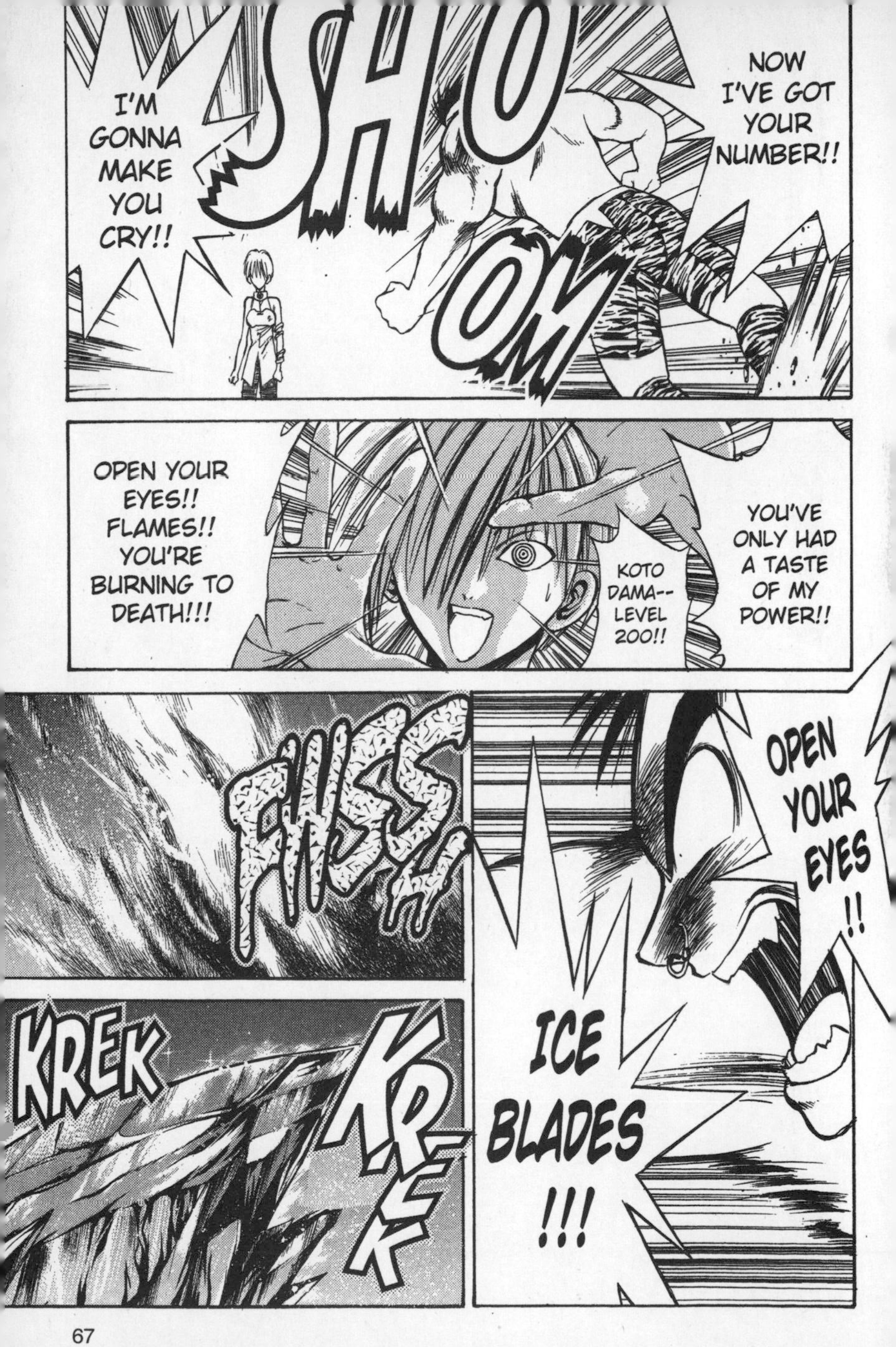
NOW I'VE GOT YOUR NUMBER!!
SHOOM
I'M GONNA MAKE YOU CRY!!
YOU'VE ONLY HAD A TASTE OF MY POWER!!
KOTO DAMA-- LEVEL 200!!
OPEN YOUR EYES!! FLAMES!! YOU'RE BURNING TO DEATH!!!
OPEN YOUR EYES!!
ICE BLADES!!!
KREK
KREK

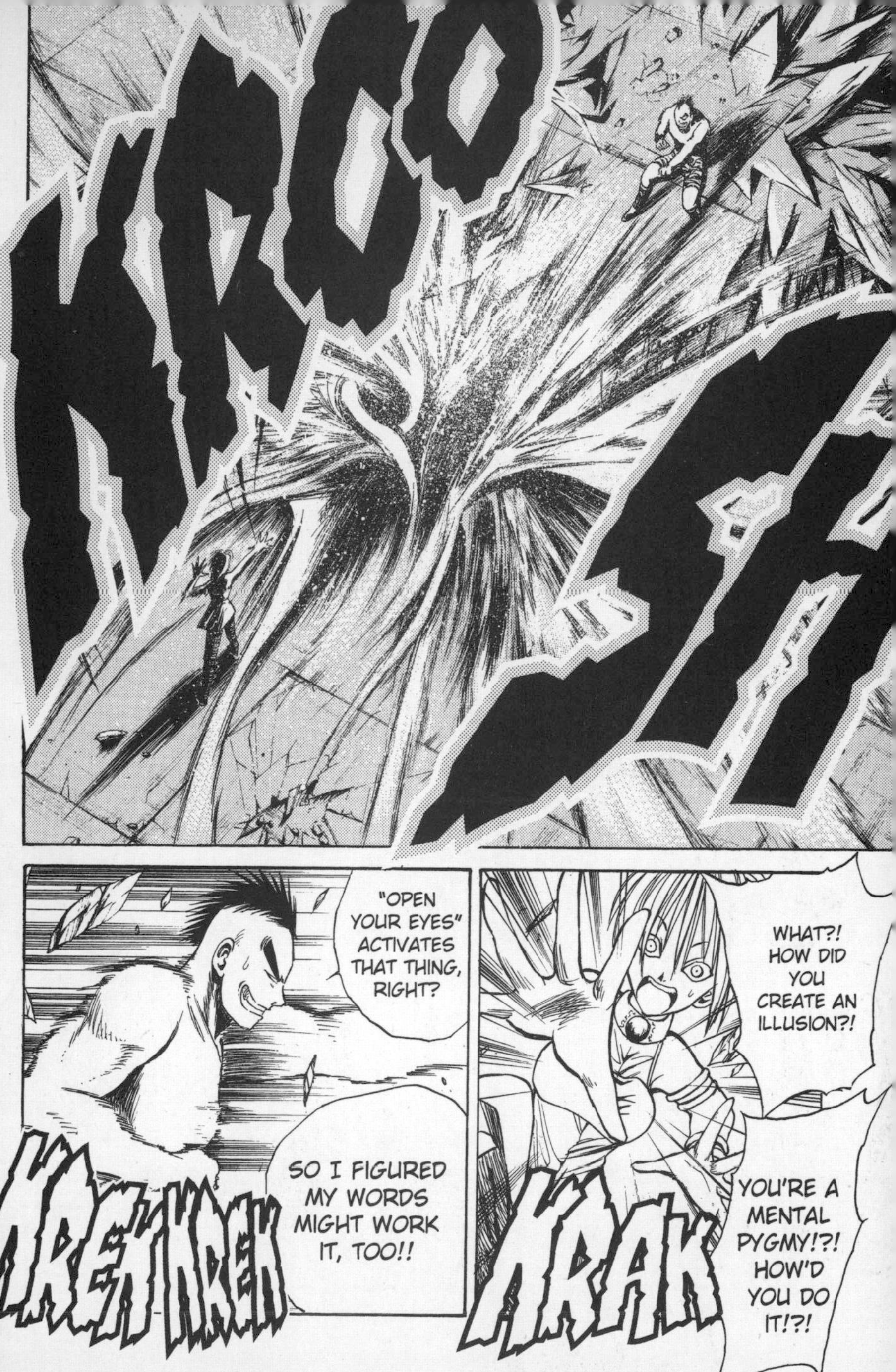
WHAT?! HOW DID YOU CREATE AN ILLUSION?!
YOU'RE A MENTAL PYGMY!?! HOW'D YOU DO IT!?!
KRAK
"OPEN YOUR EYES" ACTIVATES THAT THING, RIGHT?
SO I FIGURED MY WORDS MIGHT WORK IT, TOO!!
KREKKREK

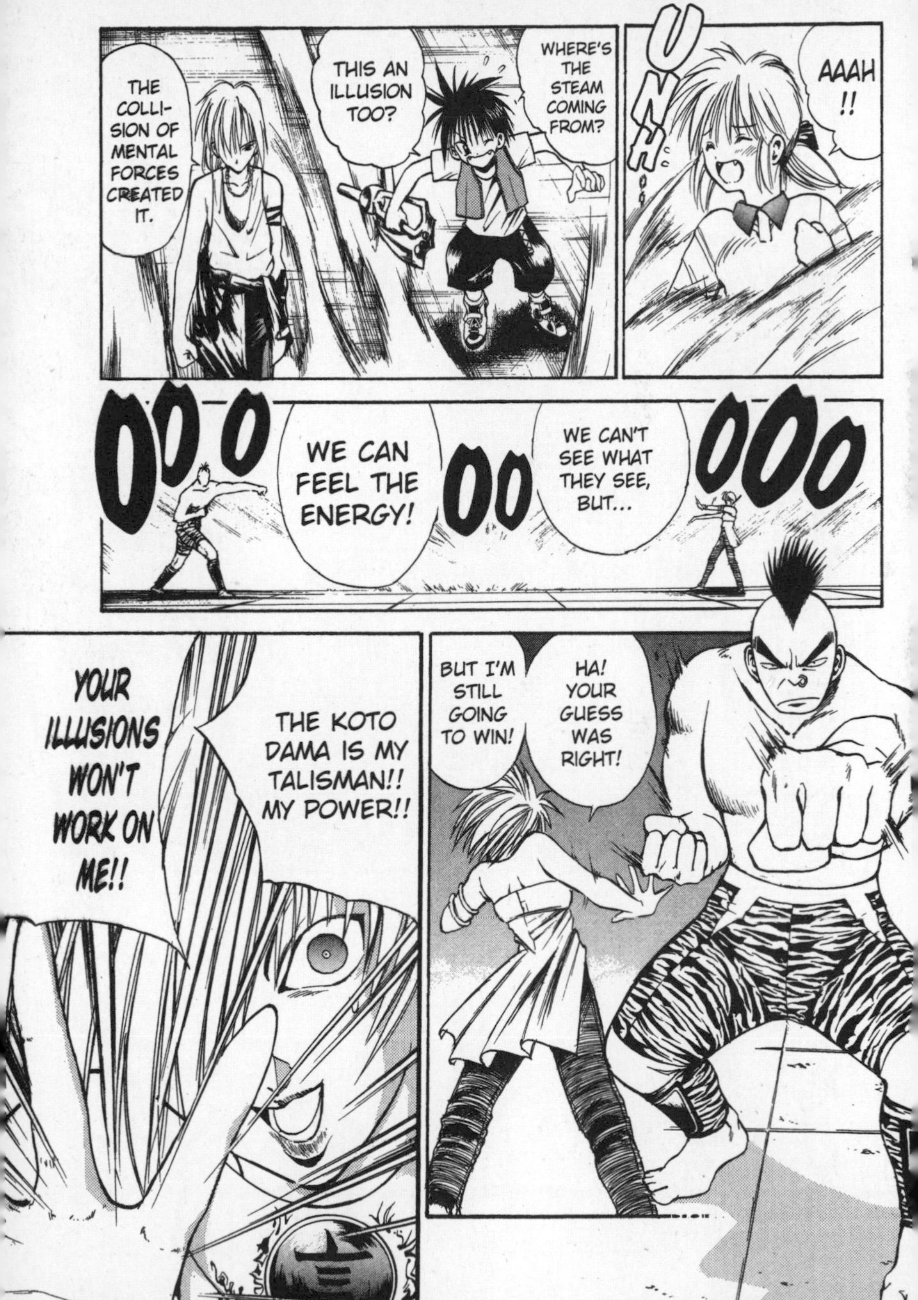
UNH...
AAAH !!
WHERE'S THE STEAM COMING FROM?
THIS AN ILLUSION TOO?
THE COLLI-SION OF MENTAL FORCES CREATED IT.
OOO
WE CAN'T SEE WHAT THEY SEE, BUT...
OO
WE CAN FEEL THE ENERGY!
OOO
HA! YOUR GUESS WAS RIGHT!
BUT I'M STILL GOING TO WIN!
THE KOTO DAMA IS MY TALISMAN!! MY POWER!!
YOUR ILLUSIONS WON'T WORK ON ME!!

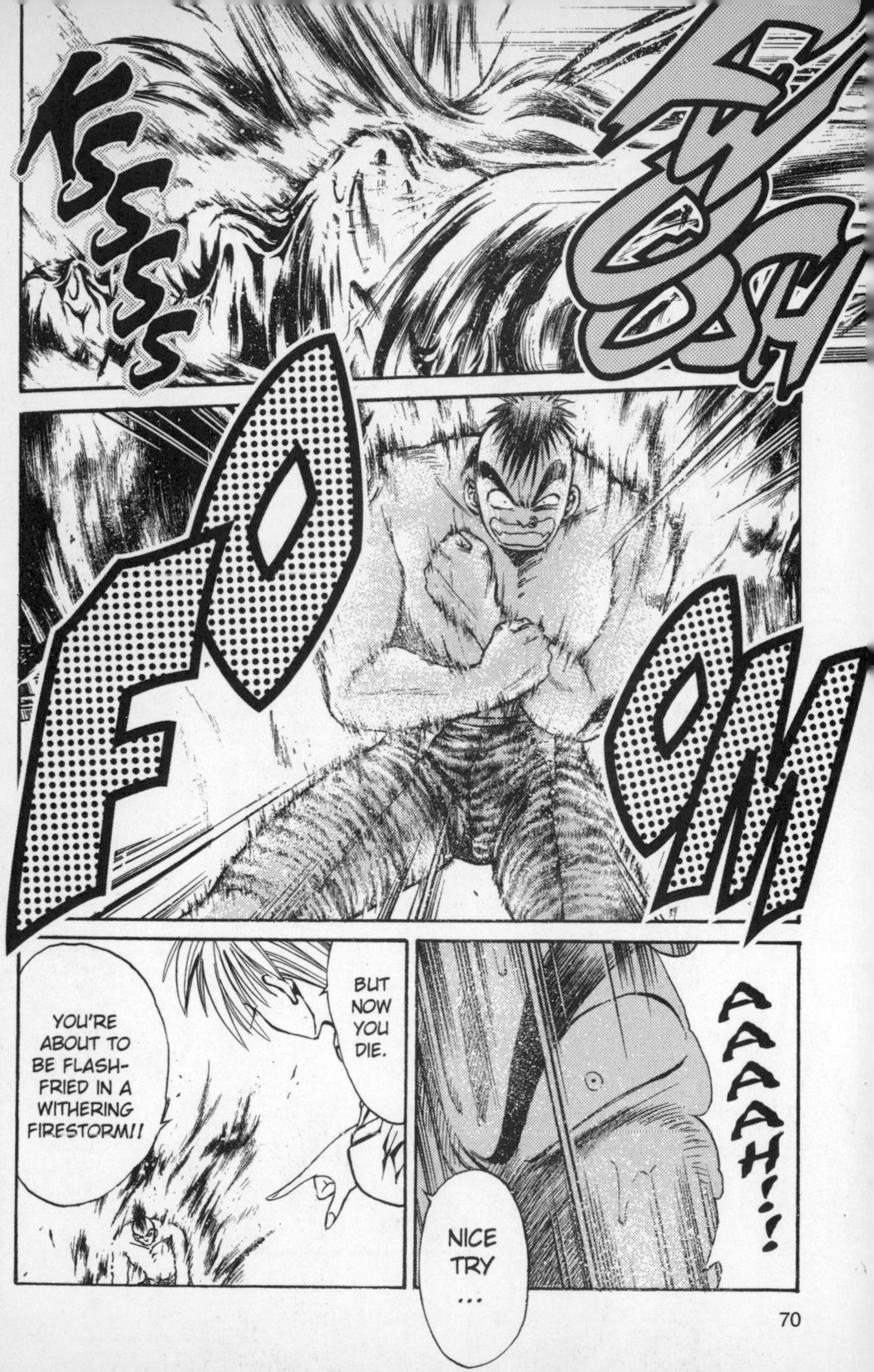
KSSSS
FOOM
AAAAH!!!
NICE TRY ...
BUT NOW YOU DIE.
YOU'RE ABOUT TO BE FLASH-FRIED IN A WITHERING FIRESTORM!!

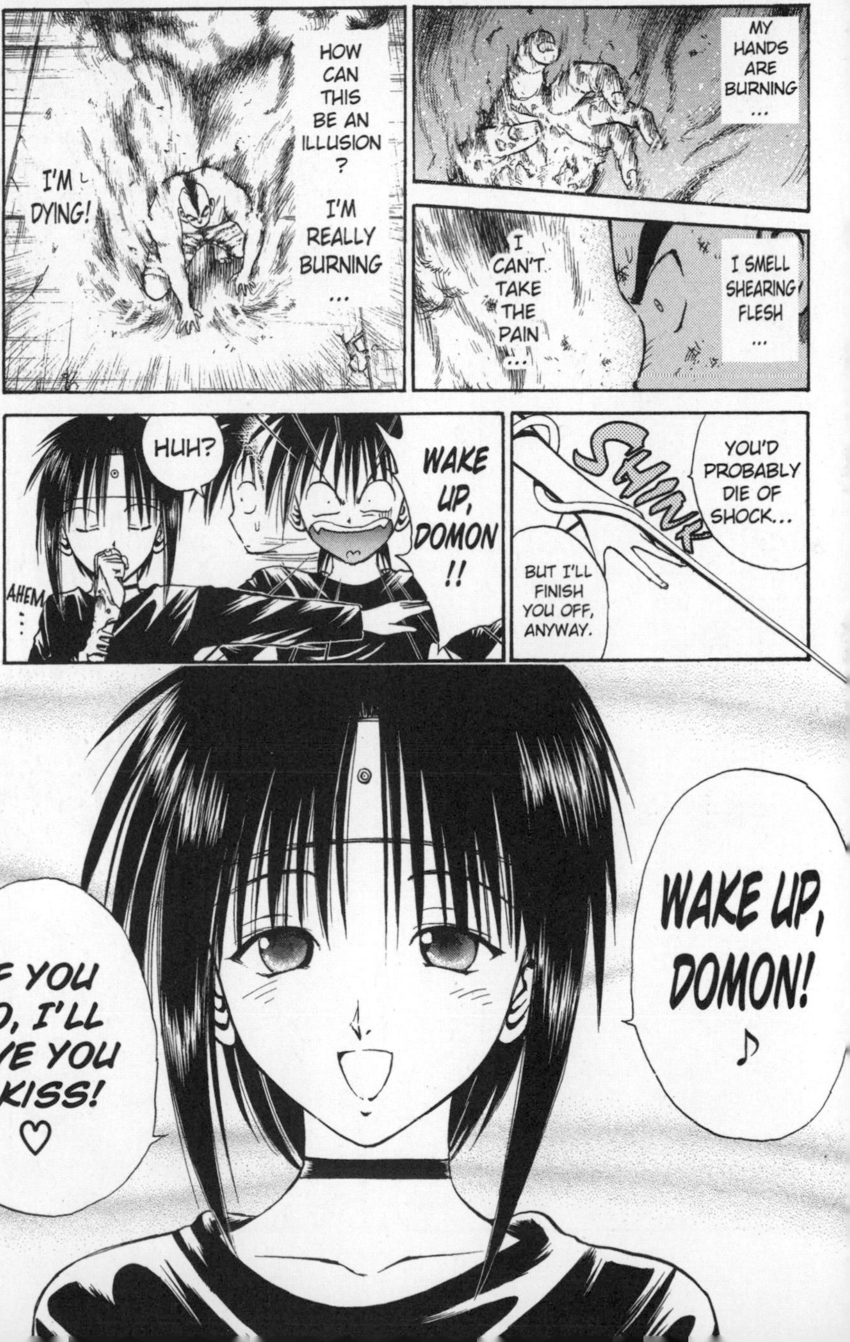
MY HANDS ARE BURNING ...
I SMELL SHEARING FLESH ...
I CAN'T TAKE THE PAIN ...
HOW CAN THIS BE AN ILLUSION ?
I'M REALLY BURNING ...
I'M DYING!
SHINK
YOU'D PROBABLY DIE OF SHOCK...
BUT I'LL FINISH YOU OFF, ANYWAY.
WAKE UP, DOMON !!
HUH?
AHEM ...
WAKE UP, DOMON! ♪
IF YOU DO, I'LL GIVE YOU A KISS! ♡

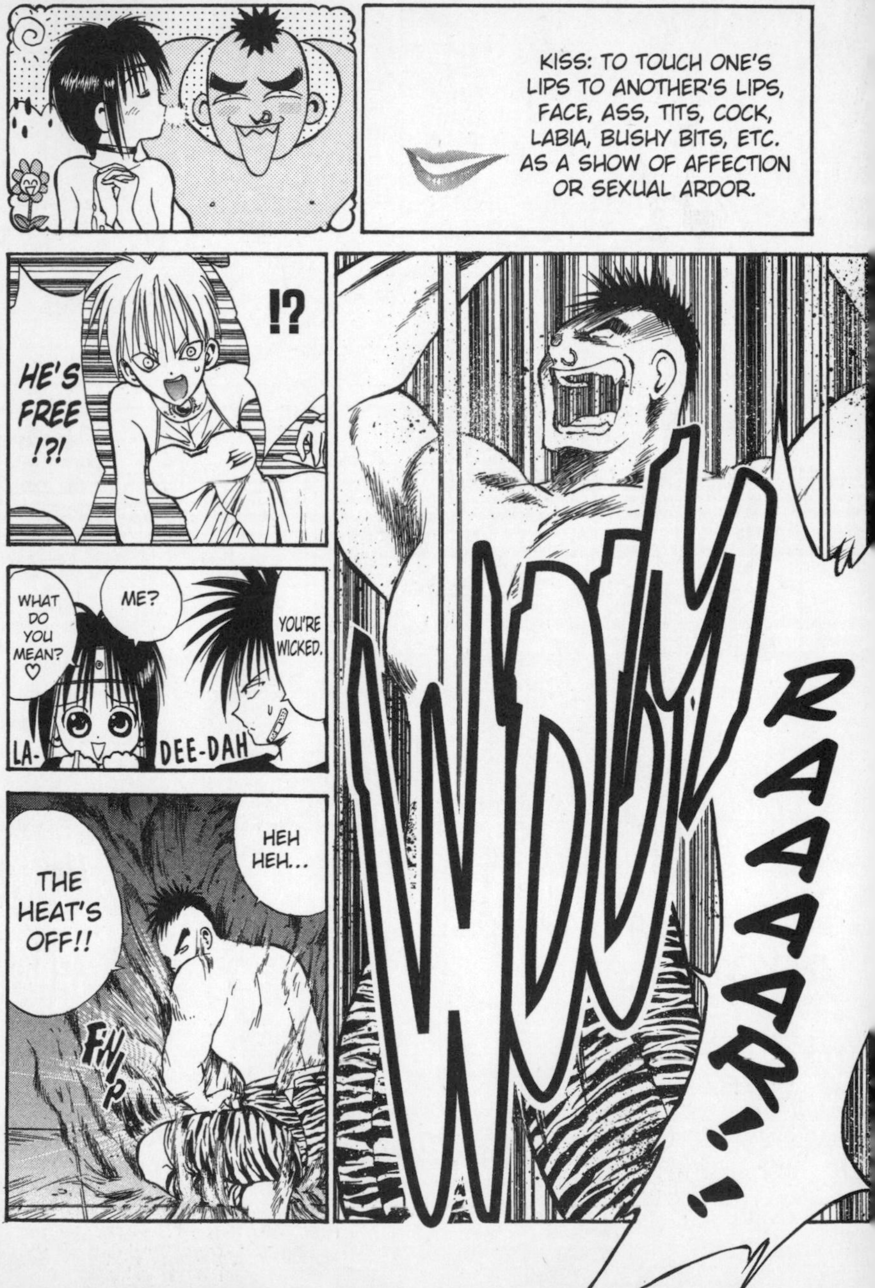
KISS: TO TOUCH ONE'S LIPS TO ANOTHER'S LIPS, FACE, ASS, TITS, COCK, LABIA, BUSHY BITS, ETC. AS A SHOW OF AFFECTION OR SEXUAL ARDOR.
RAAAAR!!
!?
HE'S FREE !?!
YOU'RE WICKED.
ME?
WHAT DO YOU MEAN? ♡
LA-
DEE-DAH
HEH HEH...
THE HEAT'S OFF!!

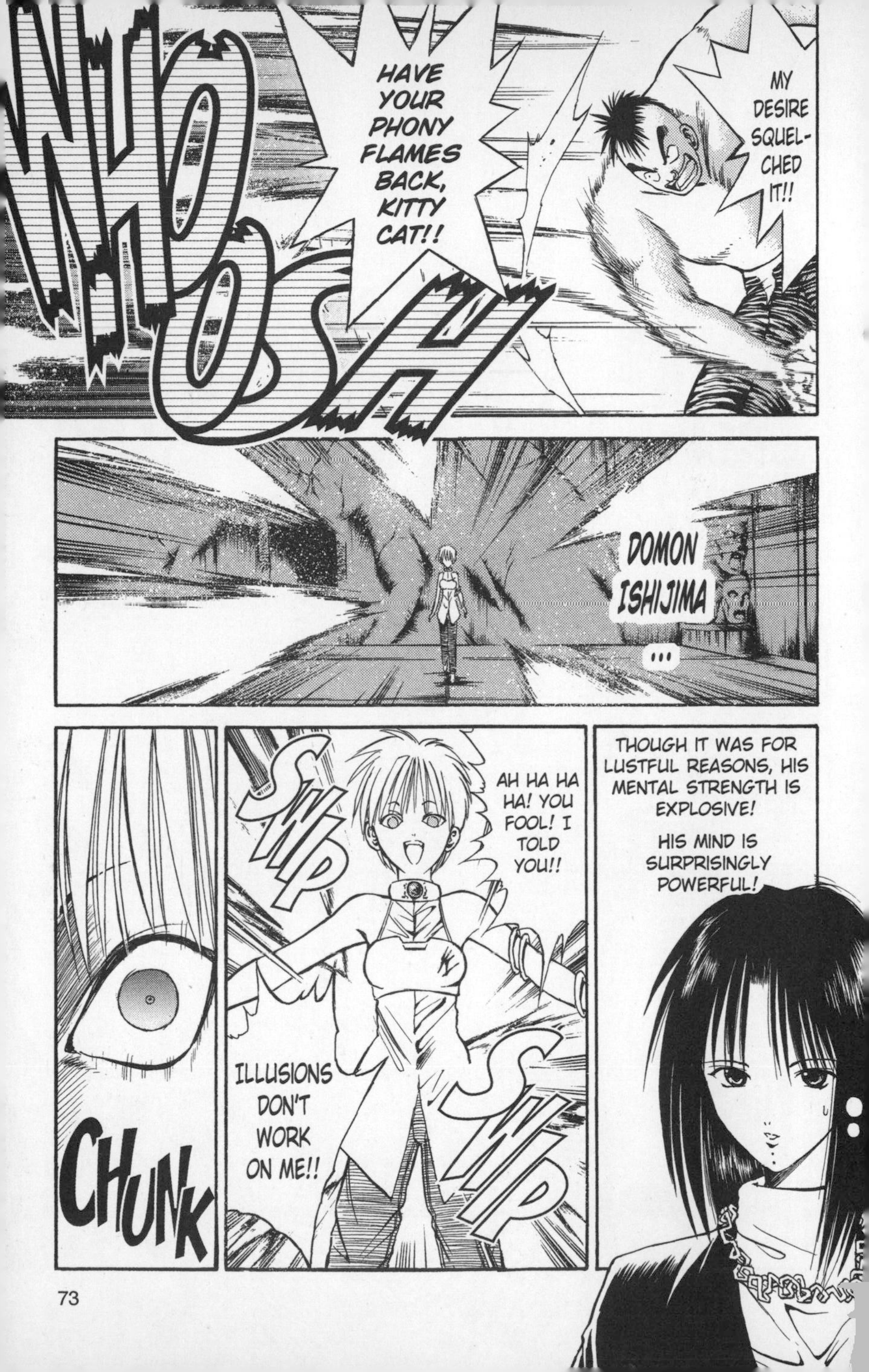
MY DESIRE SQUEL-CHED IT!!
HAVE YOUR PHONY FLAMES BACK, KITTY CAT!!
WHOOSH
DOMON ISHIJIMA
...
THOUGH IT WAS FOR LUSTFUL REASONS, HIS MENTAL STRENGTH IS EXPLOSIVE!
HIS MIND IS SURPRISINGLY POWERFUL!
AH HA HA HA! YOU FOOL! I TOLD YOU!!
SWIP
ILLUSIONS DON'T WORK ON ME!!
SWIP
CHUNK

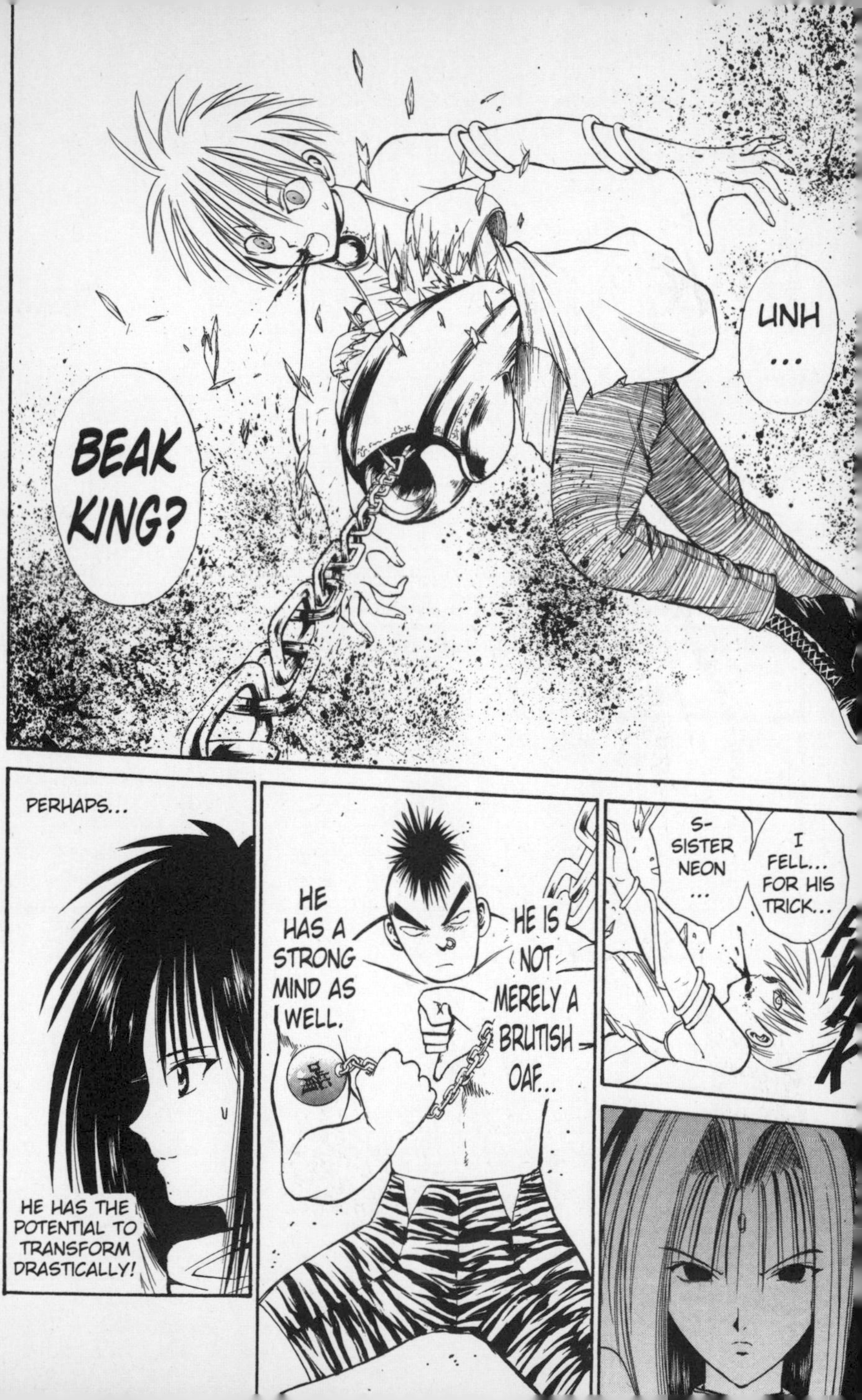
UNH ...
BEAK KING?
I FELL... FOR HIS TRICK...
S- SISTER NEON ...
HE IS NOT MERELY A BRUTISH OAF...
HE HAS A STRONG MIND AS WELL.
PERHAPS...
HE HAS THE POTENTIAL TO TRANSFORM DRASTICALLY!

Part Seventy-Two:
Live (4) Duo

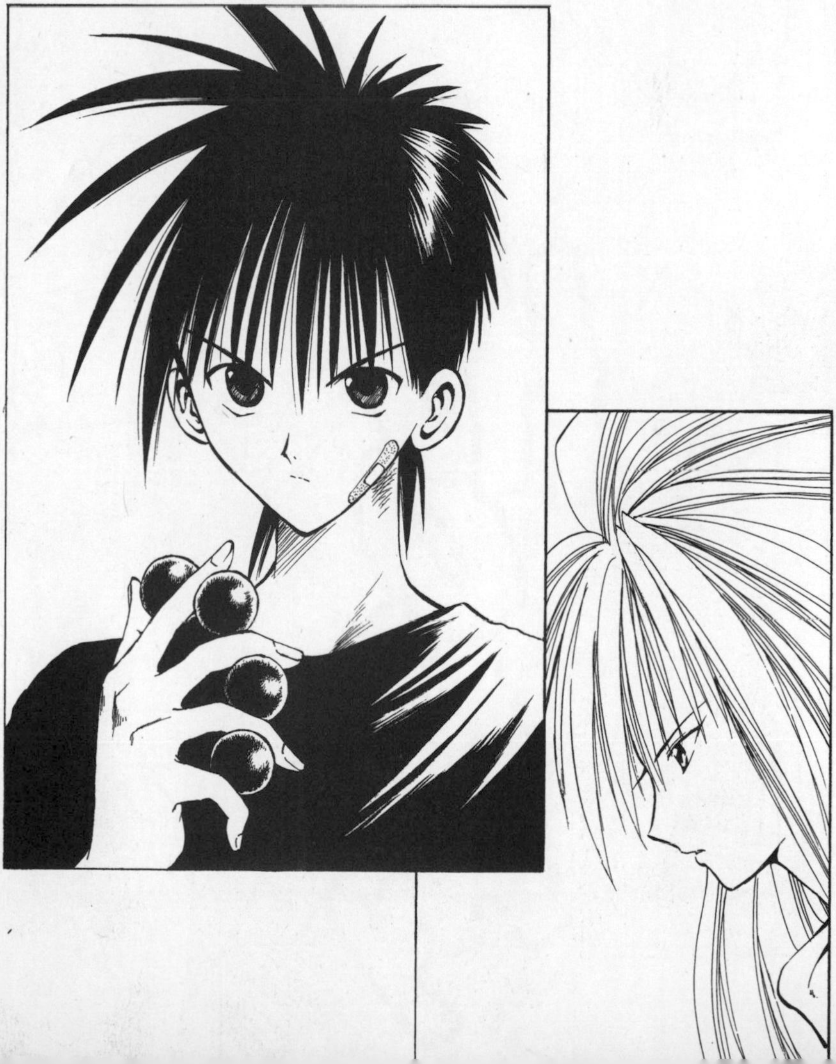

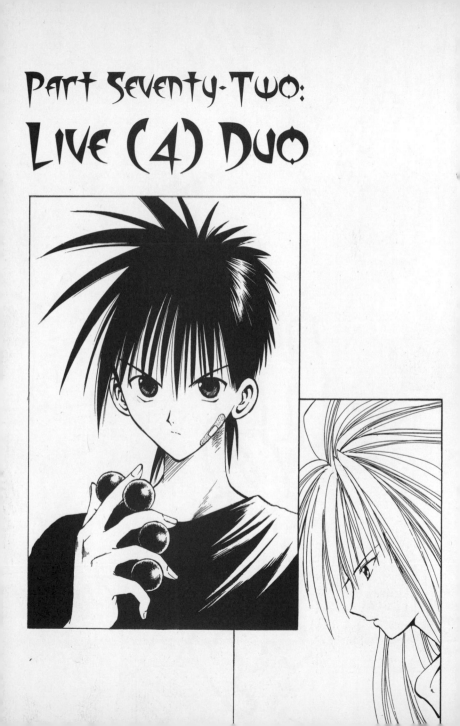

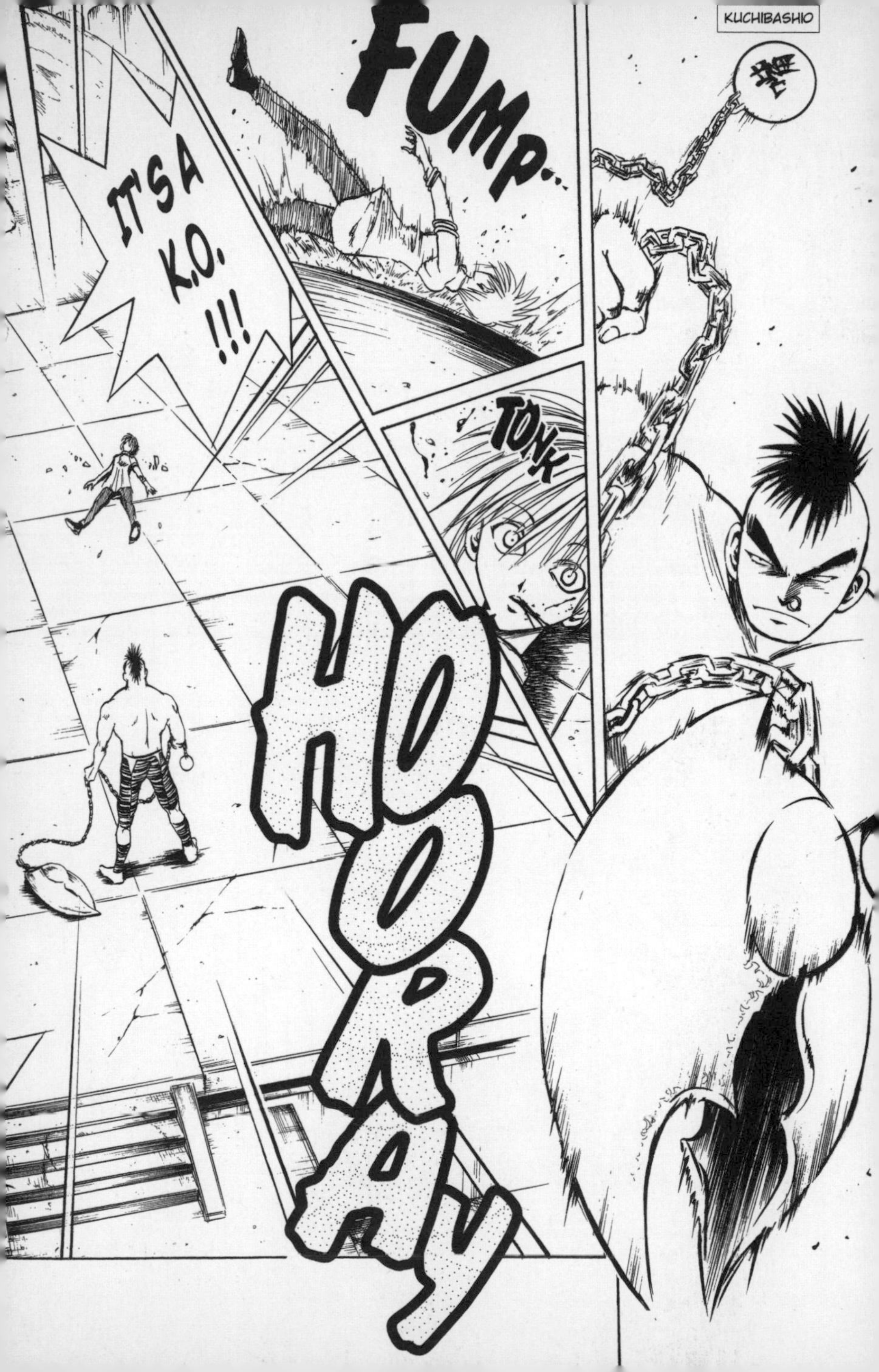
KUCHIBASHIO
FUMP...
TONK
HOORAY
IT'S A K.O. !!!

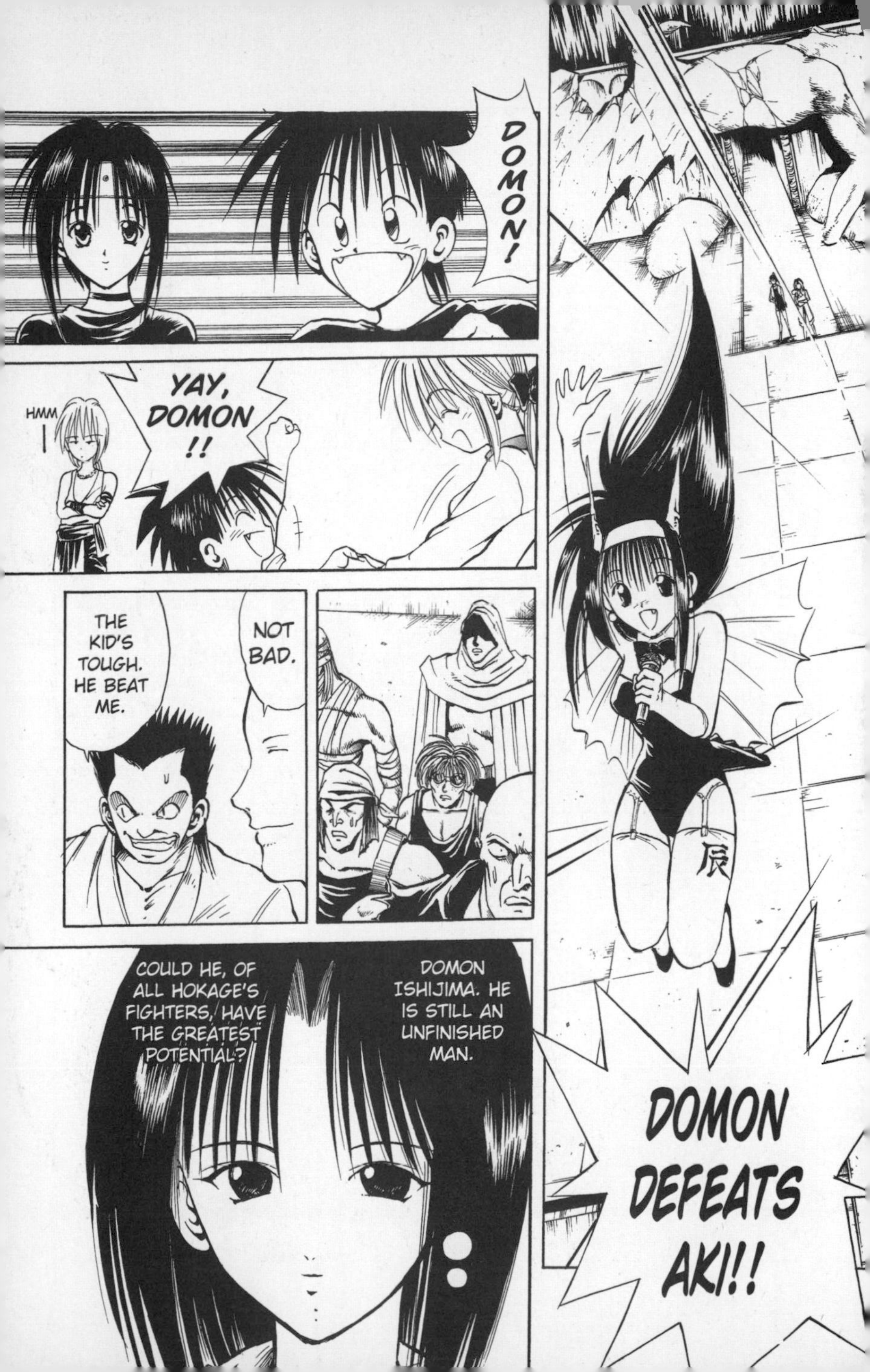
DOMON DEFEATS AKI!!
DOMON!
YAY, DOMON!!
HMM
NOT BAD.
THE KID'S TOUGH. HE BEAT ME.
DOMON ISHIJIMA. HE IS STILL AN UNFINISHED MAN.
COULD HE, OF ALL HOKAGE'S FIGHTERS, HAVE THE GREATEST POTENTIAL?

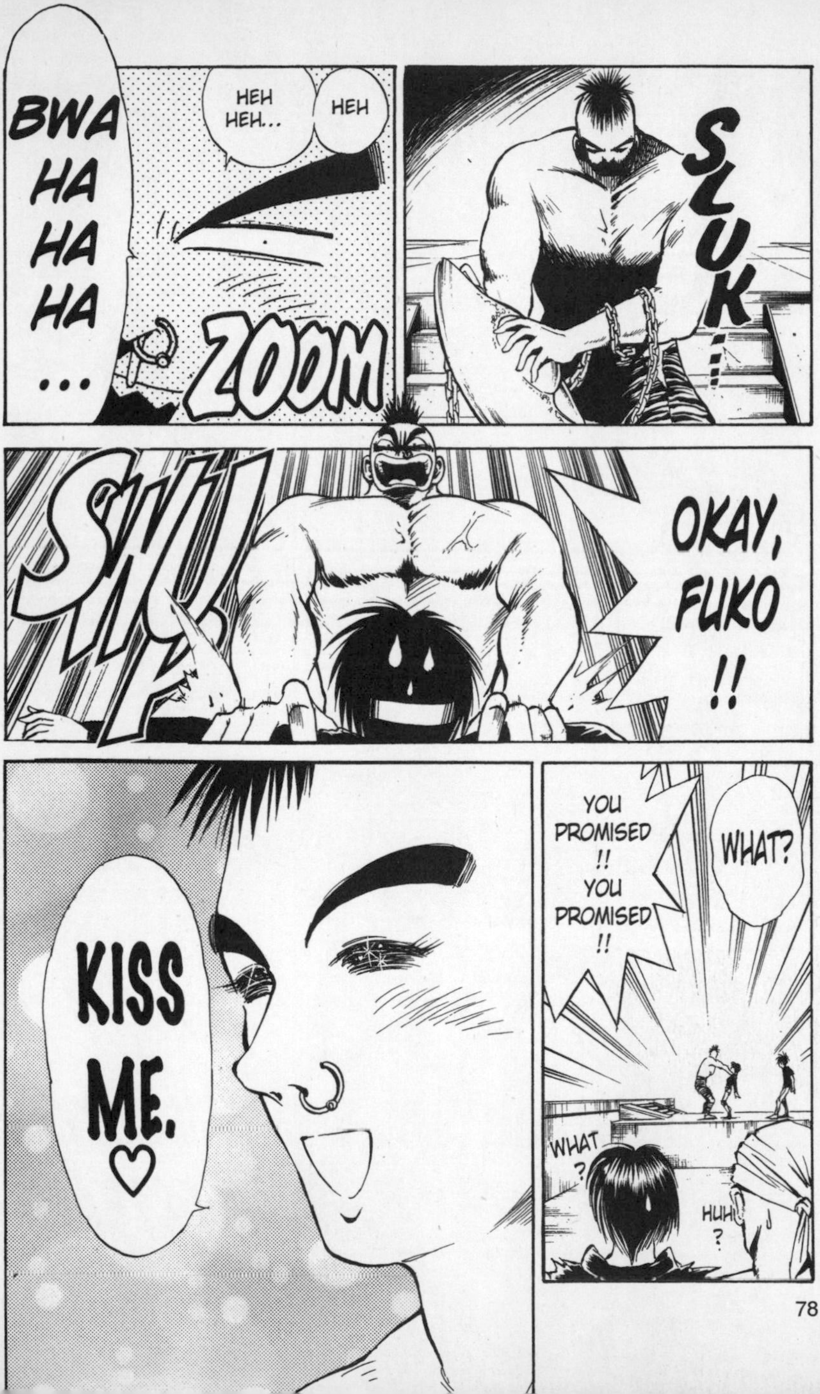
SLUK...
HEH
HEH HEH...
BWA HA HA HA HA ...
ZOOM
OKAY, FUKO !!
WHAT?
YOU PROMISED !! YOU PROMISED !!
WHAT ?
HUH ?
KISS ME. ♡

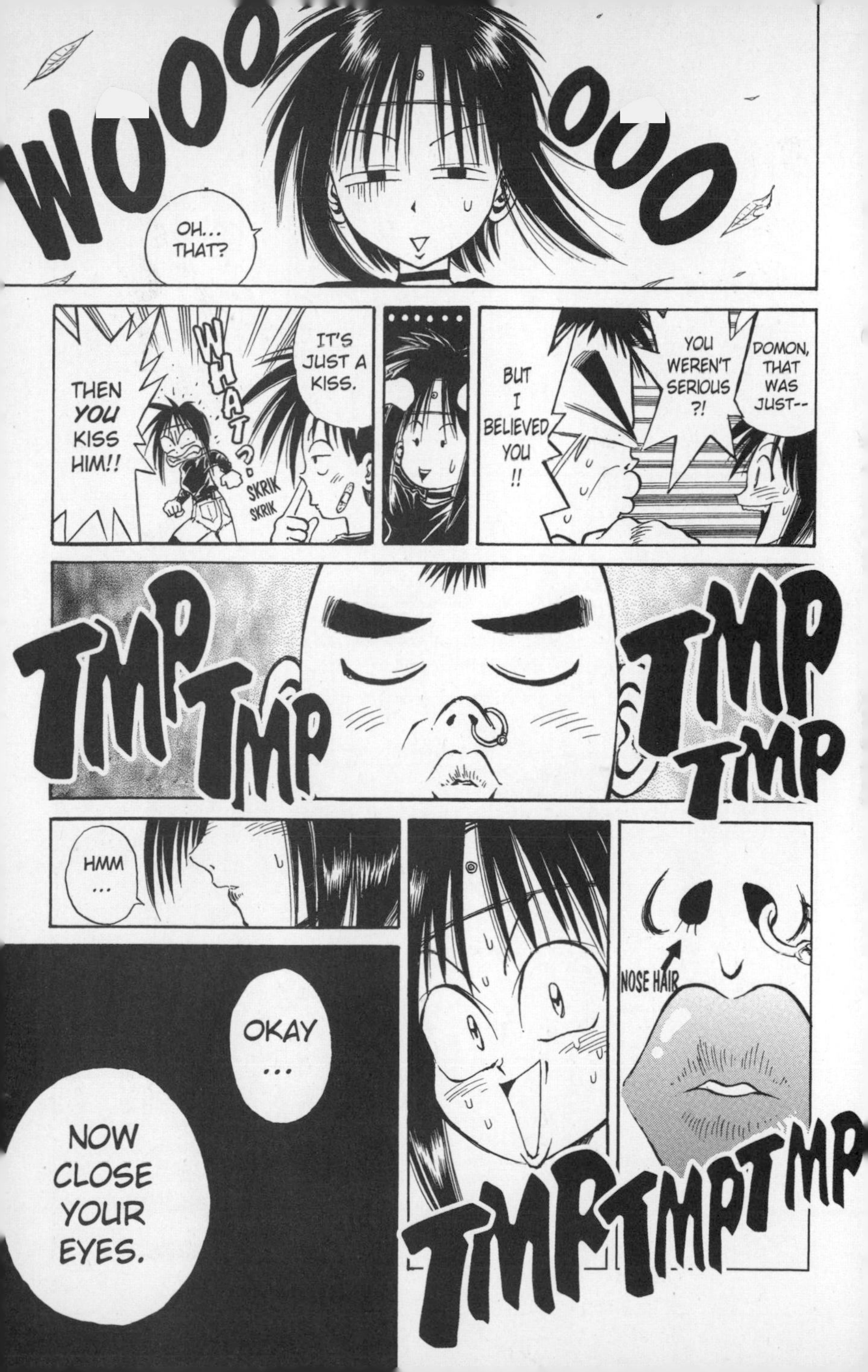
WOOOOOOO
OH... THAT?
DOMON, THAT WAS JUST--
YOU WEREN'T SERIOUS ?!
BUT I BELIEVED YOU !!
IT'S JUST A KISS.
WHAT?
THEN *YOU* KISS HIM!!
SKRIK SKRIK
TMP TMP
TMP TMP
NOSE HAIR
HMM ...
OKAY ...
NOW CLOSE YOUR EYES.
TMPTMPTMPTMP

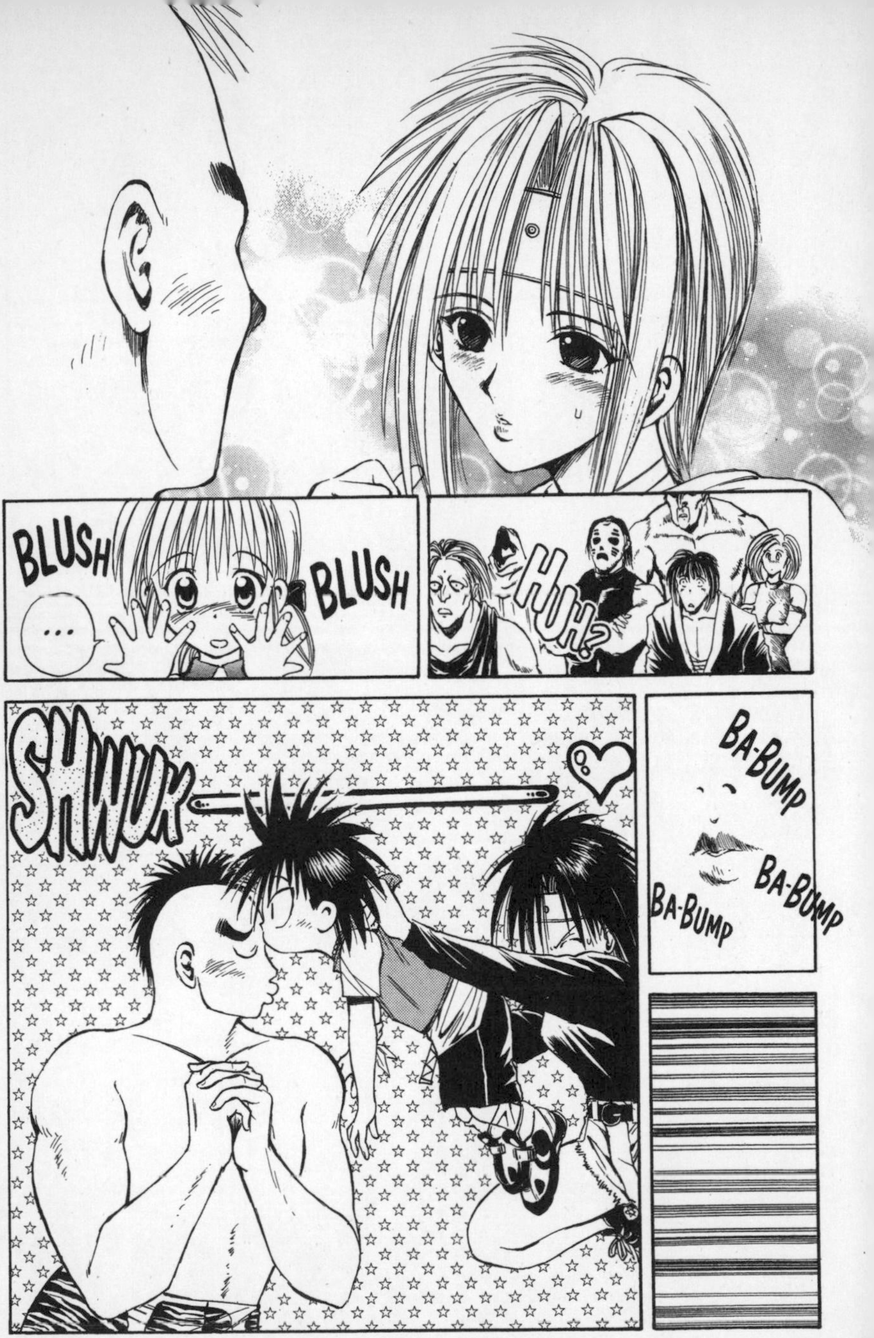
HUH?
BLUSH
BLUSH
...
BA-BUMP
BA-BUMP
BA-BUMP
SHWUK

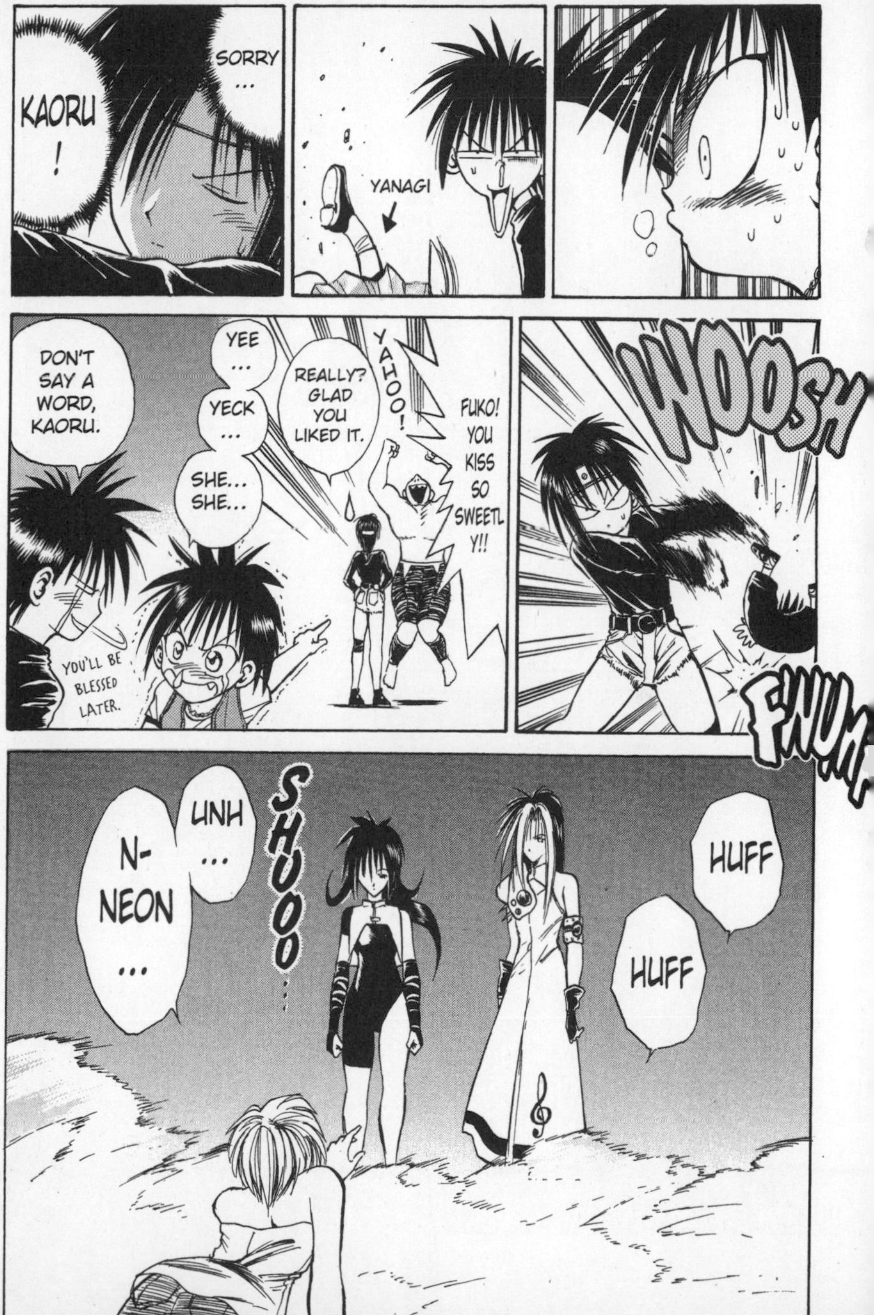
YANAGI
SORRY...
KAORU!
WOOSH
FNUH
YAHOO!
FUKO! YOU KISS SO SWEETLY!!
REALLY? GLAD YOU LIKED IT.
YEE...
YECK...
SHE... SHE...
DON'T SAY A WORD, KAORU.
YOU'LL BE BLESSED LATER.
HUFF
HUFF
SHUOOO...
UNH...
N-NEON...

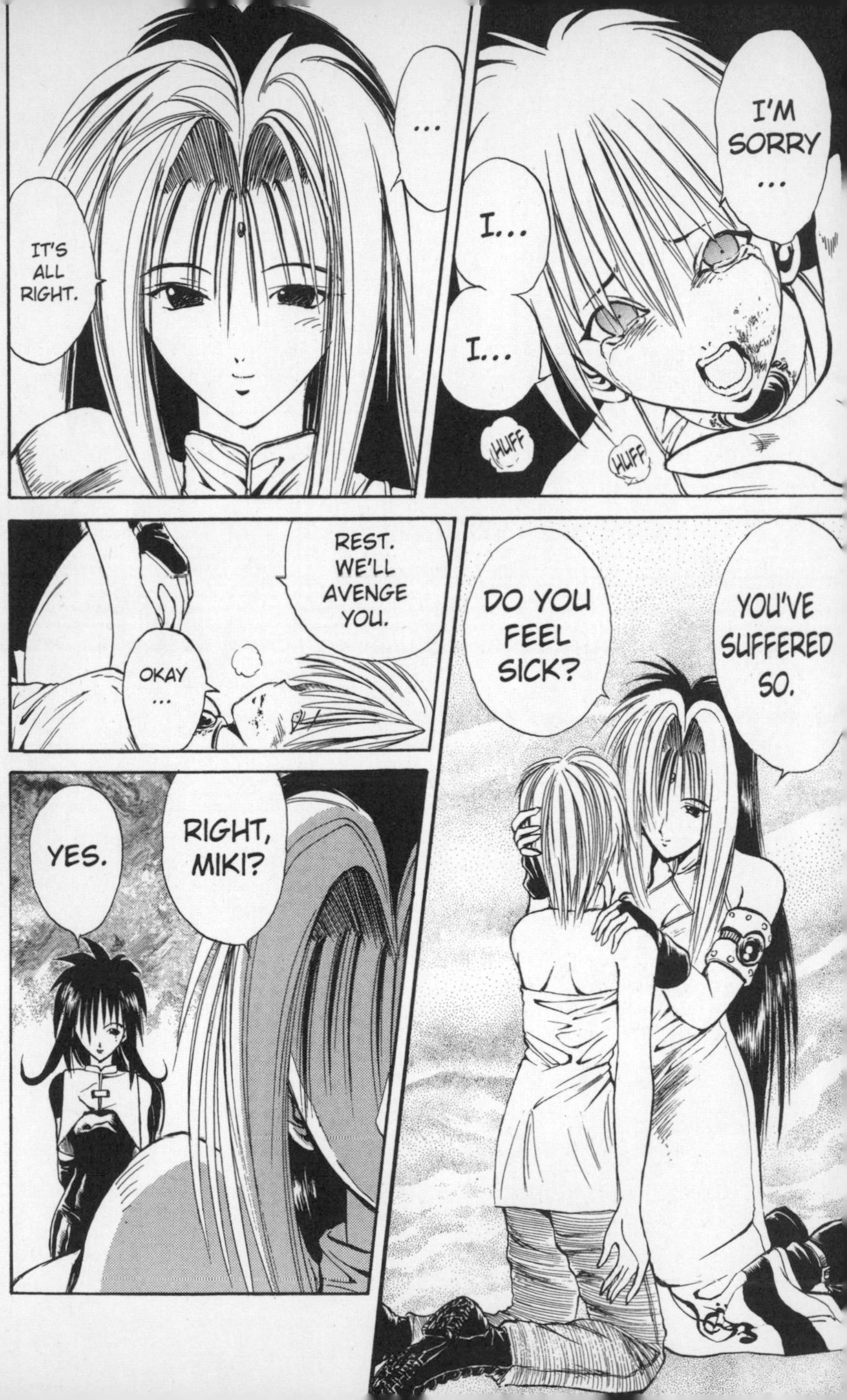
I'M SORRY ...
I...
I...
HUFF
HUFF
...
IT'S ALL RIGHT.
YOU'VE SUFFERED SO.
DO YOU FEEL SICK?
REST. WE'LL AVENGE YOU.
OKAY ...
RIGHT, MIKI?
YES.

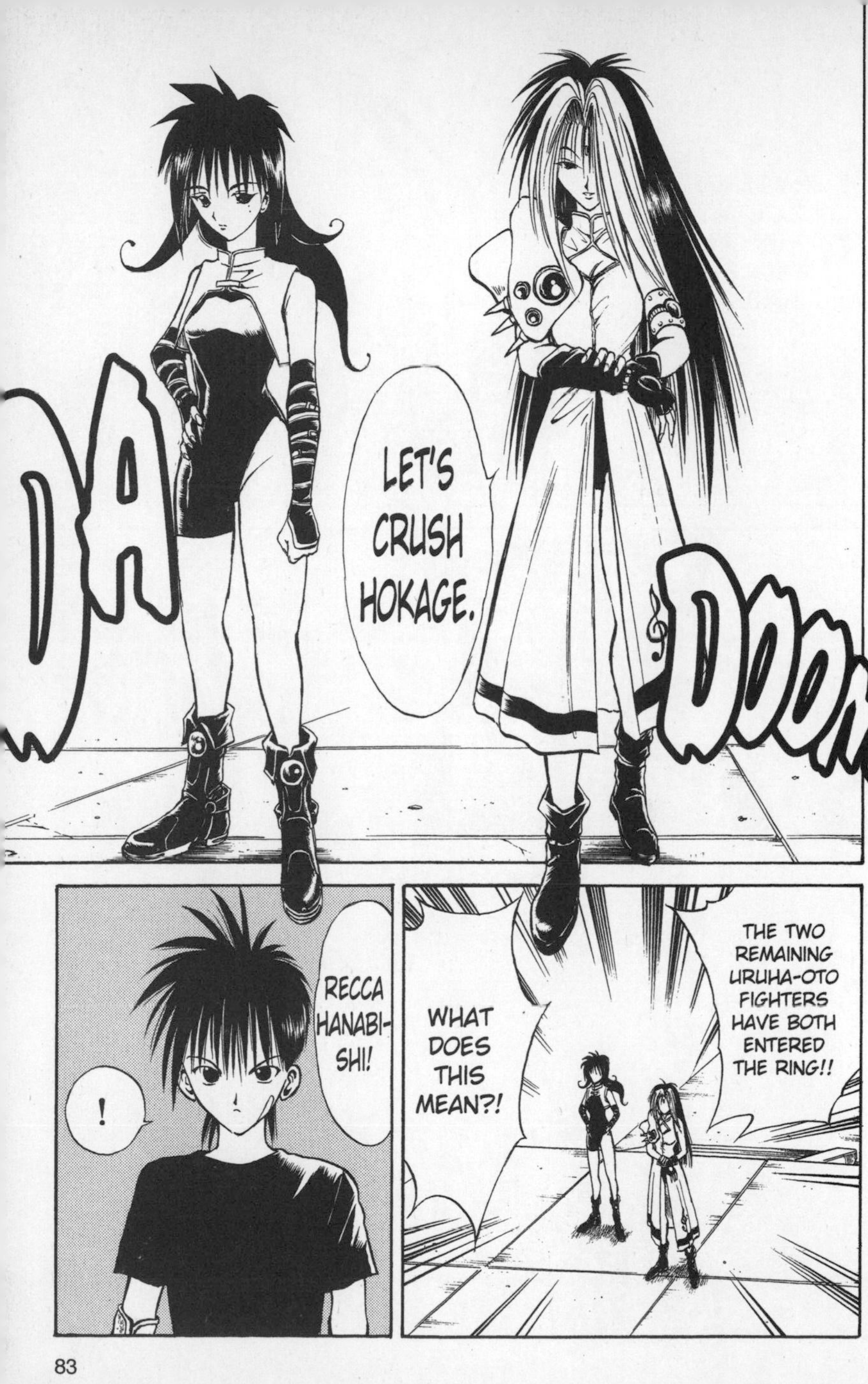
DOOM
LET'S CRUSH HOKAGE.
DA
THE TWO REMAINING URUHA-OTO FIGHTERS HAVE BOTH ENTERED THE RING!!
WHAT DOES THIS MEAN?!
RECCA HANABI-SHI!
!

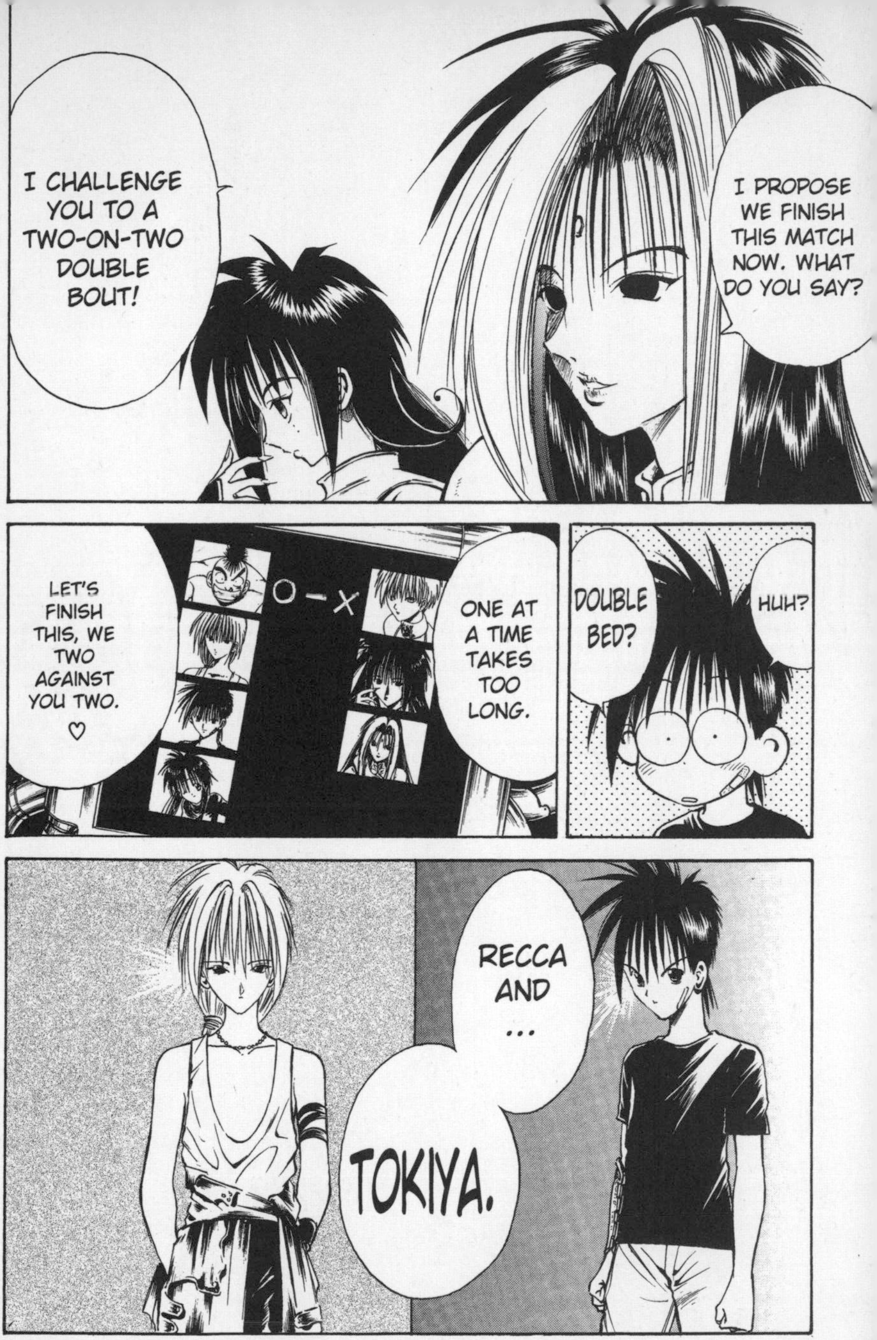
I PROPOSE WE FINISH THIS MATCH NOW. WHAT DO YOU SAY?
I CHALLENGE YOU TO A TWO-ON-TWO DOUBLE BOUT!
HUH?
DOUBLE BED?
ONE AT A TIME TAKES TOO LONG.
LET'S FINISH THIS, WE TWO AGAINST YOU TWO. ♡
O-X
RECCA AND ...
TOKIYA.

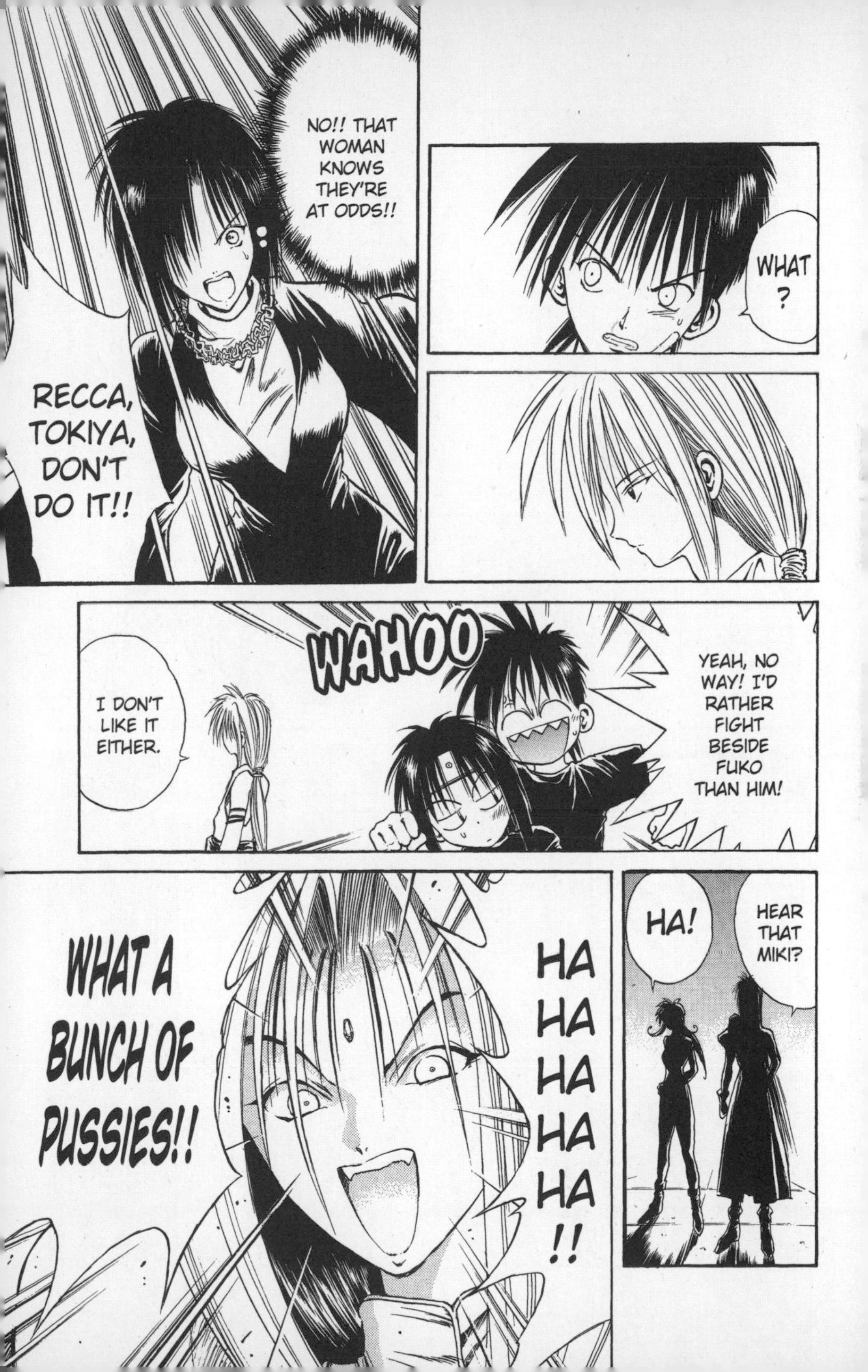
WHAT ?
NO!! THAT WOMAN KNOWS THEY'RE AT ODDS!!
RECCA, TOKIYA, DON'T DO IT!!
YEAH, NO WAY! I'D RATHER FIGHT BESIDE FUKO THAN HIM!
WAHOO
I DON'T LIKE IT EITHER.
HEAR THAT MIKI?
HA!
HA HA HA HA HA HA!!
WHAT A BUNCH OF PUSSIES!!

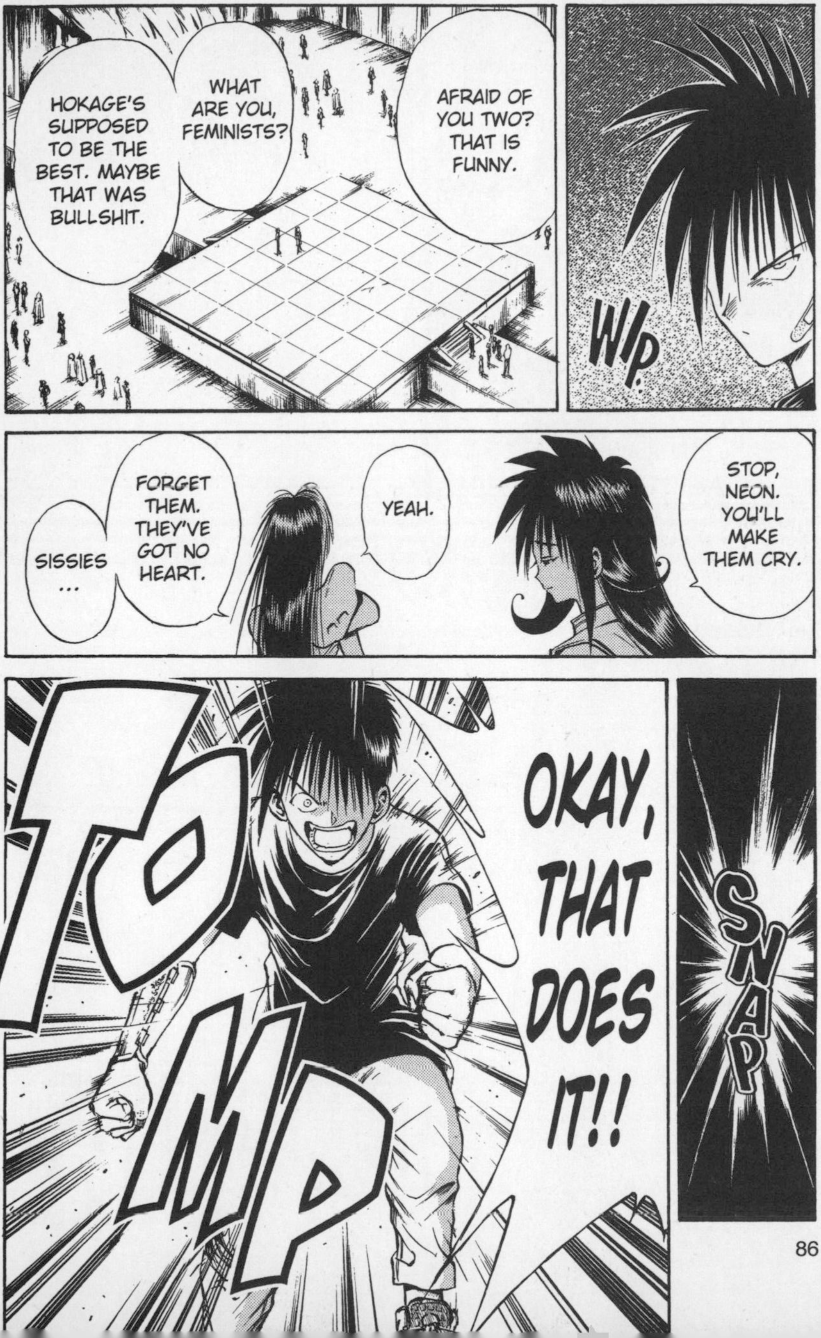
WIP.
AFRAID OF YOU TWO? THAT IS FUNNY.
WHAT ARE YOU, FEMINISTS?
HOKAGE'S SUPPOSED TO BE THE BEST. MAYBE THAT WAS BULLSHIT.
STOP, NEON. YOU'LL MAKE THEM CRY.
YEAH.
FORGET THEM. THEY'VE GOT NO HEART.
SISSIES ...
SNAP
OKAY, THAT DOES IT!!
TOMP

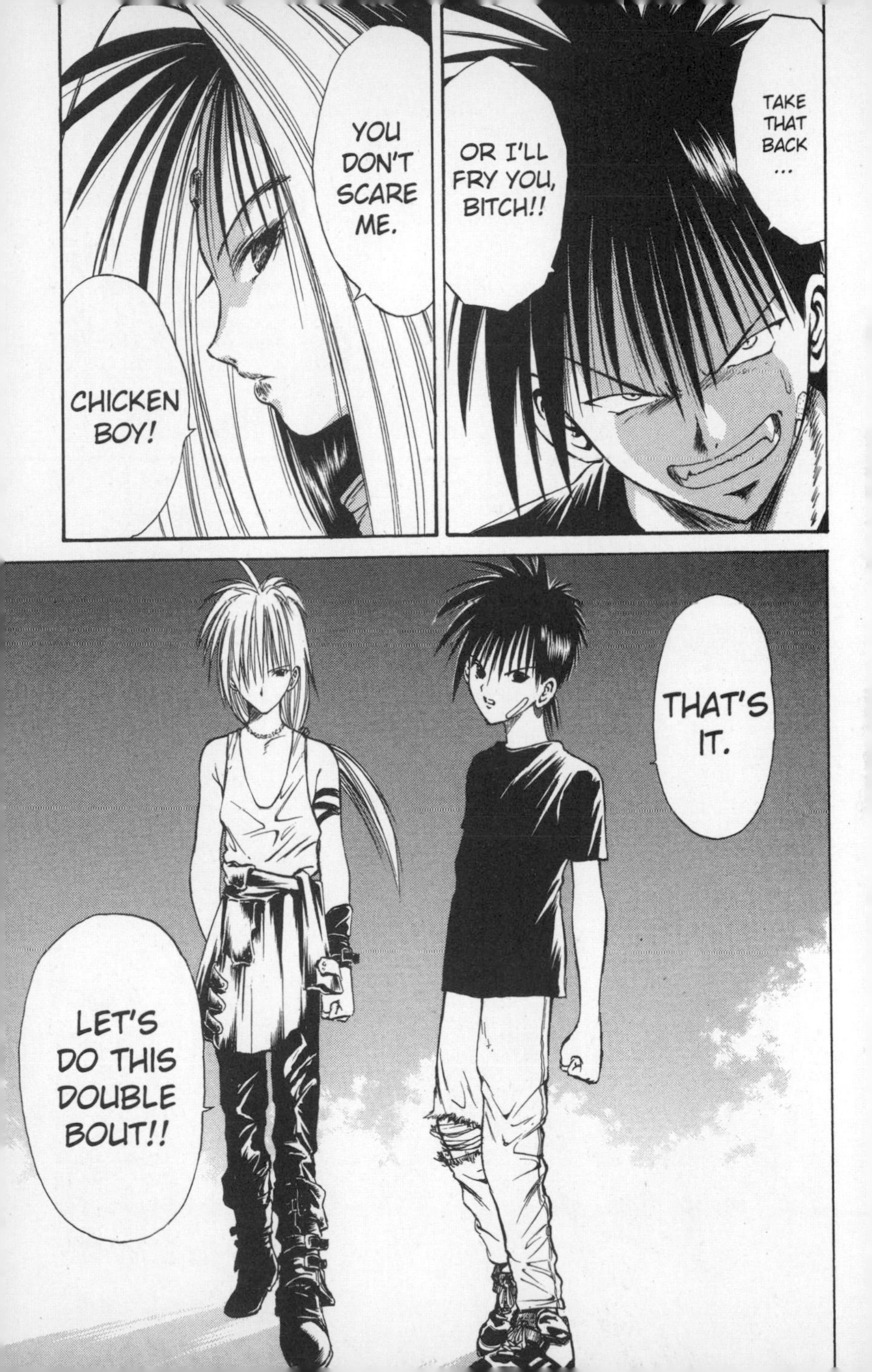
TAKE THAT BACK ...
OR I'LL FRY YOU, BITCH!!
YOU DON'T SCARE ME.
CHICKEN BOY!
THAT'S IT.
LET'S DO THIS DOUBLE BOUT!!

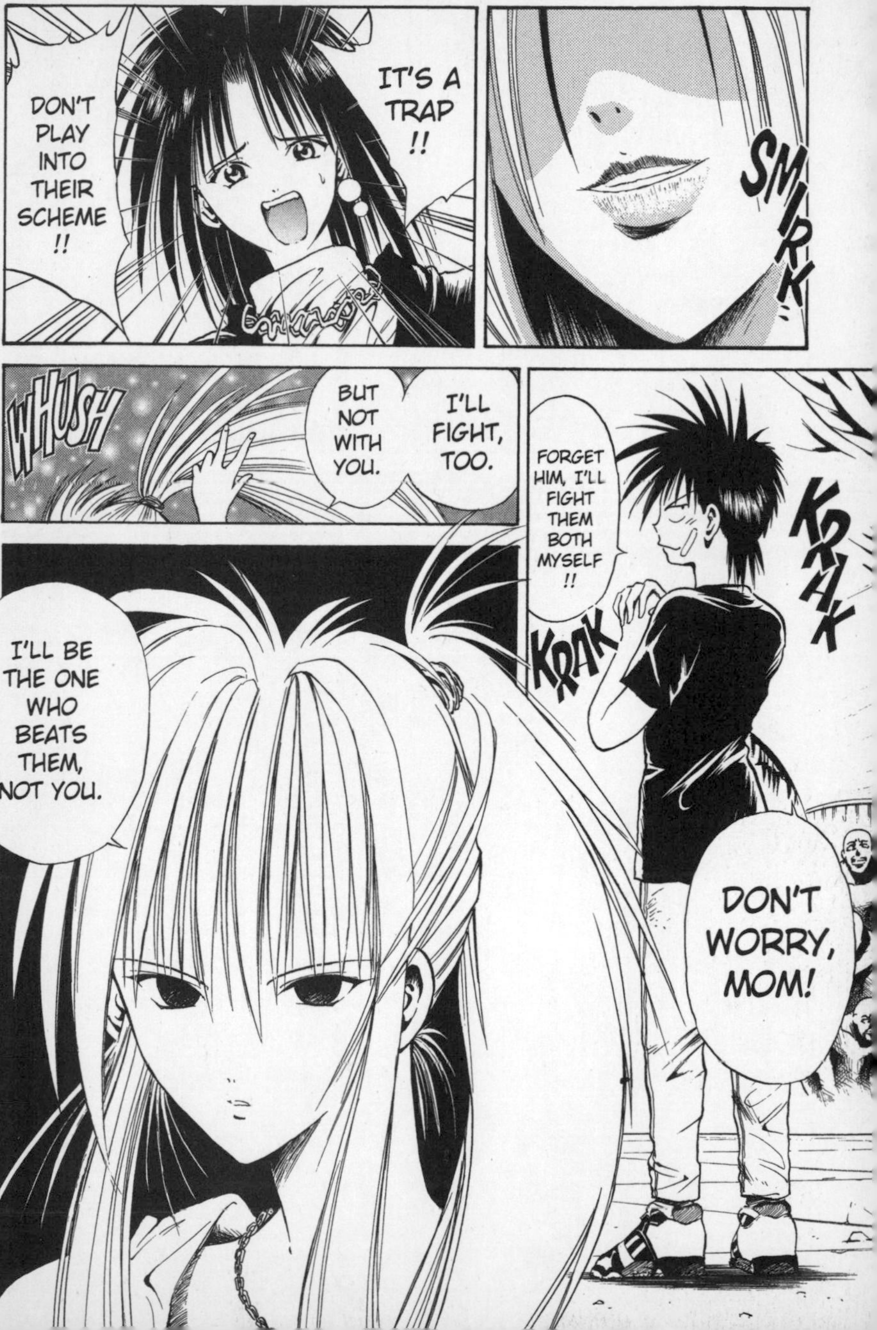
SMIRK
IT'S A TRAP !!
DON'T PLAY INTO THEIR SCHEME !!
FORGET HIM, I'LL FIGHT THEM BOTH MYSELF !!
KRAK
KRAK
DON'T WORRY, MOM!
I'LL FIGHT, TOO.
BUT NOT WITH YOU.
WHUSH
I'LL BE THE ONE WHO BEATS THEM, NOT YOU.

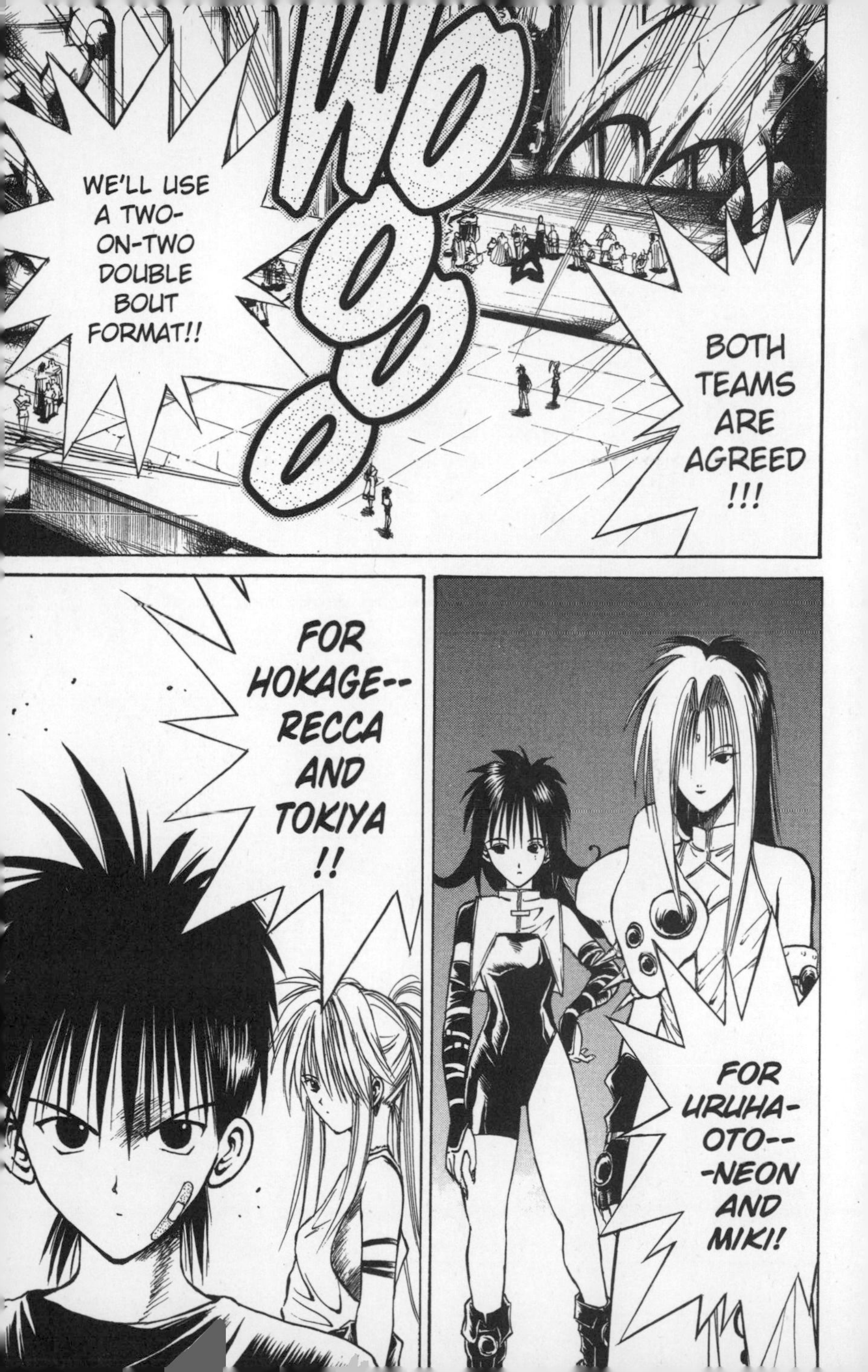
WOOOOO
WE'LL USE A TWO-ON-TWO DOUBLE BOUT FORMAT!!
BOTH TEAMS ARE AGREED!!!
FOR URUHA-OTO-- -NEON AND MIKI!
FOR HOKAGE-- RECCA AND TOKIYA !!

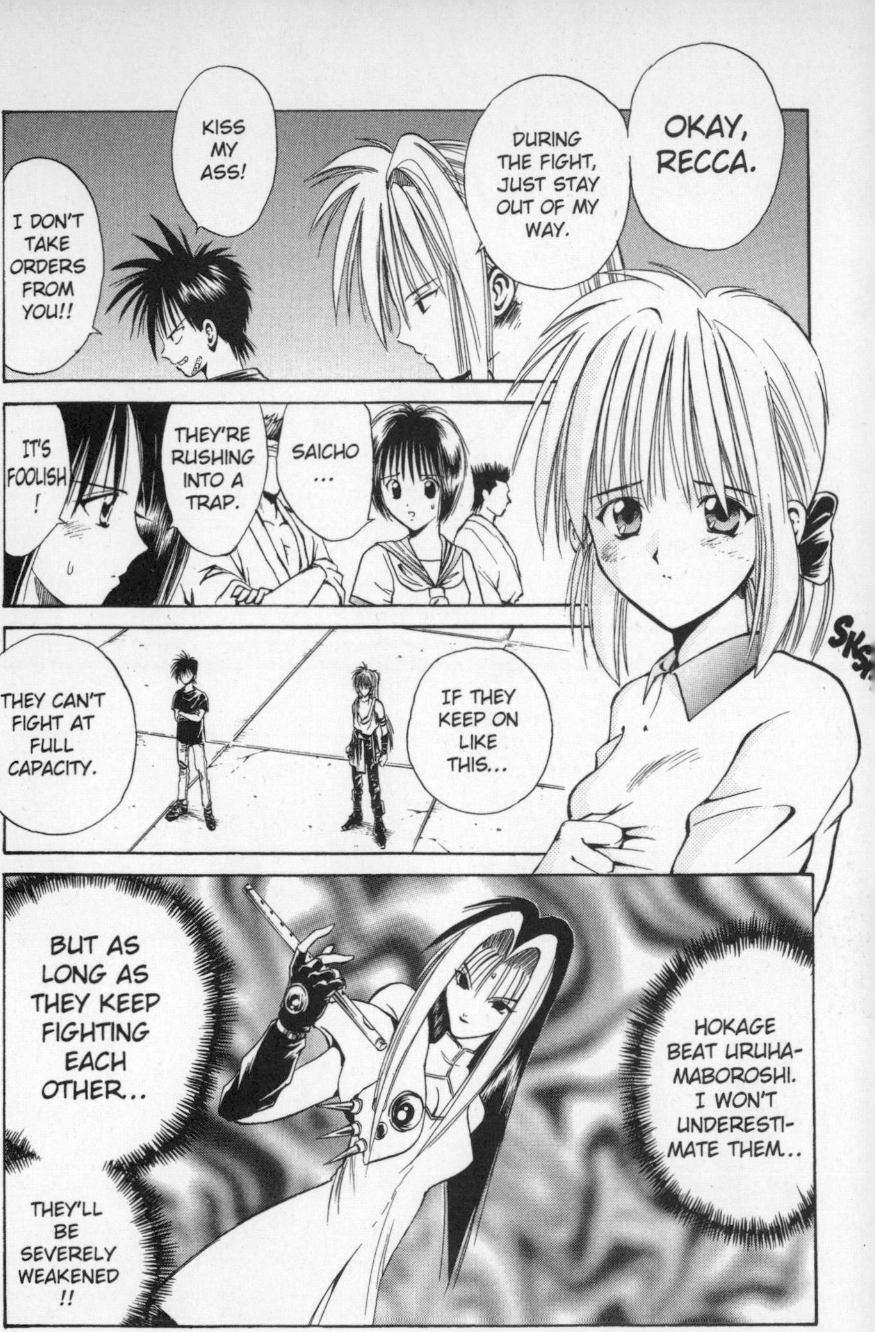
OKAY, RECCA.
DURING THE FIGHT, JUST STAY OUT OF MY WAY.
KISS MY ASS!
I DON'T TAKE ORDERS FROM YOU!!
SAICHO ...
THEY'RE RUSHING INTO A TRAP.
IT'S FOOLISH!
IF THEY KEEP ON LIKE THIS...
THEY CAN'T FIGHT AT FULL CAPACITY.
HOKAGE BEAT URUHA-MABOROSHI. I WON'T UNDERESTI-MATE THEM..
BUT AS LONG AS THEY KEEP FIGHTING EACH OTHER..
THEY'LL BE SEVERELY WEAKENED!!

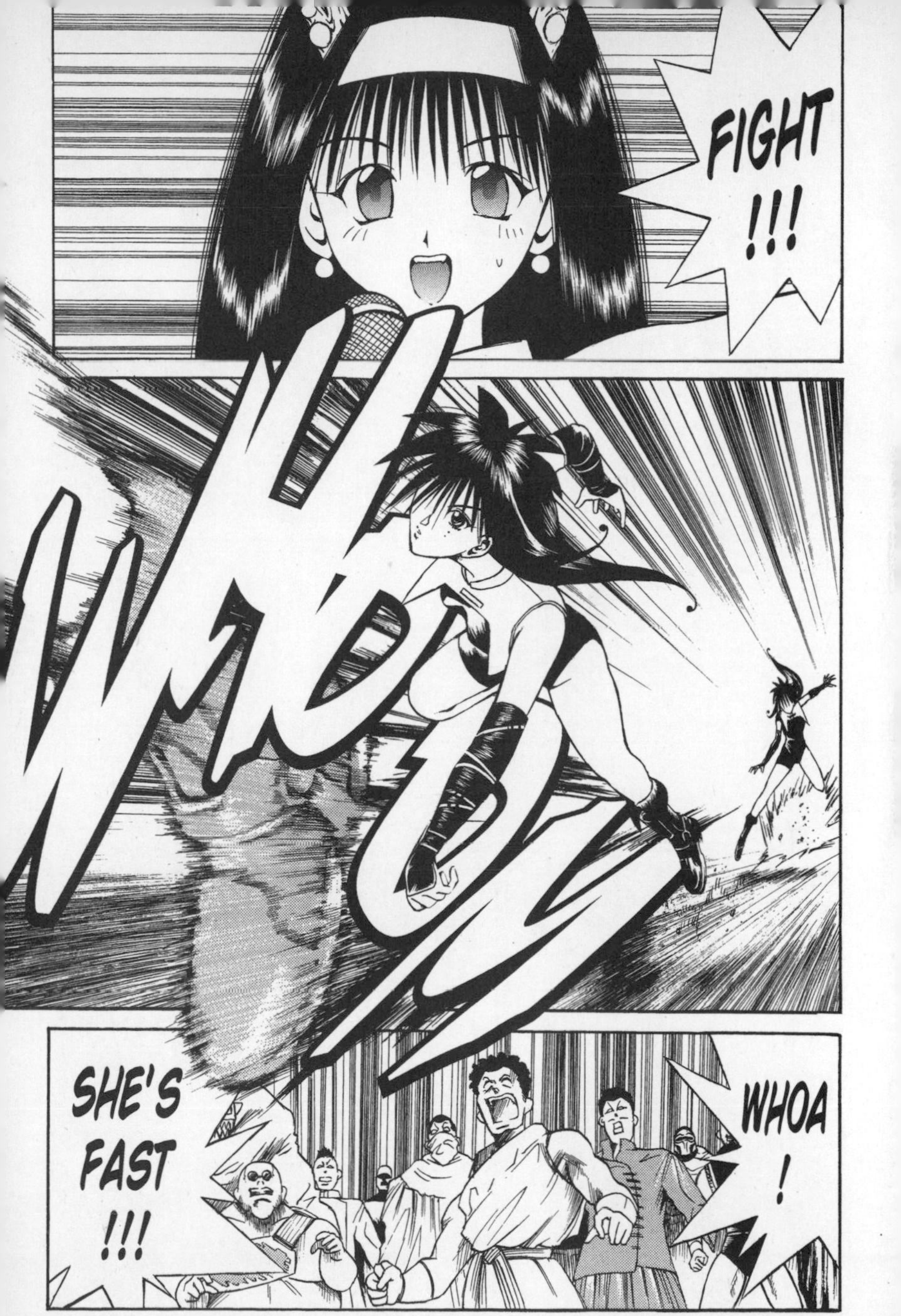
FIGHT!!!
WHOA!
SHE'S FAST!!!

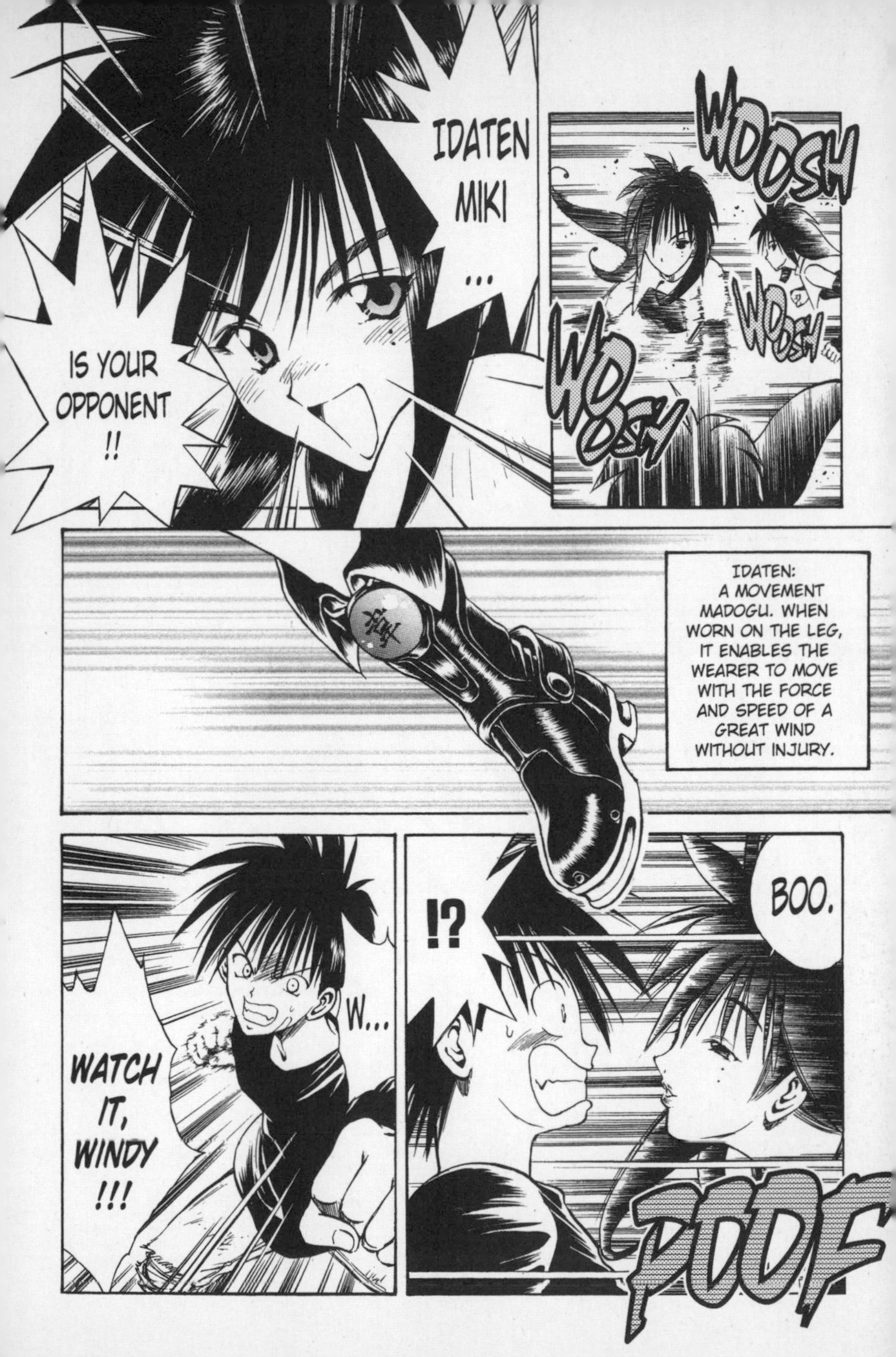
WOOSH
WOOSH
WOOOSH
IDATEN MIKI ...
IS YOUR OPPONENT !!
IDATEN: A MOVEMENT MADOGU. WHEN WORN ON THE LEG, IT ENABLES THE WEARER TO MOVE WITH THE FORCE AND SPEED OF A GREAT WIND WITHOUT INJURY.
BOO.
!?
POOF
W...
WATCH IT, WINDY !!!

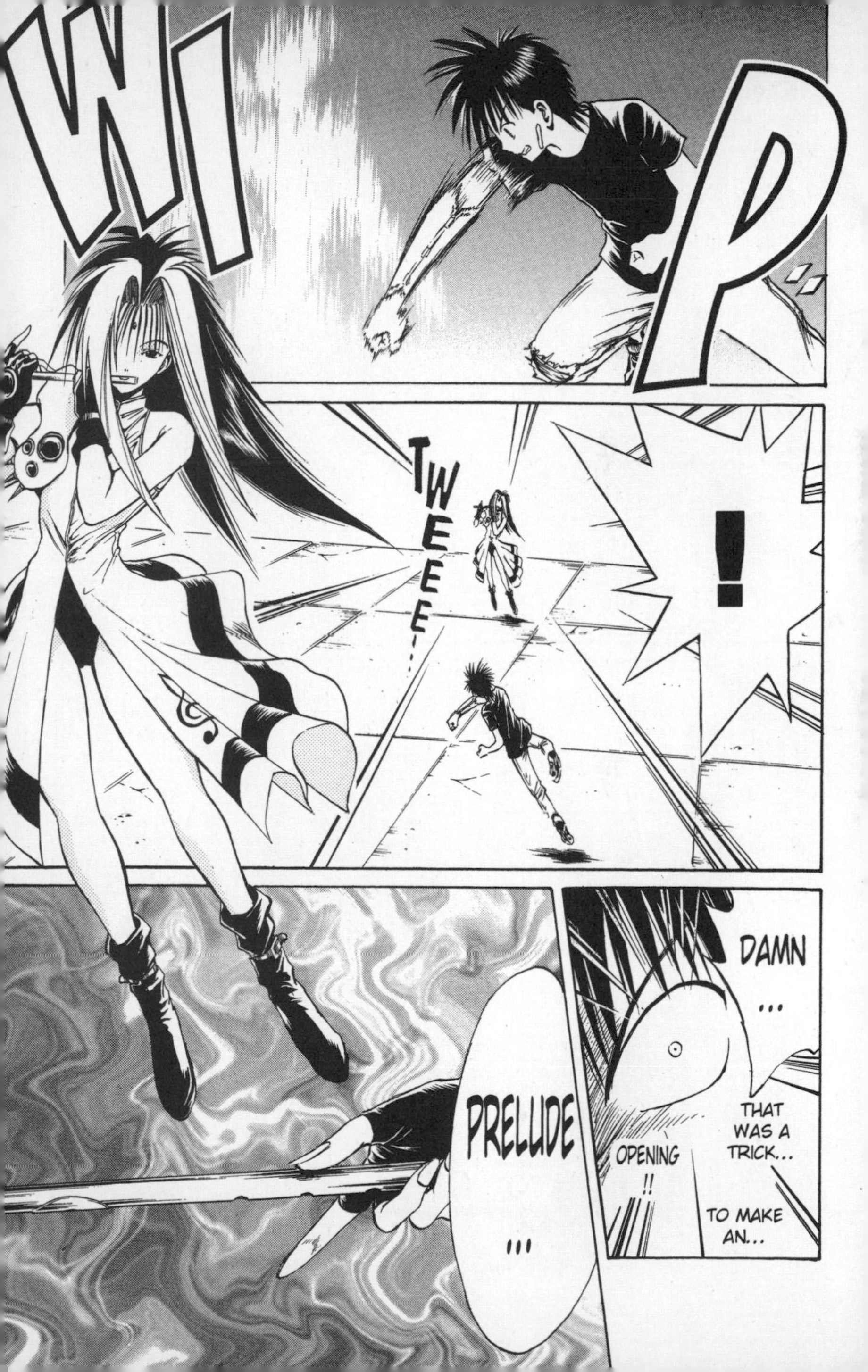
WIP
!
TWEEE...
DAMN...
THAT WAS A TRICK...
TO MAKE AN...
OPENING!!
PRELUDE...

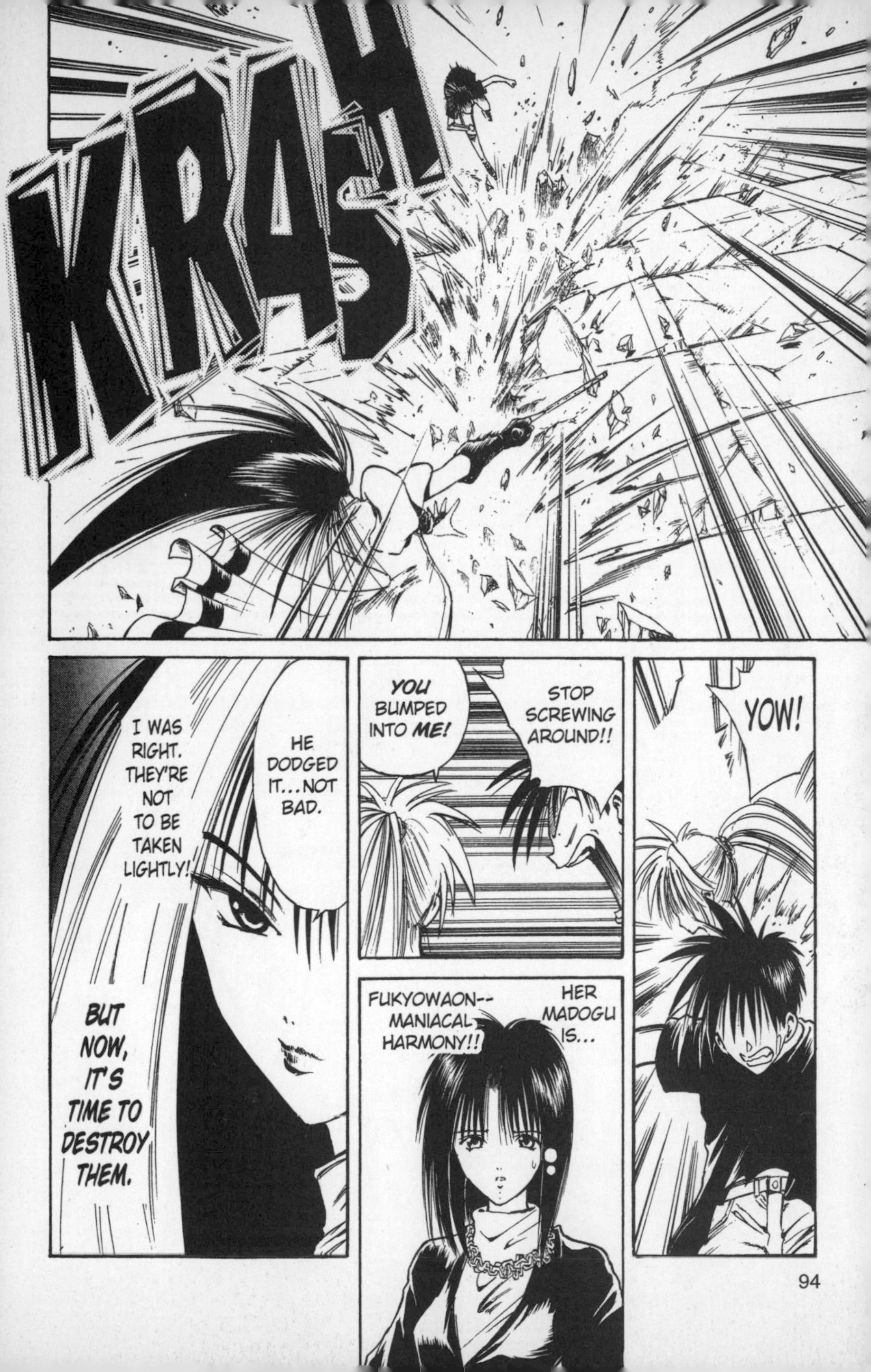
KRASH
YOW!
STOP SCREWING AROUND!!
YOU BUMPED INTO ME!
HER MADOGU IS...
FUKYOWAON--MANIACAL HARMONY!!
HE DODGED IT...NOT BAD.
I WAS RIGHT. THEY'RE NOT TO BE TAKEN LIGHTLY!
BUT NOW, IT'S TIME TO DESTROY THEM.

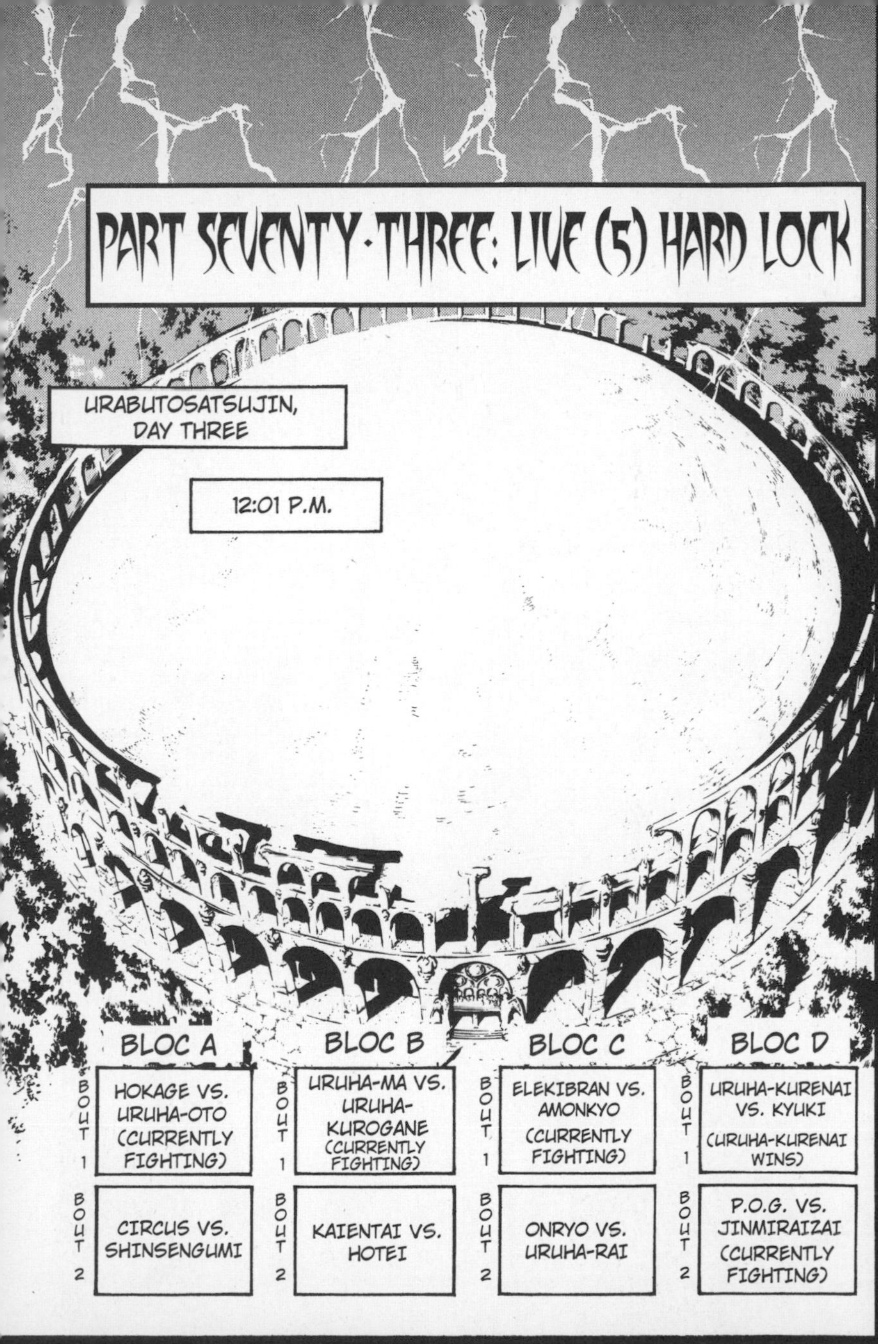
PART SEVENTY-THREE: LIVE (5) HARD LOCK
URABUTOSATSUJIN, DAY THREE
12:01 P.M.
BLOC A
BOUT 1
HOKAGE VS. URUHA-OTO (CURRENTLY FIGHTING)
BOUT 2
CIRCUS VS. SHINSENGUMI
BLOC B
BOUT 1
URUHA-MA VS. URUHA-KUROGANE (CURRENTLY FIGHTING)
BOUT 2
KAIENTAI VS. HOTEI
BLOC C
BOUT 1
ELEKIBRAN VS. AMONKYO (CURRENTLY FIGHTING)
BOUT 2
ONRYO VS. URUHA-RAI
BLOC D
BOUT 1
URUHA-KURENAI VS. KYUKI (URUHA-KURENAI WINS)
BOUT 2
P.O.G. VS. JINMIRAIZAI (CURRENTLY FIGHTING)

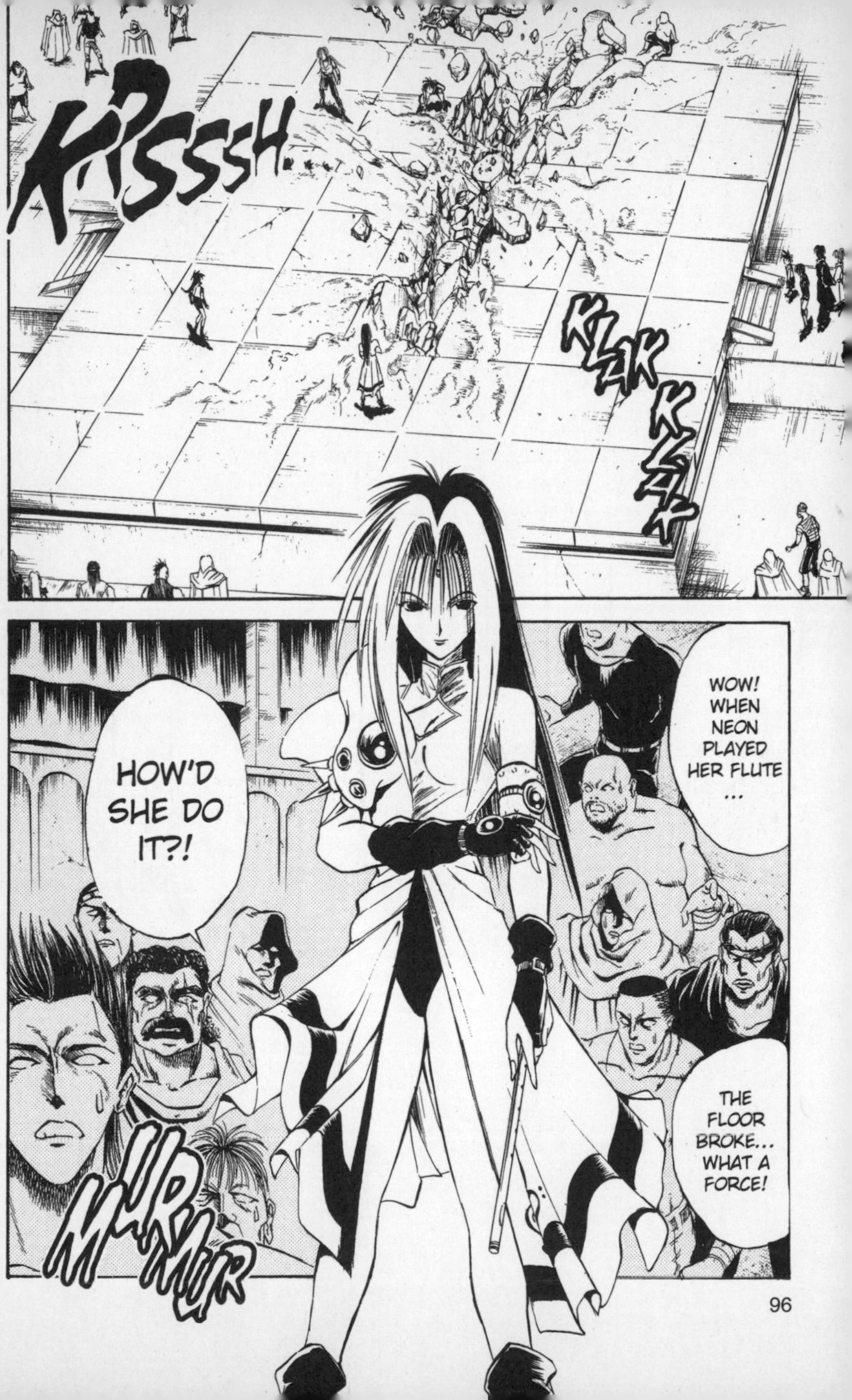
KRSSSH...
KLAK KLAK
WOW! WHEN NEON PLAYED HER FLUTE ...
THE FLOOR BROKE... WHAT A FORCE!
HOW'D SHE DO IT?!

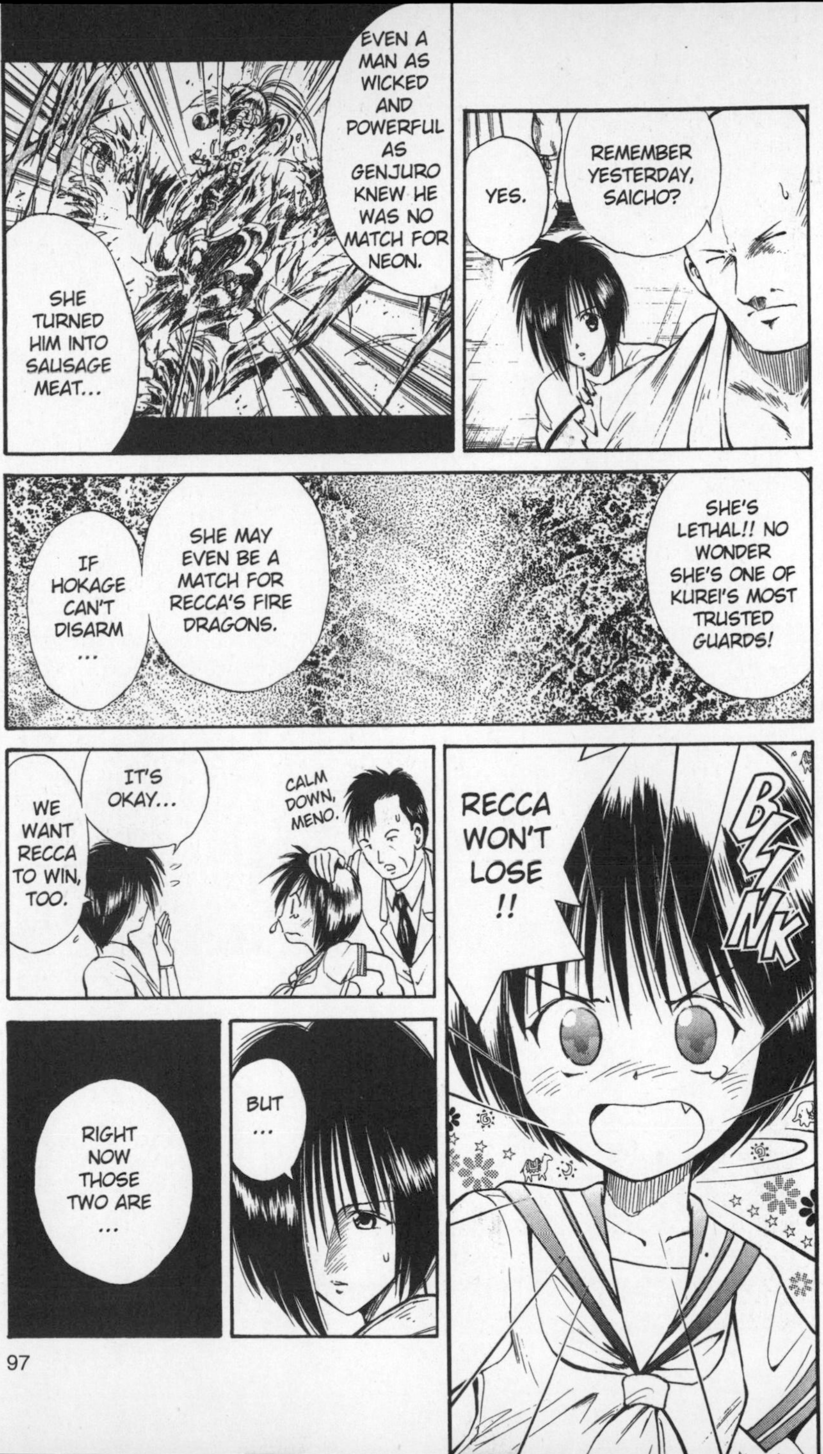
REMEMBER YESTERDAY, SAICHO?
YES.
EVEN A MAN AS WICKED AND POWERFUL AS GENJURO KNEW HE WAS NO MATCH FOR NEON.
SHE TURNED HIM INTO SAUSAGE MEAT...
SHE'S LETHAL!! NO WONDER SHE'S ONE OF KUREI'S MOST TRUSTED GUARDS!
SHE MAY EVEN BE A MATCH FOR RECCA'S FIRE DRAGONS.
IF HOKAGE CAN'T DISARM ...
RECCA WON'T LOSE !!
BLINK
CALM DOWN, MENO.
IT'S OKAY...
WE WANT RECCA TO WIN, TOO.
BUT ...
RIGHT NOW THOSE TWO ARE ...

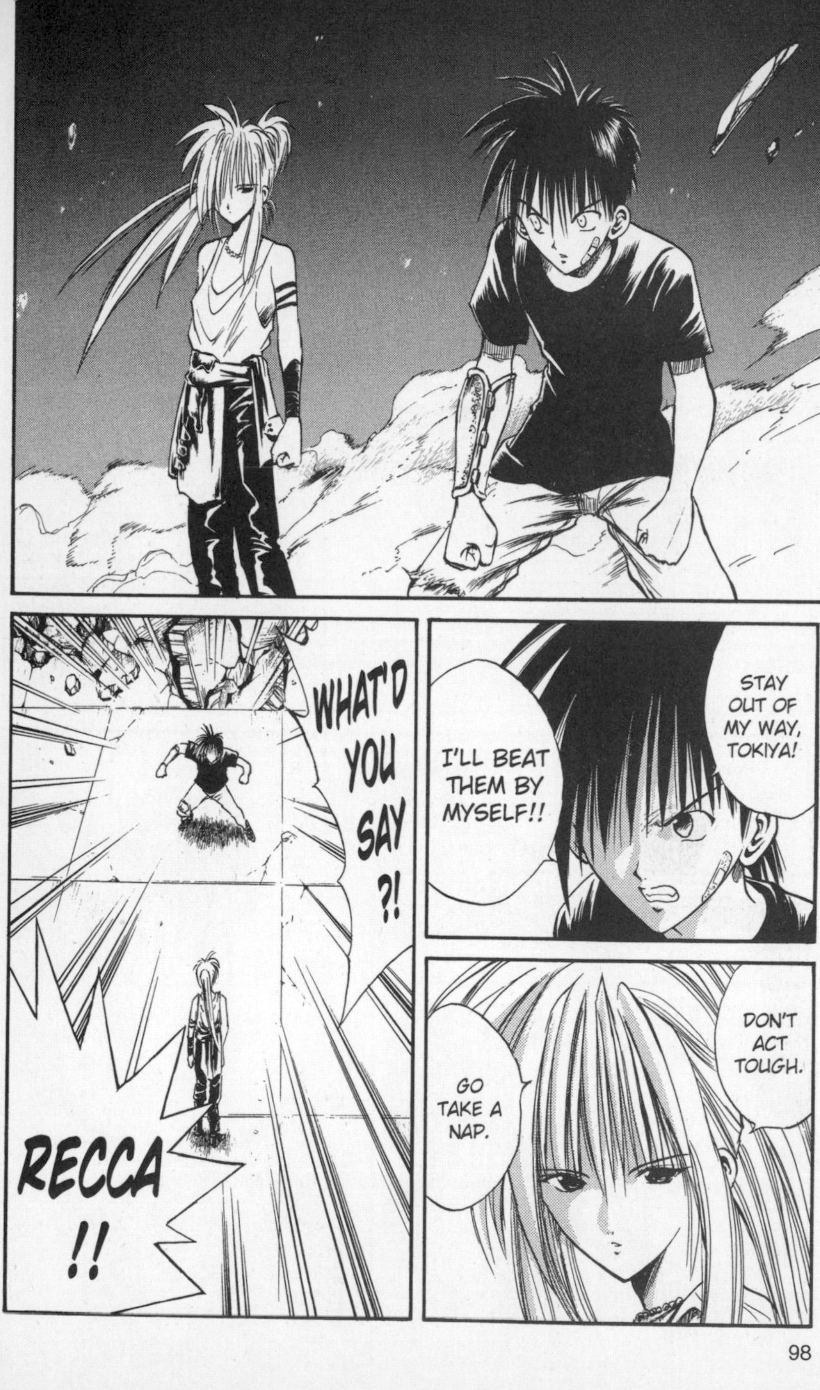
STAY OUT OF MY WAY, TOKIYA!
I'LL BEAT THEM BY MYSELF!!
DON'T ACT TOUGH.
GO TAKE A NAP.
WHAT'D YOU SAY ?!
RECCA !!

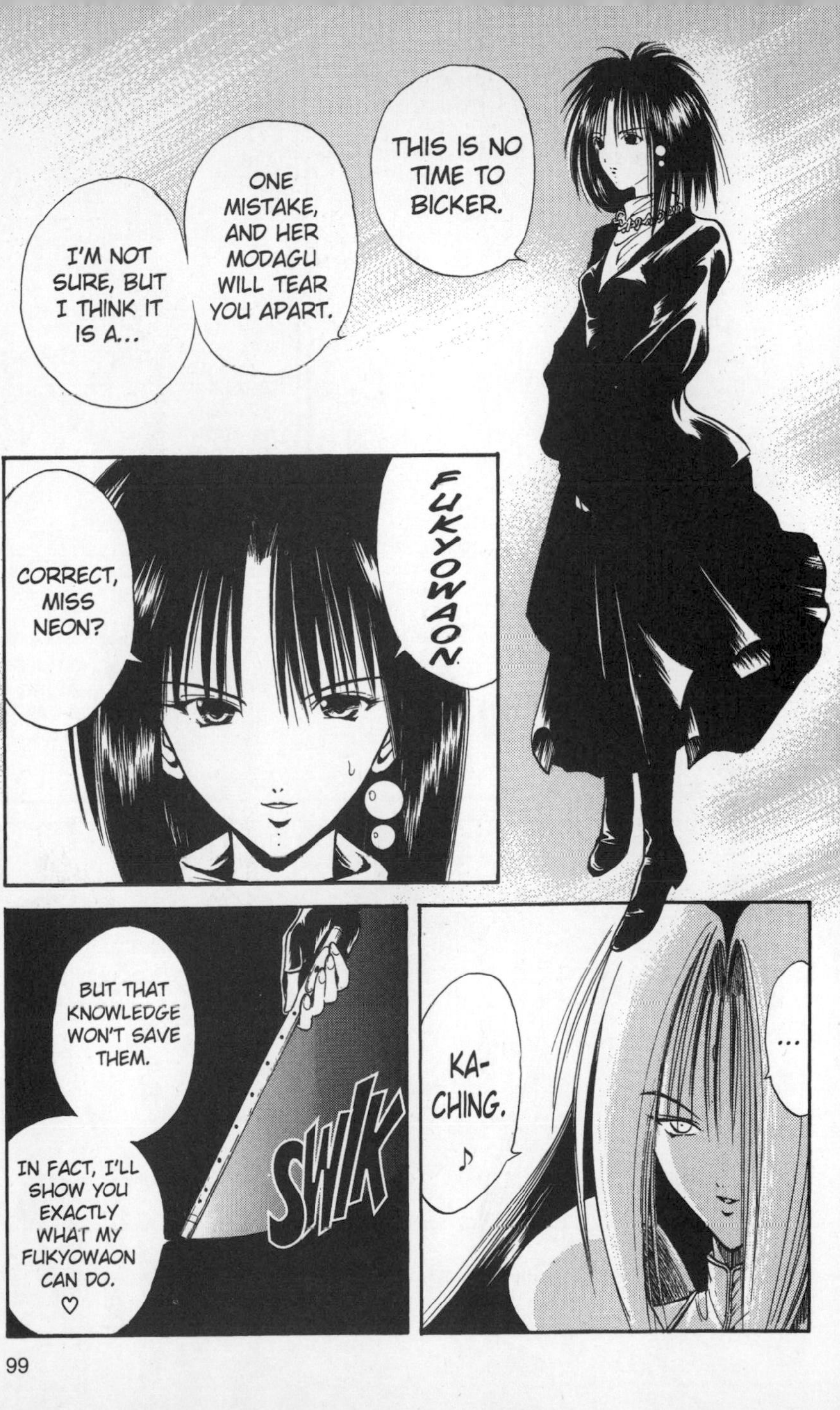
THIS IS NO TIME TO BICKER.
ONE MISTAKE, AND HER MODAGU WILL TEAR YOU APART.
I'M NOT SURE, BUT I THINK IT IS A...
FUKYOWAON.
CORRECT, MISS NEON?
...
KA-CHING. ♪
BUT THAT KNOWLEDGE WON'T SAVE THEM.
SWIK
IN FACT, I'LL SHOW YOU EXACTLY WHAT MY FUKYOWAON CAN DO. ♡

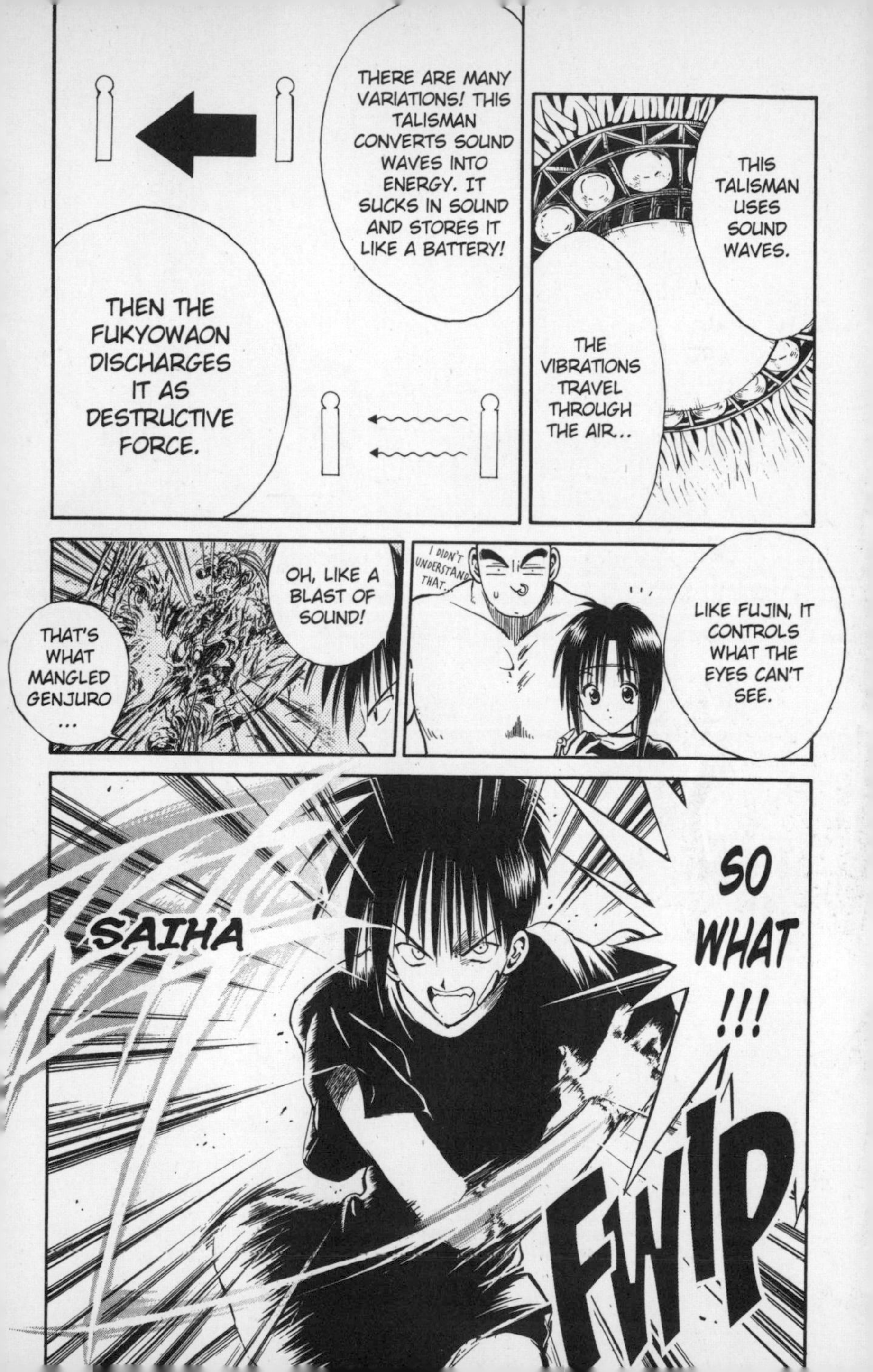
THIS TALISMAN USES SOUND WAVES.
THE VIBRATIONS TRAVEL THROUGH THE AIR..
THERE ARE MANY VARIATIONS! THIS TALISMAN CONVERTS SOUND WAVES INTO ENERGY. IT SUCKS IN SOUND AND STORES IT LIKE A BATTERY!
THEN THE FUKYOWAON DISCHARGES IT AS DESTRUCTIVE FORCE.
LIKE FUJIN, IT CONTROLS WHAT THE EYES CAN'T SEE.
I DIDN'T UNDERSTAND THAT..
...
OH, LIKE A BLAST OF SOUND!
THAT'S WHAT MANGLED GENJURO ...
SO WHAT !!!
SAIHA
FWIP

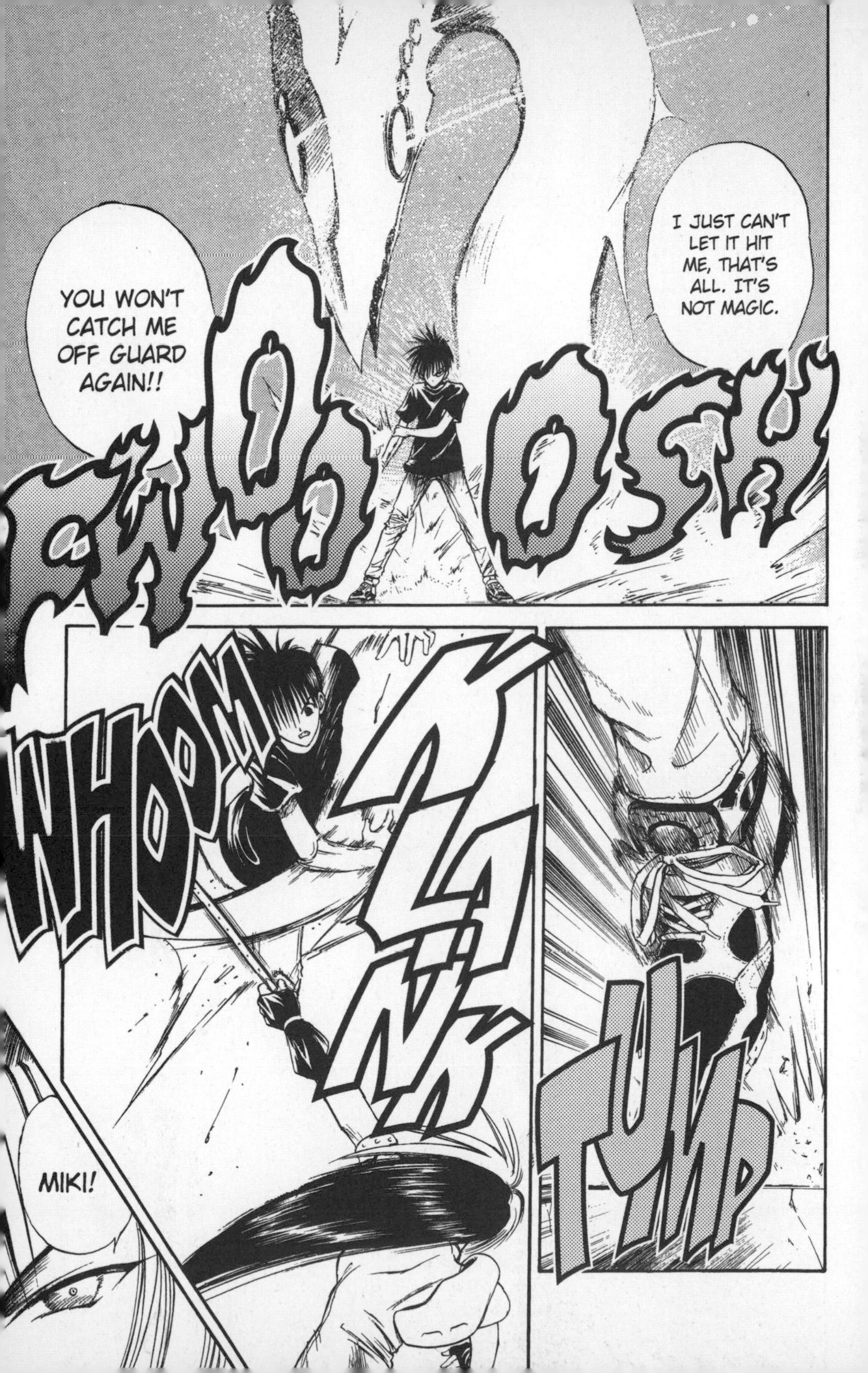
I JUST CAN'T LET IT HIT ME, THAT'S ALL. IT'S NOT MAGIC.
YOU WON'T CATCH ME OFF GUARD AGAIN!!
WHOOSH
WHOOM
MIKI!

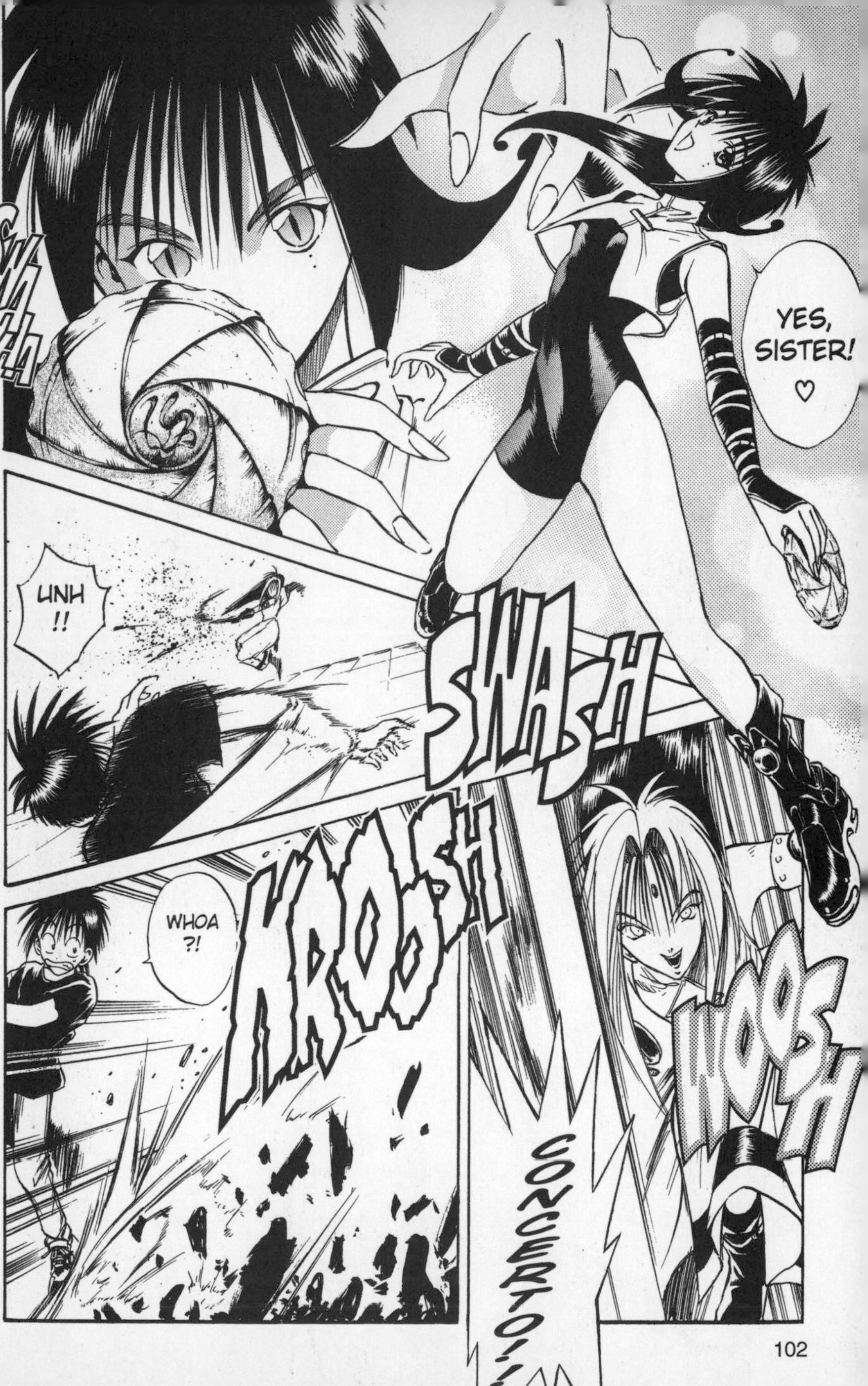
YES, SISTER! ♡
SWAAA
SWASH
UNH !!
WHOOSH
CONCERTO!!!
KROSH
WHOA ?!

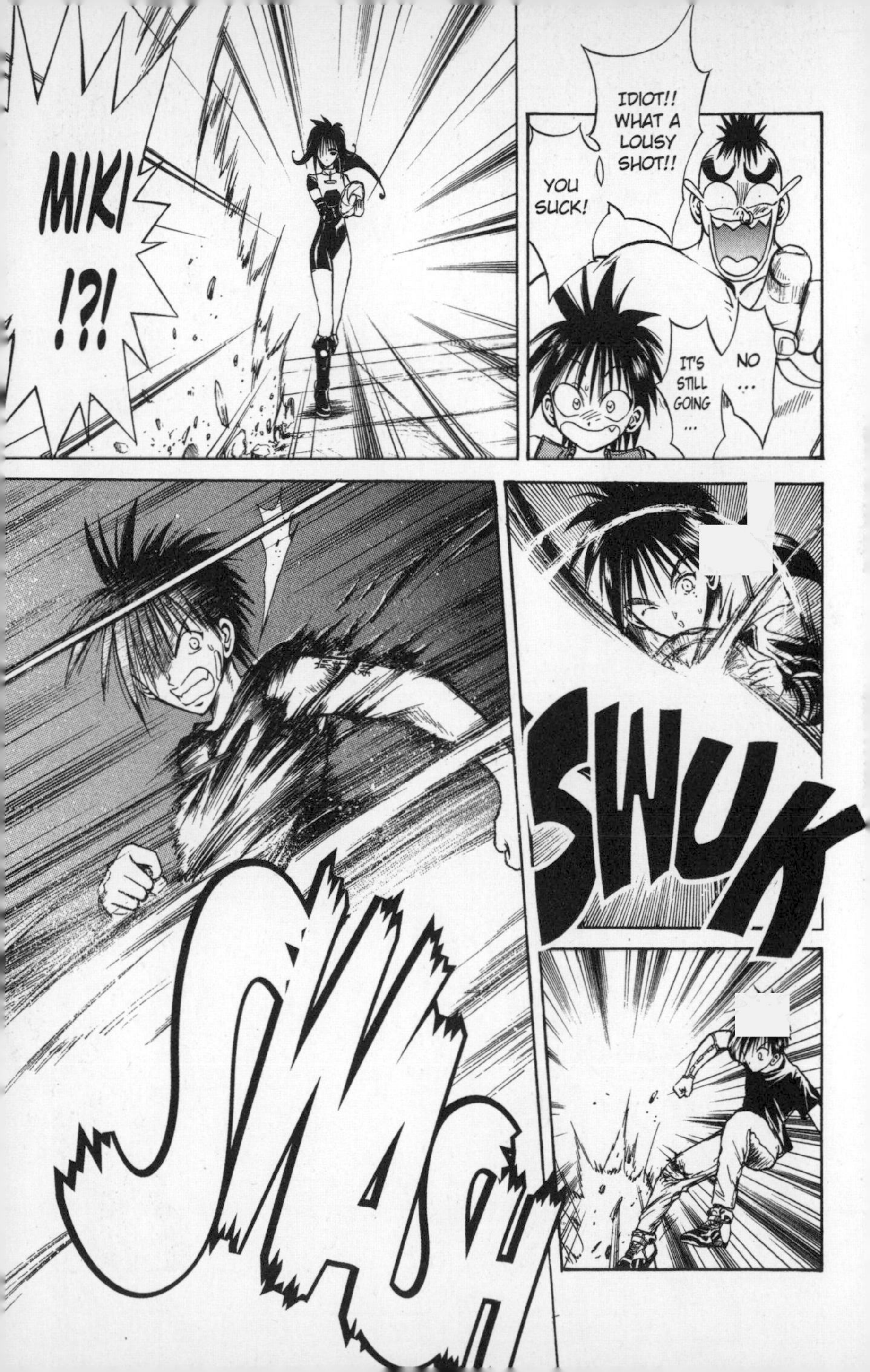
IDIOT!! WHAT A LOUSY SHOT!!
YOU SUCK!
NO ...
IT'S STILL GOING ...
MIKI !?!
SWUK
SMASH

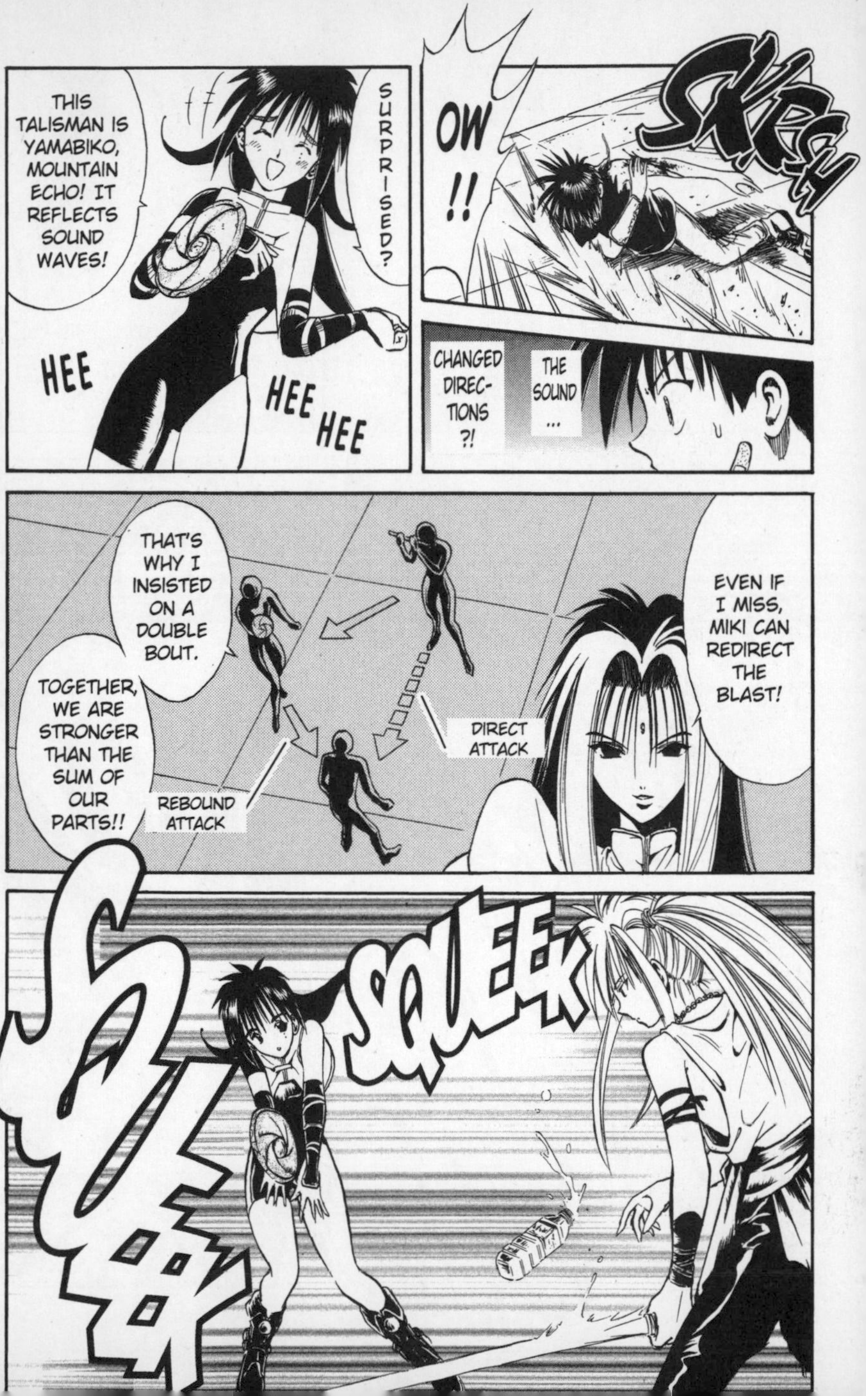
OW!!
SKECH
THE SOUND...
CHANGED DIRECTIONS?!
SURPRISED?
THIS TALISMAN IS YAMABIKO, MOUNTAIN ECHO! IT REFLECTS SOUND WAVES!
HEE HEE HEE
EVEN IF I MISS, MIKI CAN REDIRECT THE BLAST!
THAT'S WHY I INSISTED ON A DOUBLE BOUT.
TOGETHER, WE ARE STRONGER THAN THE SUM OF OUR PARTS!!
DIRECT ATTACK
REBOUND ATTACK
SQUEEK

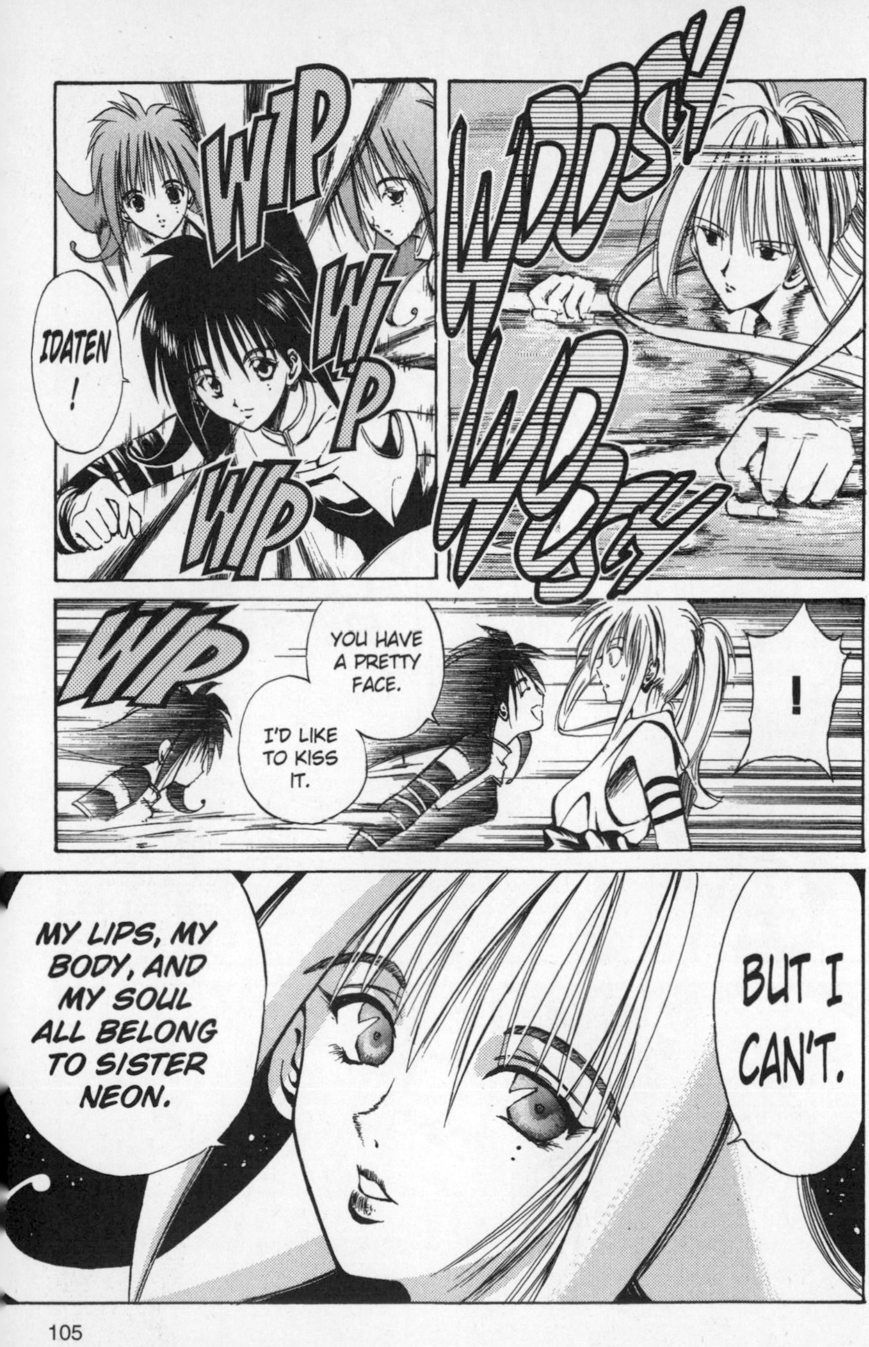
WOOSH
WOOSH
WIP
WIP
WIP
IDATEN!
!
YOU HAVE A PRETTY FACE.
I'D LIKE TO KISS IT.
WIP
BUT I CAN'T.
MY LIPS, MY BODY, AND MY SOUL ALL BELONG TO SISTER NEON.

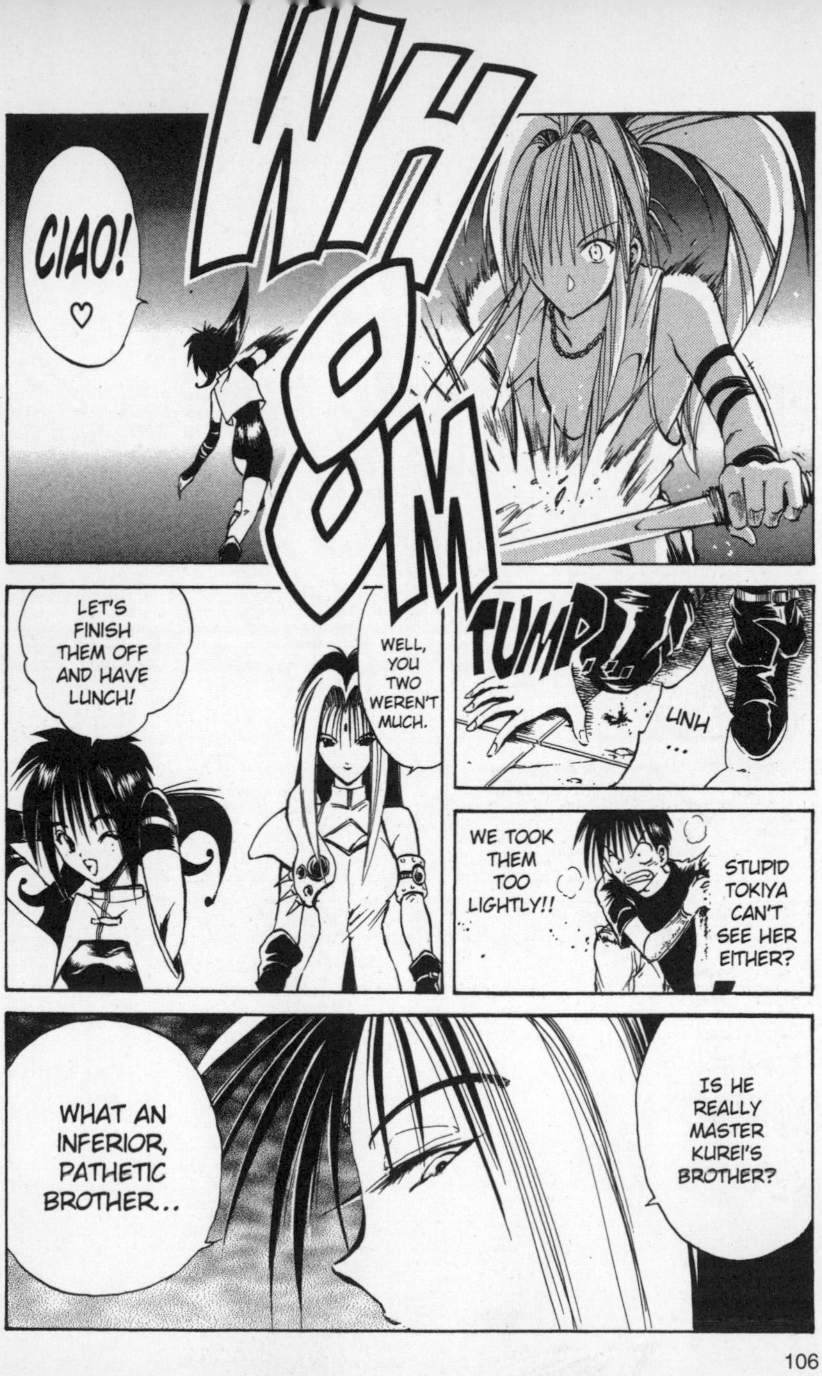
WHOOM
CIAO! ♡
TUMP
UNH ...
STUPID TOKIYA CAN'T SEE HER EITHER?
WE TOOK THEM TOO LIGHTLY!!
WELL, YOU TWO WEREN'T MUCH.
LET'S FINISH THEM OFF AND HAVE LUNCH!
IS HE REALLY MASTER KUREI'S BROTHER?
WHAT AN INFERIOR, PATHETIC BROTHER...

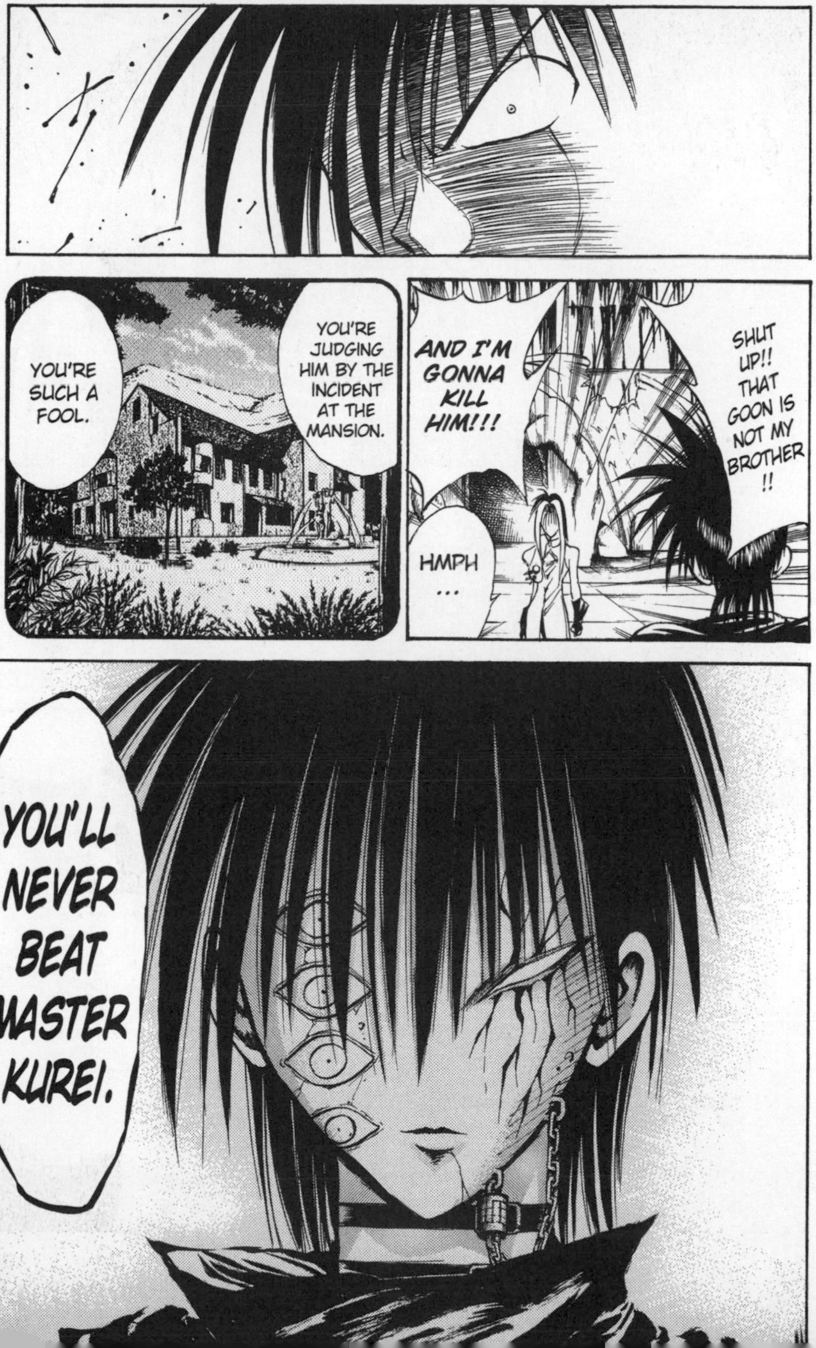
SHUT UP!! THAT GOON IS NOT MY BROTHER !!
AND I'M GONNA KILL HIM!!!
HMPH ...
YOU'RE JUDGING HIM BY THE INCIDENT AT THE MANSION.
YOU'RE SUCH A FOOL.
YOU'LL NEVER BEAT MASTER KUREI.

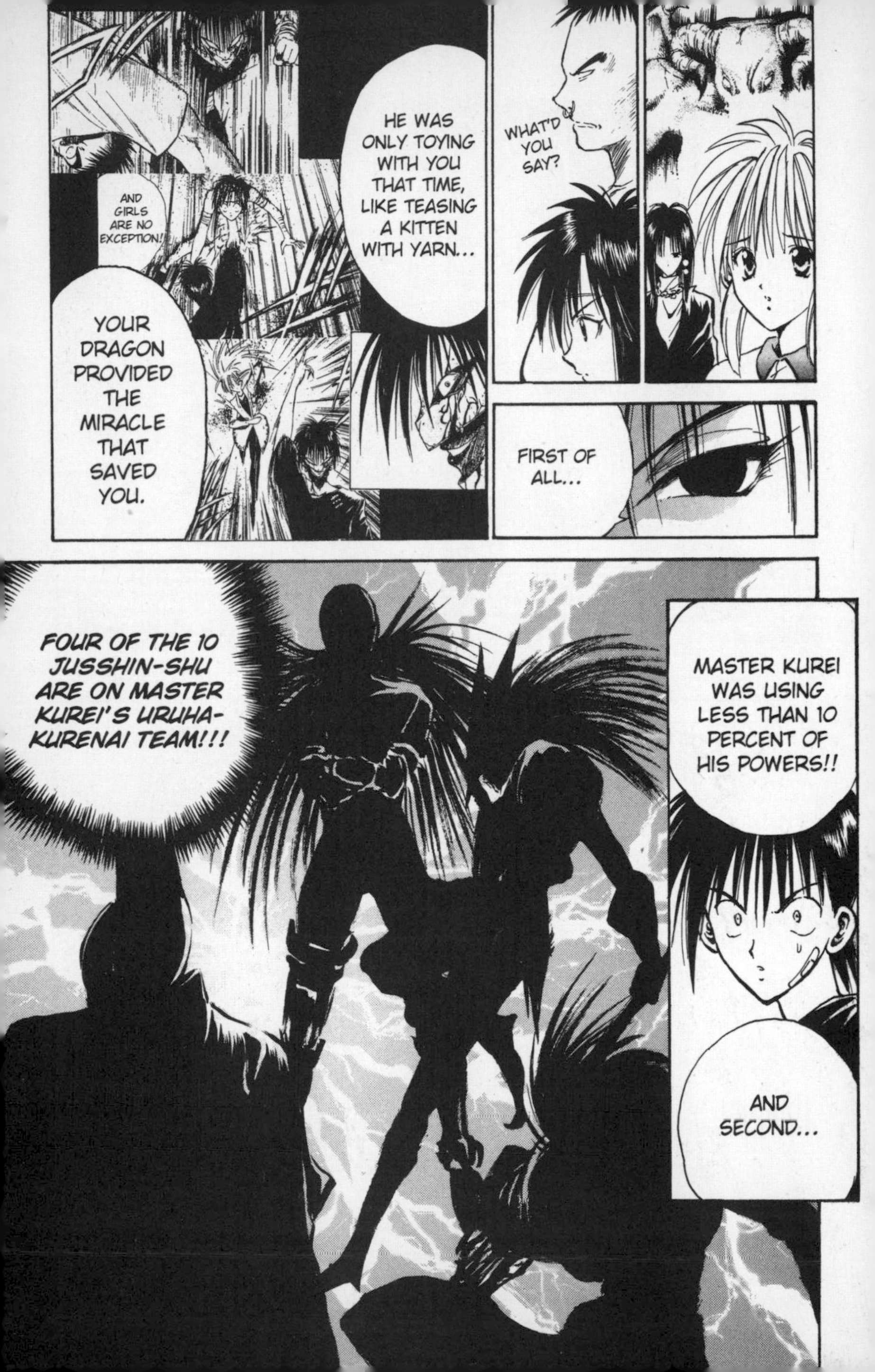
WHAT'D YOU SAY?
FIRST OF ALL...
HE WAS ONLY TOYING WITH YOU THAT TIME, LIKE TEASING A KITTEN WITH YARN...
AND GIRLS ARE NO EXCEPTION!
YOUR DRAGON PROVIDED THE MIRACLE THAT SAVED YOU.
MASTER KUREI WAS USING LESS THAN 10 PERCENT OF HIS POWERS!!
AND SECOND...
FOUR OF THE 10 JUSSHIN-SHU ARE ON MASTER KUREI'S URUHA-KURENAI TEAM!!!

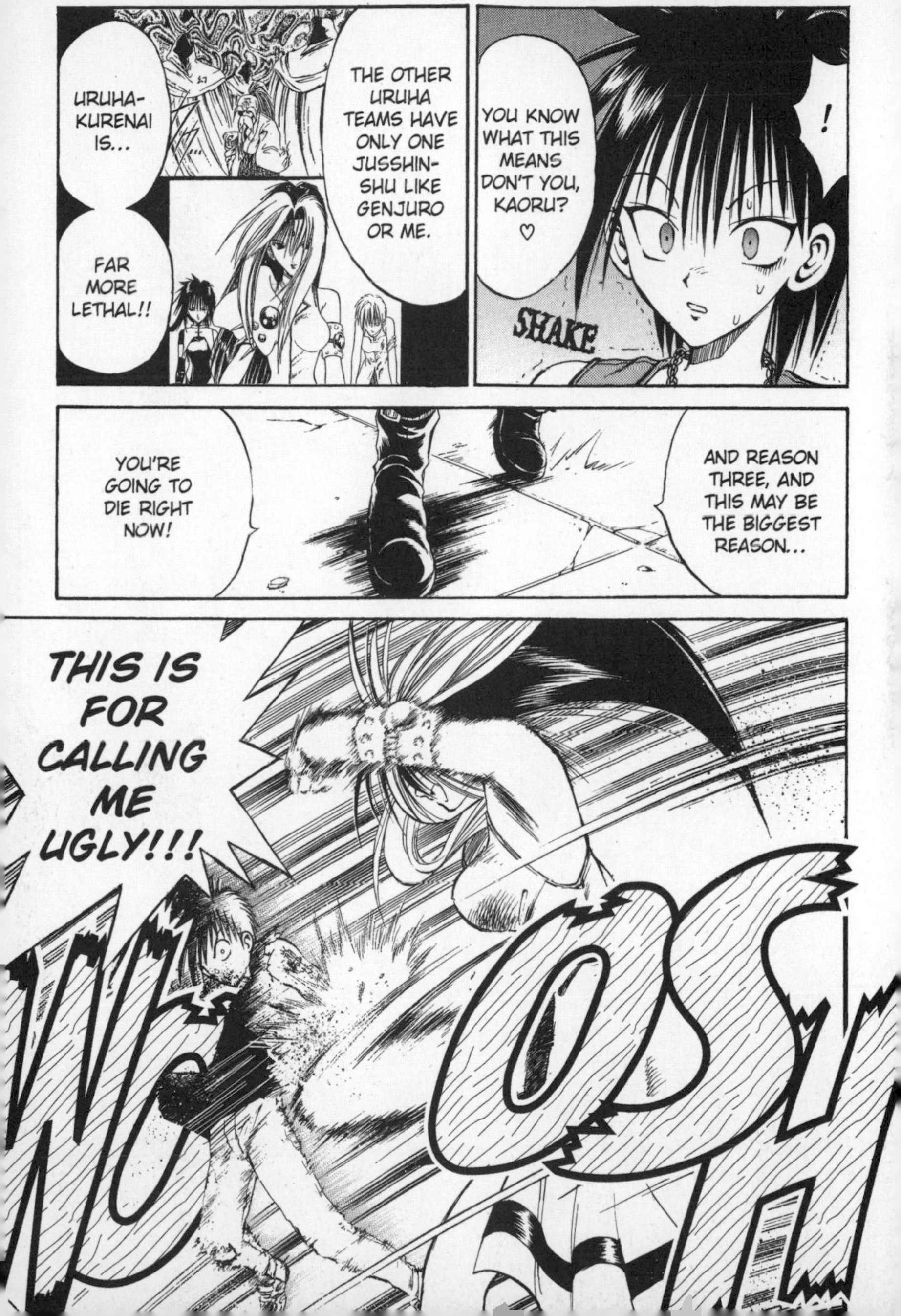
!
YOU KNOW WHAT THIS MEANS DON'T YOU, KAORU? ♡
SHAKE
THE OTHER URUHA TEAMS HAVE ONLY ONE JUSSHIN-SHU LIKE GENJURO OR ME.
URUHA-KURENAI IS...
FAR MORE LETHAL!!
AND REASON THREE, AND THIS MAY BE THE BIGGEST REASON...
YOU'RE GOING TO DIE RIGHT NOW!
THIS IS FOR CALLING ME UGLY!!!

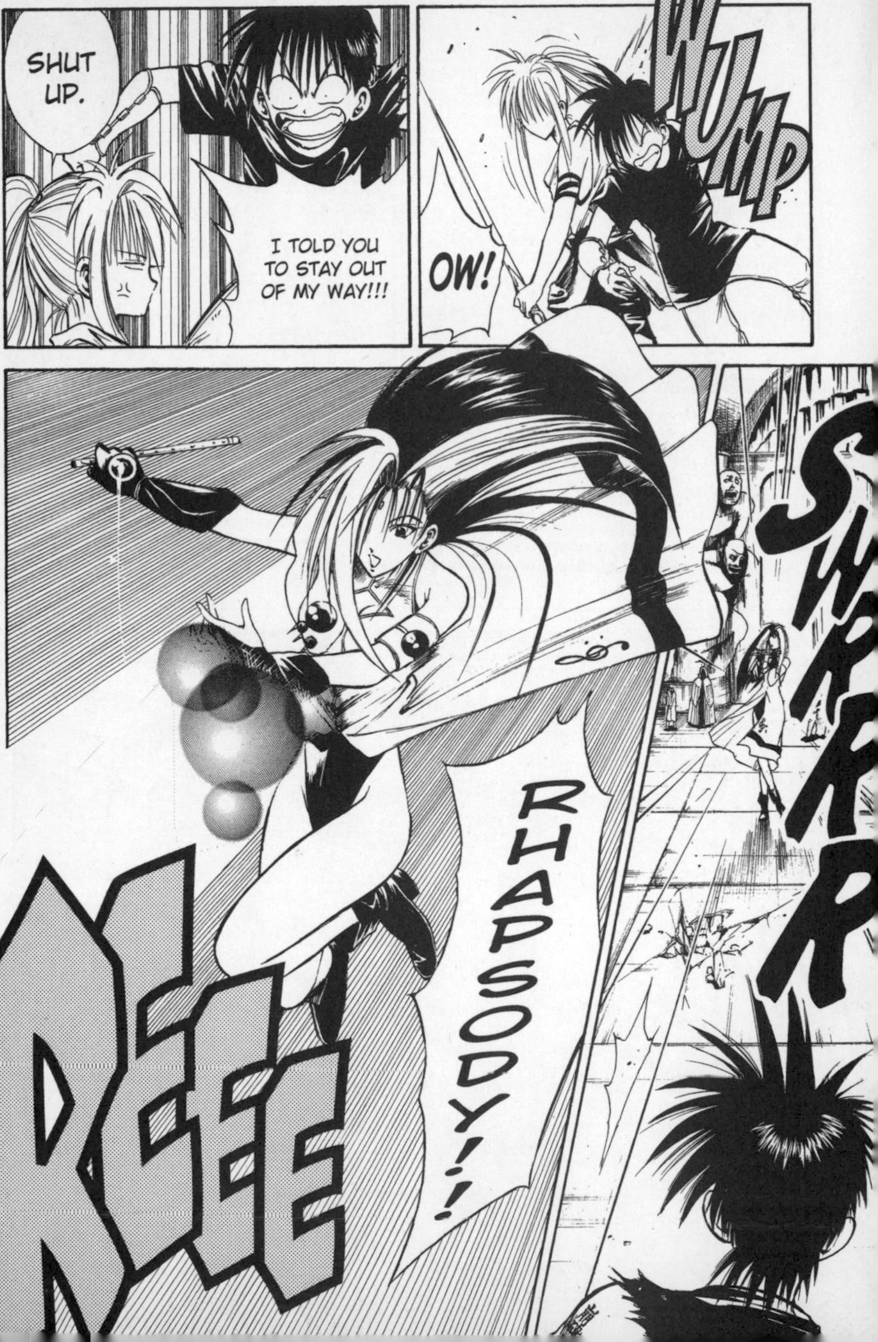
WUMP
OW!
SHUT UP.
I TOLD YOU TO STAY OUT OF MY WAY!!!
SHRRR
RHAPSODY!!!
REEE

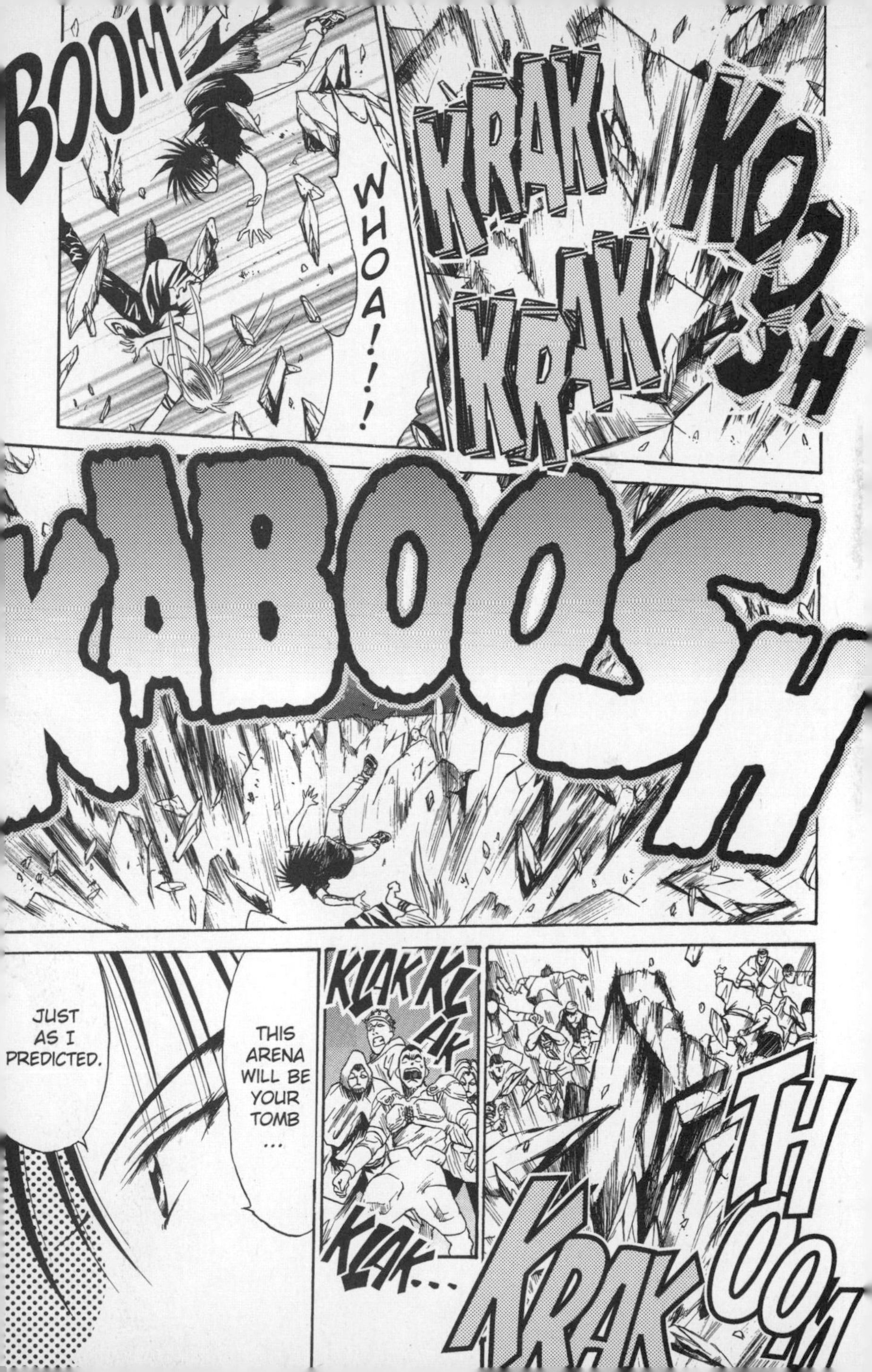
KOSH
KRAK
KRAK
WHOA!!!!
BOOM
ABOOSH
THOOOM
KRAK
KLAK KLAK
KLAK...
THIS ARENA WILL BE YOUR TOMB ...
JUST AS I PREDICTED.

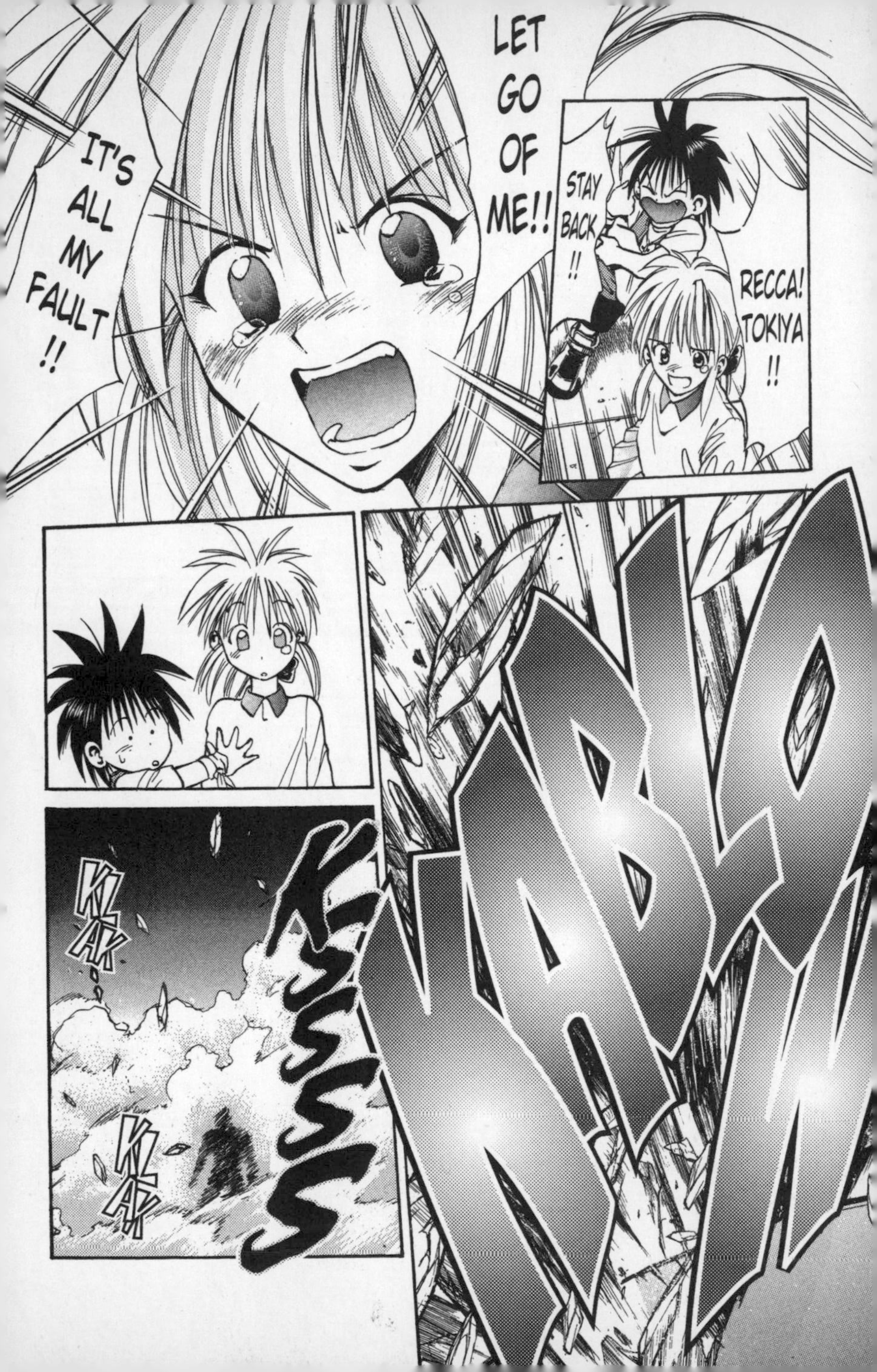
LET GO OF ME!!
RECCA! TOKIYA!!
STAY BACK!!
IT'S ALL MY FAULT!!
KLAK
KLAK

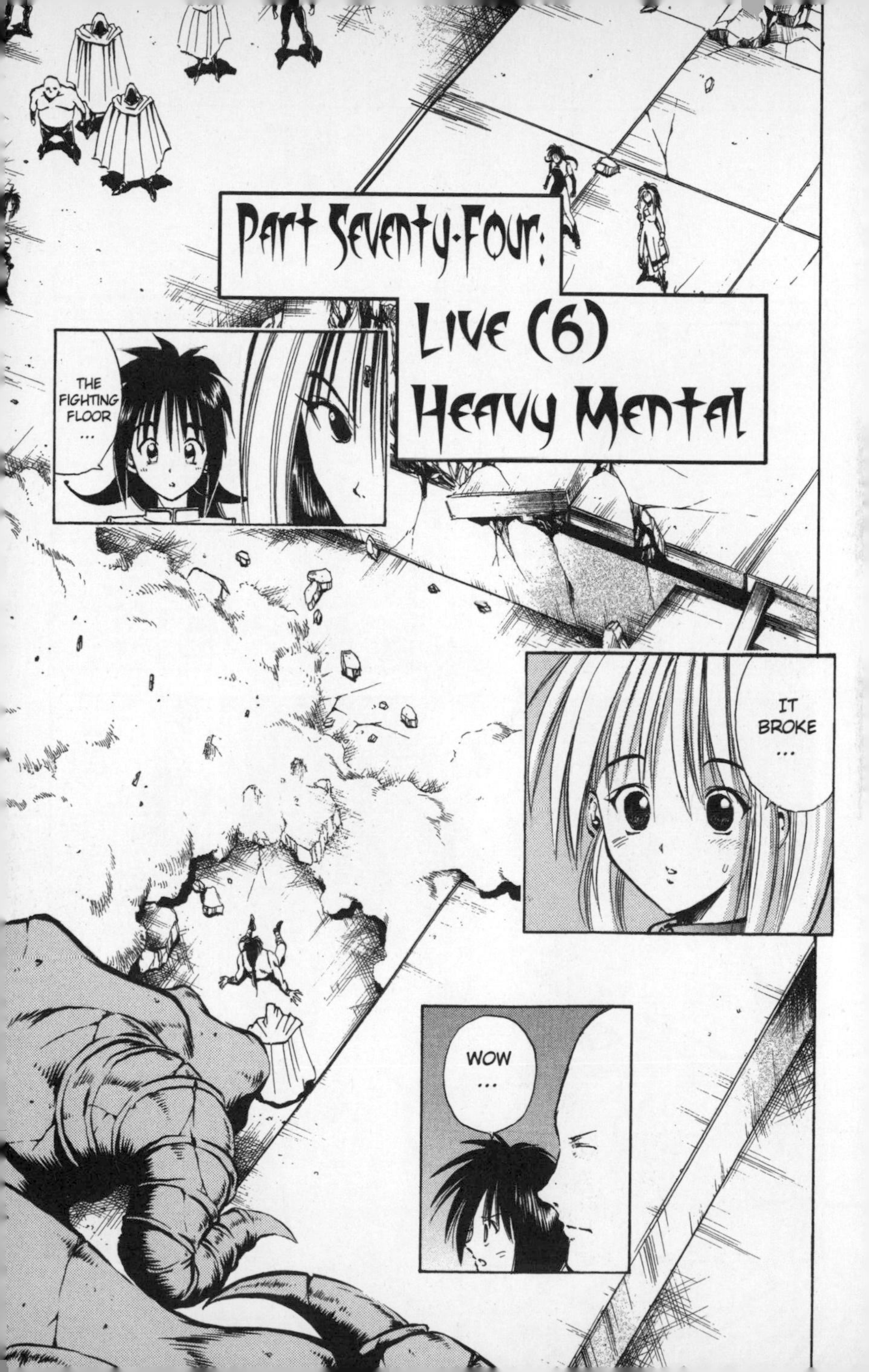
Part Seventy-Four:
Live (6)
Heavy Mental
THE FIGHTING FLOOR ...
IT BROKE ...
WOW ...

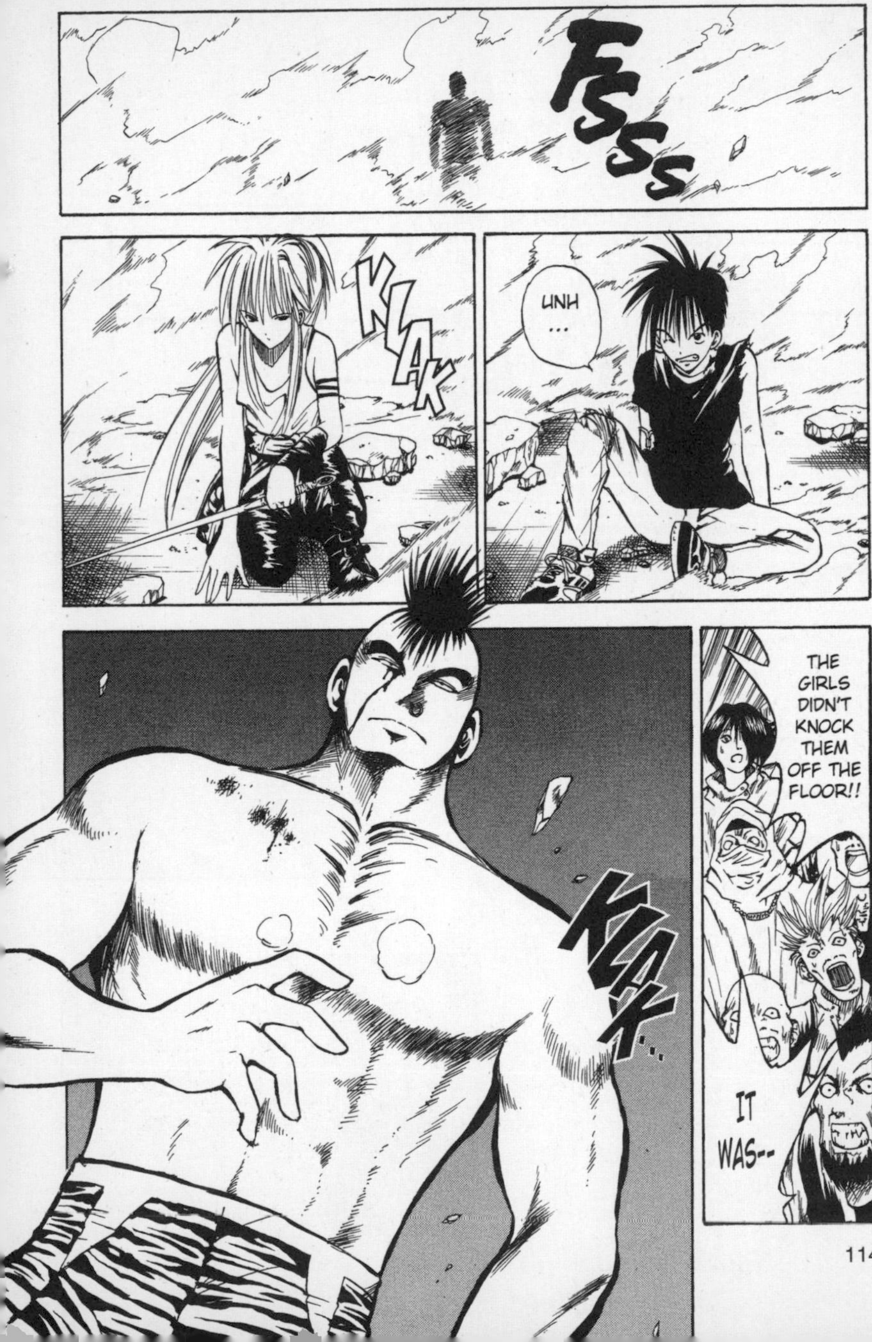
FSSS
UNH ...
KLAK
THE GIRLS DIDN'T KNOCK THEM OFF THE FLOOR!!
IT WAS--
KLAK...

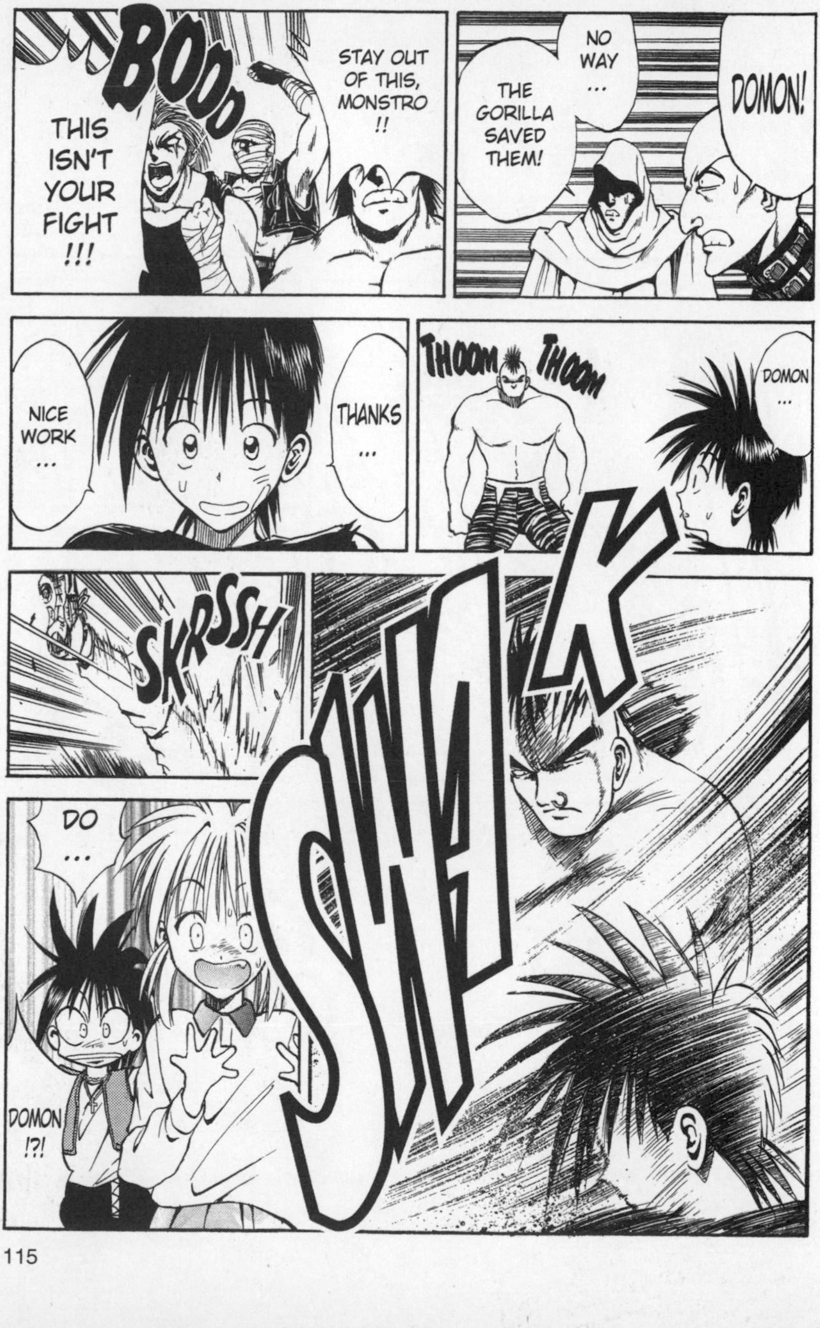
DOMON!
NO WAY ...
THE GORILLA SAVED THEM!
BOOO
STAY OUT OF THIS, MONSTRO !!
THIS ISN'T YOUR FIGHT !!!
THOOM THOOM
DOMON ...
THANKS ...
NICE WORK ...
SHAK
SKRSSH
DO ...
DOMON !?!

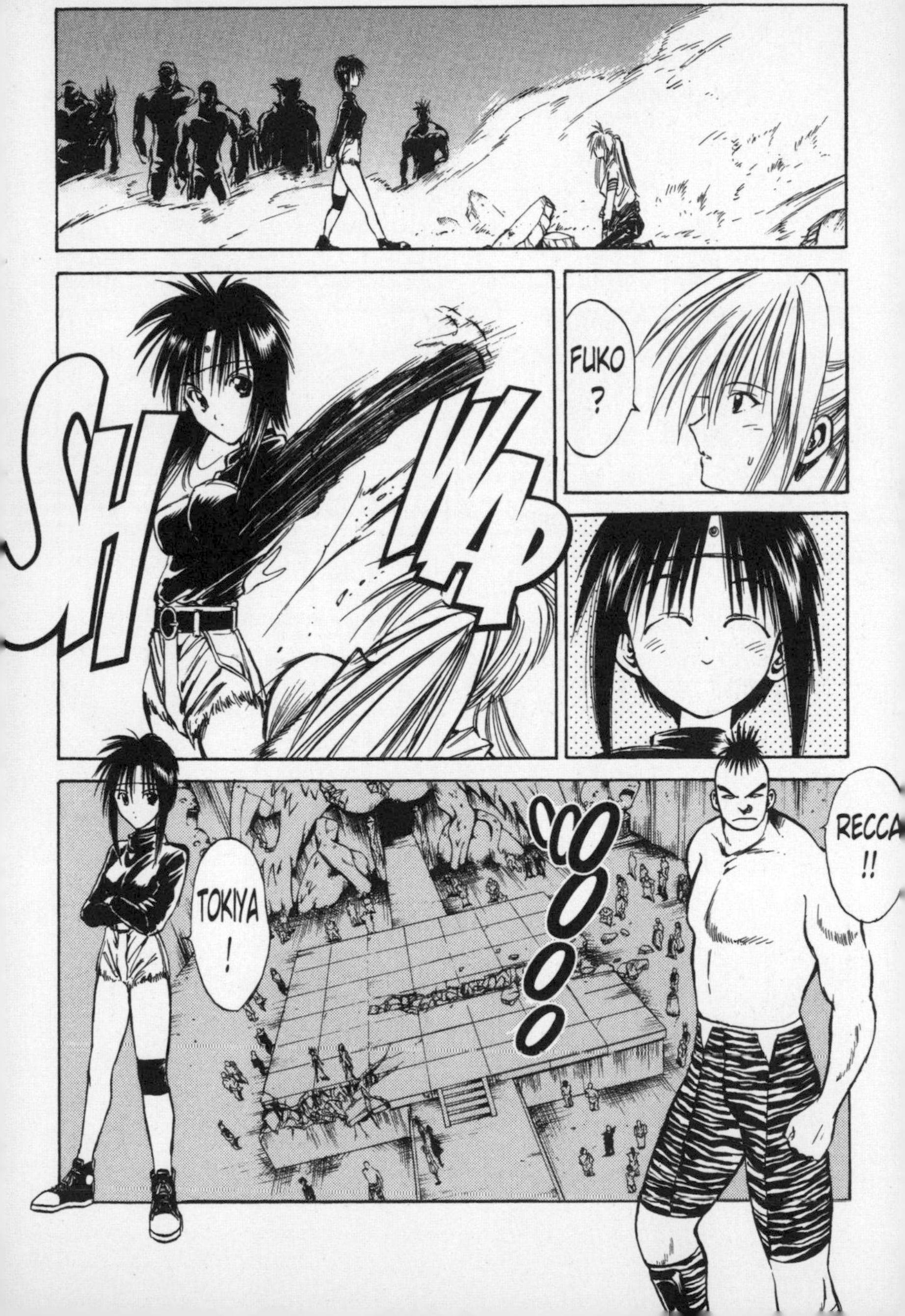
FUKO ?
SHWAP
RECCA !!
OOOOOOO
TOKIYA !

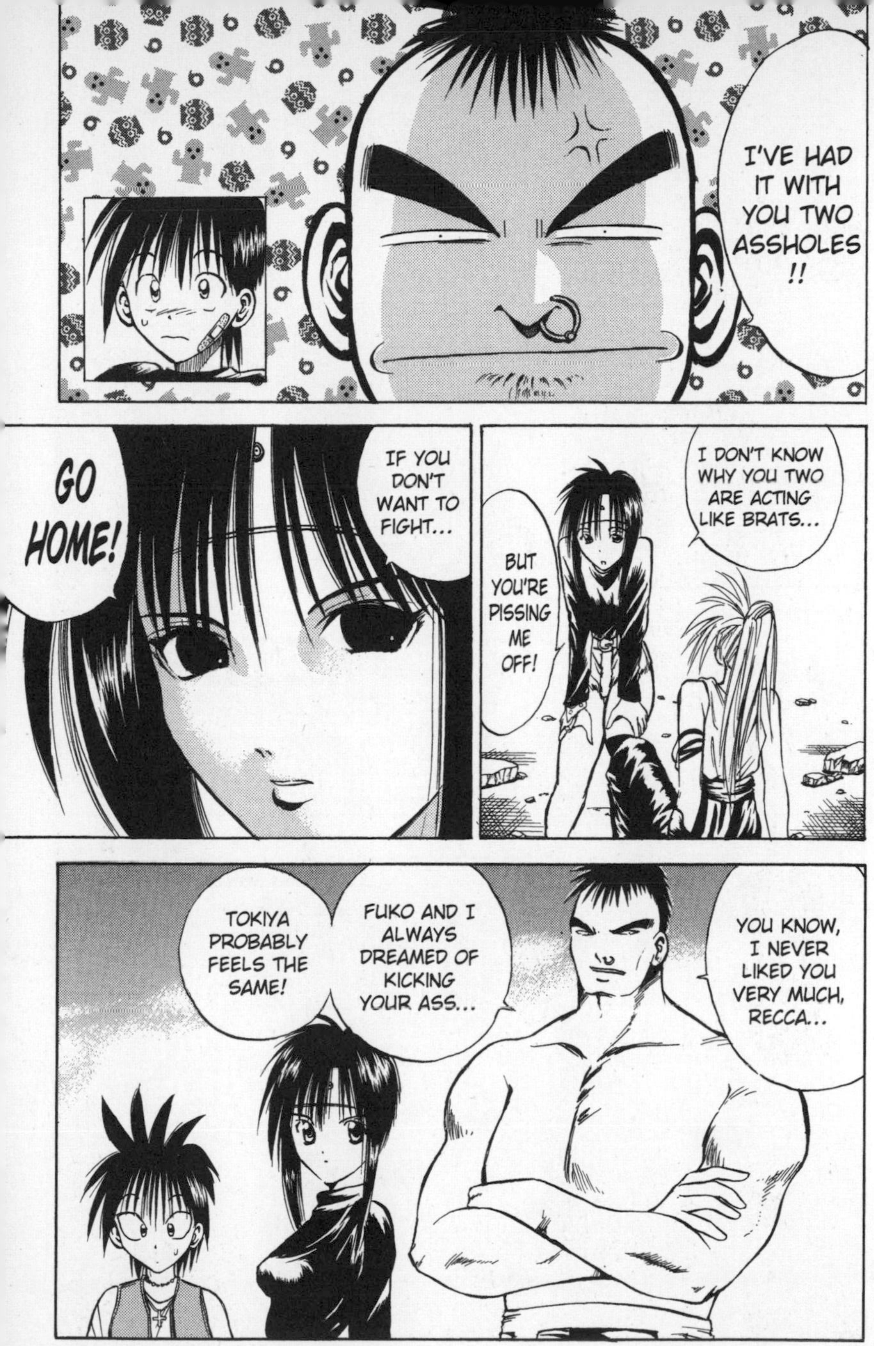
I'VE HAD IT WITH YOU TWO ASSHOLES !!
I DON'T KNOW WHY YOU TWO ARE ACTING LIKE BRATS...
BUT YOU'RE PISSING ME OFF!
IF YOU DON'T WANT TO FIGHT...
GO HOME!
YOU KNOW, I NEVER LIKED YOU VERY MUCH, RECCA...
FUKO AND I ALWAYS DREAMED OF KICKING YOUR ASS...
TOKIYA PROBABLY FEELS THE SAME!

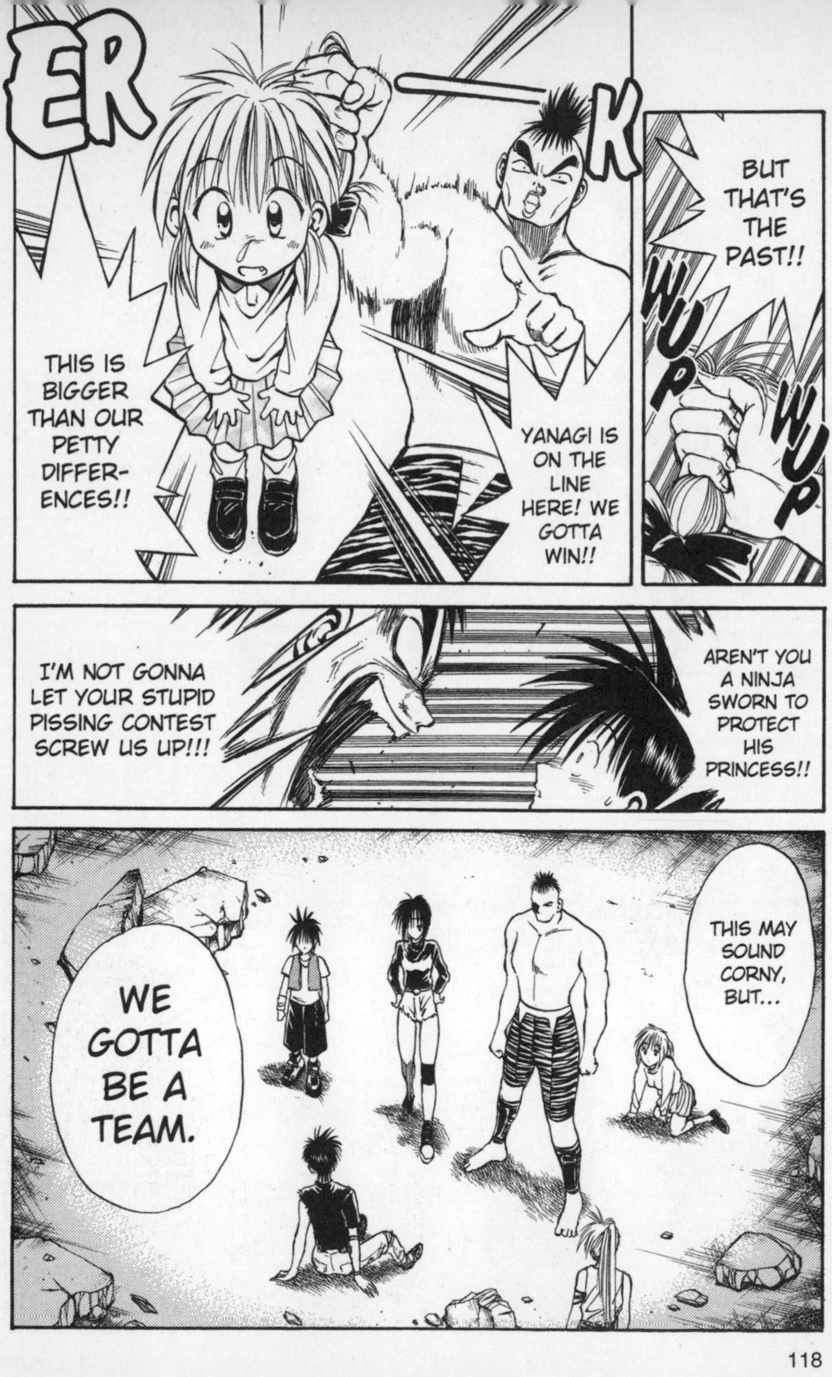
BUT THAT'S THE PAST!!
WUP WUP
WUP WUP
ER
K
YANAGI IS ON THE LINE HERE! WE GOTTA WIN!!
THIS IS BIGGER THAN OUR PETTY DIFFER-ENCES!!
AREN'T YOU A NINJA SWORN TO PROTECT HIS PRINCESS!!
I'M NOT GONNA LET YOUR STUPID PISSING CONTEST SCREW US UP!!!
THIS MAY SOUND CORNY, BUT...
WE GOTTA BE A TEAM.

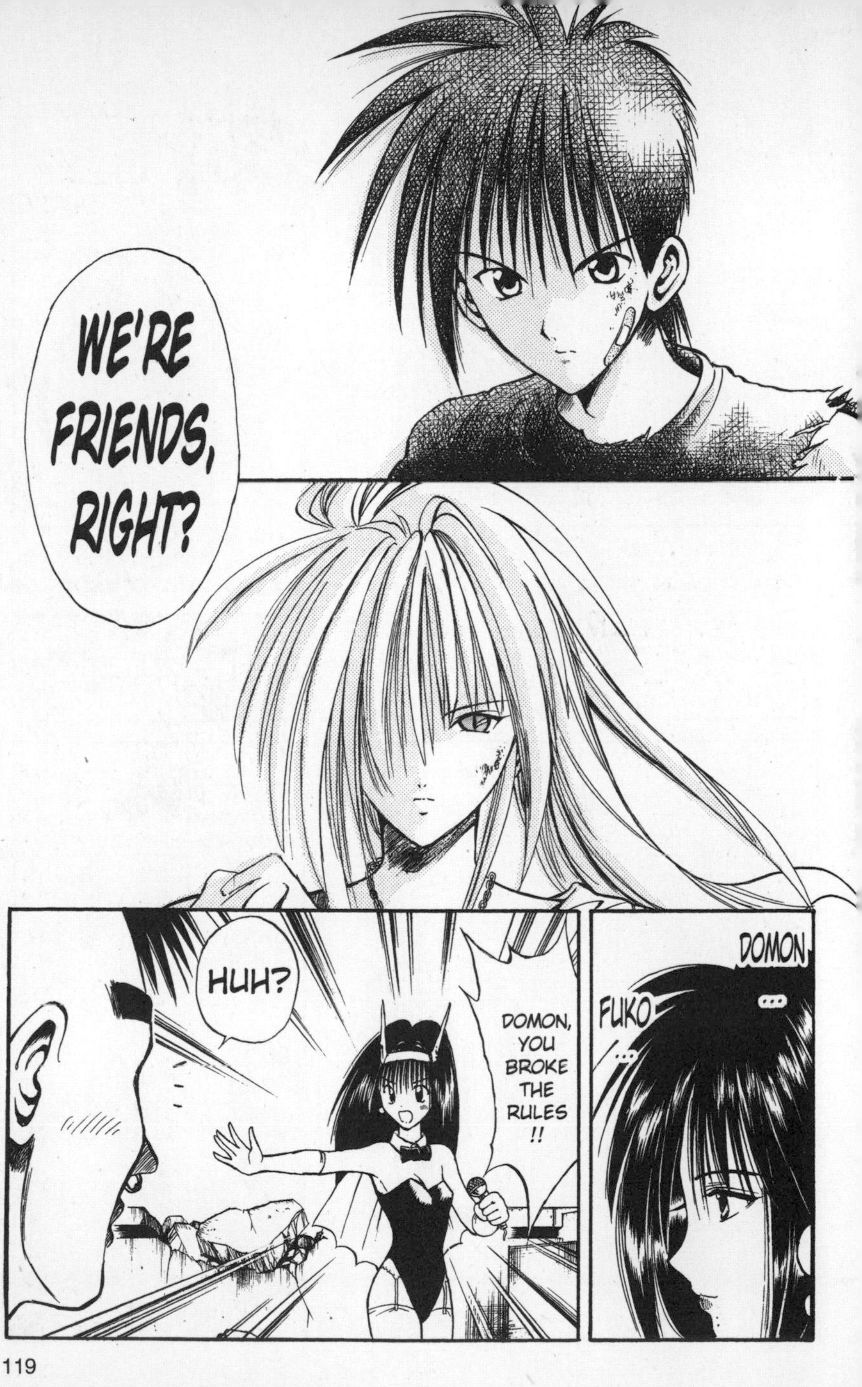
WE'RE FRIENDS, RIGHT?
DOMON
...
FUKO
...
DOMON, YOU BROKE THE RULES !!
HUH?

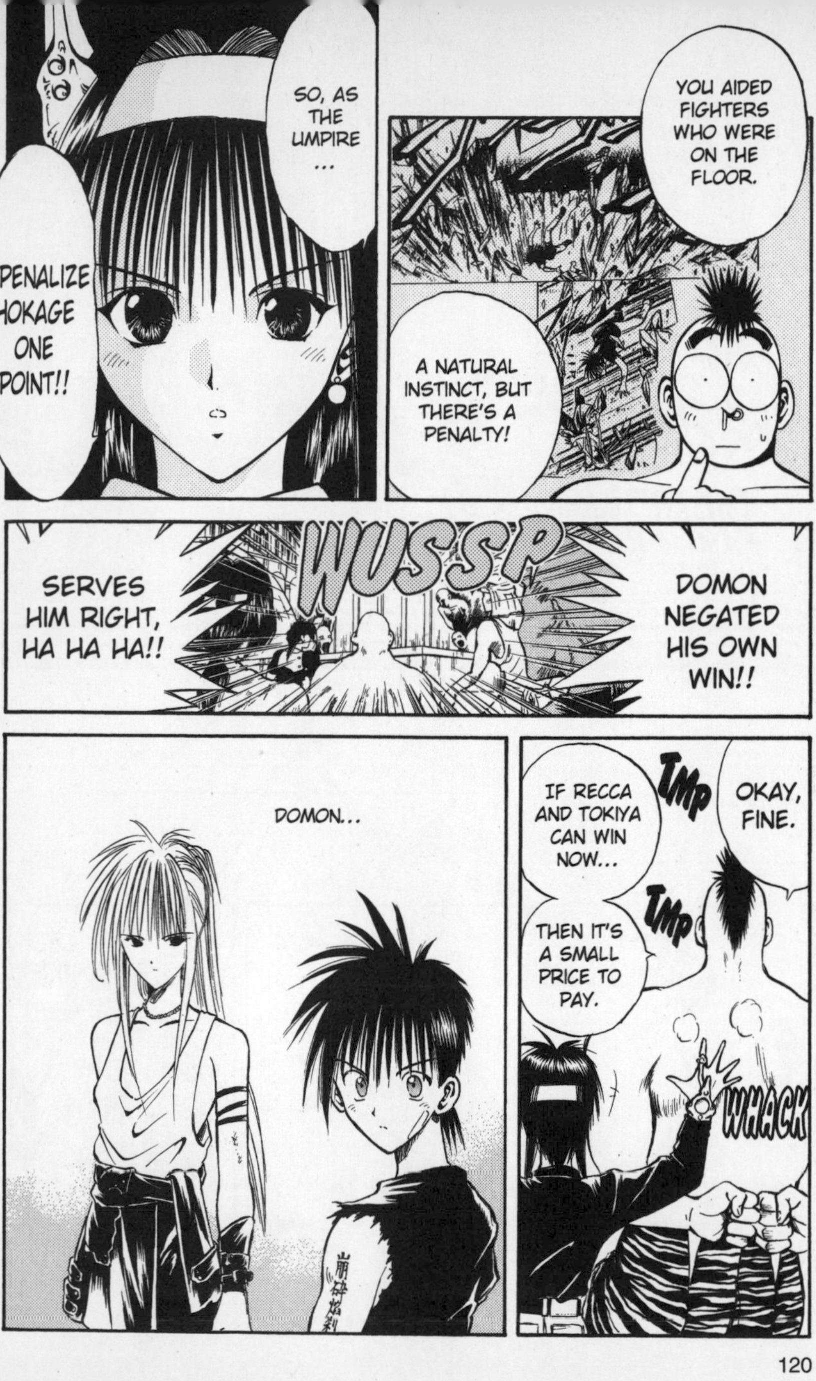
YOU AIDED FIGHTERS WHO WERE ON THE FLOOR.
A NATURAL INSTINCT, BUT THERE'S A PENALTY!
SO, AS THE UMPIRE ...
I PENALIZE HOKAGE ONE POINT!!
DOMON NEGATED HIS OWN WIN!!
WUSSP
SERVES HIM RIGHT, HA HA HA!!
OKAY, FINE.
TMP
IF RECCA AND TOKIYA CAN WIN NOW...
TMP
THEN IT'S A SMALL PRICE TO PAY.
WHACK
DOMON...

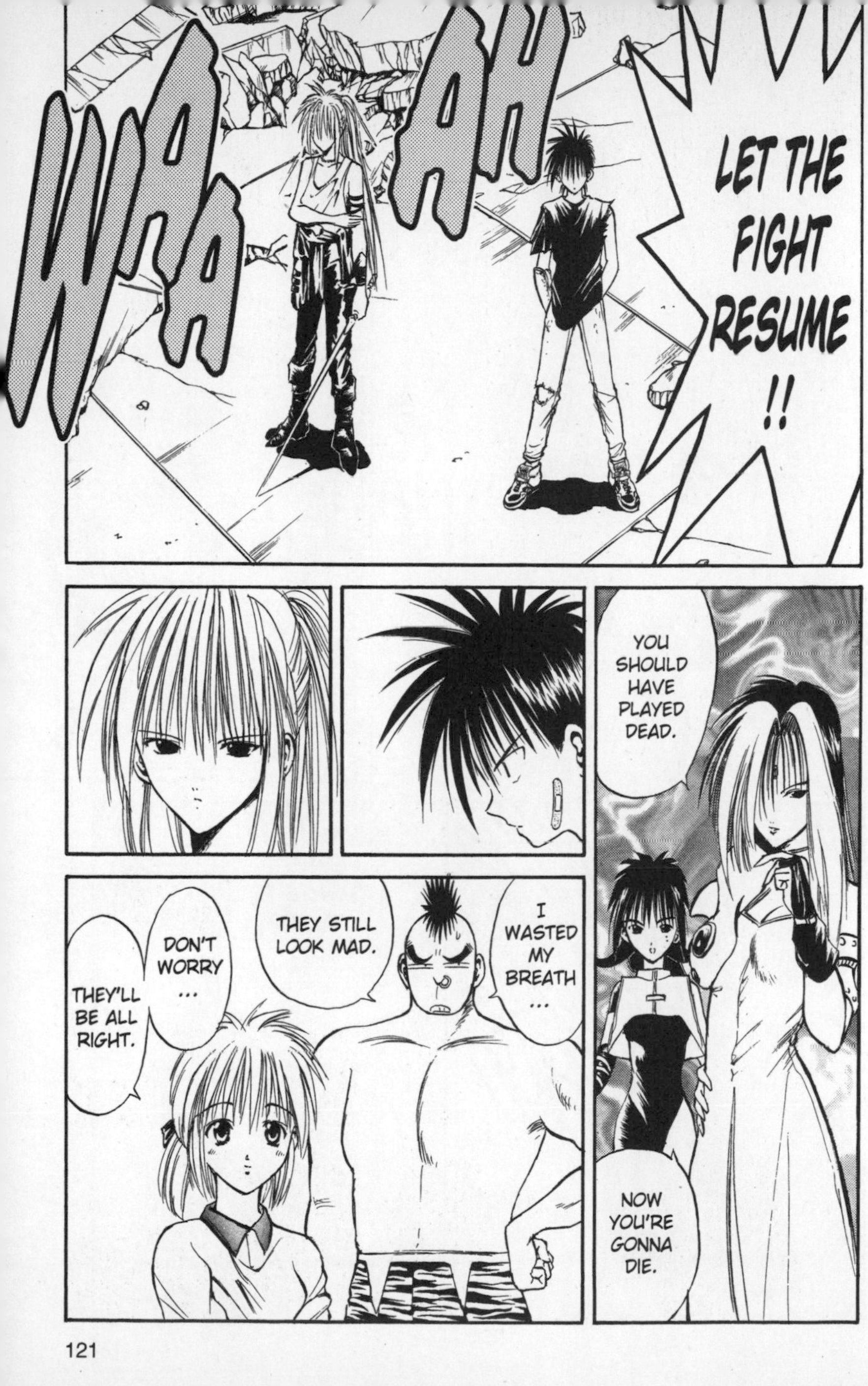
LET THE FIGHT RESUME !!
WAAAH
YOU SHOULD HAVE PLAYED DEAD.
NOW YOU'RE GONNA DIE.
I WASTED MY BREATH ...
THEY STILL LOOK MAD.
DON'T WORRY ...
THEY'LL BE ALL RIGHT.

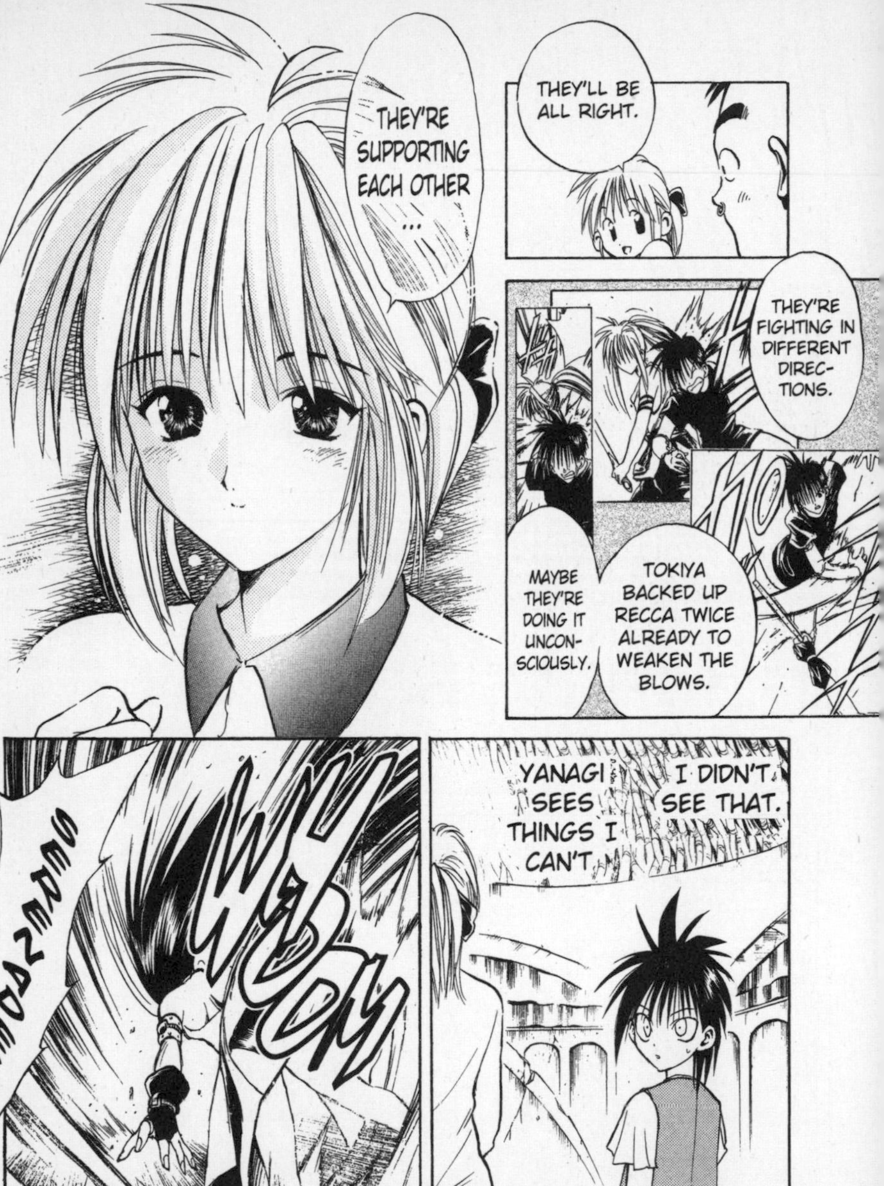
THEY'LL BE ALL RIGHT.
THEY'RE FIGHTING IN DIFFERENT DIREC-TIONS.
TOKIYA BACKED UP RECCA TWICE ALREADY TO WEAKEN THE BLOWS.
MAYBE THEY'RE DOING IT UNCON-SCIOUSLY.
THEY'RE SUPPORTING EACH OTHER ...
I DIDN'T SEE THAT.
YANAGI SEES THINGS I CAN'T
WHOOM
SEREZADE!!

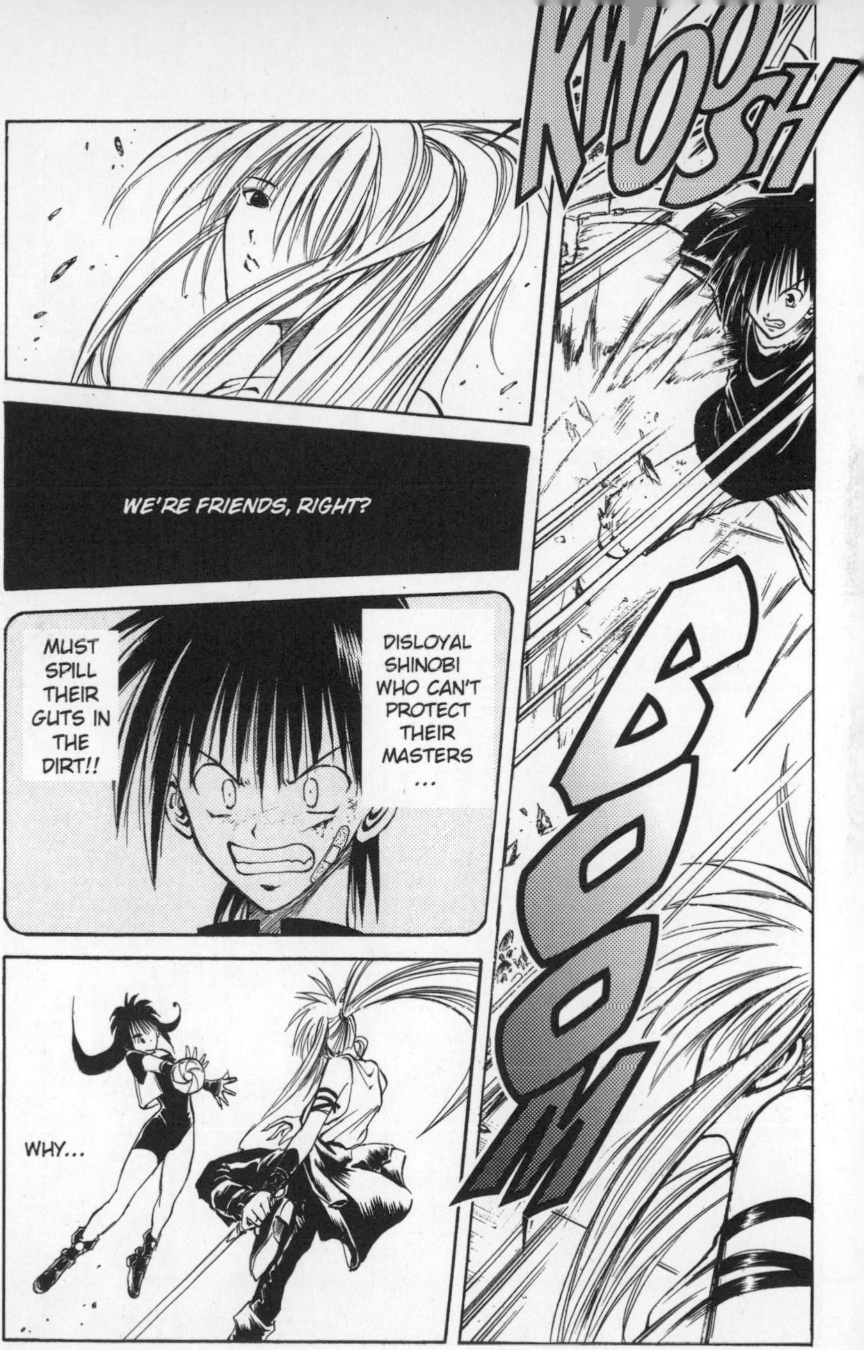
KWOOSH
BOOM
WE'RE FRIENDS, RIGHT?
DISLOYAL SHINOBI WHO CAN'T PROTECT THEIR MASTERS ...
MUST SPILL THEIR GUTS IN THE DIRT!!
WHY...

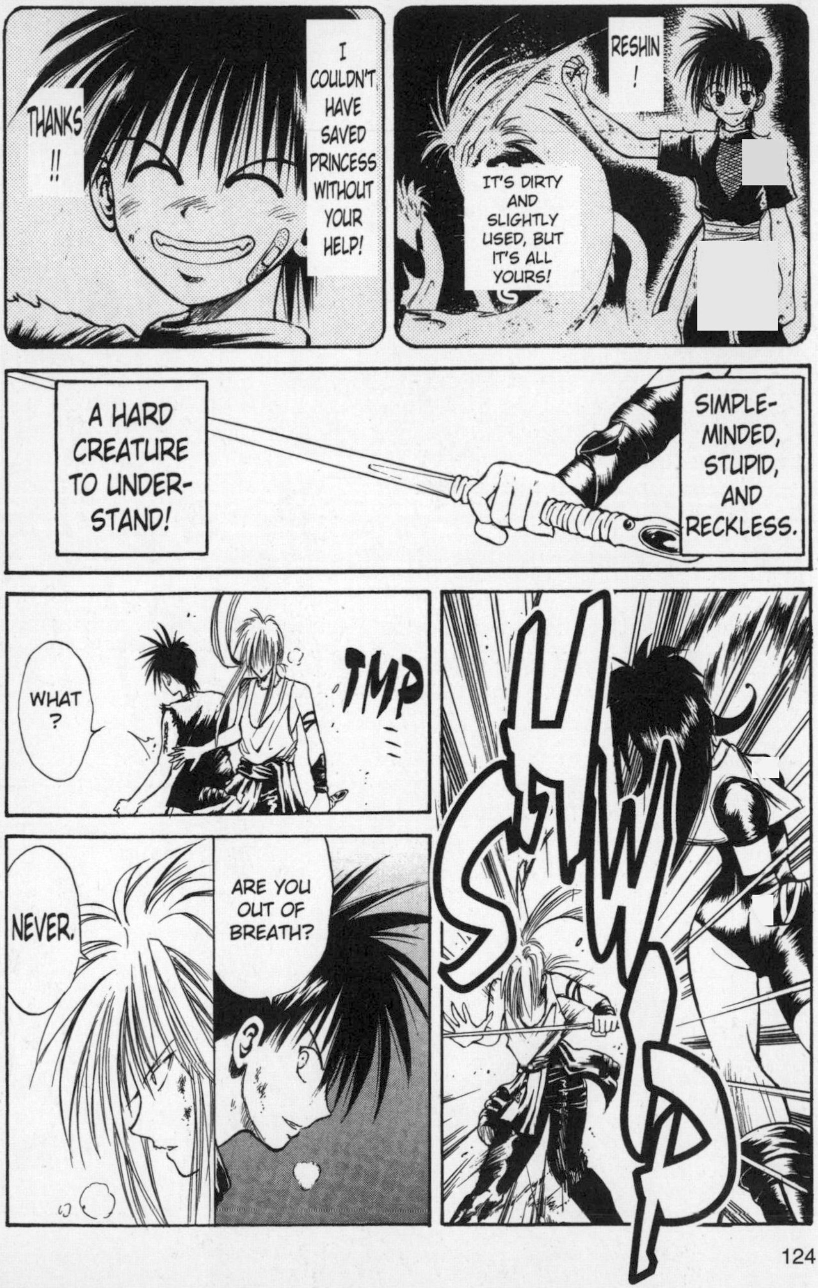
RESHIN !
IT'S DIRTY AND SLIGHTLY USED, BUT IT'S ALL YOURS!
I COULDN'T HAVE SAVED PRINCESS WITHOUT YOUR HELP!
THANKS !!
SIMPLE-MINDED, STUPID, AND RECKLESS.
A HARD CREATURE TO UNDER-STAND!
SHWP
TMP
WHAT ?
ARE YOU OUT OF BREATH?
NEVER.

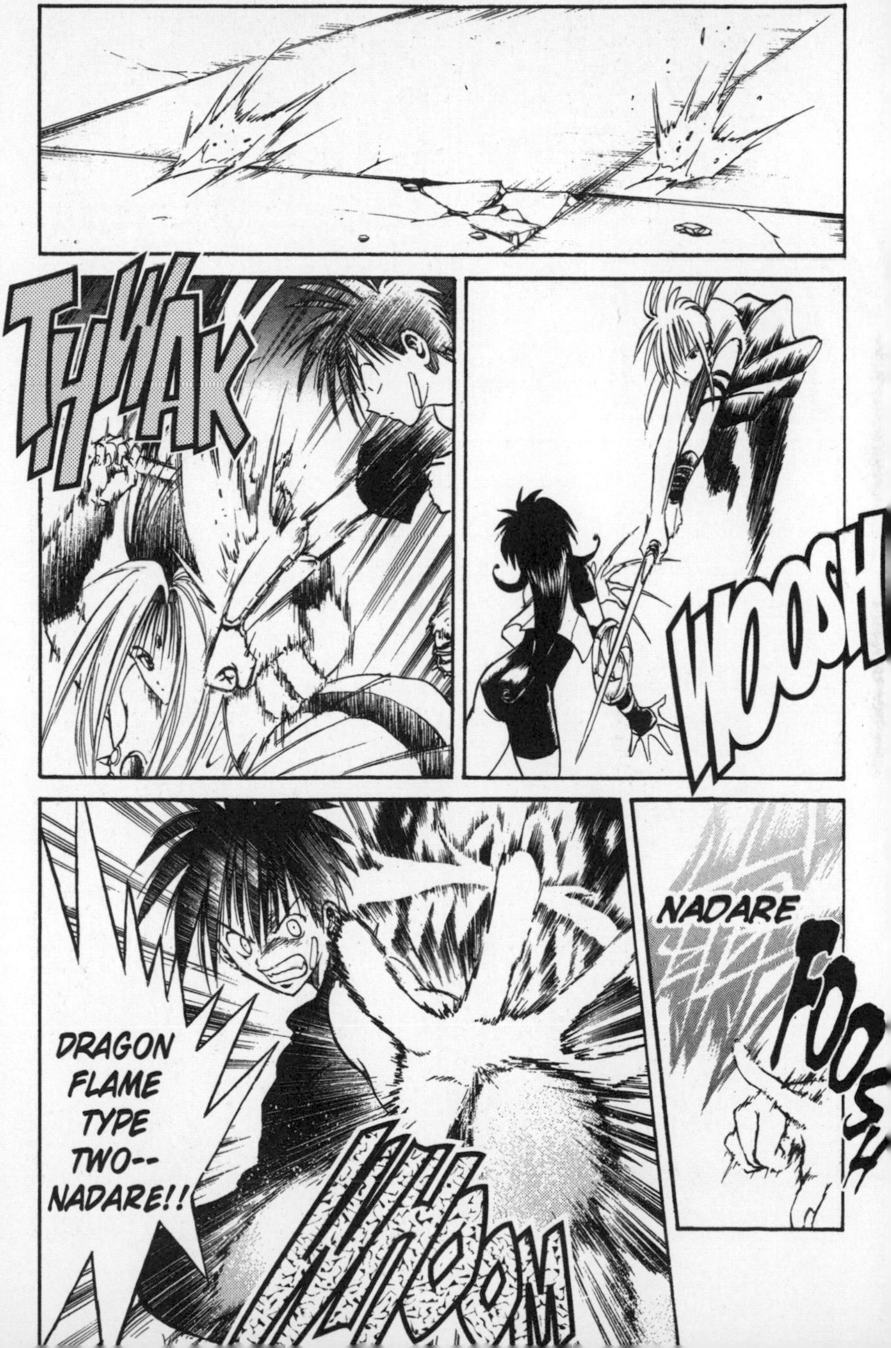
WOOSH
THWAK
NADARE
FOOSH
DRAGON FLAME TYPE TWO-- NADARE!!
WHOOM

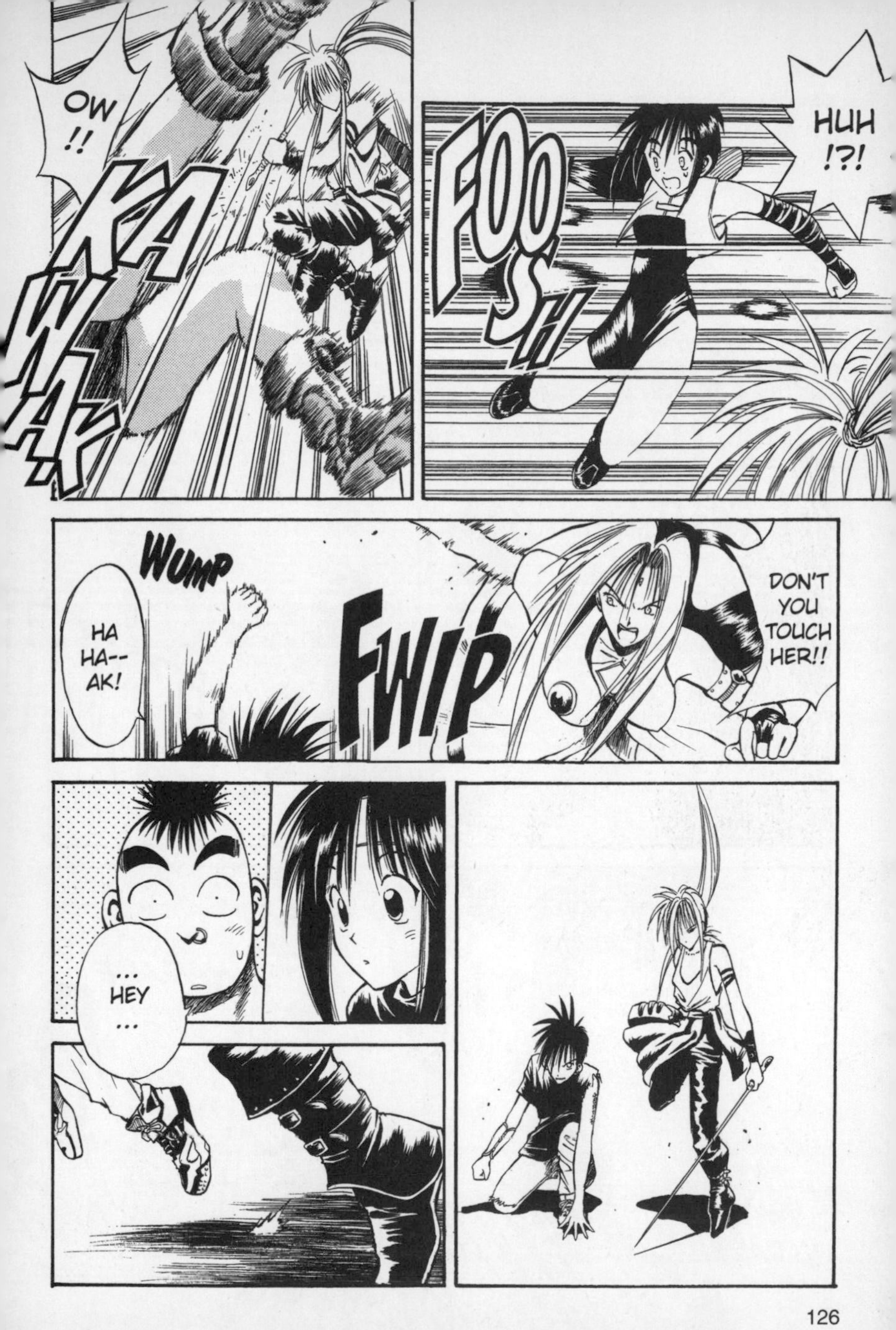
HUH !?!
FOOSH!
OW !!
KAWHAK
DON'T YOU TOUCH HER!!
FWIP
WUMP
HA HA-- AK!
... HEY ...

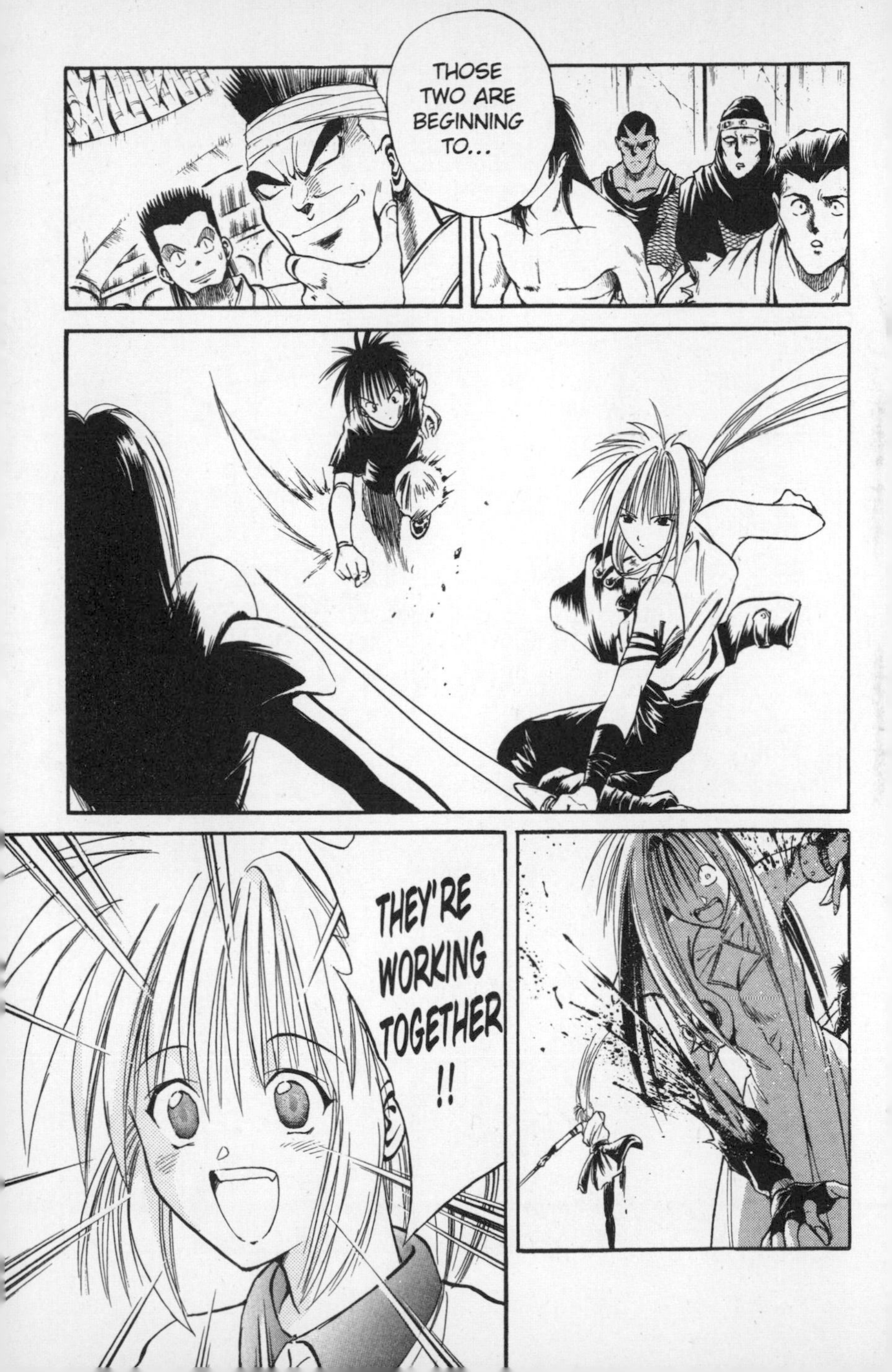
THOSE TWO ARE BEGINNING TO...
THEY'RE WORKING TOGETHER !!

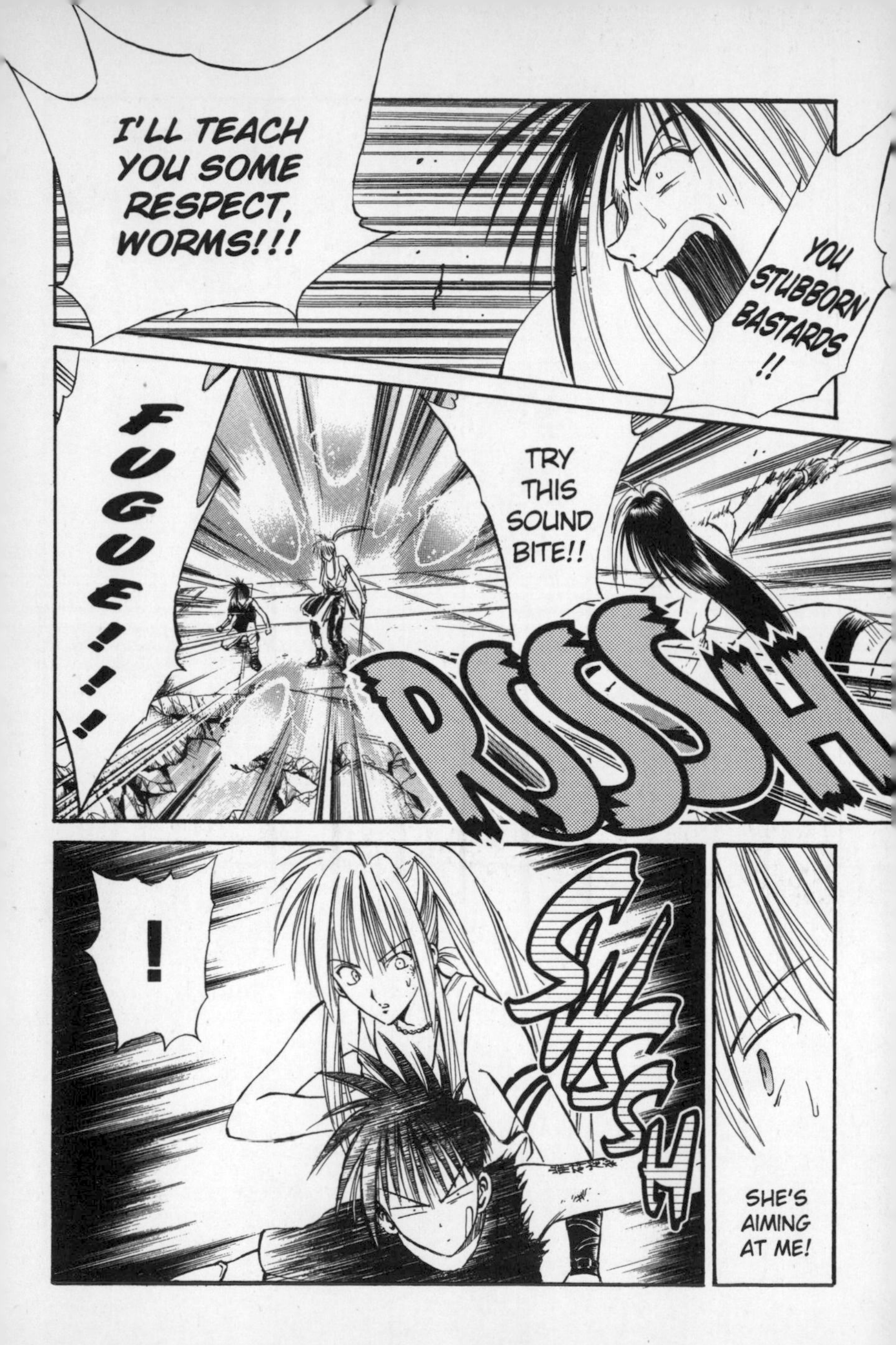
YOU STUBBORN BASTARDS!!
I'LL TEACH YOU SOME RESPECT, WORMS!!!
TRY THIS SOUND BITE!!
RUSSH
FUGUE!!!!
SHE'S AIMING AT ME!
SWISH
!

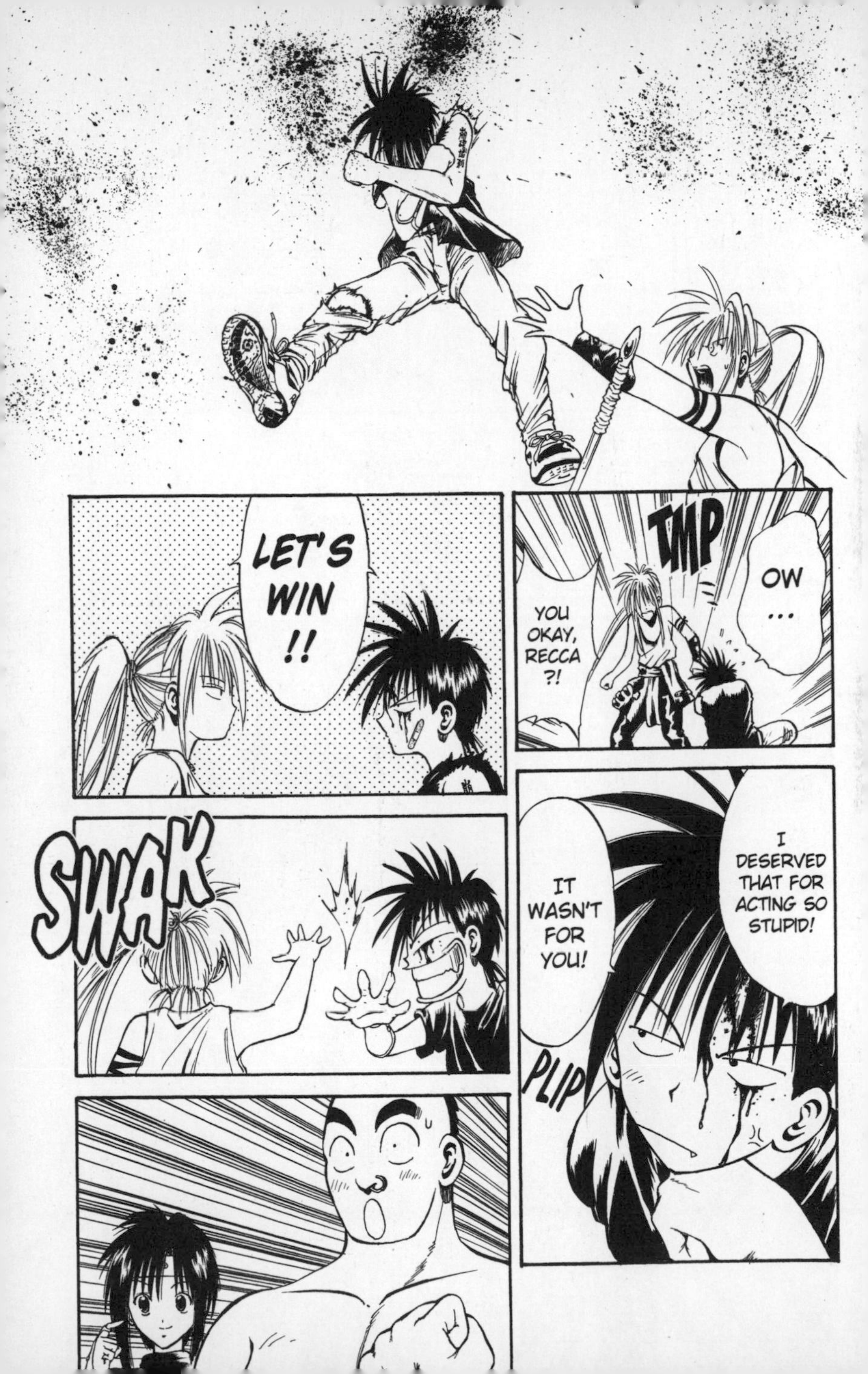
OW ...
TMP
YOU OKAY, RECCA?!
LET'S WIN!!
I DESERVED THAT FOR ACTING SO STUPID!
IT WASN'T FOR YOU!
PLIP
SWAK

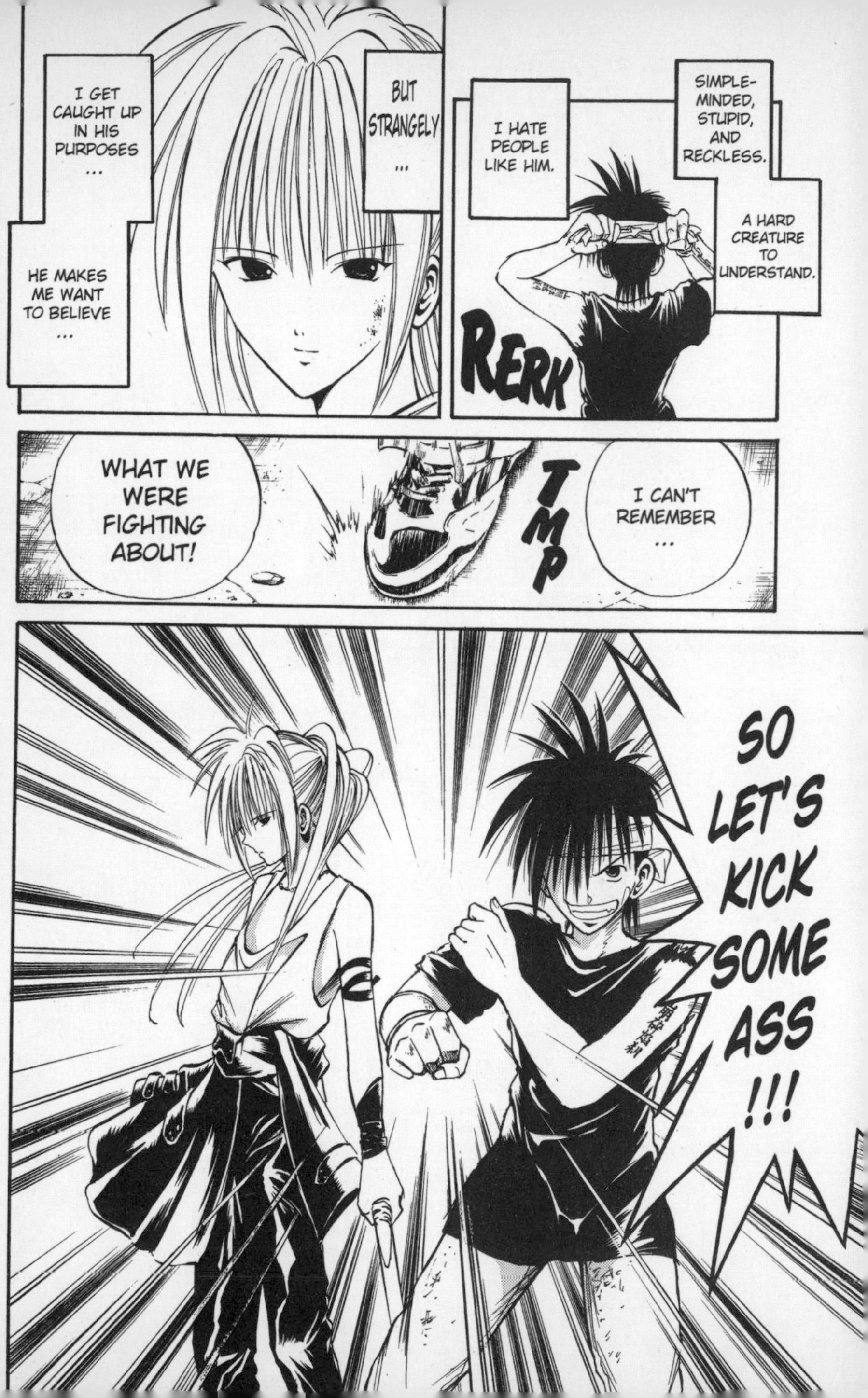
SIMPLE-MINDED, STUPID, AND RECKLESS.
A HARD CREATURE TO UNDERSTAND.
I HATE PEOPLE LIKE HIM.
RERK
BUT STRANGELY ...
I GET CAUGHT UP IN HIS PURPOSES ...
HE MAKES ME WANT TO BELIEVE ...
I CAN'T REMEMBER ...
TMP
WHAT WE WERE FIGHTING ABOUT!
SO LET'S KICK SOME ASS !!!

Part Seventy-Five:
Live (7) Kurei, My Love

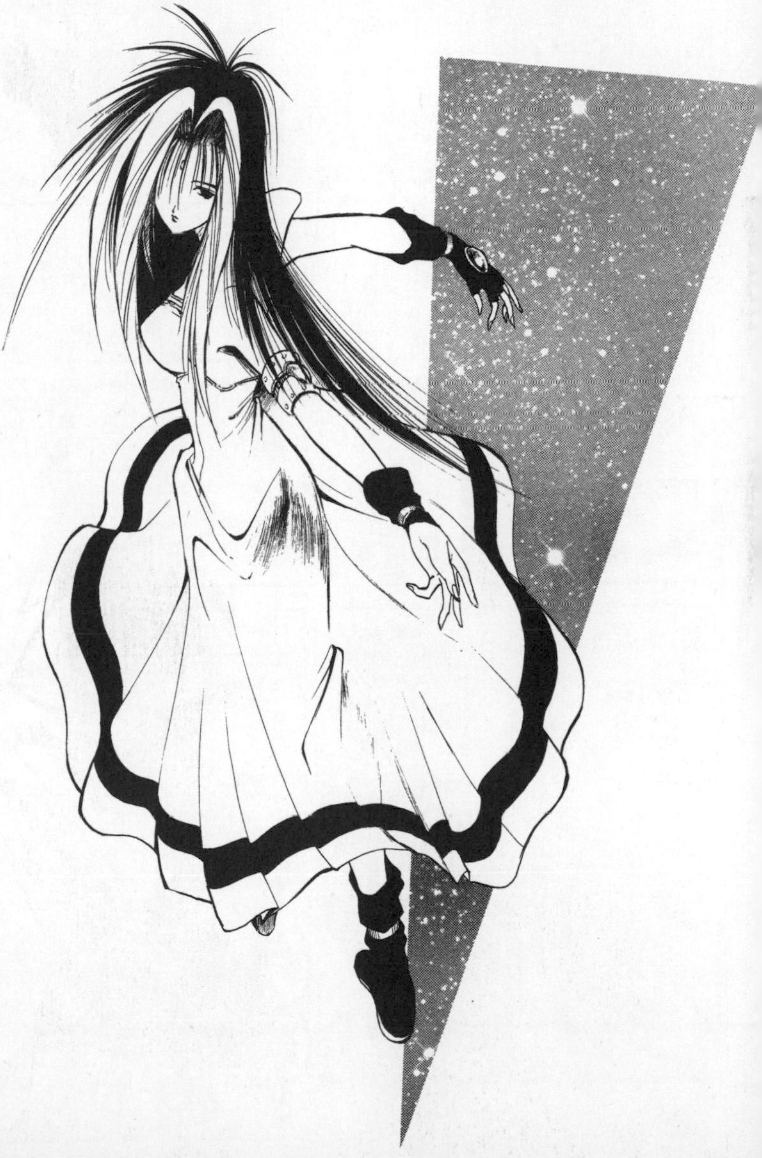

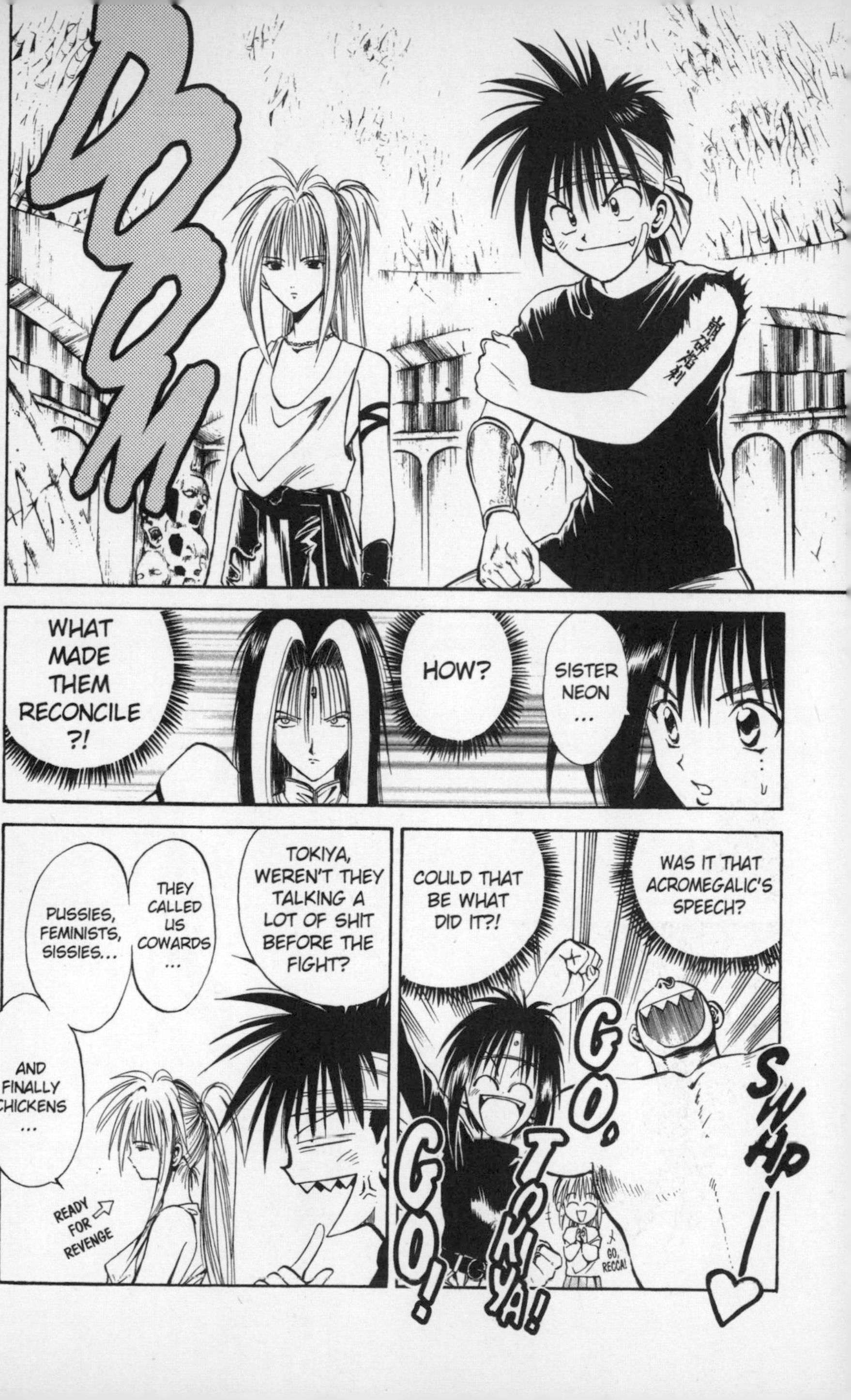
DOOM
SISTER NEON ...
HOW?
WHAT MADE THEM RECONCILE ?!
WAS IT THAT ACROMEGALIC'S SPEECH?
COULD THAT BE WHAT DID IT?!
SHAP!
GO, TOKIYA!
GO, GO!
GO, RECCA!
TOKIYA, WEREN'T THEY TALKING A LOT OF SHIT BEFORE THE FIGHT?
THEY CALLED US COWARDS ...
PUSSIES, FEMINISTS, SISSIES...
AND FINALLY CHICKENS ...
READY FOR REVENGE

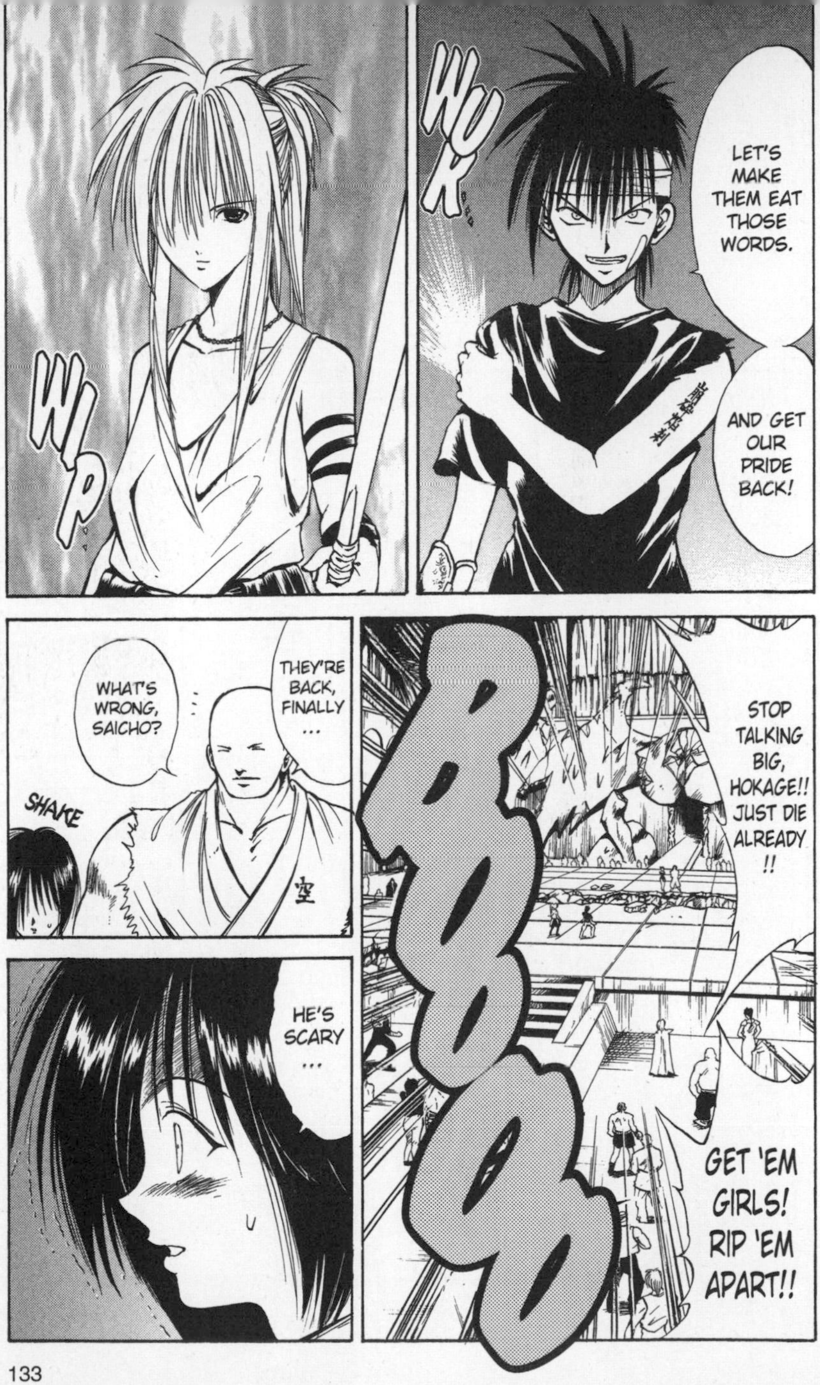
WUK
LET'S MAKE THEM EAT THOSE WORDS.
AND GET OUR PRIDE BACK!
WIP
STOP TALKING BIG, HOKAGE!! JUST DIE ALREADY !!
GET 'EM GIRLS! RIP 'EM APART!!
THEY'RE BACK, FINALLY ...
WHAT'S WRONG, SAICHO?
SHAKE
HE'S SCARY ...

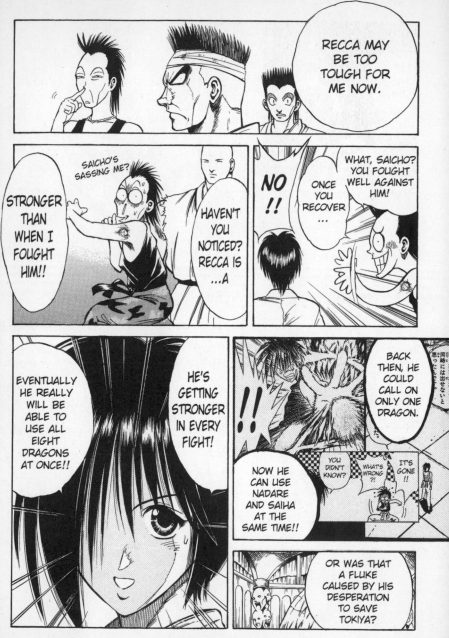

RECCA MAY BE TOO TOUGH FOR ME NOW.
WHAT, SAICHO? YOU FOUGHT WELL AGAINST HIM!
ONCE YOU RECOVER ...
NO !!
HAVEN'T YOU NOTICED? RECCA IS ...A
SAICHO'S SASSING ME?
STRONGER THAN WHEN I FOUGHT HIM!!
BACK THEN, HE COULD CALL ON ONLY ONE DRAGON.
!!
IT'S GONE !!
WHAT'S WRONG ?!
YOU DIDN'T KNOW?
NOW HE CAN USE NADARE AND SAIHA AT THE SAME TIME!!
OR WAS THAT A FLUKE CAUSED BY HIS DESPERATION TO SAVE TOKIYA?
HE'S GETTING STRONGER IN EVERY FIGHT!
EVENTUALLY HE REALLY WILL BE ABLE TO USE ALL EIGHT DRAGONS AT ONCE!!

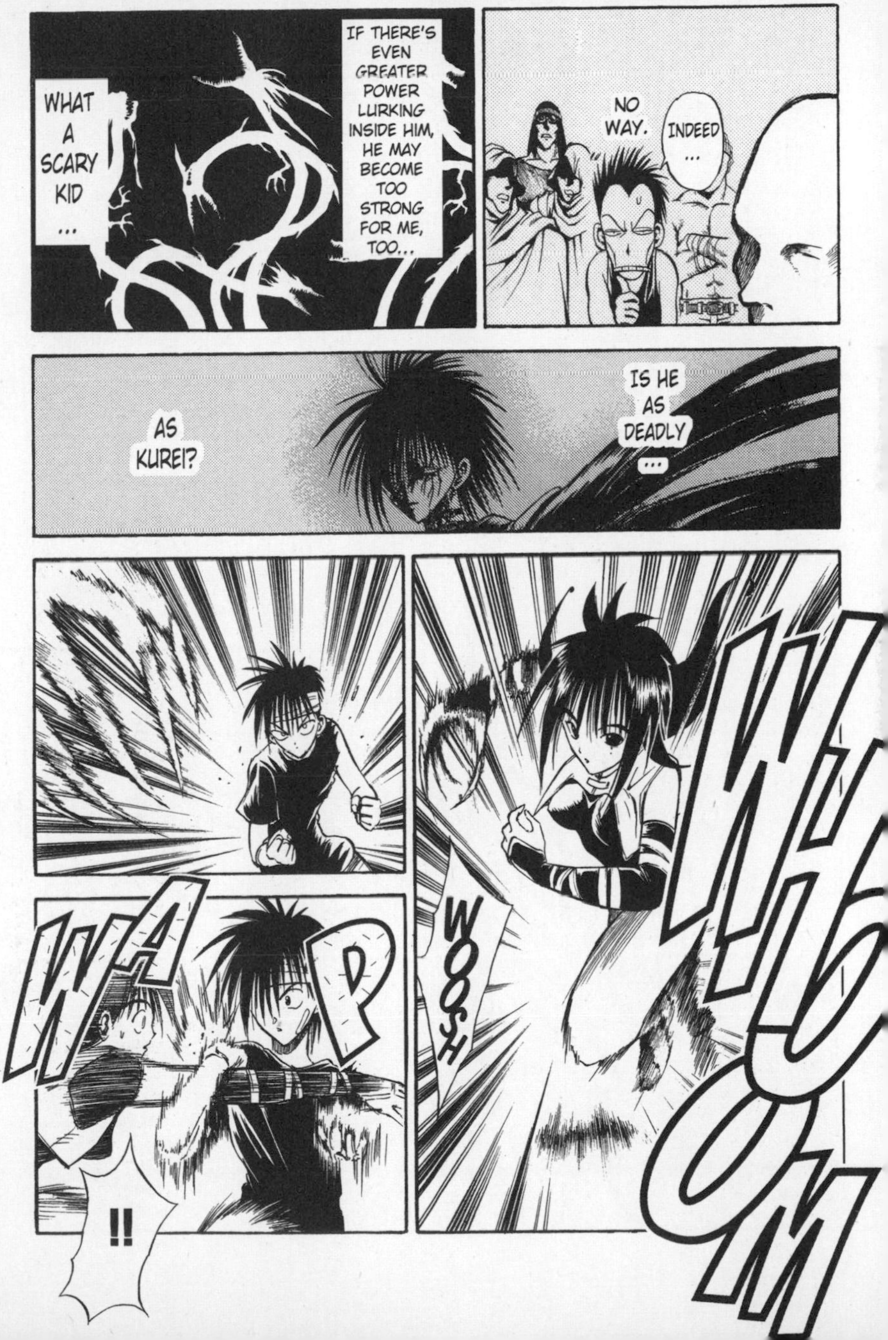
INDEED...
NO WAY.
IF THERE'S EVEN GREATER POWER LURKING INSIDE HIM, HE MAY BECOME TOO STRONG FOR ME, TOO...
WHAT A SCARY KID...
IS HE AS DEADLY...
AS KUREI?
WHOOOM
WOOSH
WAP
!!

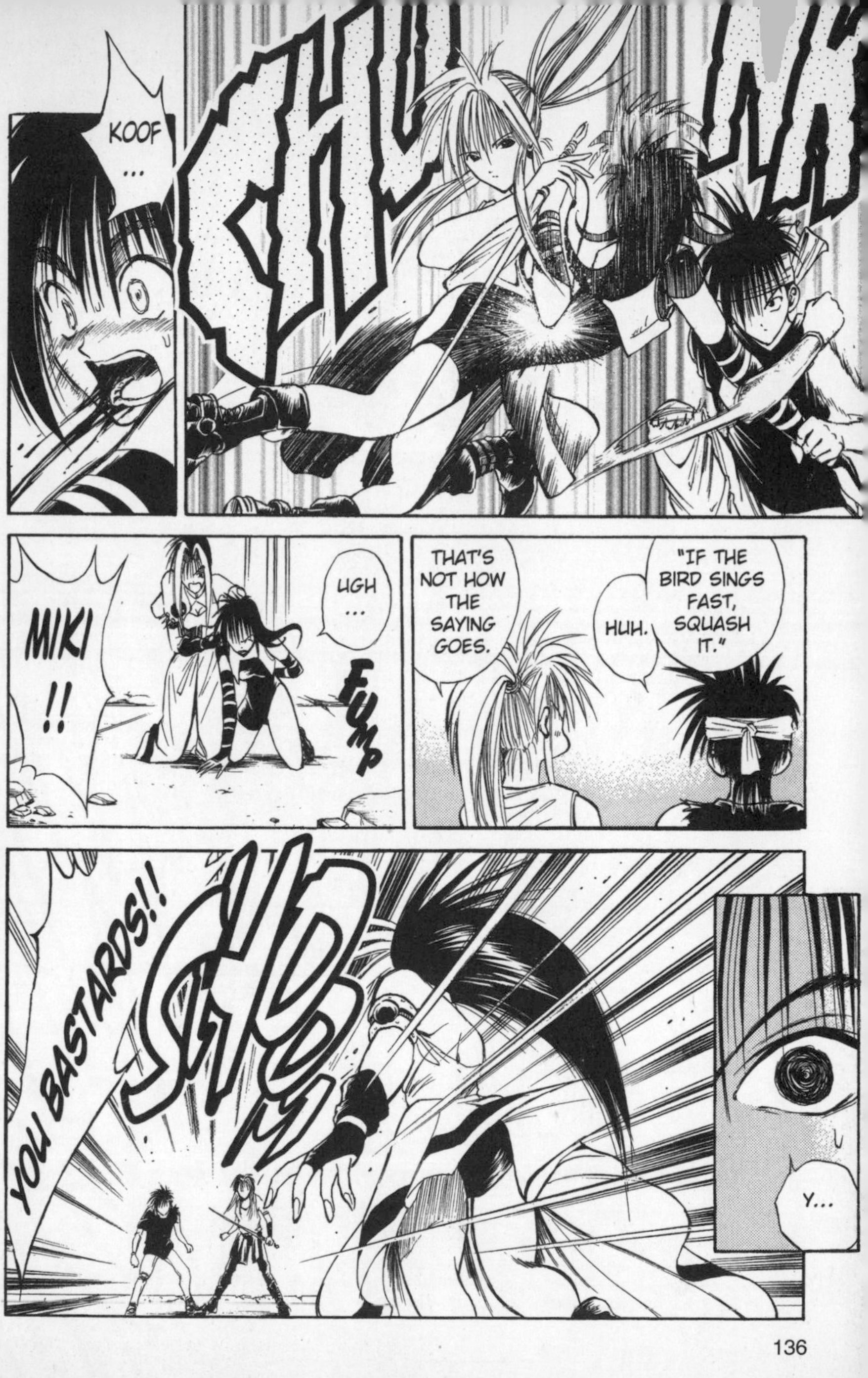
KOOF ...
"IF THE BIRD SINGS FAST, SQUASH IT."
HUH.
THAT'S NOT HOW THE SAYING GOES.
UGH ...
FUMP
MIKI !!
Y...
YOU BASTARDS!!

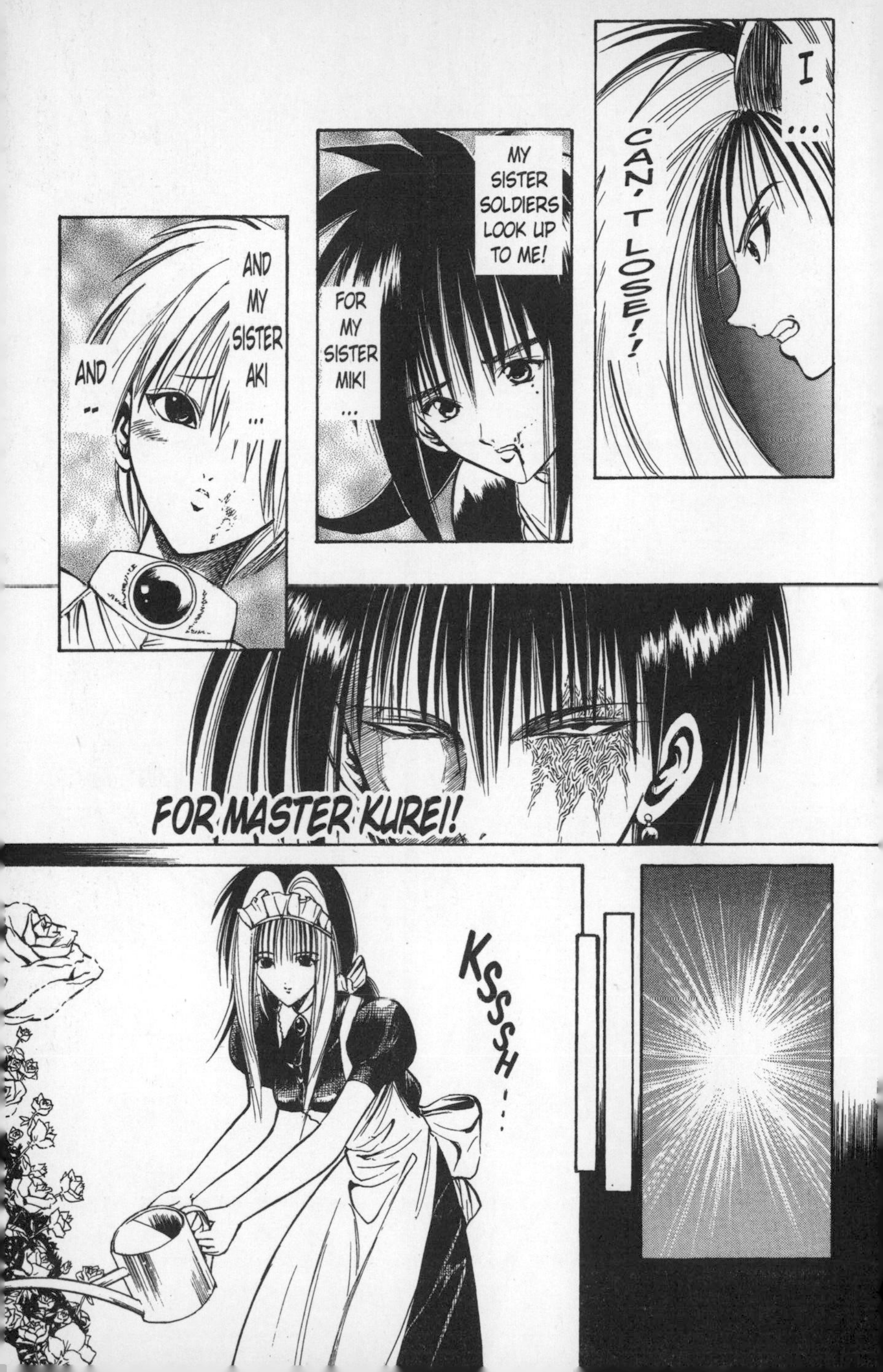
I ...
CAN'T LOSE!!
MY SISTER SOLDIERS LOOK UP TO ME!
FOR MY SISTER MIKI ...
AND MY SISTER AKI ...
AND --
FOR MASTER KUREI!
KSSSH ...

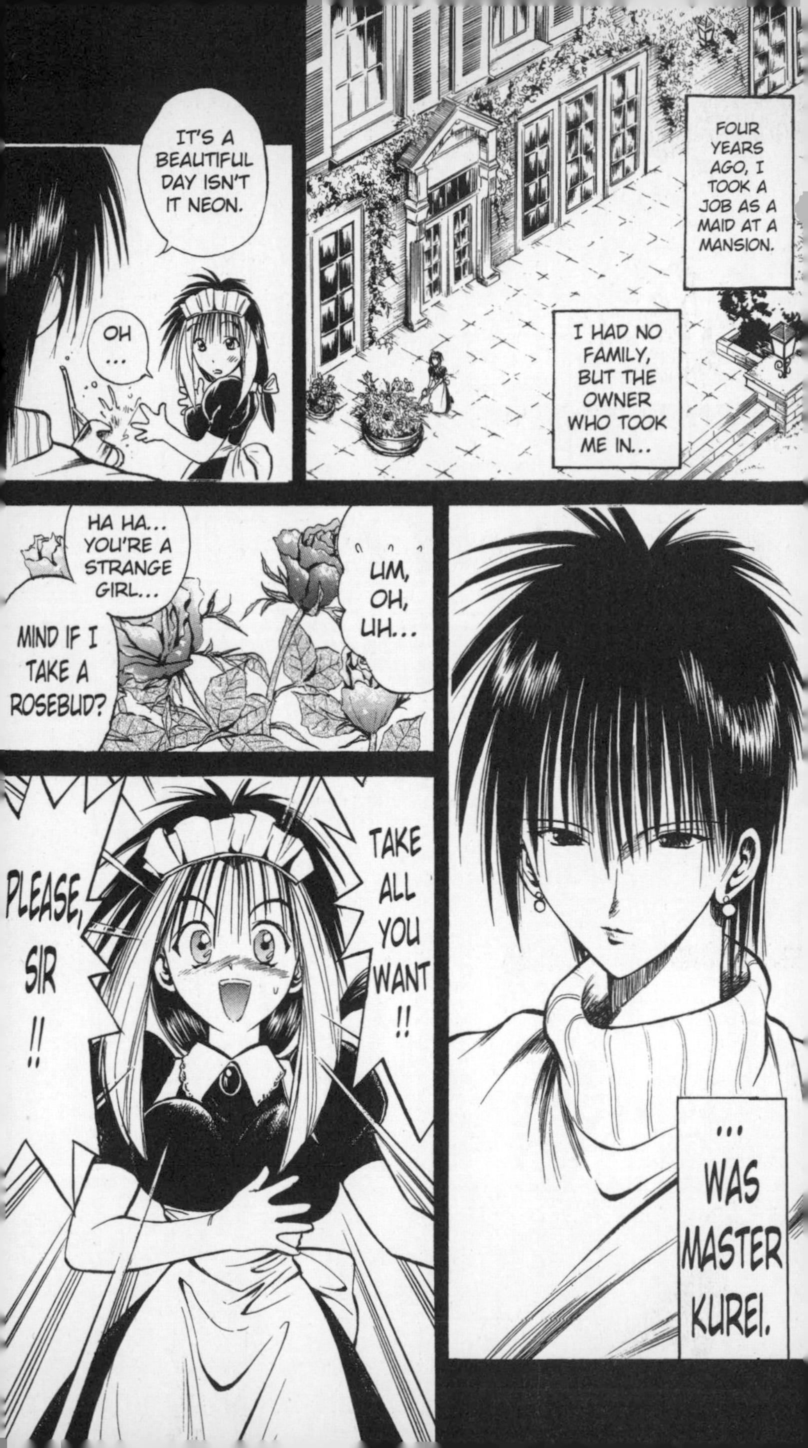
FOUR YEARS AGO, I TOOK A JOB AS A MAID AT A MANSION.
I HAD NO FAMILY, BUT THE OWNER WHO TOOK ME IN...
IT'S A BEAUTIFUL DAY ISN'T IT NEON.
OH ...
... WAS MASTER KUREI.
HA HA... YOU'RE A STRANGE GIRL...
MIND IF I TAKE A ROSEBUD?
UM, OH, UH...
TAKE ALL YOU WANT !!
PLEASE, SIR !!

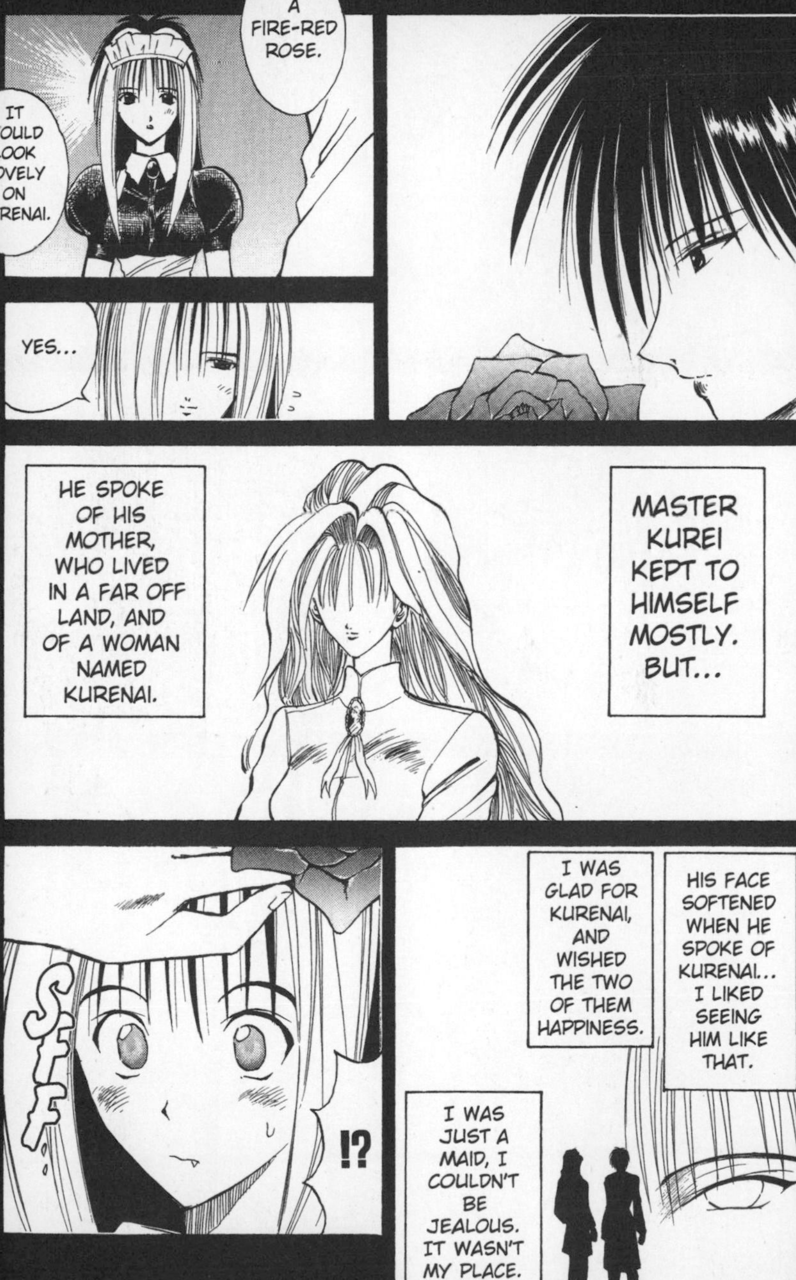
A FIRE-RED ROSE.
IT WOULD LOOK LOVELY ON KURENAI.
YES...
MASTER KUREI KEPT TO HIMSELF MOSTLY. BUT...
HE SPOKE OF HIS MOTHER, WHO LIVED IN A FAR OFF LAND, AND OF A WOMAN NAMED KURENAI.
HIS FACE SOFTENED WHEN HE SPOKE OF KURENAI... I LIKED SEEING HIM LIKE THAT.
I WAS GLAD FOR KURENAI, AND WISHED THE TWO OF THEM HAPPINESS.
I WAS JUST A MAID, I COULDN'T BE JEALOUS. IT WASN'T MY PLACE.
!?
SFF

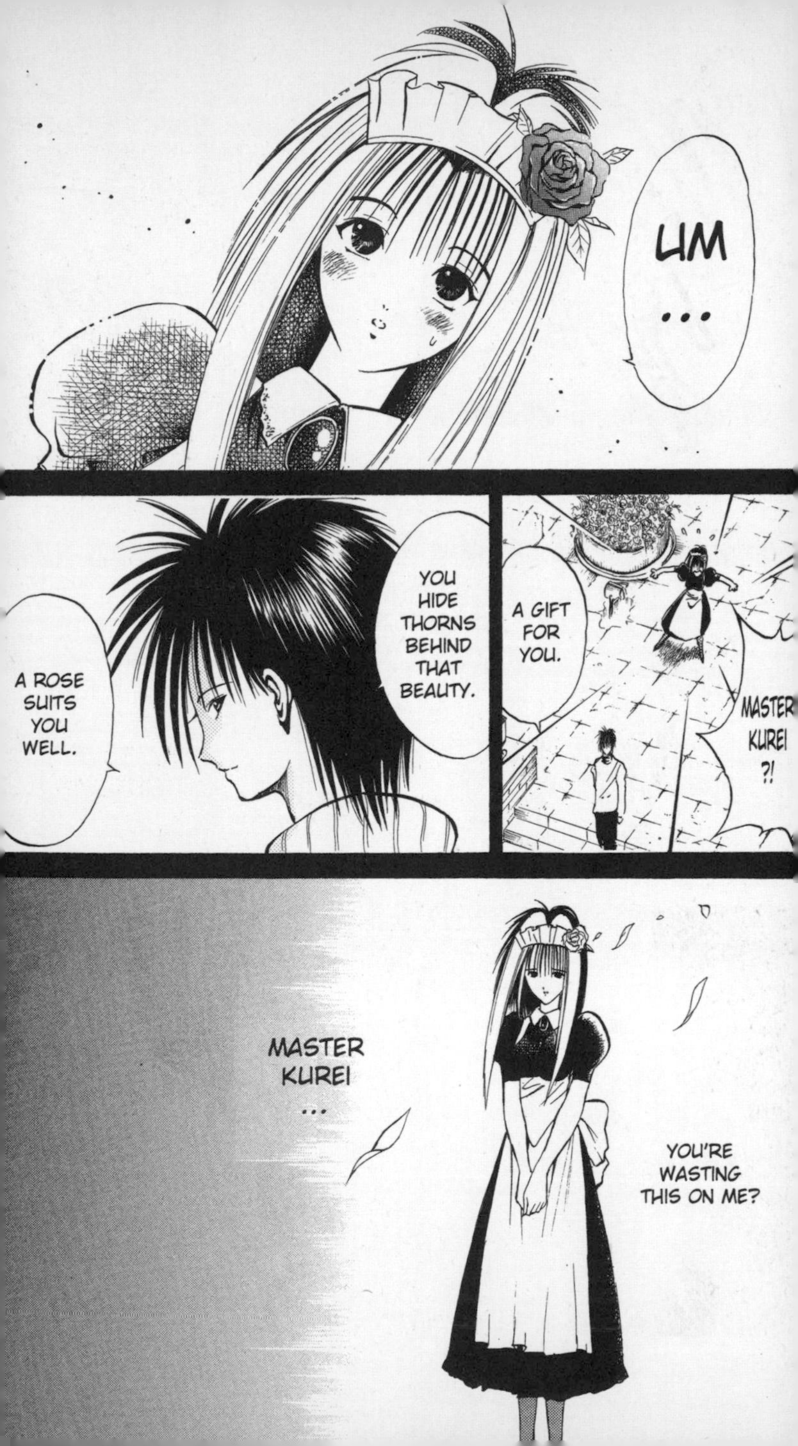
UM ...
MASTER KUREI ?!
A GIFT FOR YOU.
YOU HIDE THORNS BEHIND THAT BEAUTY.
A ROSE SUITS YOU WELL.
MASTER KUREI ...
YOU'RE WASTING THIS ON ME?

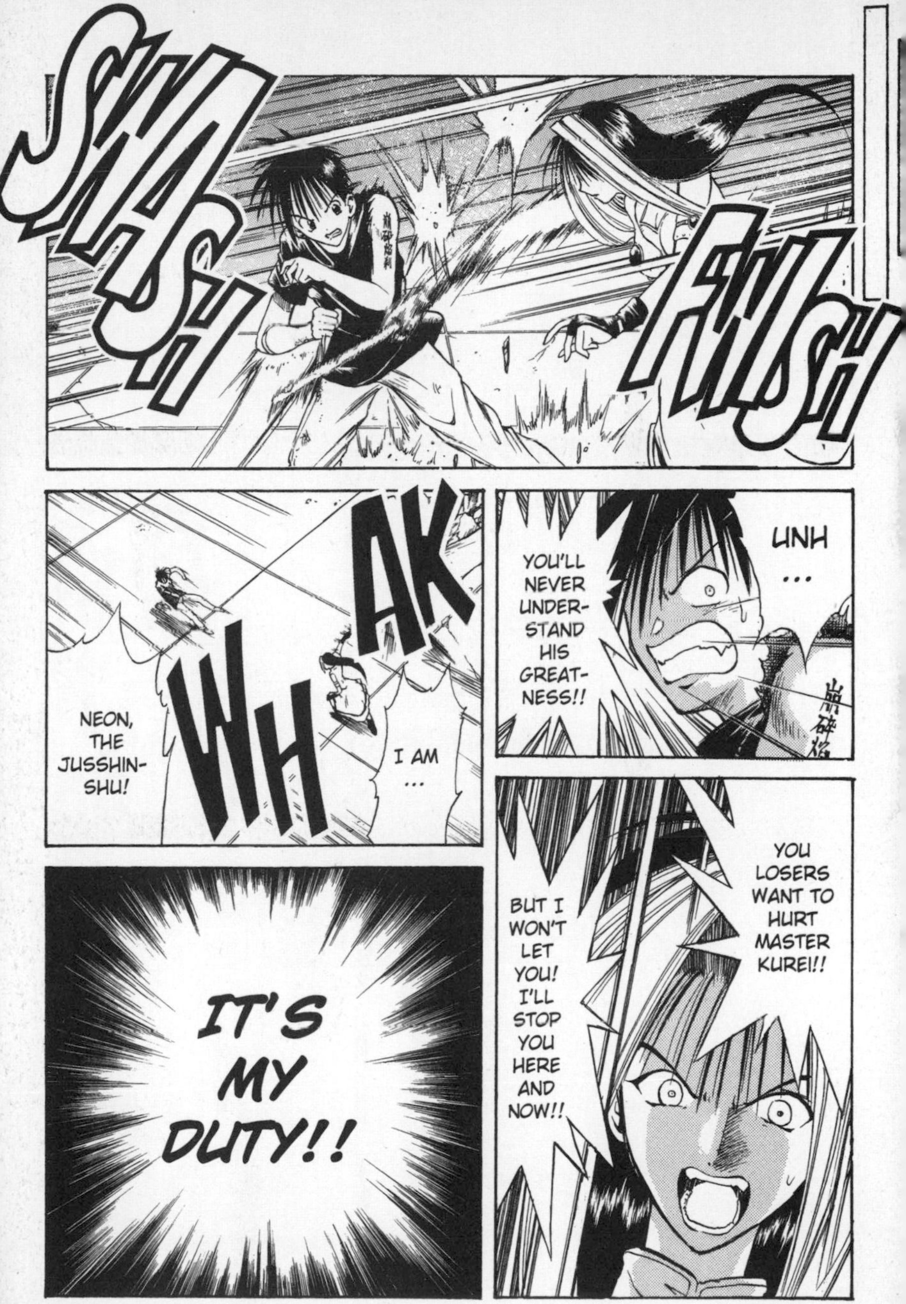
FWISH
SMASH
UNH ...
YOU'LL NEVER UNDER-STAND HIS GREAT-NESS!!
I AM ...
WHAK
NEON, THE JUSSHIN-SHU!
YOU LOSERS WANT TO HURT MASTER KUREI!!
BUT I WON'T LET YOU! I'LL STOP YOU HERE AND NOW!!
IT'S MY DUTY!!

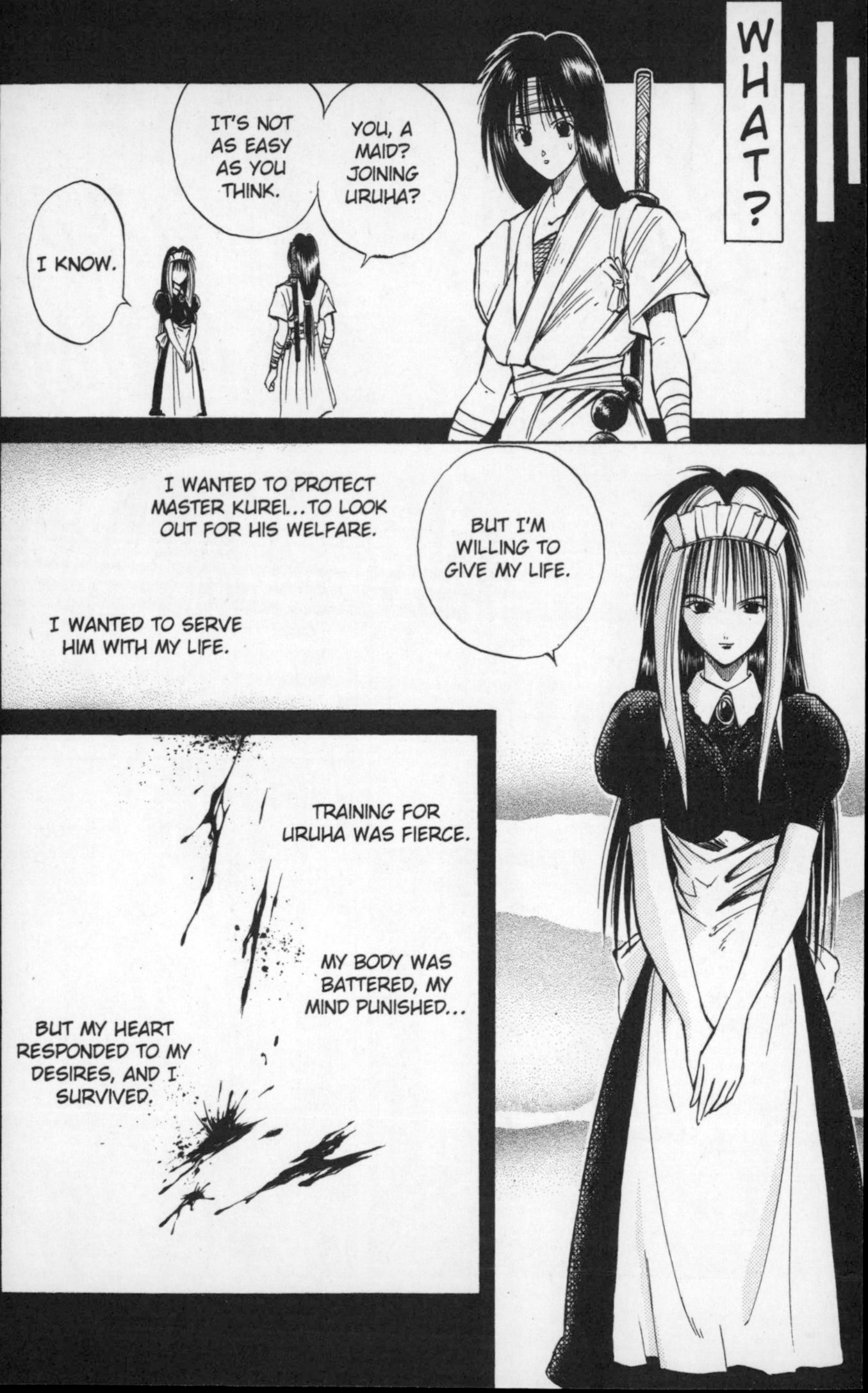
WHAT?
YOU, A MAID? JOINING URUHA?
IT'S NOT AS EASY AS YOU THINK.
I KNOW.
BUT I'M WILLING TO GIVE MY LIFE.
I WANTED TO PROTECT MASTER KUREI...TO LOOK OUT FOR HIS WELFARE.
I WANTED TO SERVE HIM WITH MY LIFE.
TRAINING FOR URUHA WAS FIERCE.
MY BODY WAS BATTERED, MY MIND PUNISHED...
BUT MY HEART RESPONDED TO MY DESIRES, AND I SURVIVED.

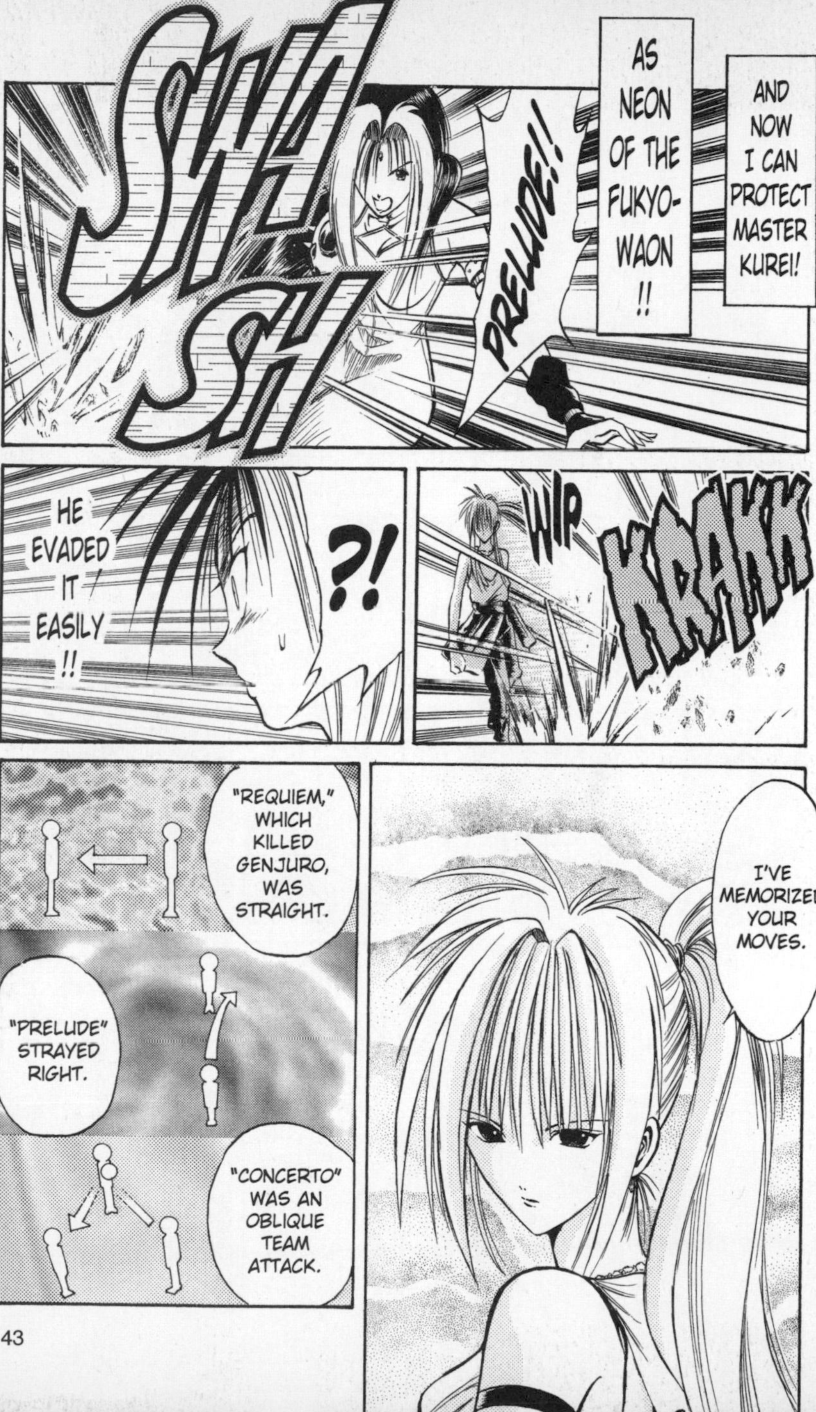
AND NOW I CAN PROTECT MASTER KUREI!
AS NEON OF THE FUKYO-WAON !!
PRELUDE!!
SWASH
WIP
KRAKK
?!
HE EVADED IT EASILY !!
I'VE MEMORIZED YOUR MOVES.
"REQUIEM," WHICH KILLED GENJURO, WAS STRAIGHT.
"PRELUDE" STRAYED RIGHT.
"CONCERTO" WAS AN OBLIQUE TEAM ATTACK.

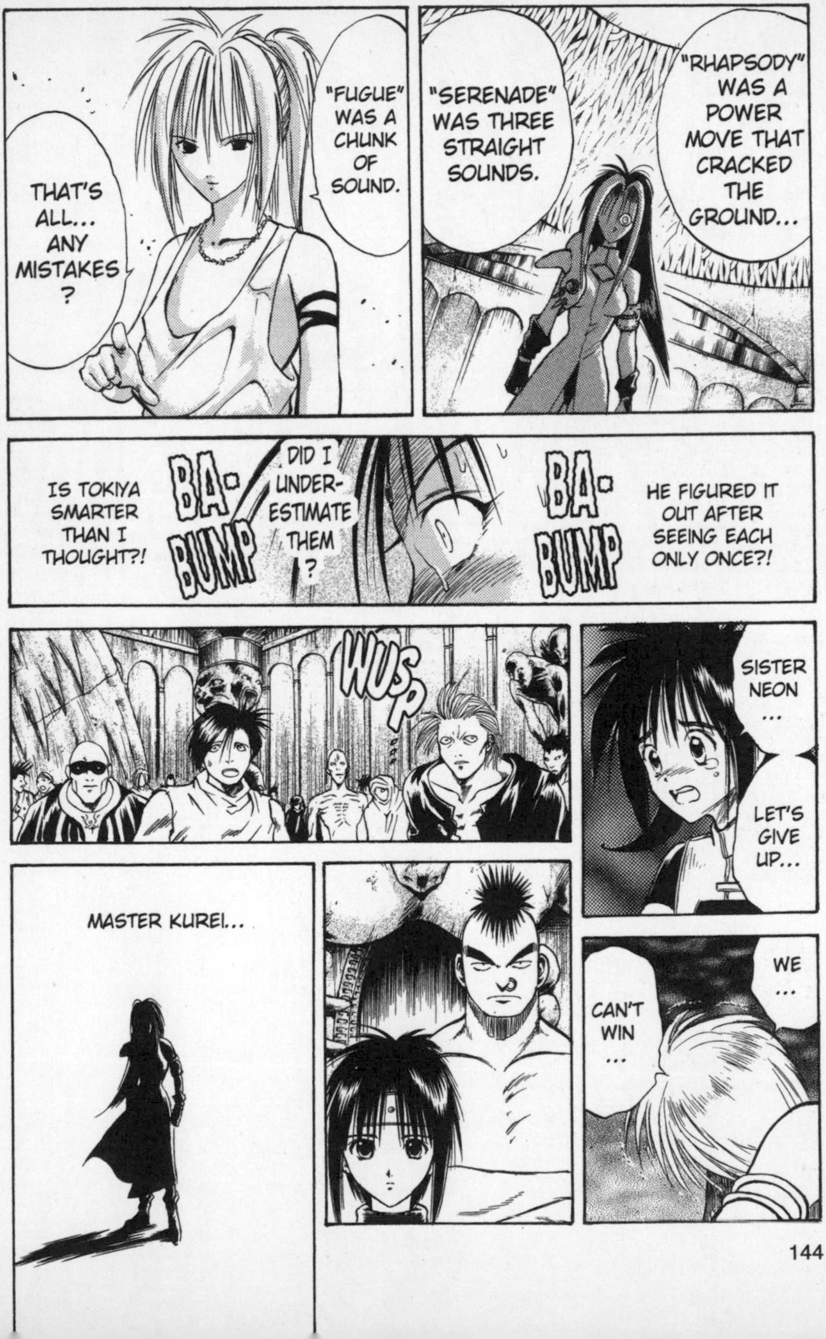
"RHAPSODY" WAS A POWER MOVE THAT CRACKED THE GROUND...
"SERENADE" WAS THREE STRAIGHT SOUNDS.
"FUGUE" WAS A CHUNK OF SOUND.
THAT'S ALL... ANY MISTAKES ?
HE FIGURED IT OUT AFTER SEEING EACH ONLY ONCE?!
BA-BUMP
DID I UNDER-ESTIMATE THEM ?
BA-BUMP
IS TOKIYA SMARTER THAN I THOUGHT?!
SISTER NEON ...
LET'S GIVE UP...
WUSP
WE ...
CAN'T WIN ...
MASTER KUREI...

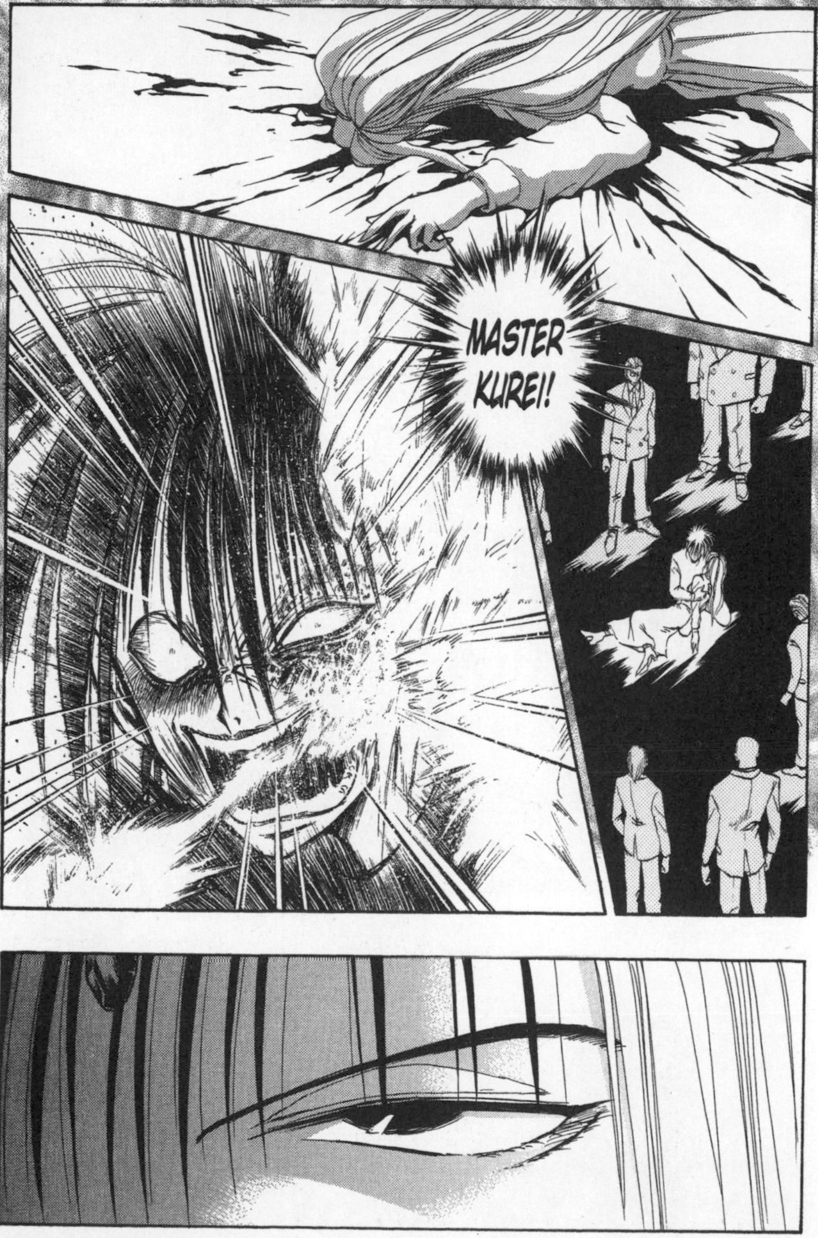
MASTER KUREI!

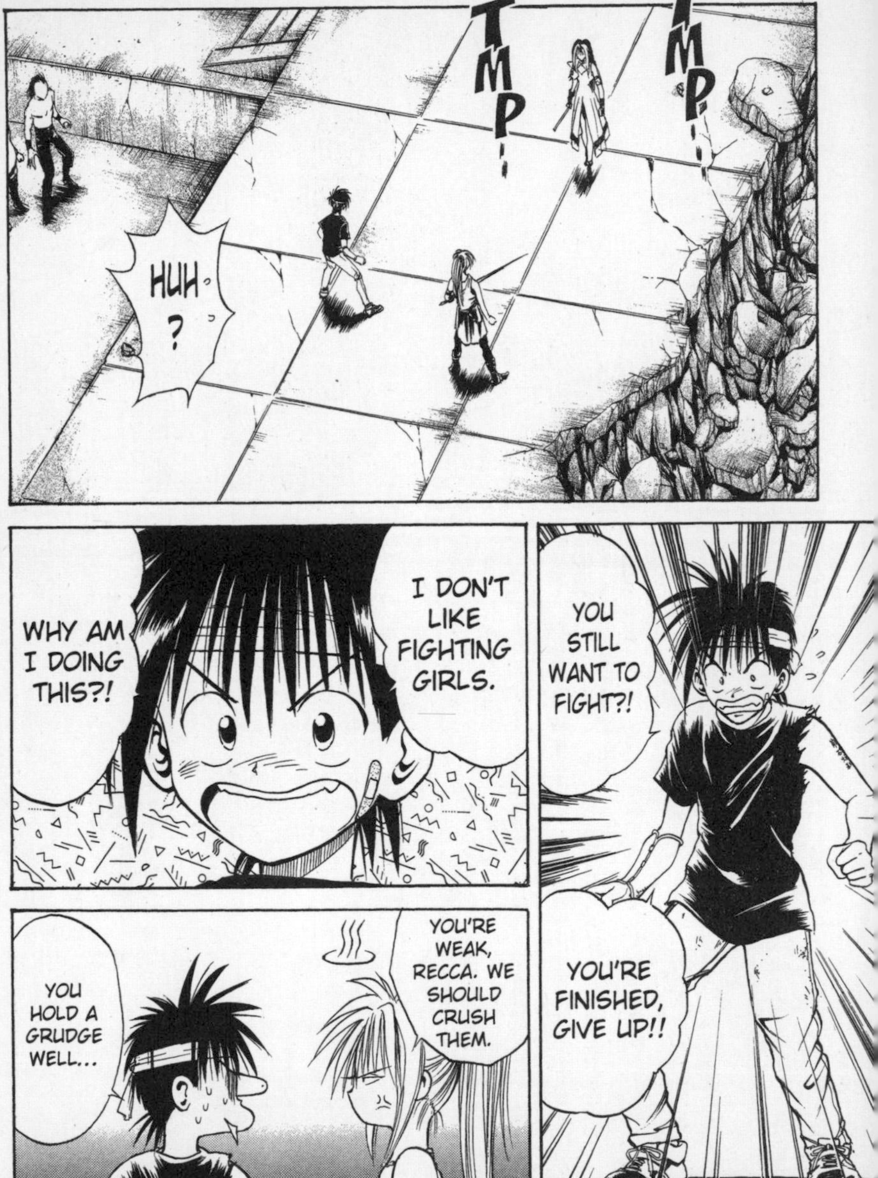
TMP...
TMP...
HUH?
YOU STILL WANT TO FIGHT?!
YOU'RE FINISHED, GIVE UP!!
I DON'T LIKE FIGHTING GIRLS.
WHY AM I DOING THIS?!
YOU'RE WEAK, RECCA. WE SHOULD CRUSH THEM.
YOU HOLD A GRUDGE WELL...

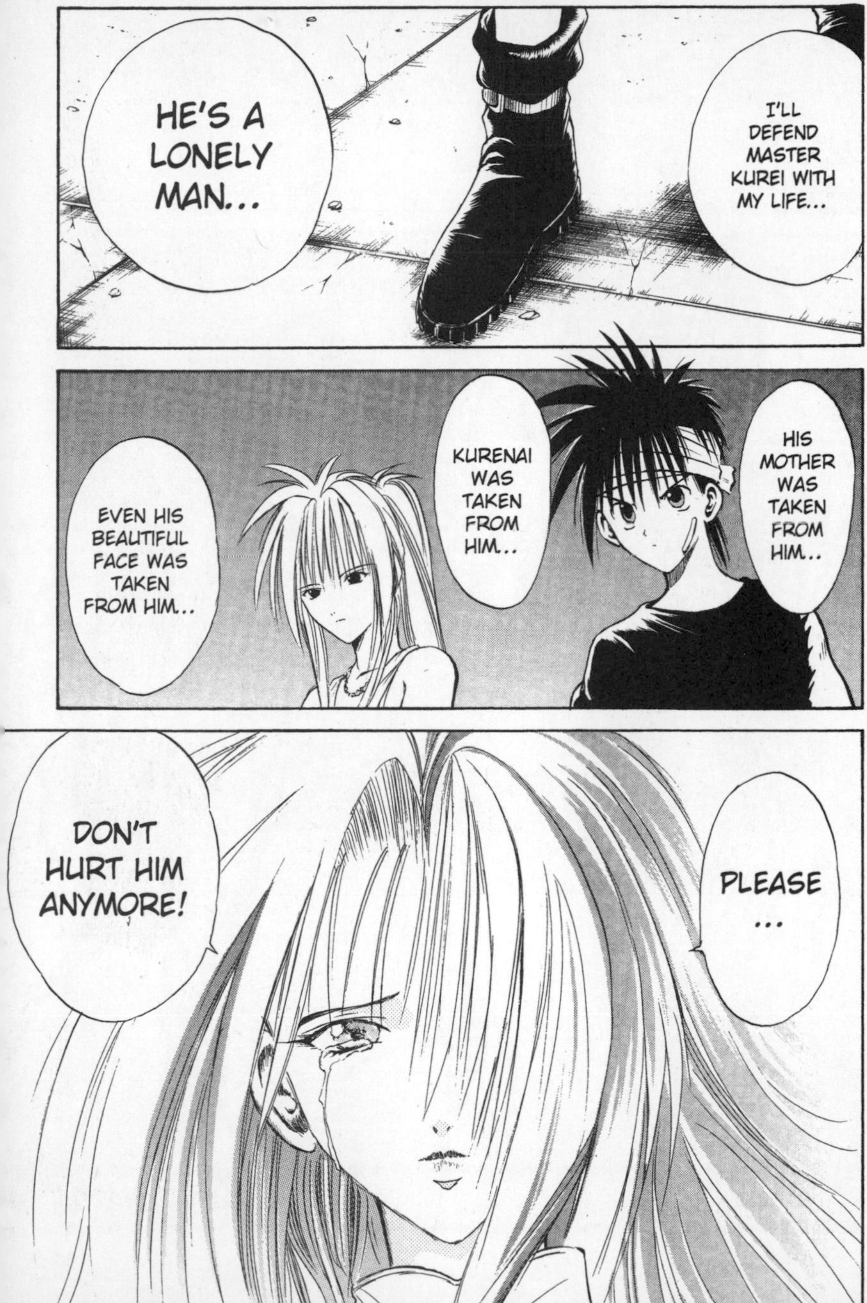
I'LL DEFEND MASTER KUREI WITH MY LIFE...
HE'S A LONELY MAN...
HIS MOTHER WAS TAKEN FROM HIM...
KURENAI WAS TAKEN FROM HIM...
EVEN HIS BEAUTIFUL FACE WAS TAKEN FROM HIM...
PLEASE ...
DON'T HURT HIM ANYMORE!

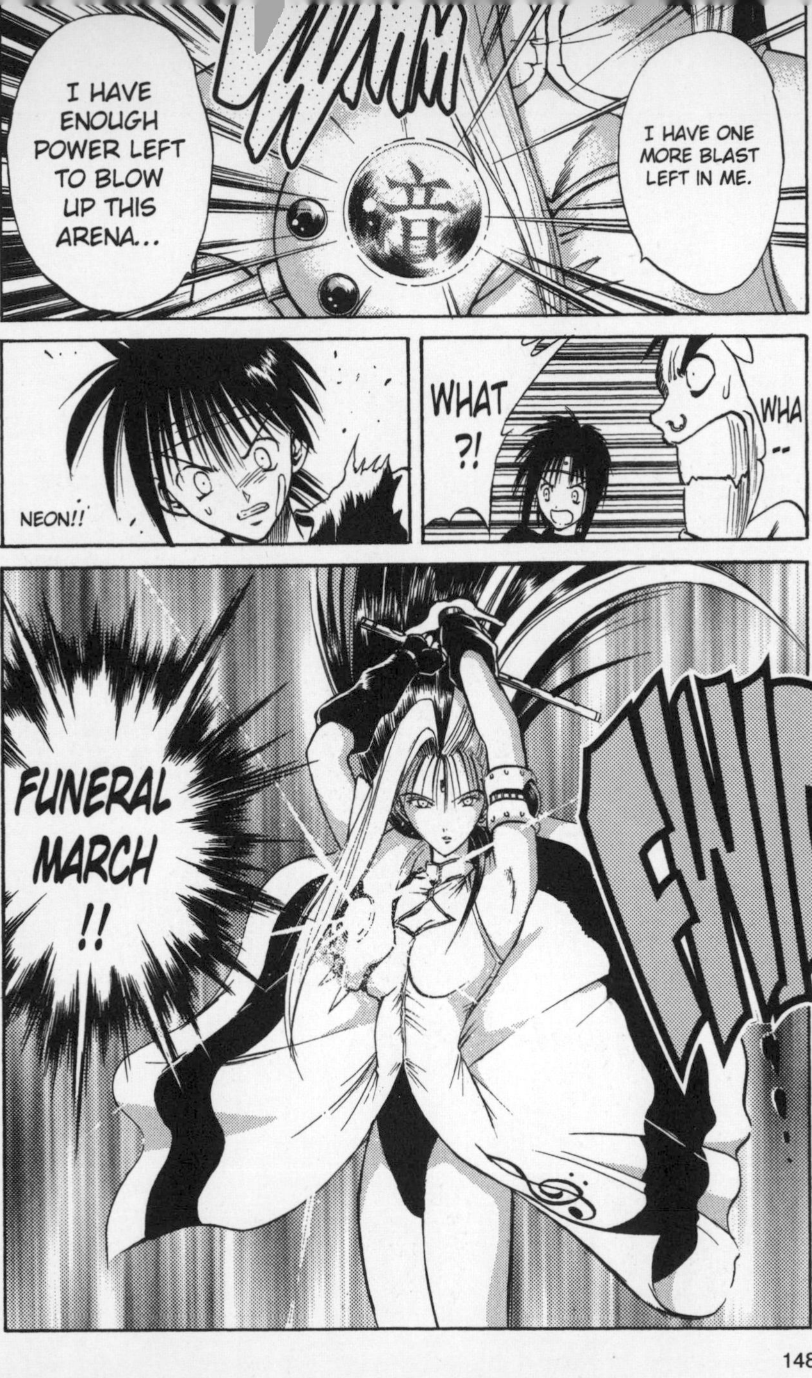
I HAVE ONE MORE BLAST LEFT IN ME.
I HAVE ENOUGH POWER LEFT TO BLOW UP THIS ARENA...
WHA --
WHAT ?!
NEON!!
FUNERAL MARCH !!

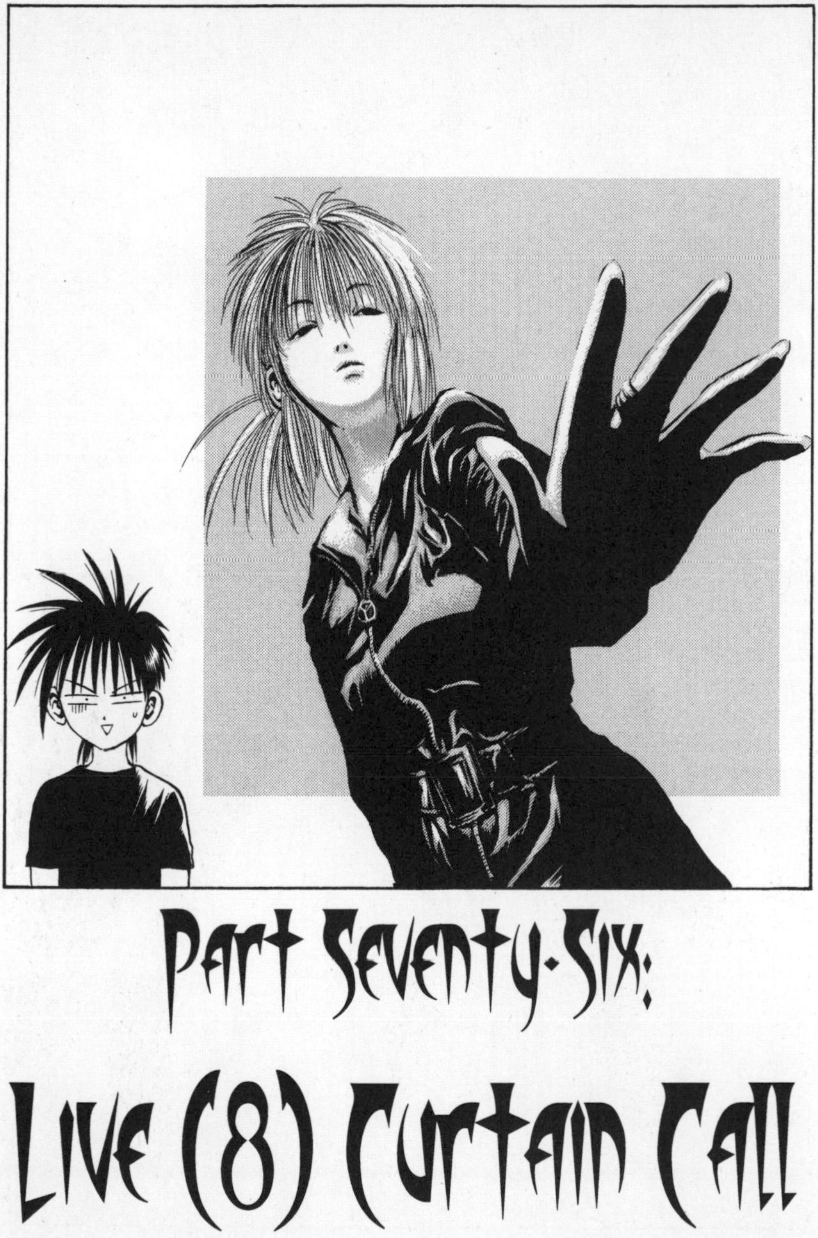

Part Seventy-Six:

Live (8) Curtain Call

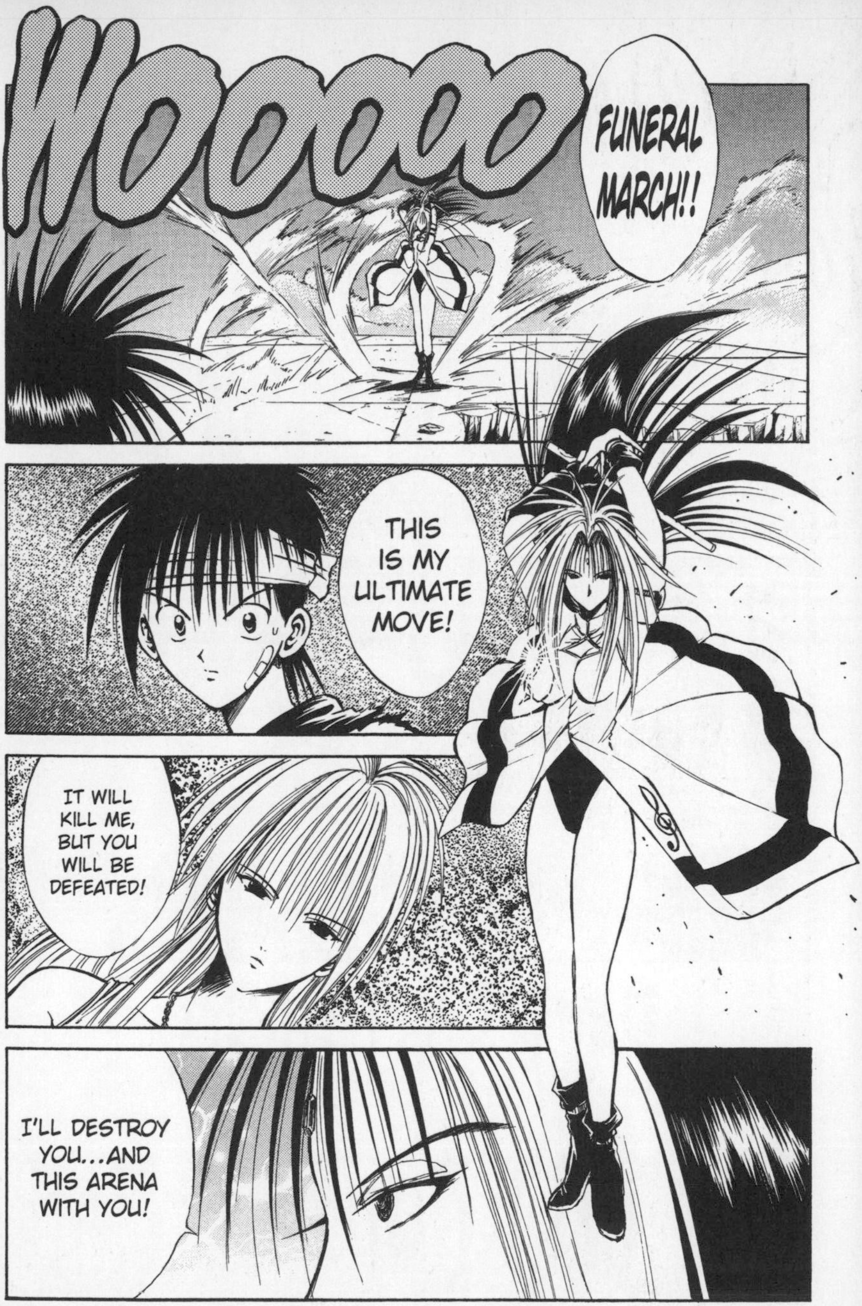
WOOOOO
FUNERAL MARCH!!
THIS IS MY ULTIMATE MOVE!
IT WILL KILL ME, BUT YOU WILL BE DEFEATED!
I'LL DESTROY YOU...AND THIS ARENA WITH YOU!

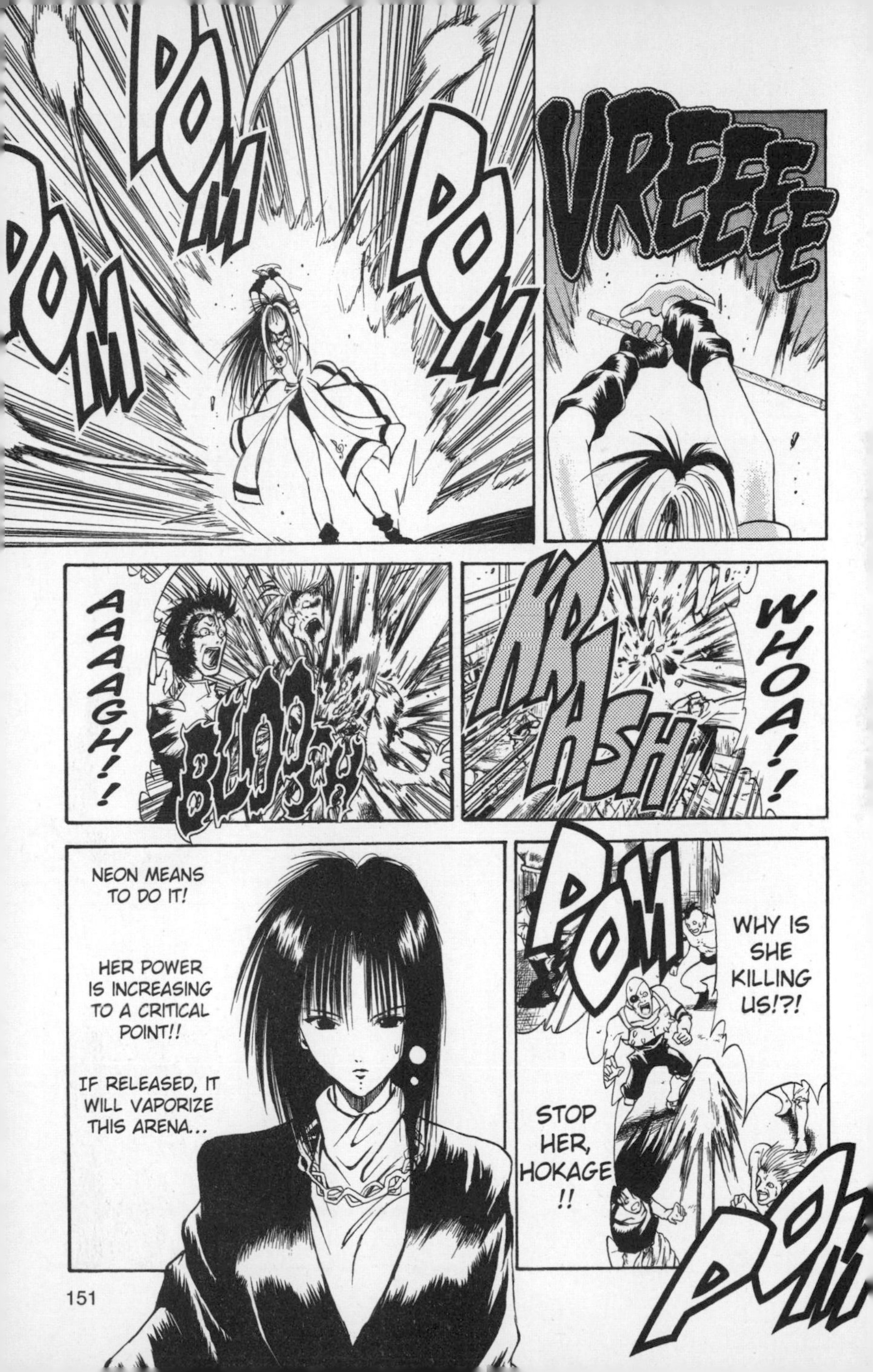
VREEEE
POM
POM
POM
POM
KRASH
WHOA!!
AAAAGH!!
BLOOSH
POM
WHY IS SHE KILLING US!?!
STOP HER, HOKAGE!!
POM
NEON MEANS TO DO IT!
HER POWER IS INCREASING TO A CRITICAL POINT!!
IF RELEASED, IT WILL VAPORIZE THIS ARENA...

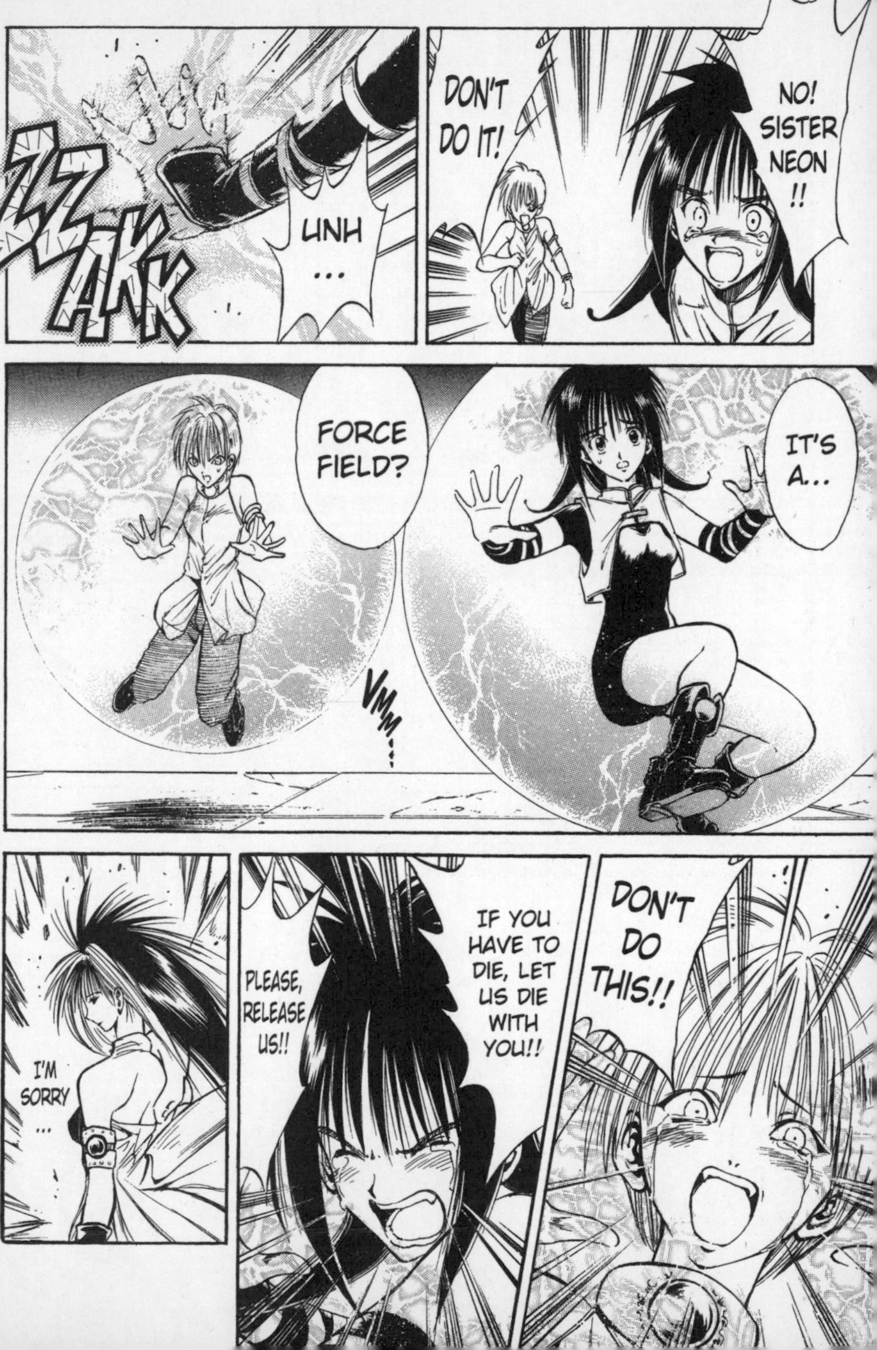
NO! SISTER NEON !!
DON'T DO IT!
UNH ...
ZZAKK
IT'S A...
FORCE FIELD?
VMMM
DON'T DO THIS!!
IF YOU HAVE TO DIE, LET US DIE WITH YOU!!
PLEASE, RELEASE US!!
I'M SORRY ...

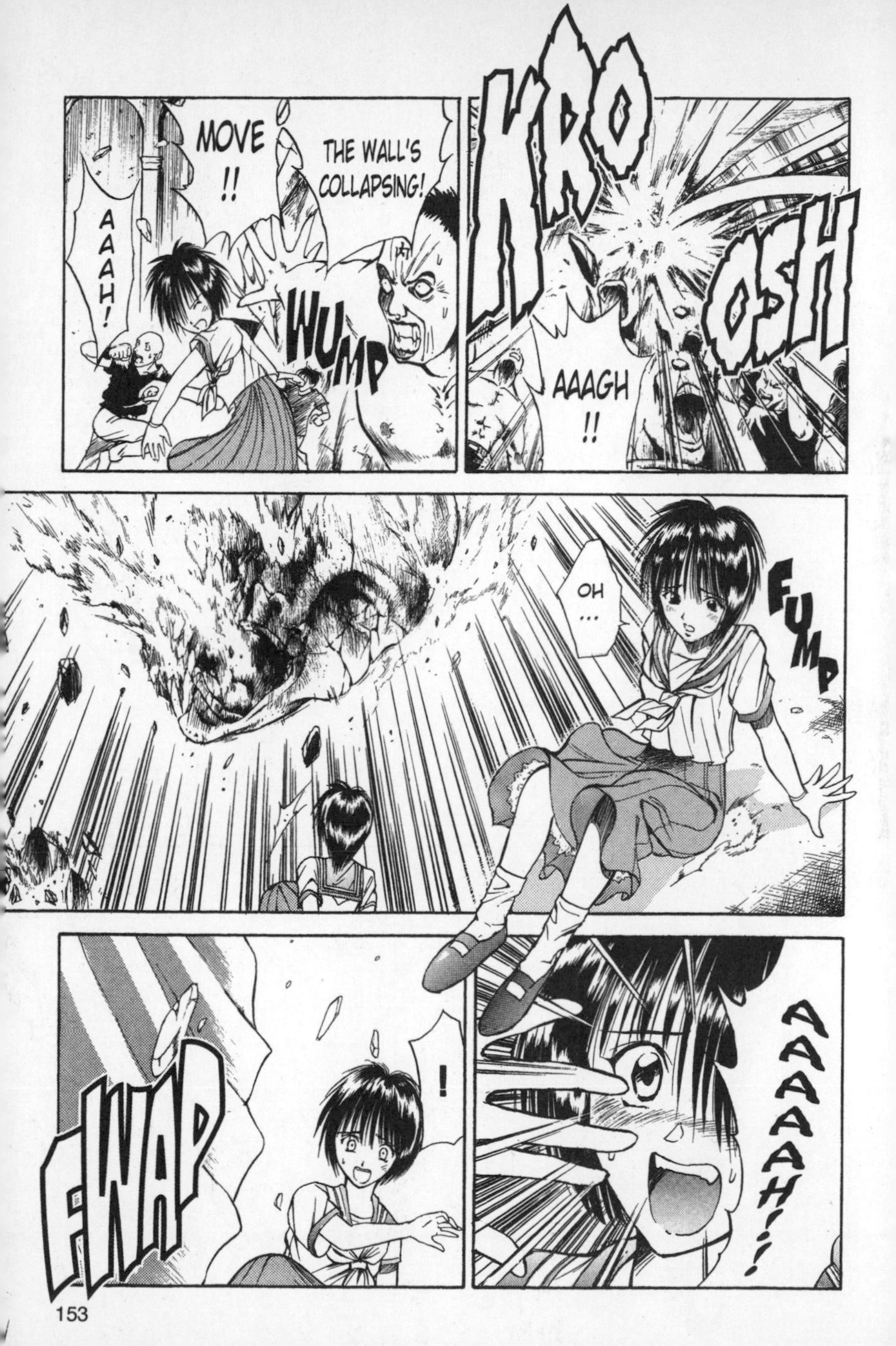
KROOSH
AAAGH !!
THE WALL'S COLLAPSING!
MOVE !!
AAAAH!
WUMP
FUMP
OH ...
AAAAAAH!!!
!
FWAP

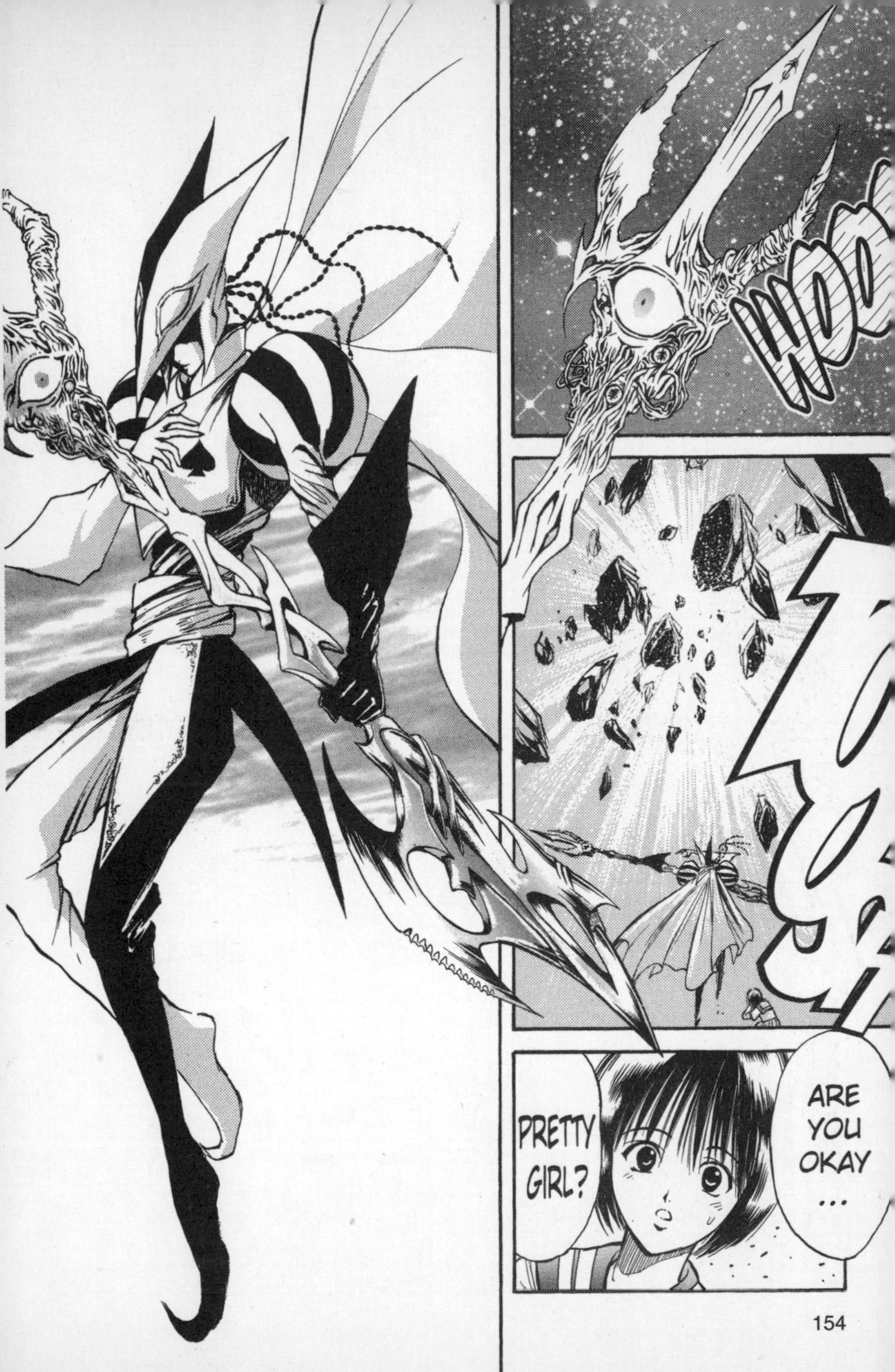
WHOO
ARE YOU OKAY ...
PRETTY GIRL?

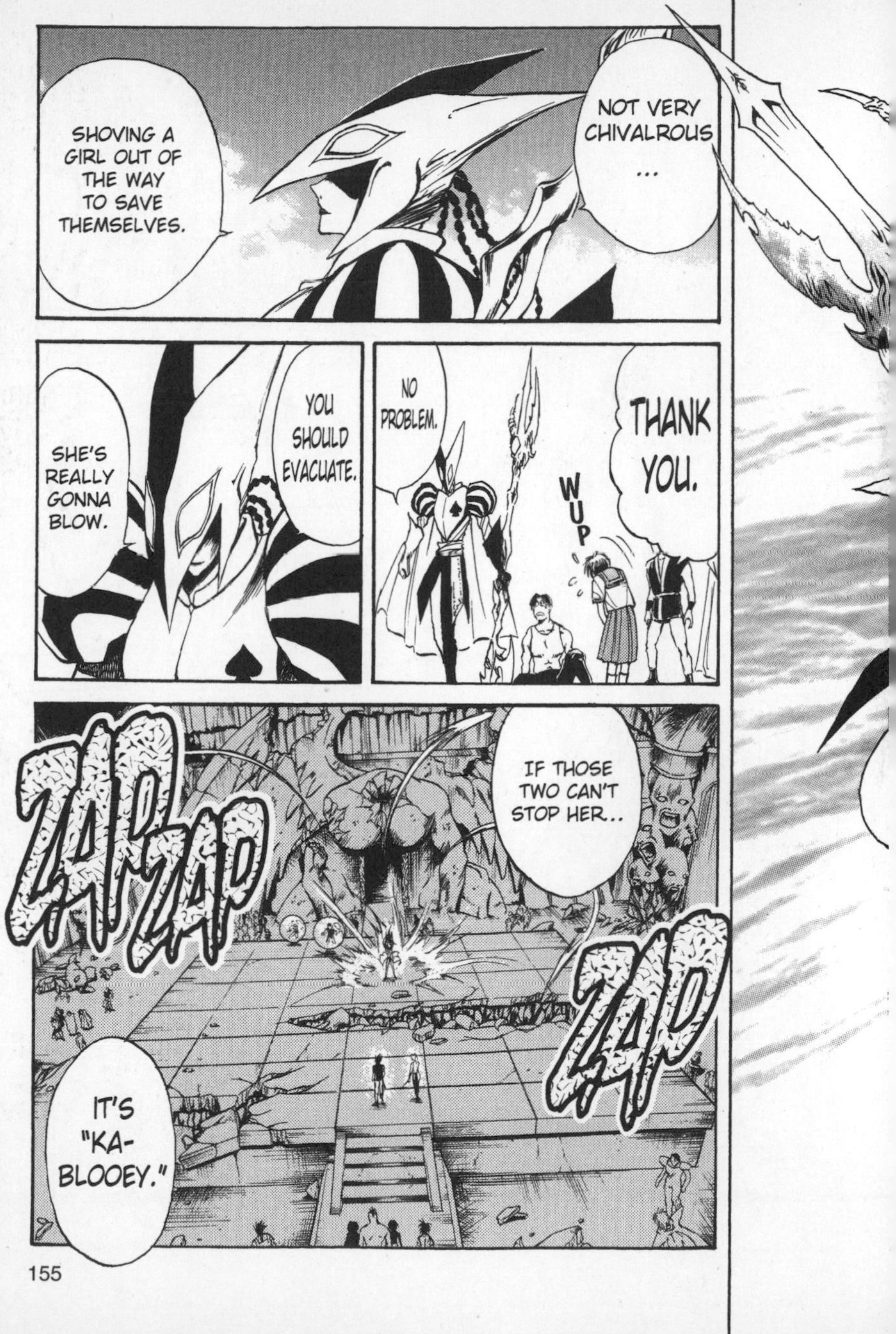
NOT VERY CHIVALROUS ...
SHOVING A GIRL OUT OF THE WAY TO SAVE THEMSELVES.
THANK YOU.
WUP
NO PROBLEM.
YOU SHOULD EVACUATE.
SHE'S REALLY GONNA BLOW.
ZAP
IF THOSE TWO CAN'T STOP HER..
ZAP ZAP
IT'S "KA-BLOOEY."

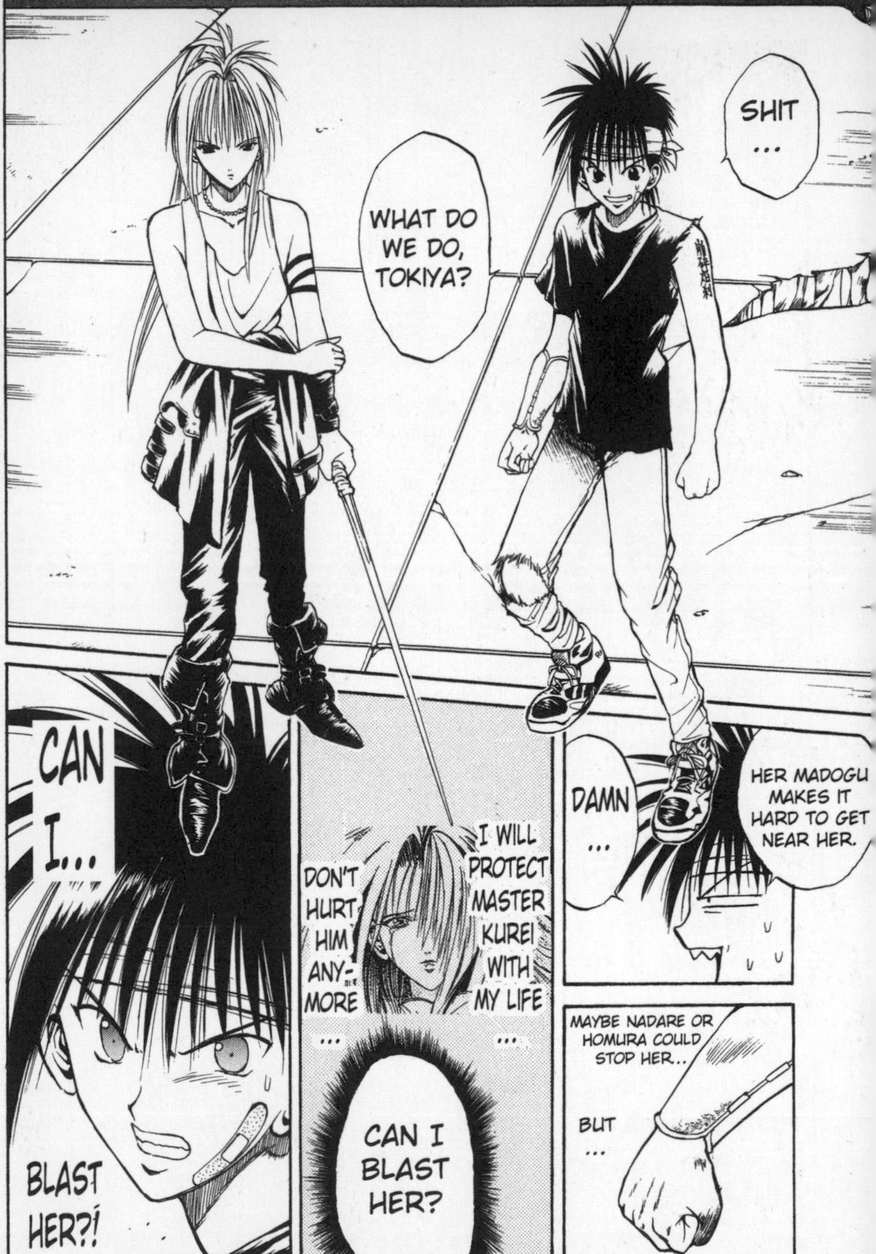
SHIT ...
WHAT DO WE DO, TOKIYA?
HER MADOGU MAKES IT HARD TO GET NEAR HER.
DAMN ...
MAYBE NADARE OR HOMURA COULD STOP HER..
BUT ...
I WILL PROTECT MASTER KUREI WITH MY LIFE ...
DON'T HURT HIM ANY-MORE ...
CAN I BLAST HER?
CAN I...
BLAST HER?!

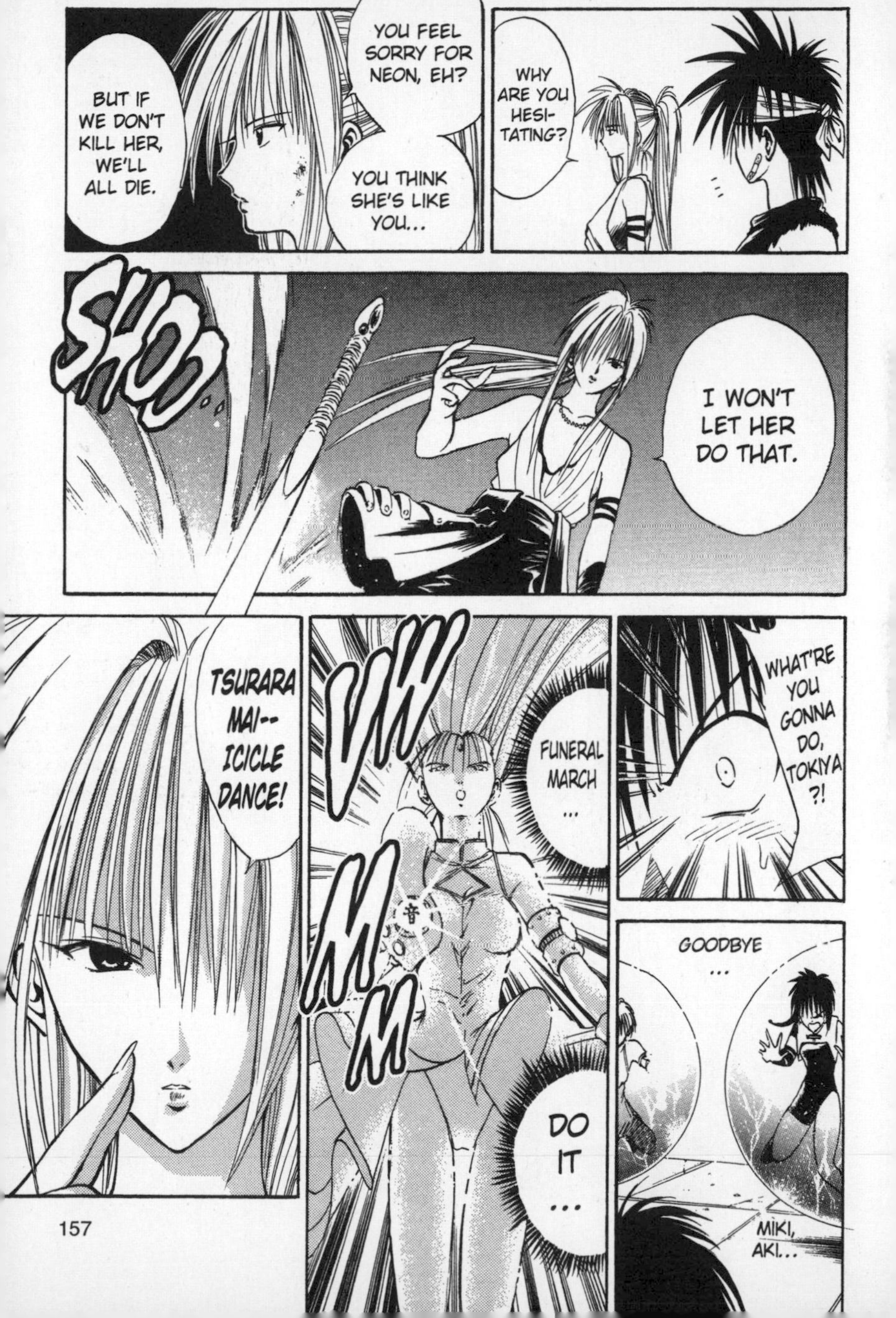
WHY ARE YOU HESI-TATING?
YOU FEEL SORRY FOR NEON, EH?
YOU THINK SHE'S LIKE YOU...
BUT IF WE DON'T KILL HER, WE'LL ALL DIE.
I WON'T LET HER DO THAT.
SHOO
WHAT'RE YOU GONNA DO, TOKIYA?!
GOODBYE...
MIKI, AKI...
VMMM
FUNERAL MARCH...
音
DO IT...
TSURARA MAI-- ICICLE DANCE!

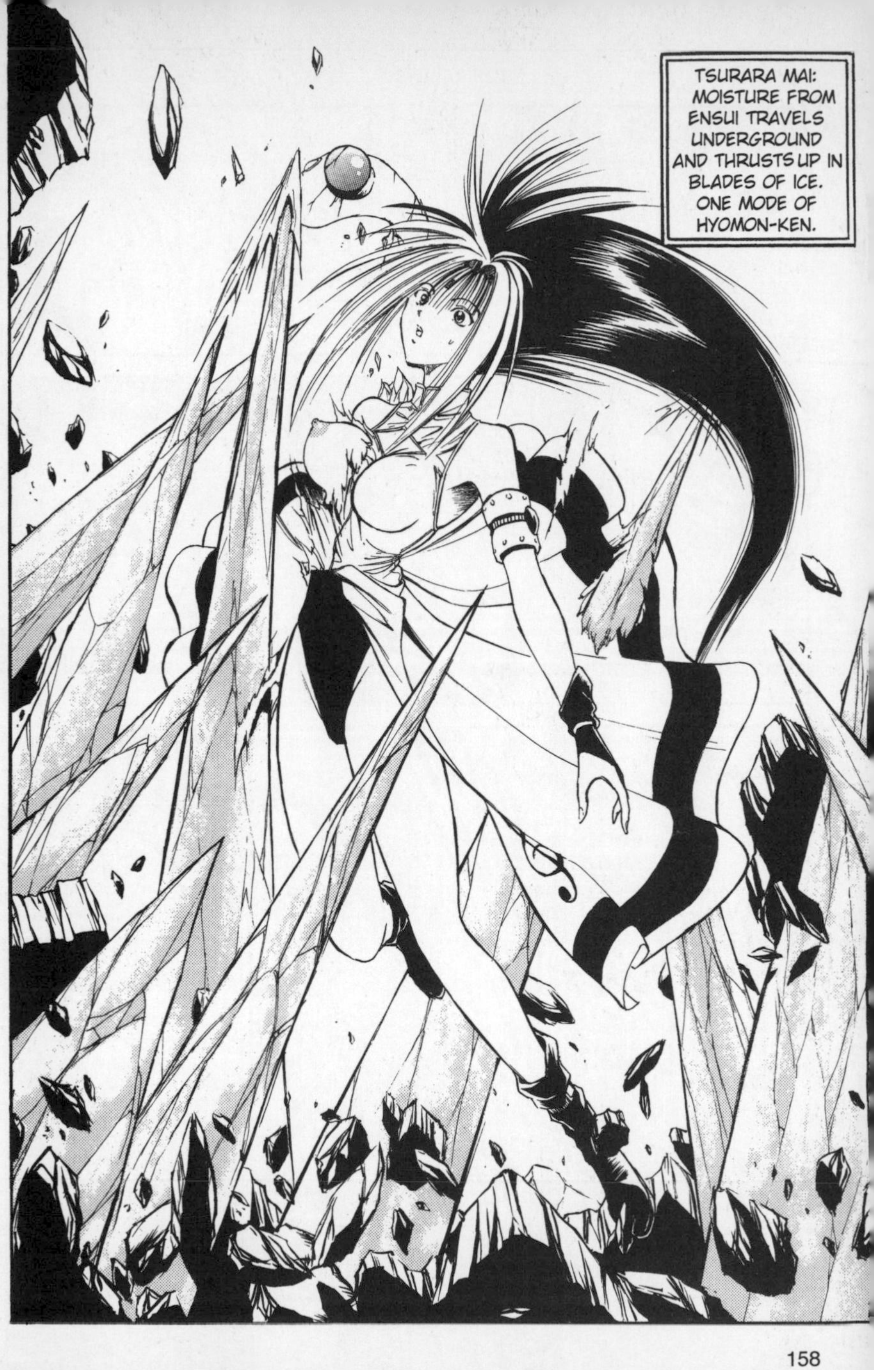
TSURARA MAI: MOISTURE FROM ENSUI TRAVELS UNDERGROUND AND THRUSTS UP IN BLADES OF ICE. ONE MODE OF HYOMON-KEN.

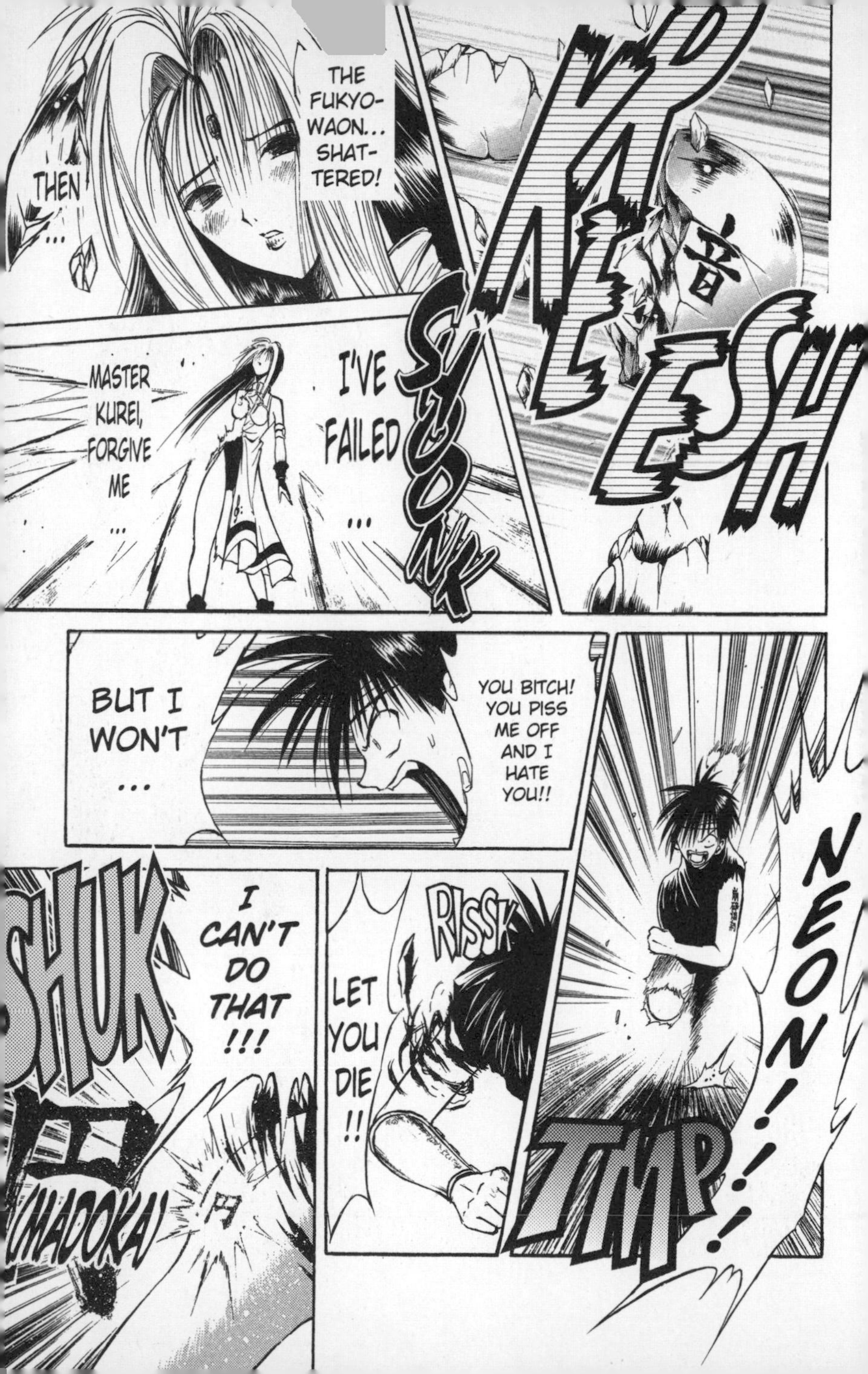
THE FUKYO-WAON... SHATTERED!
THEN ...
I'VE FAILED ...
MASTER KUREI, FORGIVE ME ...
NEON!!!!
THMP
YOU BITCH! YOU PISS ME OFF AND I HATE YOU!!
BUT I WON'T ...
RISSK
LET YOU DIE !!
I CAN'T DO THAT !!!
SHUK
(MADOKA)

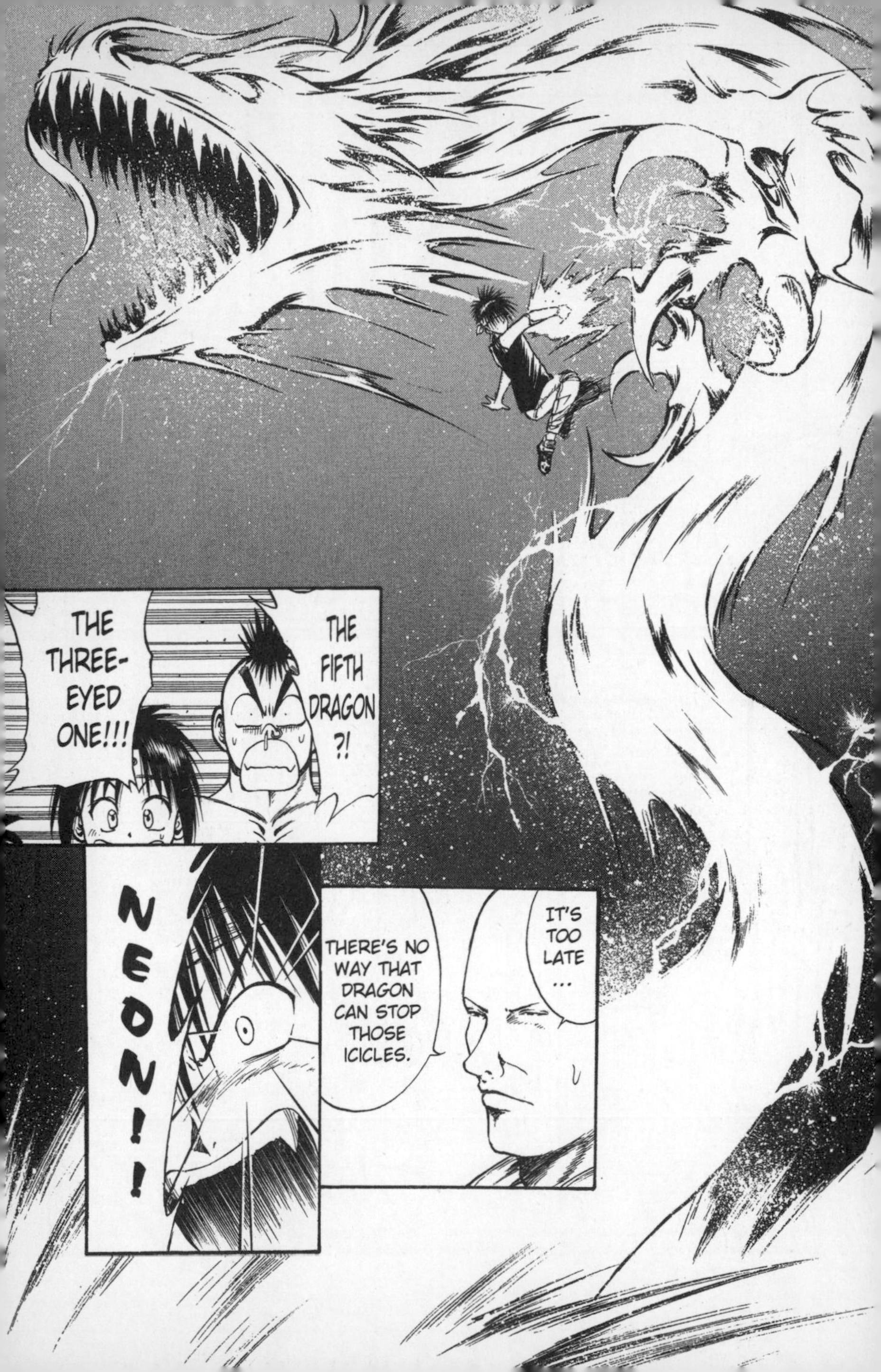
THE FIFTH DRAGON ?!
THE THREE-EYED ONE!!!
IT'S TOO LATE ...
THERE'S NO WAY THAT DRAGON CAN STOP THOSE ICICLES.
NEON!!

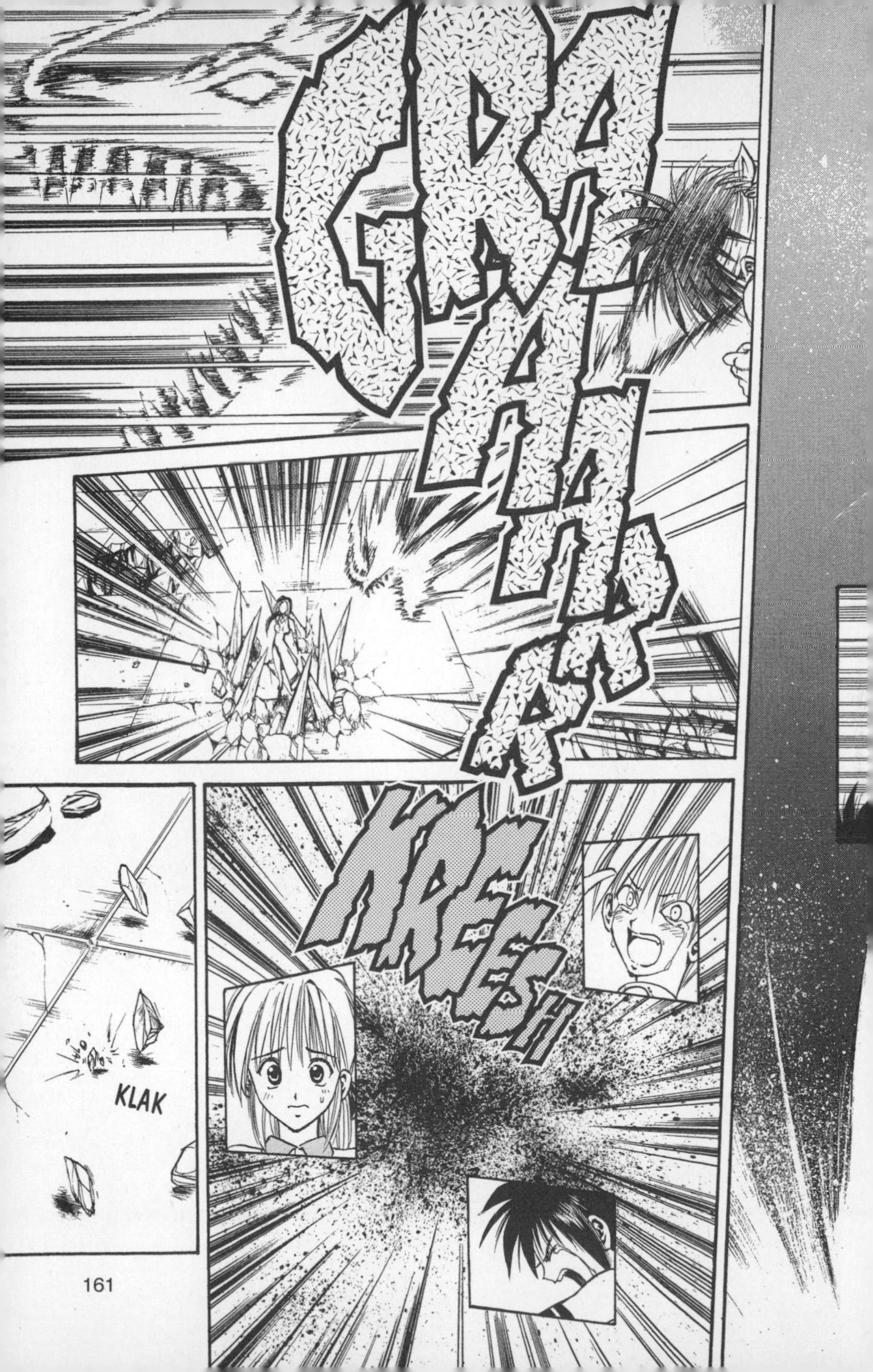
KREESH
KLAK

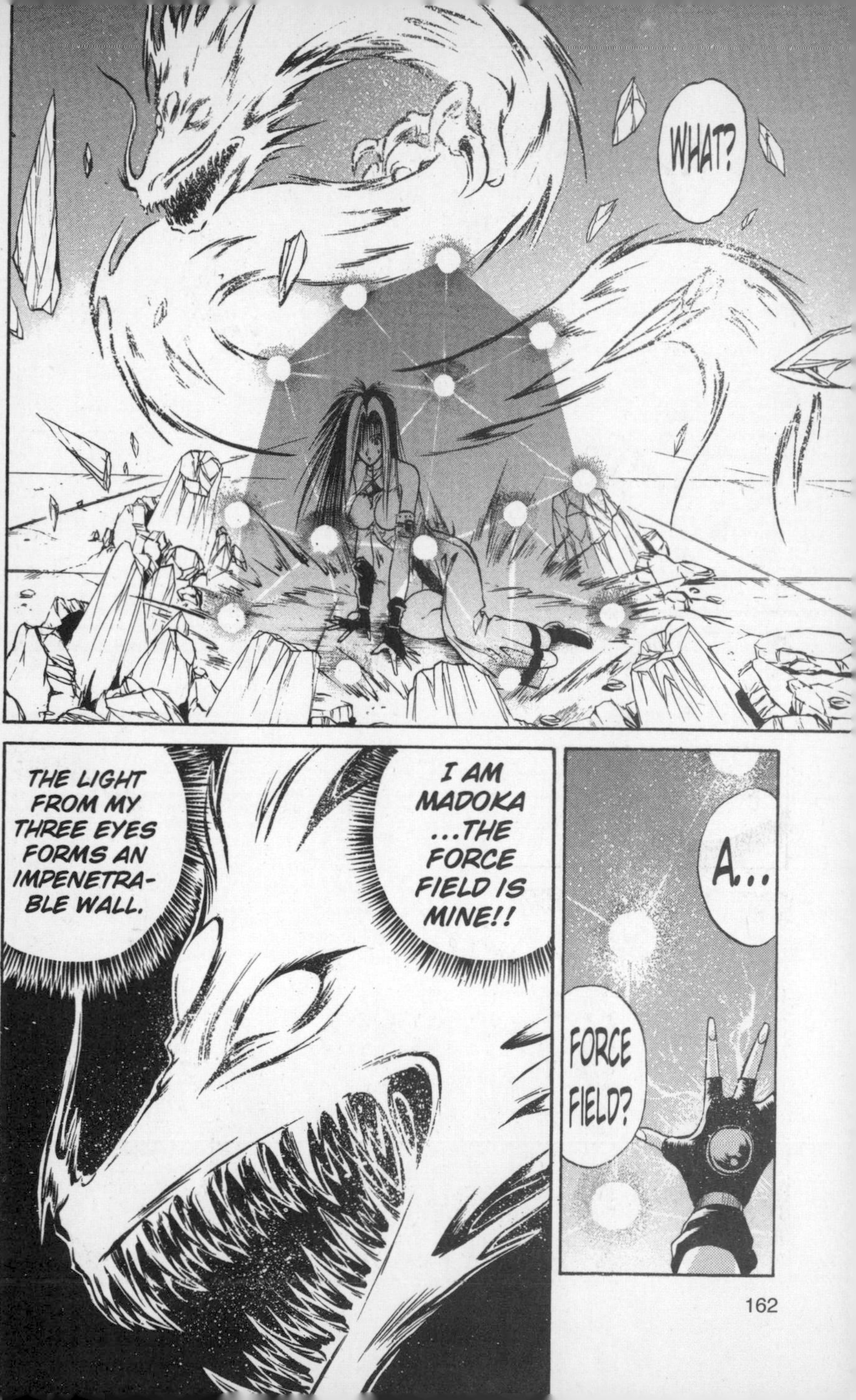
WHAT?
A...
FORCE FIELD?
I AM MADOKA ...THE FORCE FIELD IS MINE!!
THE LIGHT FROM MY THREE EYES FORMS AN IMPENETRA-BLE WALL.

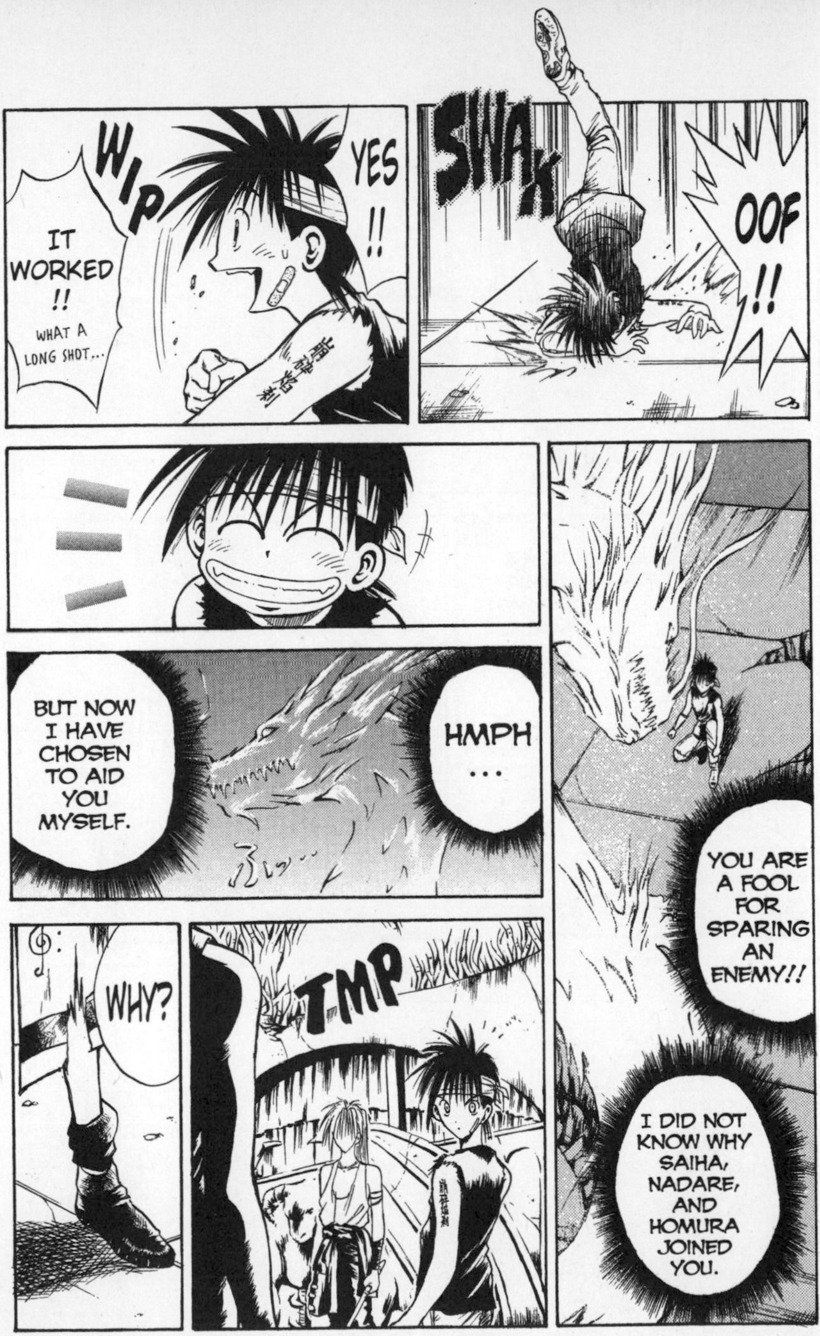
SWAK
OOF!!
WIP
YES!!
IT WORKED!!
WHAT A LONG SHOT...
YOU ARE A FOOL FOR SPARING AN ENEMY!!
I DID NOT KNOW WHY SAIHA, NADARE, AND HOMURA JOINED YOU.
HMPH...
BUT NOW I HAVE CHOSEN TO AID YOU MYSELF.
TMP
WHY?

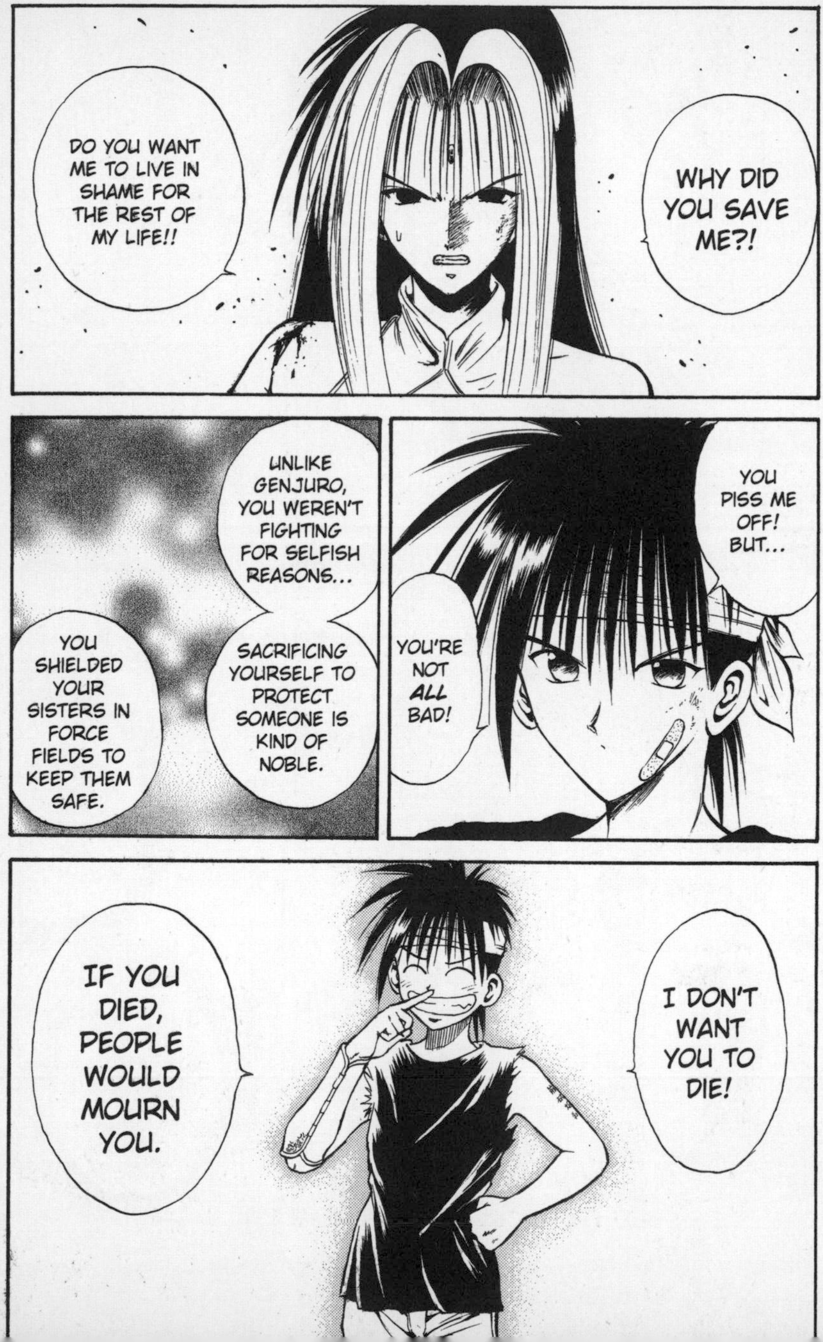
WHY DID YOU SAVE ME?!
DO YOU WANT ME TO LIVE IN SHAME FOR THE REST OF MY LIFE!!
YOU PISS ME OFF! BUT...
YOU'RE NOT ALL BAD!
UNLIKE GENJURO, YOU WEREN'T FIGHTING FOR SELFISH REASONS...
SACRIFICING YOURSELF TO PROTECT SOMEONE IS KIND OF NOBLE.
YOU SHIELDED YOUR SISTERS IN FORCE FIELDS TO KEEP THEM SAFE.
I DON'T WANT YOU TO DIE!
IF YOU DIED, PEOPLE WOULD MOURN YOU.

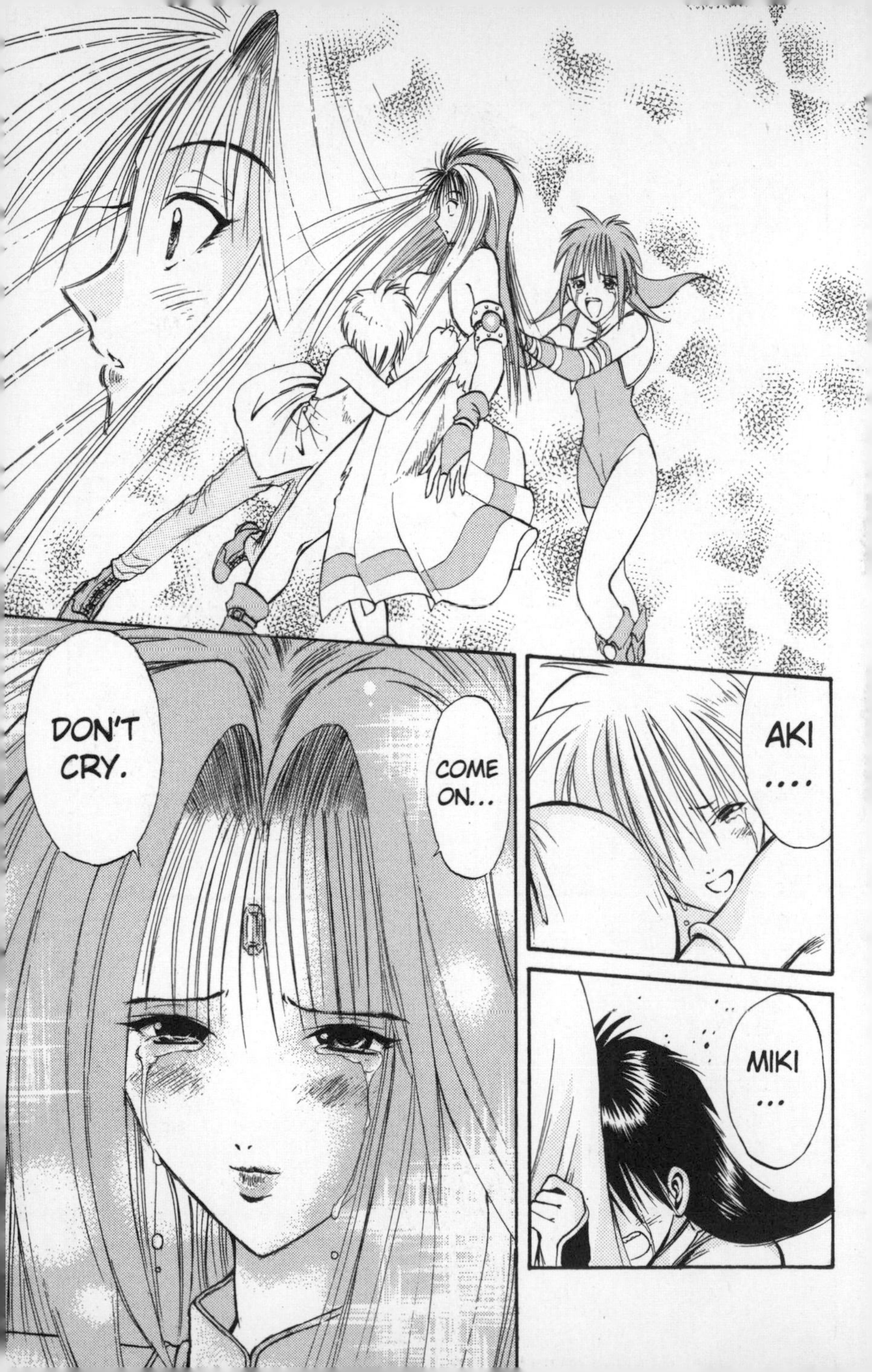
AKI ....
MIKI ...
COME ON...
DON'T CRY.

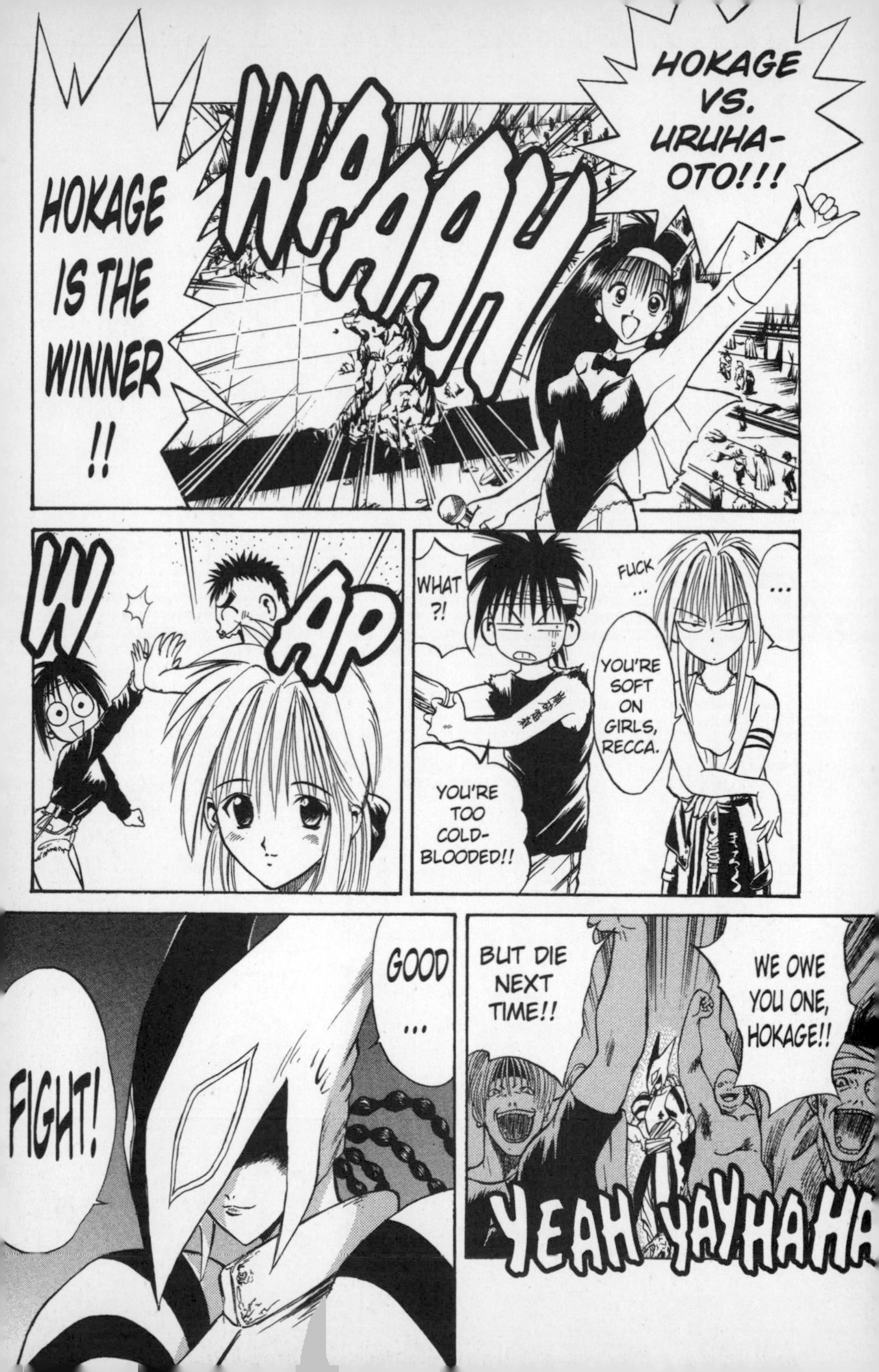
HOKAGE VS. URUHA-OTO!!!
WAAAH
HOKAGE IS THE WINNER !!
...
FUCK ...
WHAT ?!
YOU'RE SOFT ON GIRLS, RECCA.
YOU'RE TOO COLD-BLOODED!!
W AP
WE OWE YOU ONE, HOKAGE!!
BUT DIE NEXT TIME!!
YEAH YAYHAHA
GOOD ...
FIGHT!

Part Seventy-Seven: Beautiful Monster..Deadly Talk

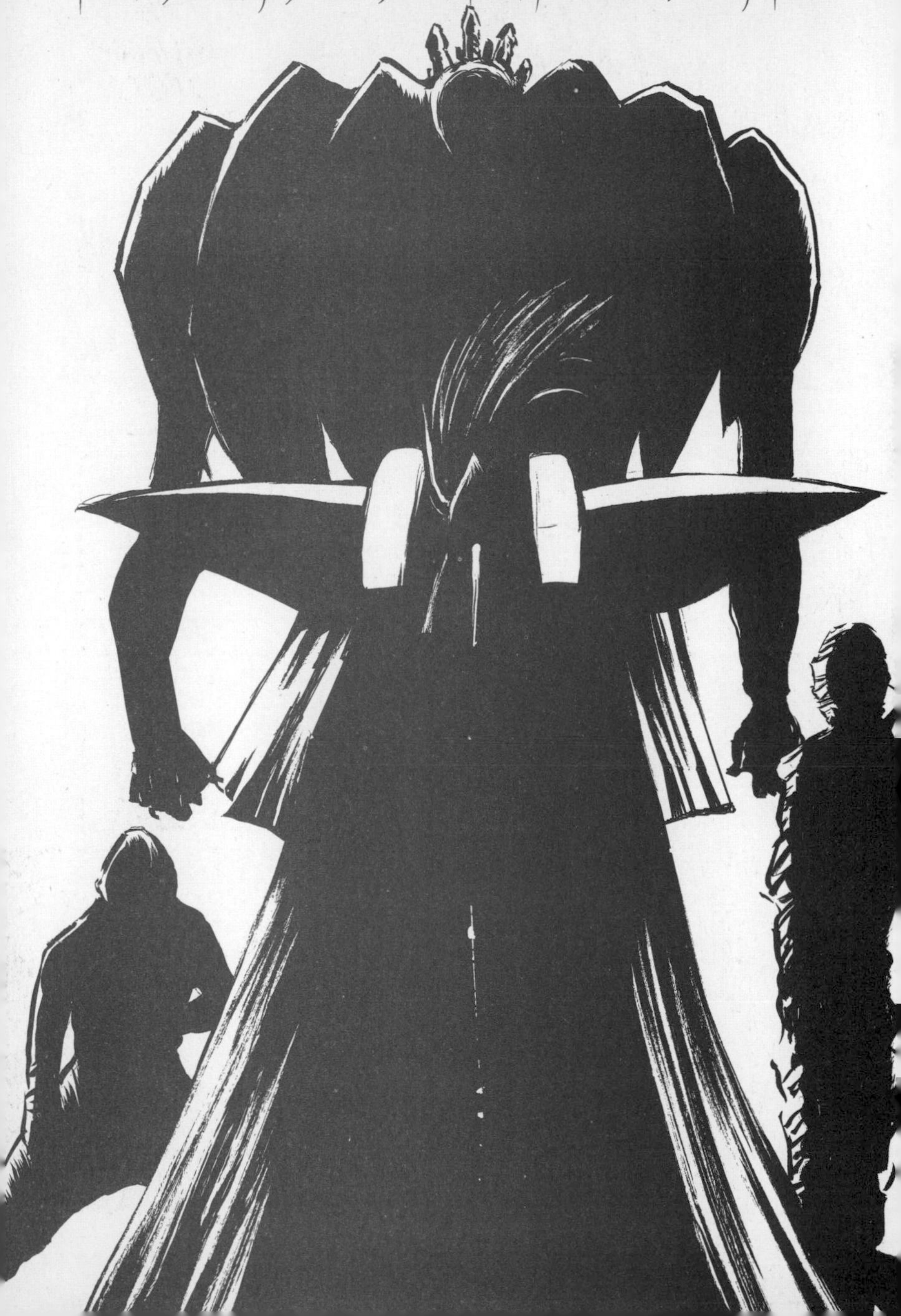

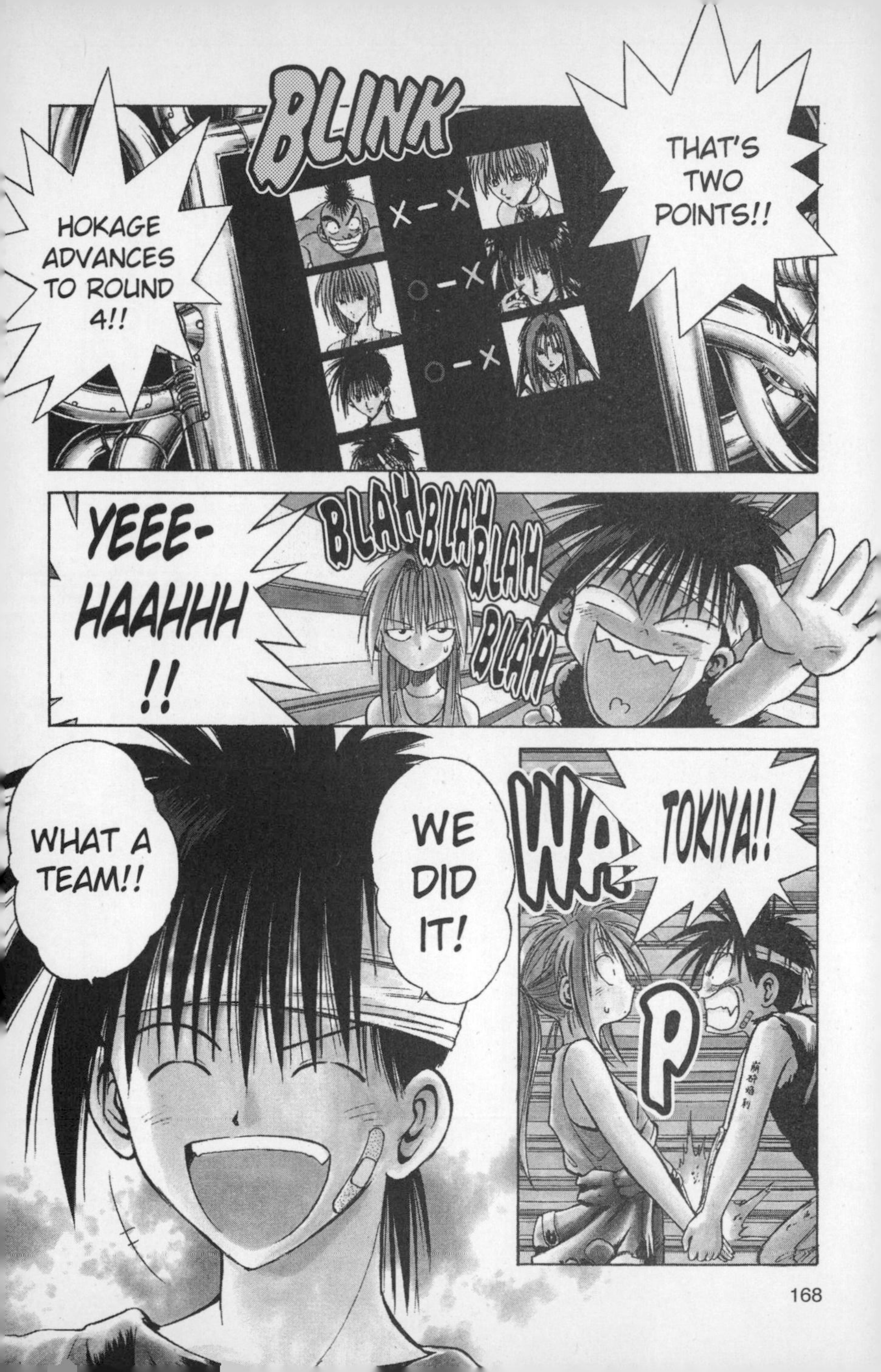
THAT'S TWO POINTS!!
BLINK
HOKAGE ADVANCES TO ROUND 4!!
BLAH BLAH BLAH BLAH
YEEE-HAAHHH!!
TOKIYA!!
WAP
WE DID IT!
WHAT A TEAM!!

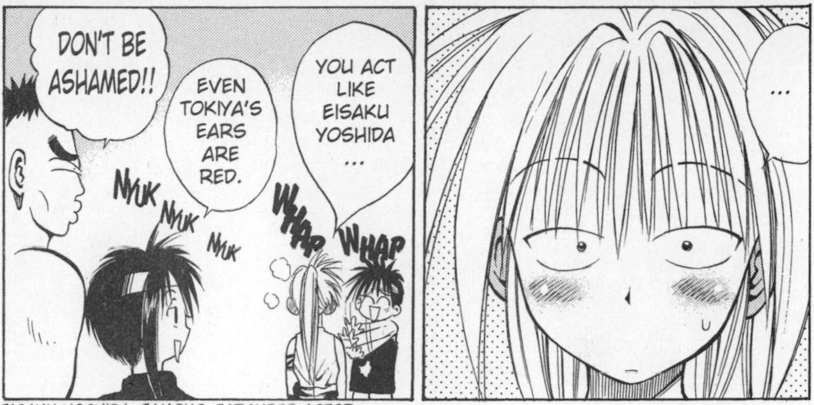
...
YOU ACT LIKE EISAKU YOSHIDA ...
WHAP
WHAP
EVEN TOKIYA'S EARS ARE RED.
NYUK NYUK NYUK
DON'T BE ASHAMED!!

EISAKU YOSHIDA: FAMOUS JAPANESE ACTOR

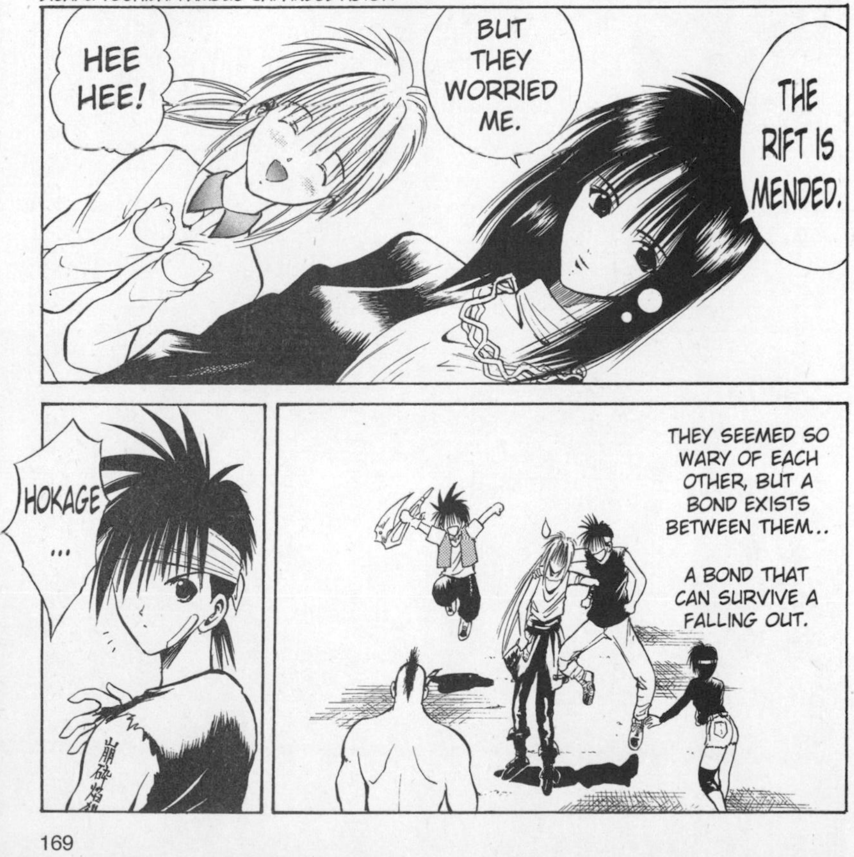
THE RIFT IS MENDED.
BUT THEY WORRIED ME.
HEE HEE!
THEY SEEMED SO WARY OF EACH OTHER, BUT A BOND EXISTS BETWEEN THEM...
A BOND THAT CAN SURVIVE A FALLING OUT.
HOKAGE ...

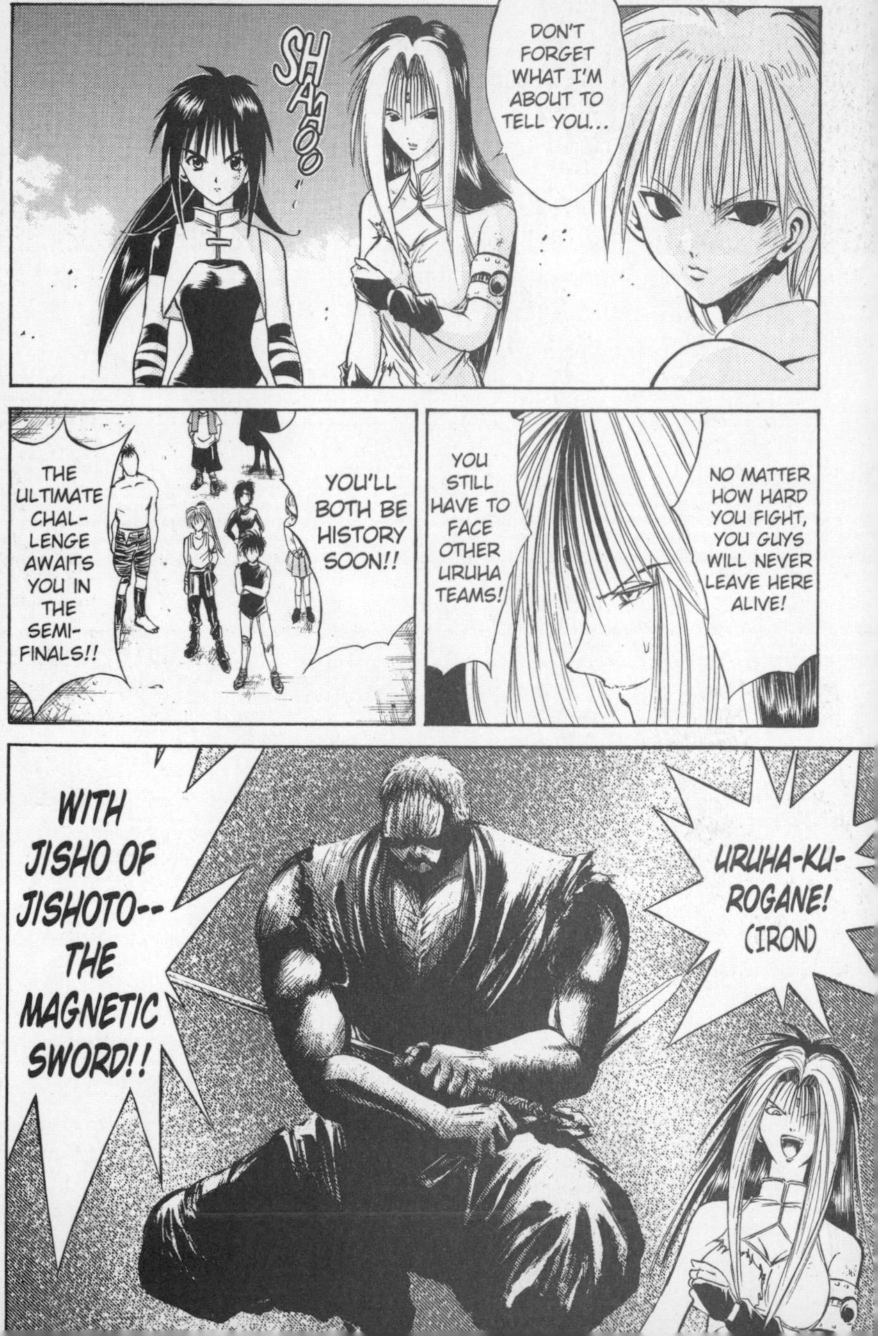
DON'T FORGET WHAT I'M ABOUT TO TELL YOU...
SHAAOO
NO MATTER HOW HARD YOU FIGHT, YOU GUYS WILL NEVER LEAVE HERE ALIVE!
YOU STILL HAVE TO FACE OTHER URUHA TEAMS!
YOU'LL BOTH BE HISTORY SOON!!
THE ULTIMATE CHAL-LENGE AWAITS YOU IN THE SEMI-FINALS!!
URUHA-KU-ROGANE! (IRON)
WITH JISHO OF JISHOTO-- THE MAGNETIC SWORD!!

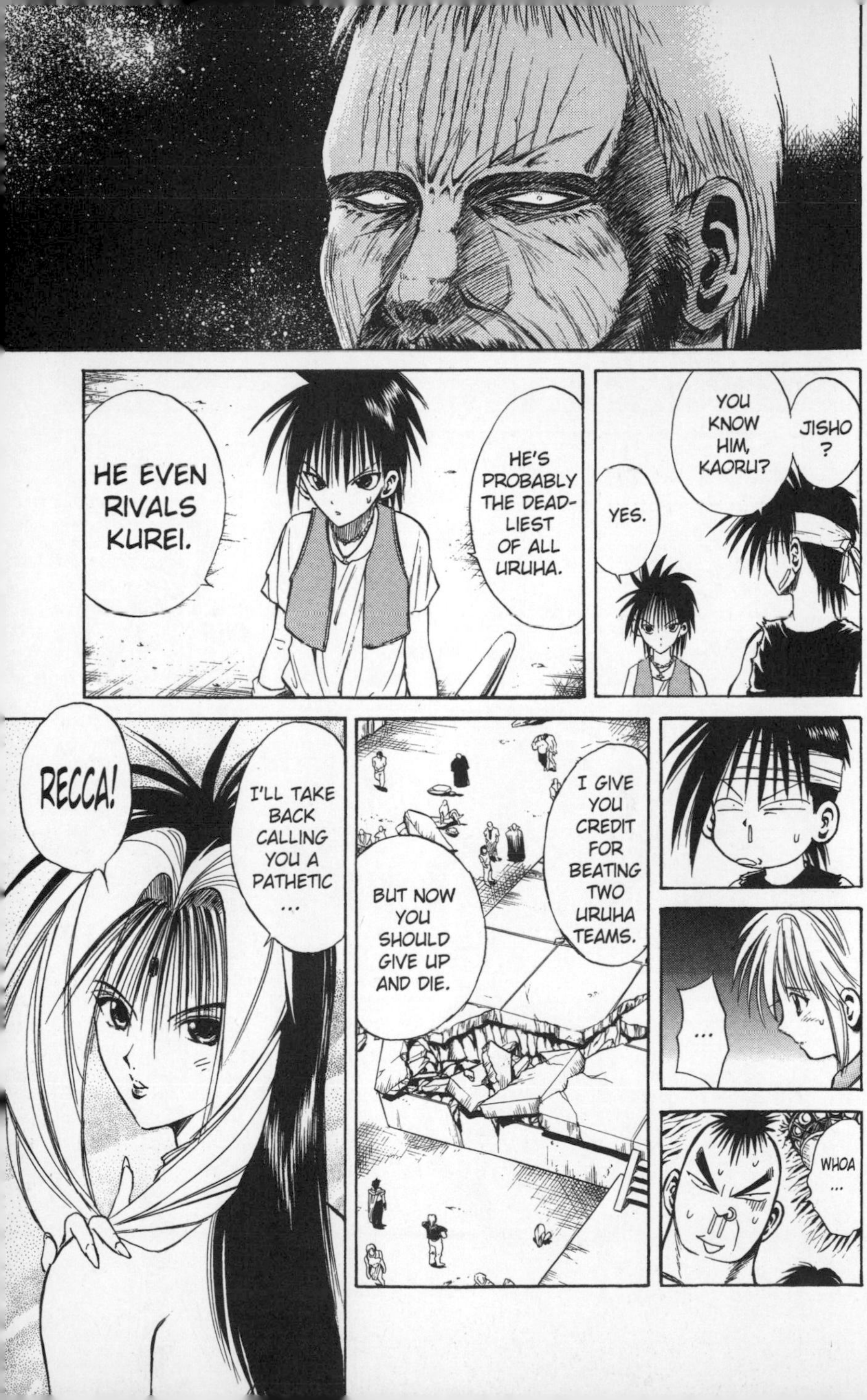
JISHO ?
YOU KNOW HIM, KAORU?
YES.
HE'S PROBABLY THE DEAD-LIEST OF ALL URUHA.
HE EVEN RIVALS KUREI.
...
WHOA ...
I GIVE YOU CREDIT FOR BEATING TWO URUHA TEAMS.
BUT NOW YOU SHOULD GIVE UP AND DIE.
I'LL TAKE BACK CALLING YOU A PATHETIC ...
RECCA!

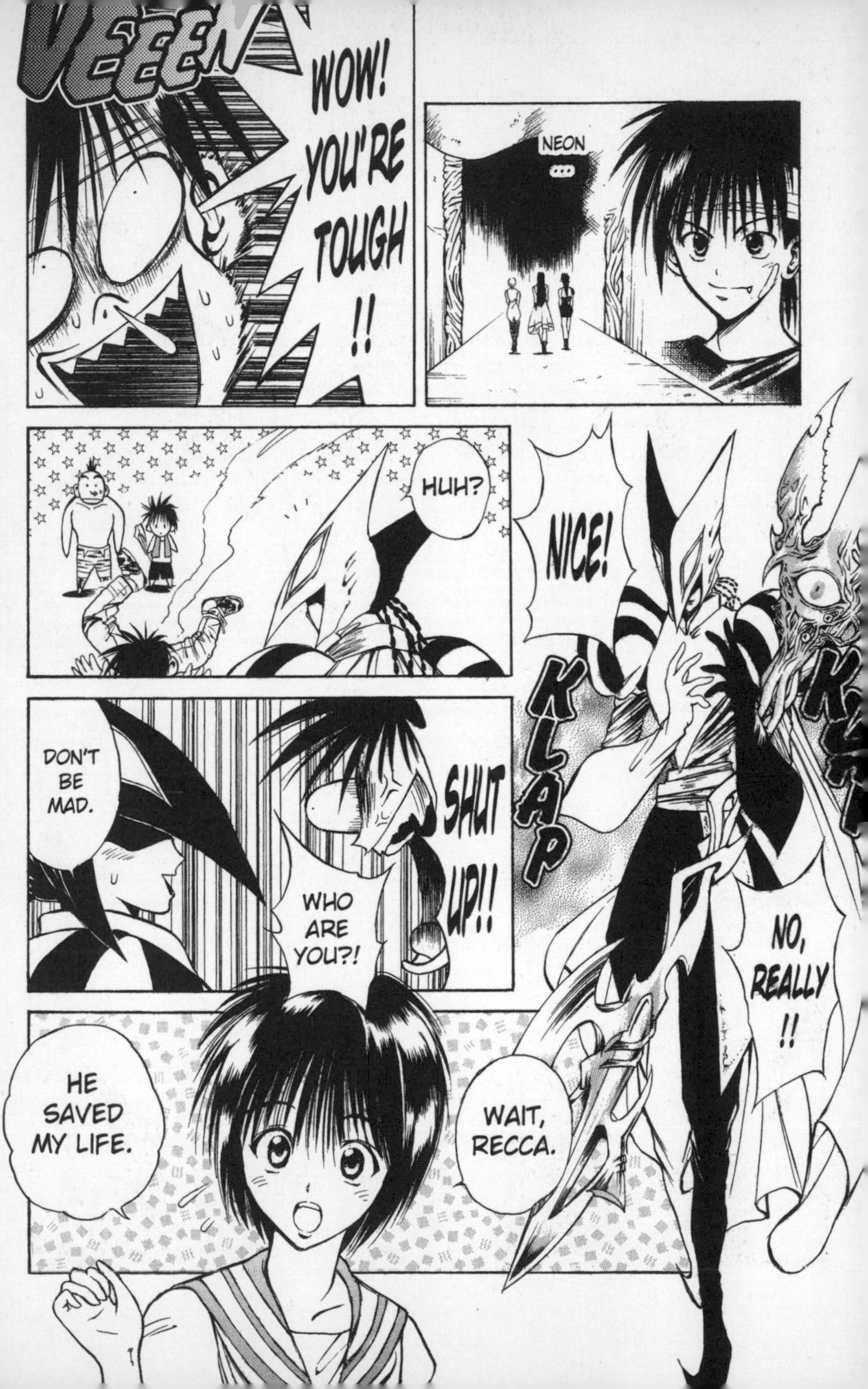
NEON
...
VEEEN
WOW! YOU'RE TOUGH!!
NICE!
KLAP
NO, REALLY!!
HUH?
SHUT UP!!
WHO ARE YOU?!
DON'T BE MAD.
WAIT, RECCA.
HE SAVED MY LIFE.

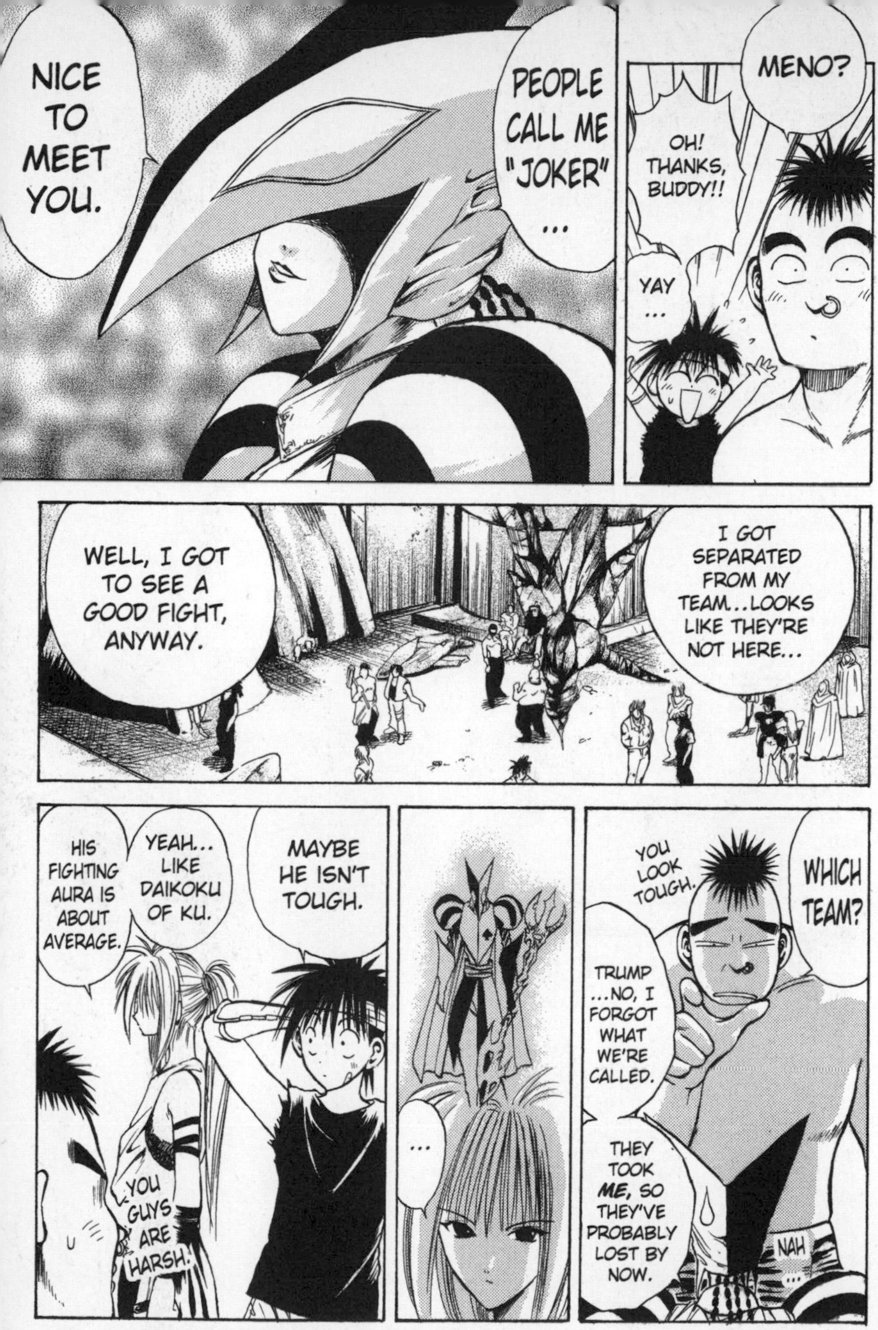
MENO?
OH! THANKS, BUDDY!!
YAY ...
PEOPLE CALL ME "JOKER" ...
NICE TO MEET YOU.
I GOT SEPARATED FROM MY TEAM...LOOKS LIKE THEY'RE NOT HERE...
WELL, I GOT TO SEE A GOOD FIGHT, ANYWAY.
WHICH TEAM?
YOU LOOK TOUGH.
TRUMP ...NO, I FORGOT WHAT WE'RE CALLED.
THEY TOOK *ME*, SO THEY'VE PROBABLY LOST BY NOW.
NAH ...
...
MAYBE HE ISN'T TOUGH.
YEAH... LIKE DAIKOKU OF KU.
HIS FIGHTING AURA IS ABOUT AVERAGE.
YOU GUYS ARE HARSH!

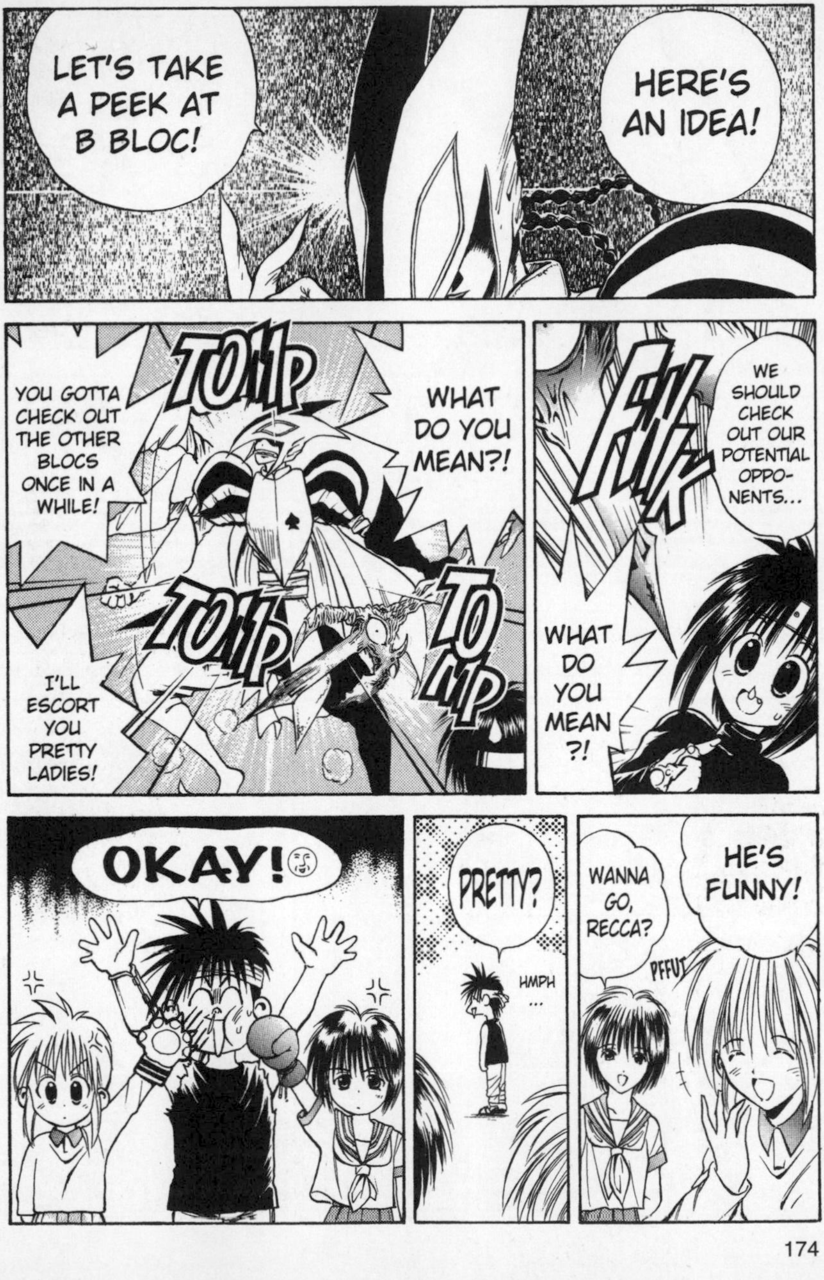
HERE'S AN IDEA!
LET'S TAKE A PEEK AT B BLOC!
WE SHOULD CHECK OUT OUR POTENTIAL OPPO-NENTS...
FLIK
WHAT DO YOU MEAN ?!
WHAT DO YOU MEAN?!
TOMP
YOU GOTTA CHECK OUT THE OTHER BLOCS ONCE IN A WHILE!
TOMP
TOMP
I'LL ESCORT YOU PRETTY LADIES!
HE'S FUNNY!
WANNA GO, RECCA?
PRETTY?
HMPH ...
OKAY!

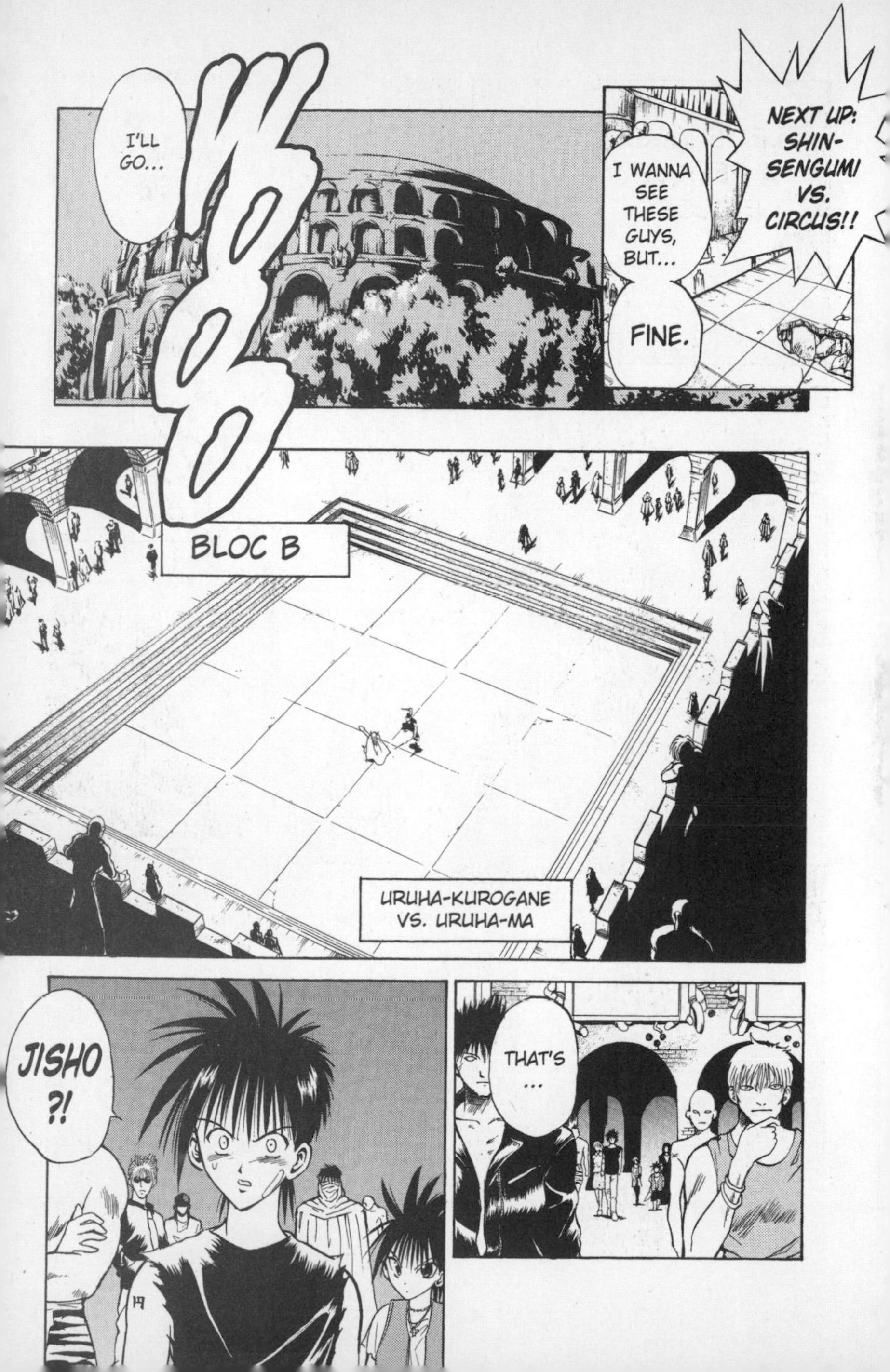
NEXT UP: SHIN-SENGUMI VS. CIRCUS!!
I WANNA SEE THESE GUYS, BUT...
FINE.
I'LL GO...
BLOC B
URUHA-KUROGANE VS. URUHA-MA
THAT'S ...
JISHO ?!

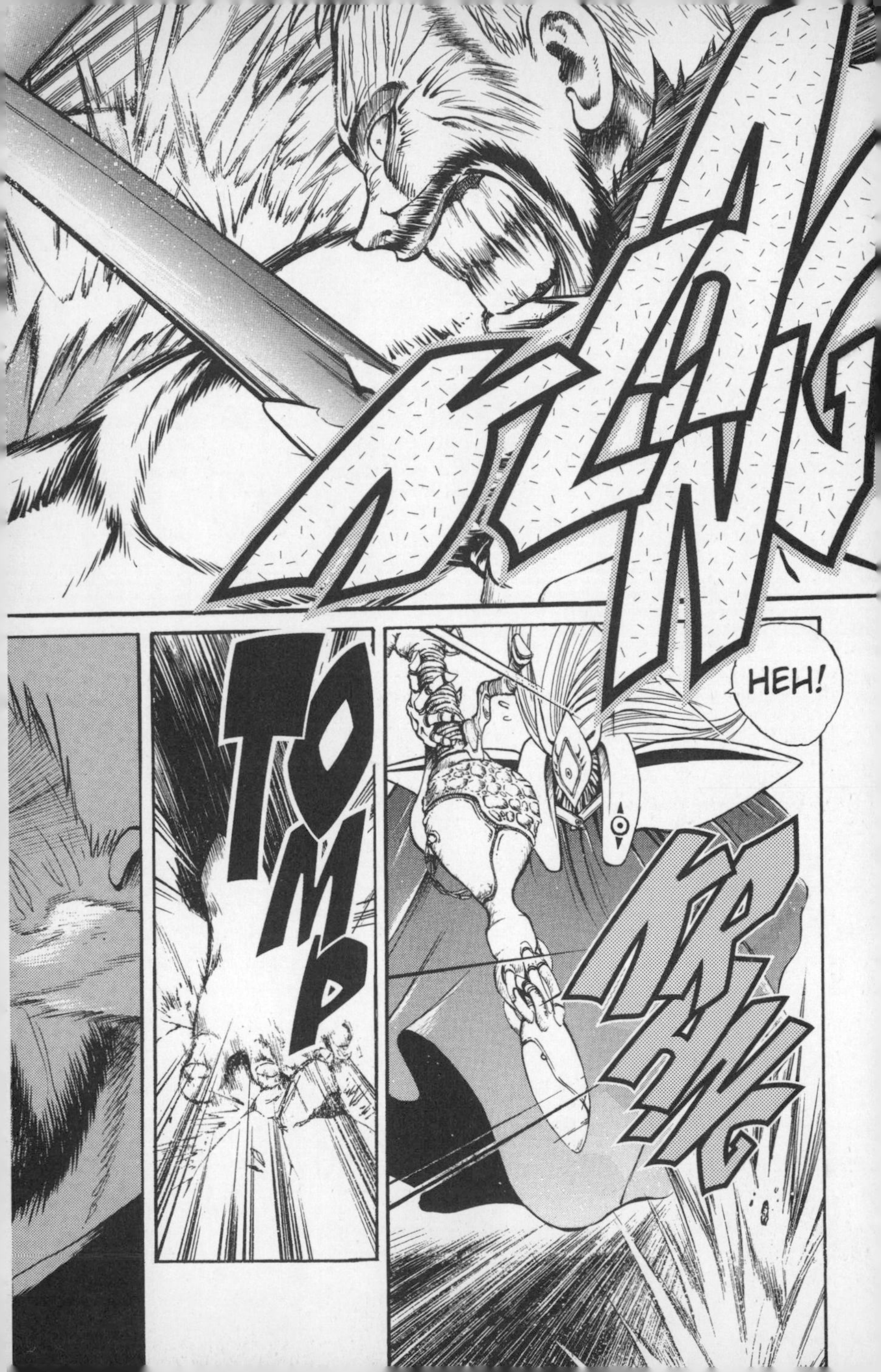
CLANG
HEH!
KRANG
TOMP

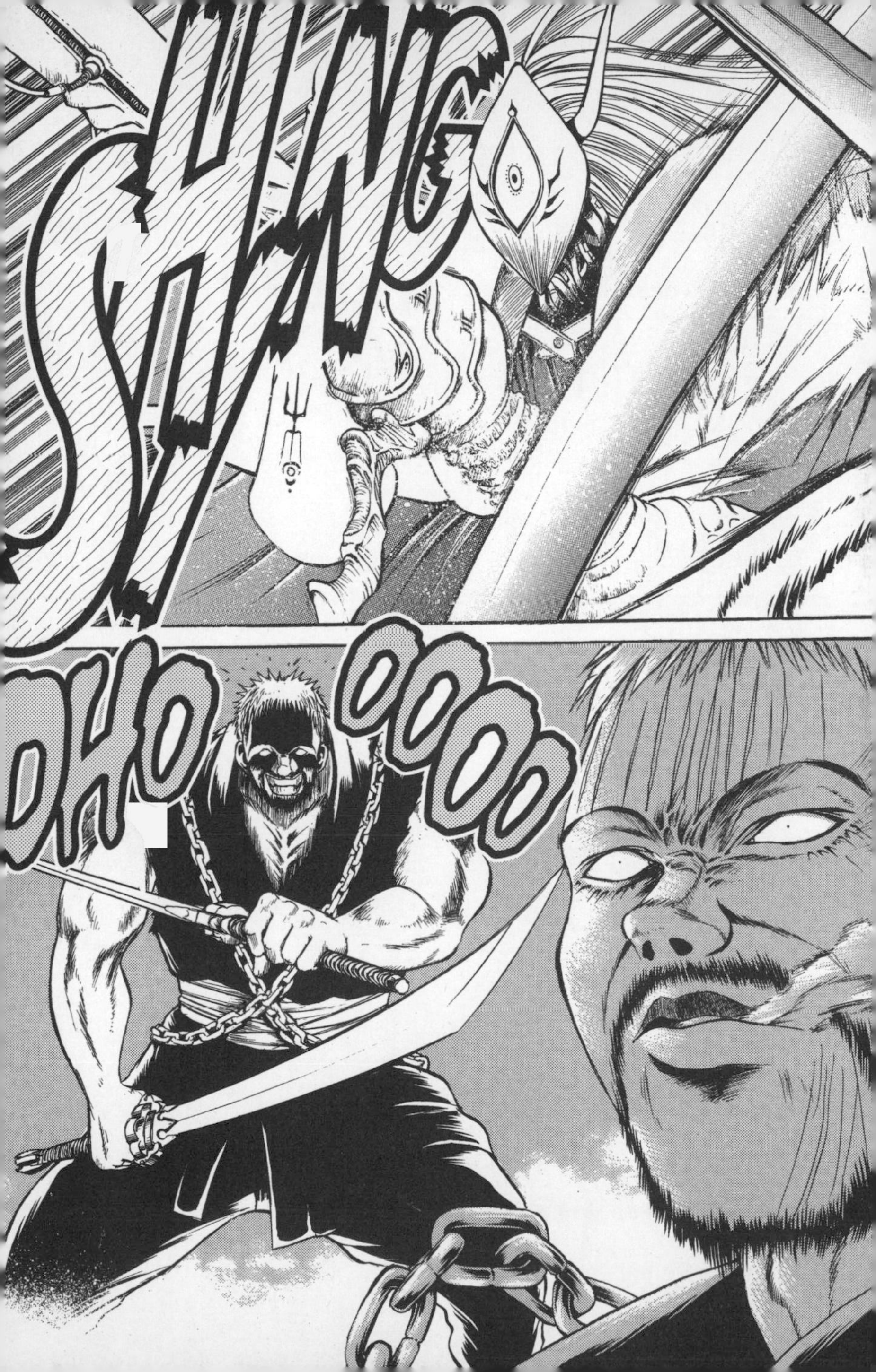
SHING
OHOOOOO

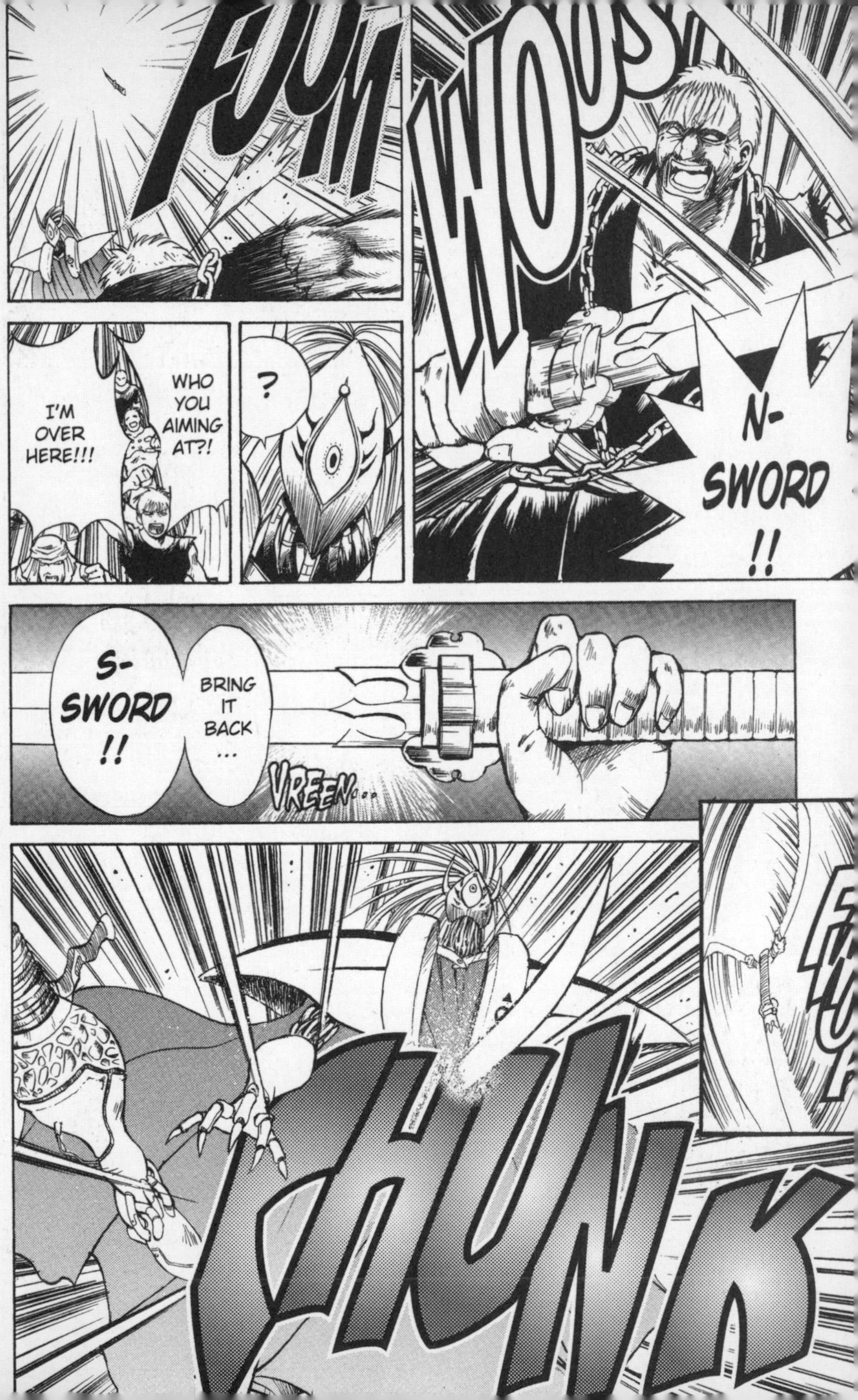
WHOOS
FOOM
N- SWORD !!
?
WHO YOU AIMING AT?!
I'M OVER HERE!!!
BRING IT BACK ...
S- SWORD !!
VREEN...
CHUNK

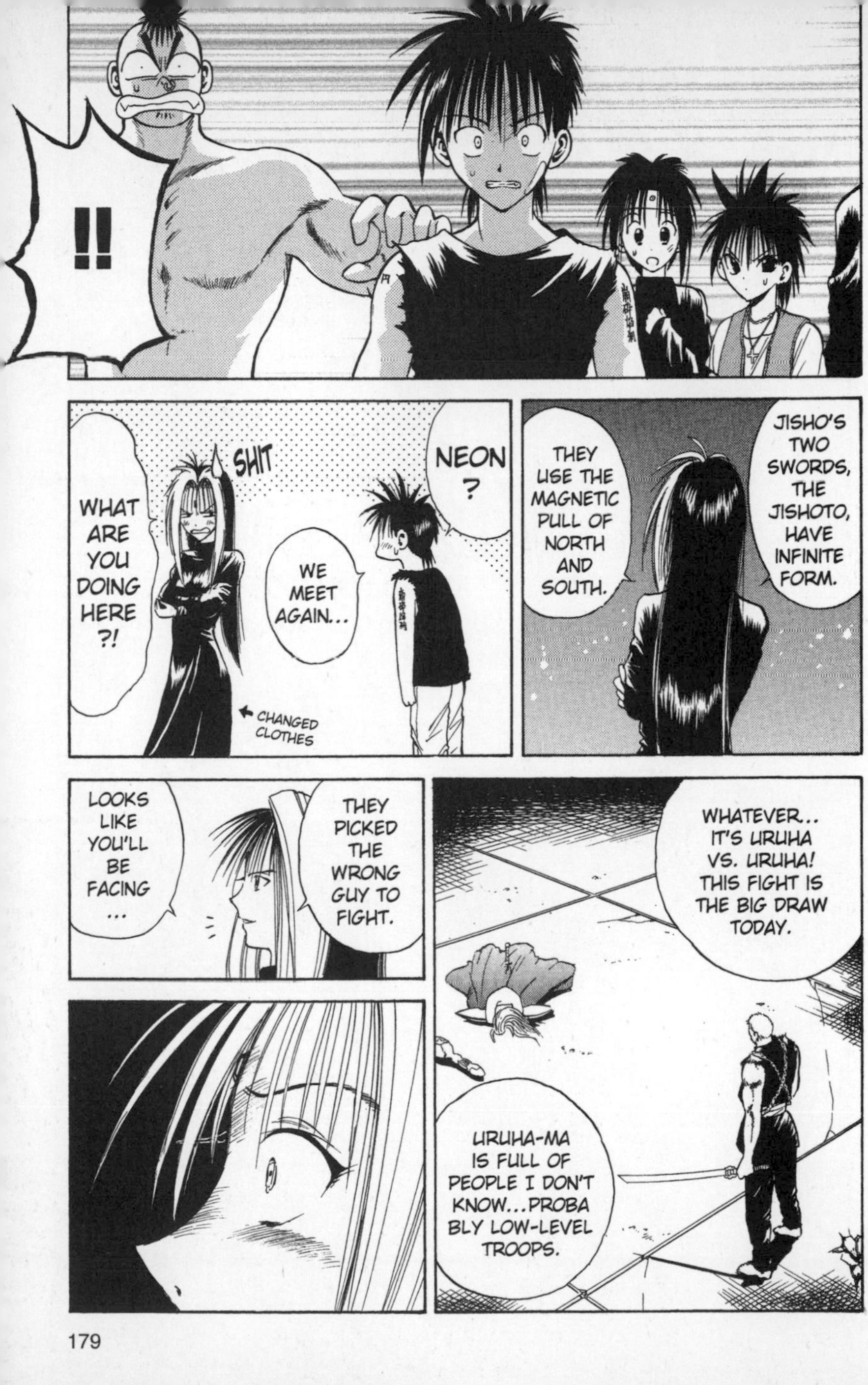
!!
JISHO'S TWO SWORDS, THE JISHOTO, HAVE INFINITE FORM.
THEY USE THE MAGNETIC PULL OF NORTH AND SOUTH.
NEON ?
SHIT
WE MEET AGAIN...
WHAT ARE YOU DOING HERE ?!
CHANGED CLOTHES
WHATEVER.. IT'S URUHA VS. URUHA! THIS FIGHT IS THE BIG DRAW TODAY.
URUHA-MA IS FULL OF PEOPLE I DON'T KNOW...PROBA BLY LOW-LEVEL TROOPS.
THEY PICKED THE WRONG GUY TO FIGHT.
LOOKS LIKE YOU'LL BE FACING ...

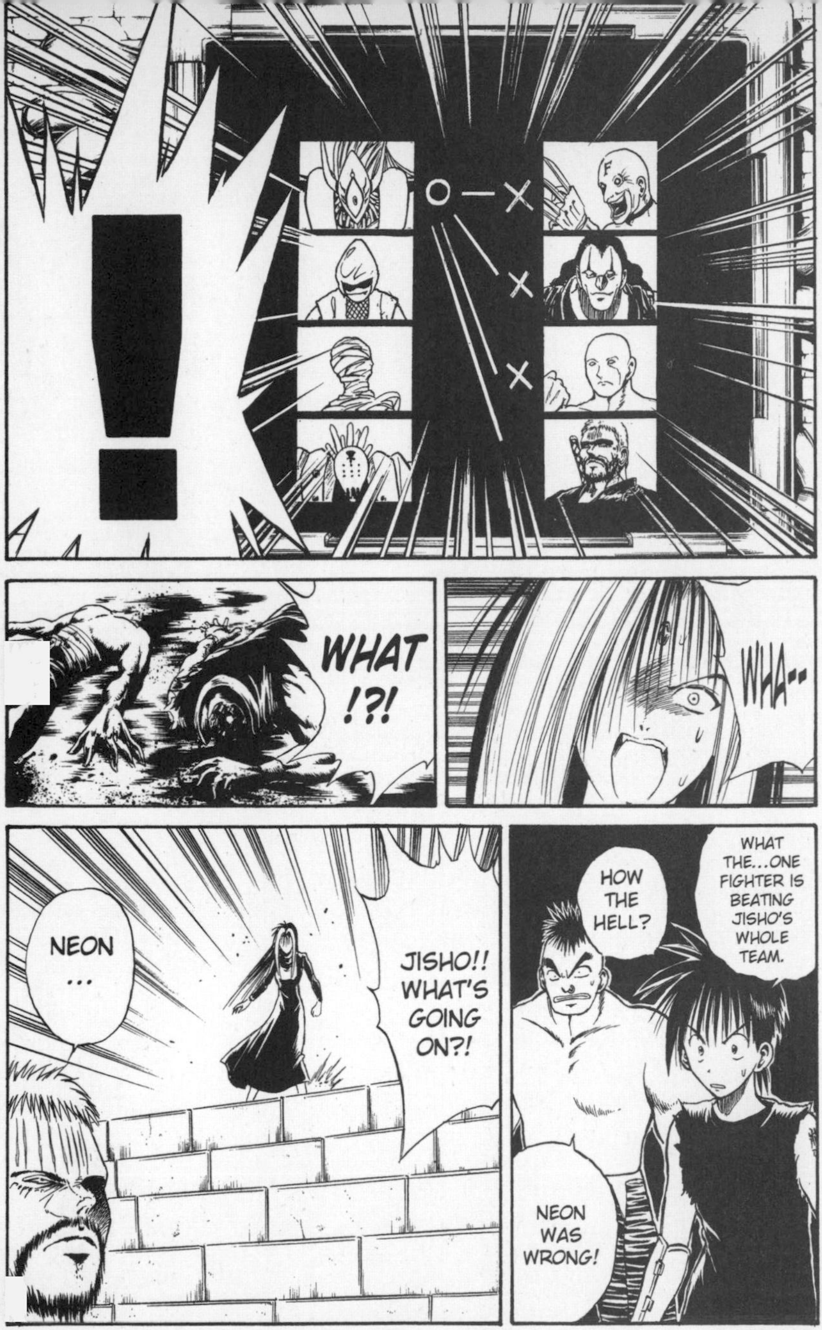
!
WHA--
WHAT !?!
WHAT THE...ONE FIGHTER IS BEATING JISHO'S WHOLE TEAM.
HOW THE HELL?
NEON WAS WRONG!
JISHO!! WHAT'S GOING ON?!
NEON ...

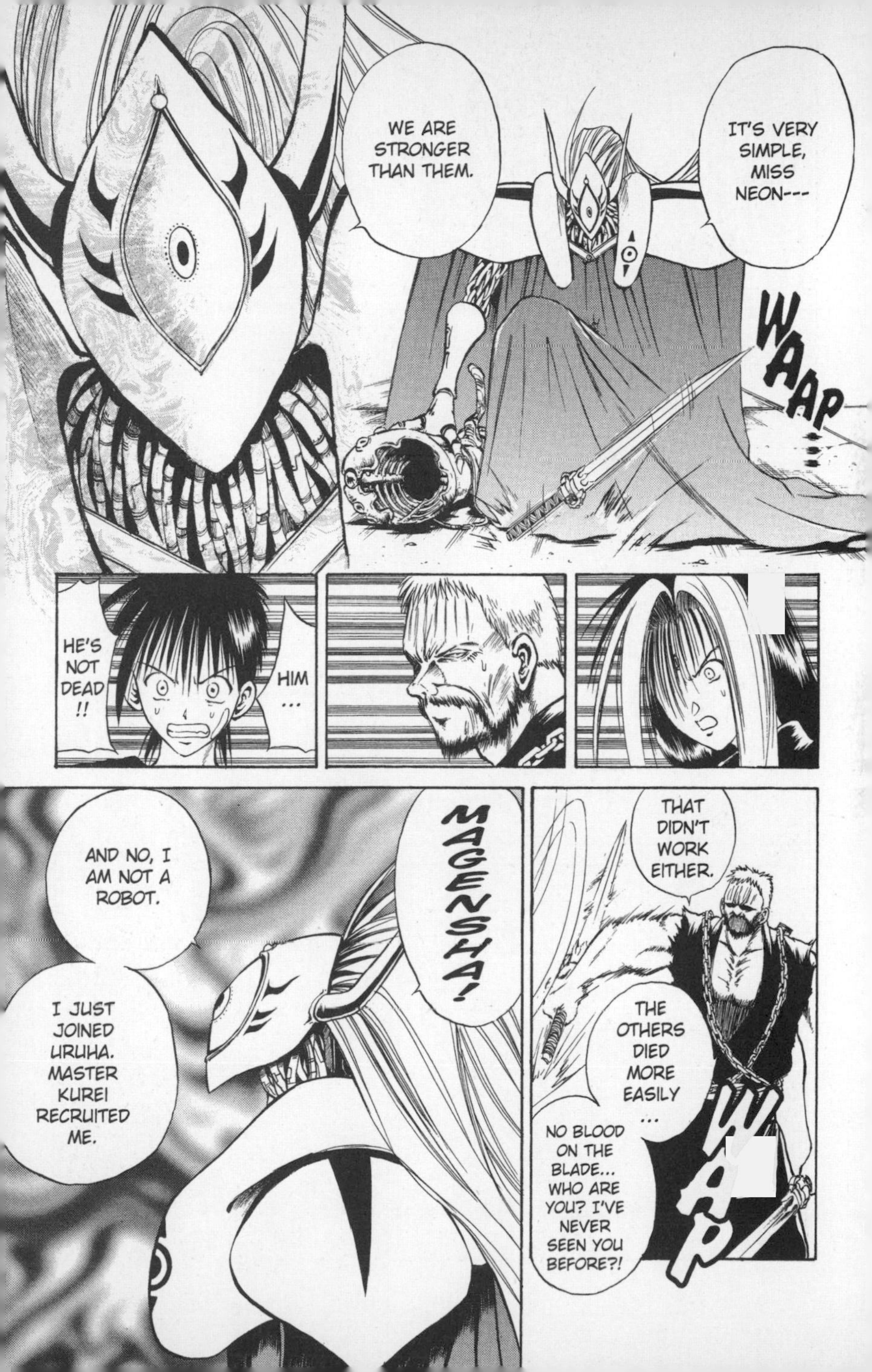
IT'S VERY SIMPLE, MISS NEON---
WE ARE STRONGER THAN THEM.
WAAP
HIM ...
HE'S NOT DEAD !!
THAT DIDN'T WORK EITHER.
THE OTHERS DIED MORE EASILY ...
WAP
NO BLOOD ON THE BLADE... WHO ARE YOU? I'VE NEVER SEEN YOU BEFORE?!
MAGENSHA!
AND NO, I AM NOT A ROBOT.
I JUST JOINED URUHA. MASTER KUREI RECRUITED ME.

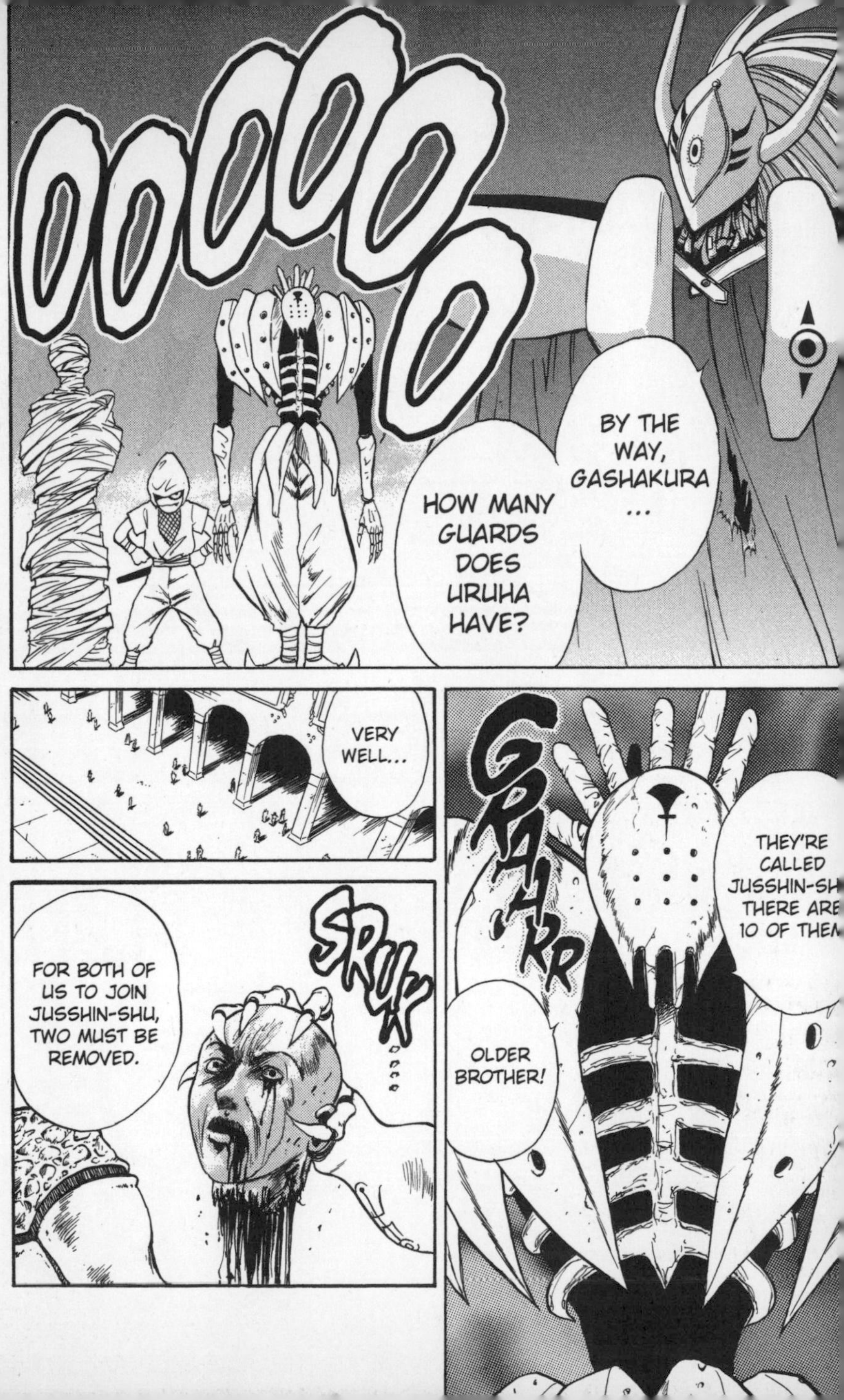
OOOOOOOO
BY THE WAY, GASHAKURA ...
HOW MANY GUARDS DOES URUHA HAVE?
GRAHRR
THEY'RE CALLED JUSSHIN-SH THERE ARE 10 OF THEM
OLDER BROTHER!
VERY WELL...
SRUK
FOR BOTH OF US TO JOIN JUSSHIN-SHU, TWO MUST BE REMOVED.

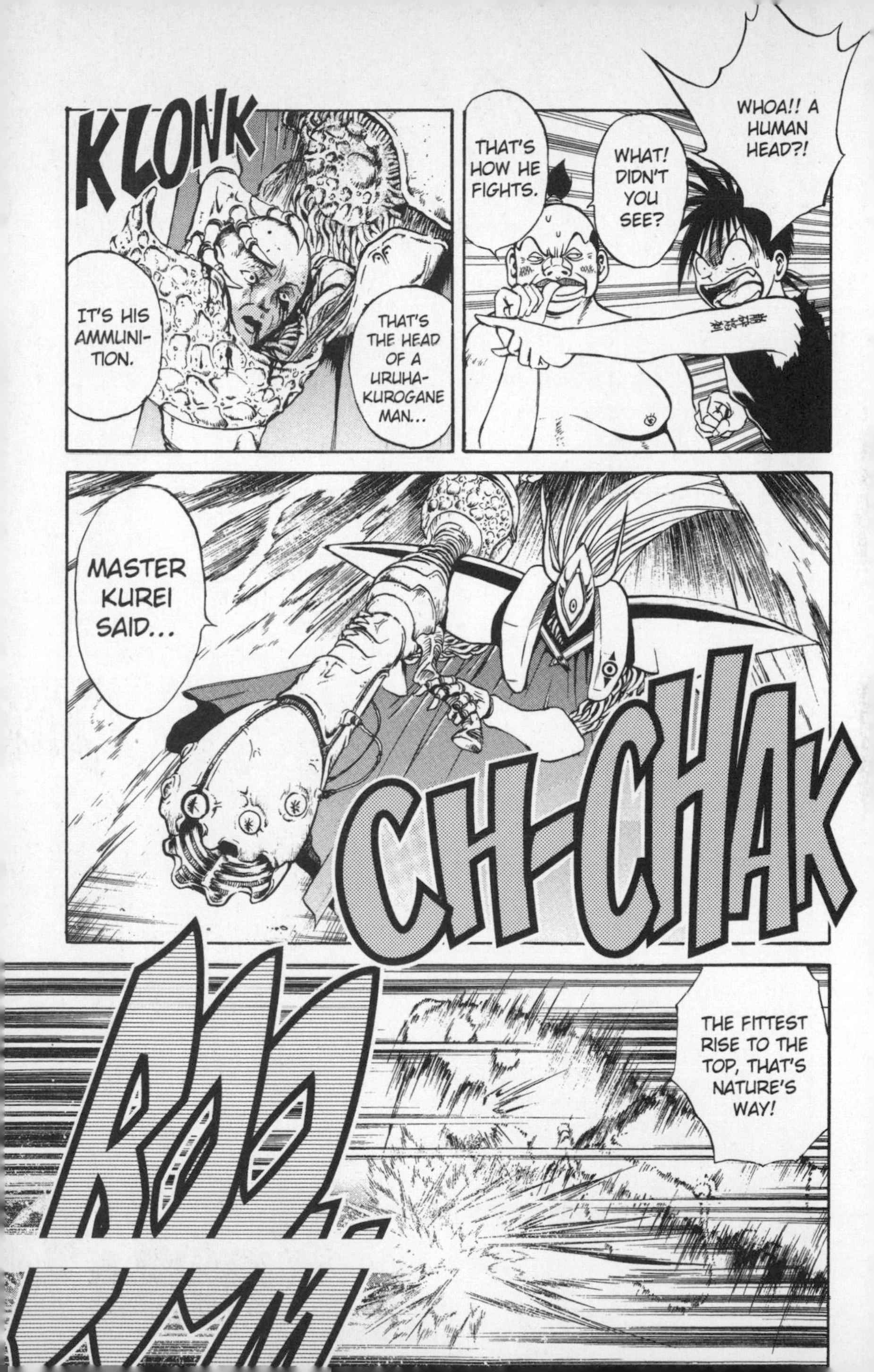
WHOA!! A HUMAN HEAD?!
WHAT! DIDN'T YOU SEE?
THAT'S HOW HE FIGHTS.
KLONK
THAT'S THE HEAD OF A URUHA-KUROGANE MAN...
IT'S HIS AMMUNITION.
MASTER KUREI SAID...
CH-CHAK
THE FITTEST RISE TO THE TOP, THAT'S NATURE'S WAY!

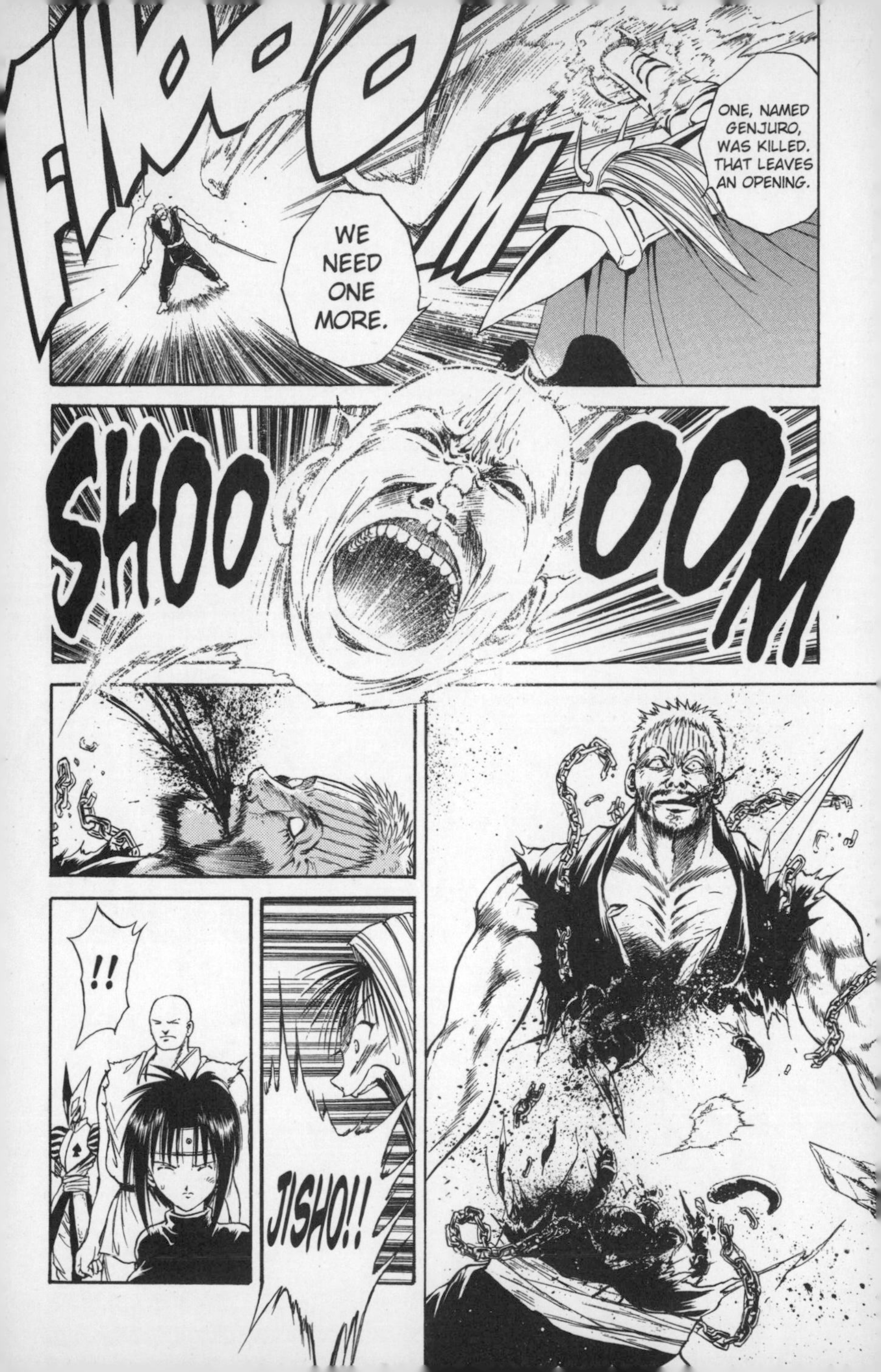
ONE, NAMED GENJURO, WAS KILLED. THAT LEAVES AN OPENING.
WE NEED ONE MORE.
FWOOOOM
SHOO
OOM
JISHO!!
!!

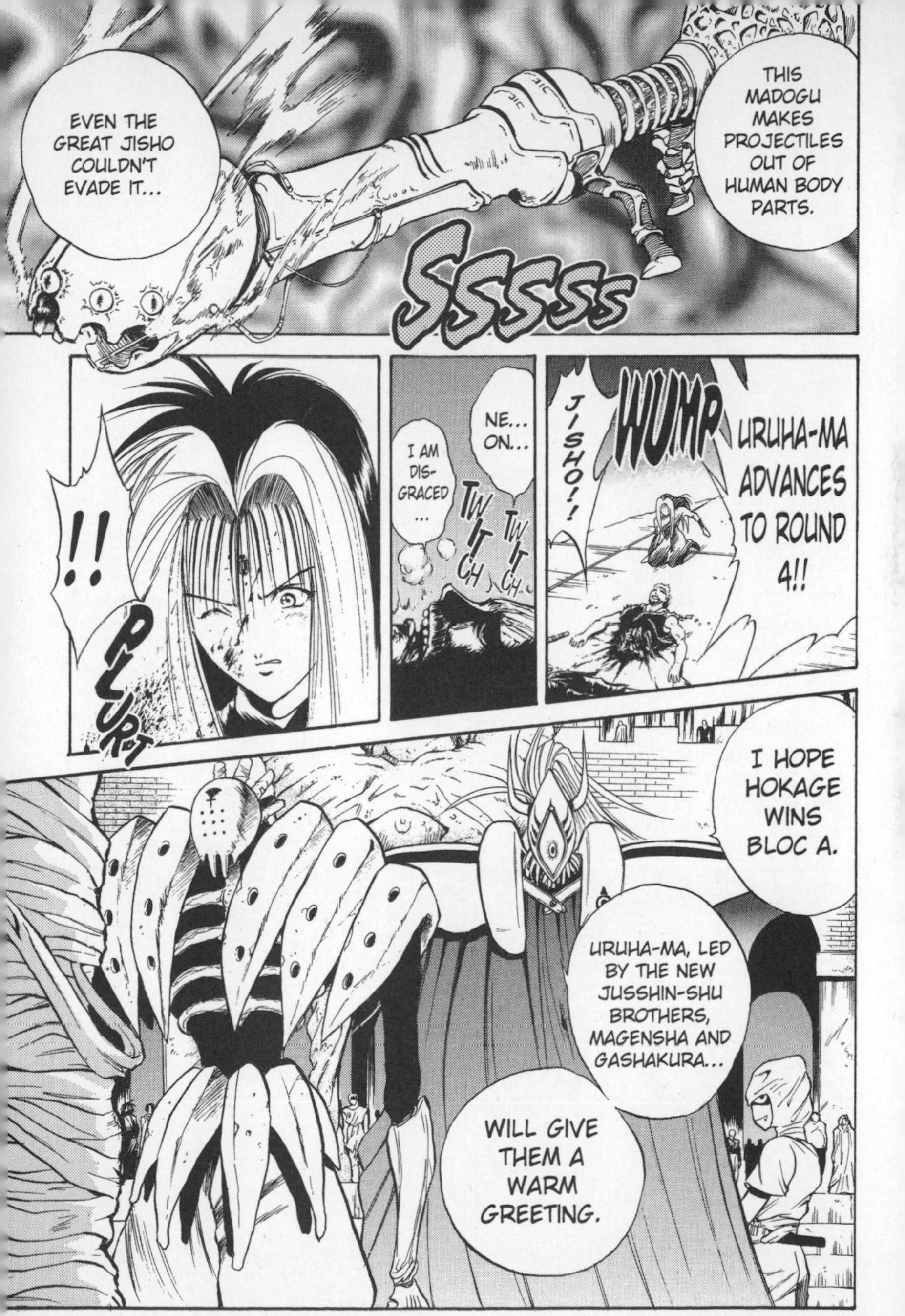
THIS MADOGU MAKES PROJECTILES OUT OF HUMAN BODY PARTS.
EVEN THE GREAT JISHO COULDN'T EVADE IT...
SSSSS
URUHA-MA ADVANCES TO ROUND 4!!
WUMP
JISHO!!
NE... ON...
TWITCH
I AM DIS-GRACED...
TWITCH
!!
PLURT
I HOPE HOKAGE WINS BLOC A.
URUHA-MA, LED BY THE NEW JUSSHIN-SHU BROTHERS, MAGENSHA AND GASHAKURA...
WILL GIVE THEM A WARM GREETING.

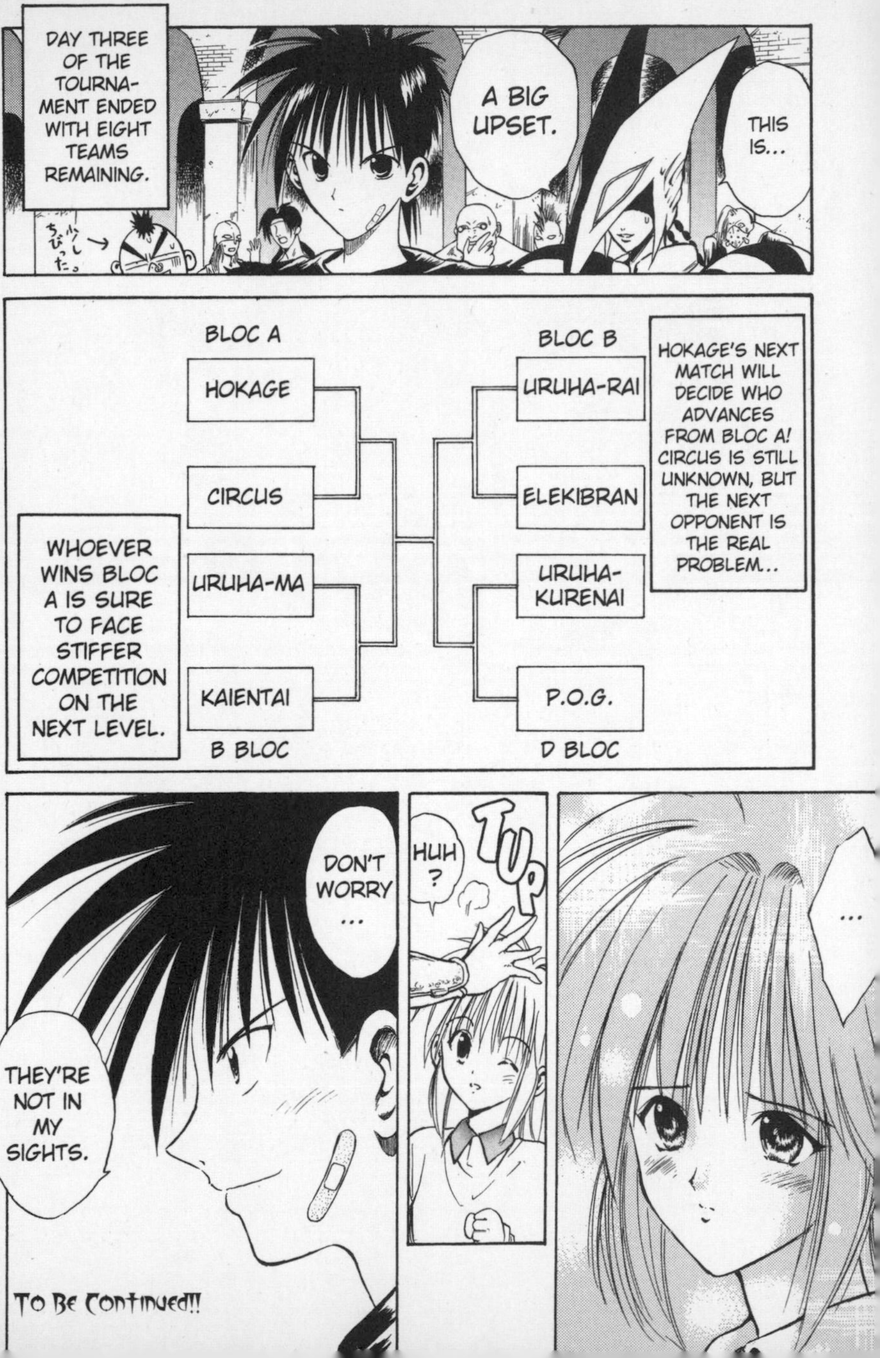
THIS IS...
A BIG UPSET.
DAY THREE OF THE TOURNAMENT ENDED WITH EIGHT TEAMS REMAINING.
少しちびった。
HOKAGE'S NEXT MATCH WILL DECIDE WHO ADVANCES FROM BLOC A! CIRCUS IS STILL UNKNOWN, BUT THE NEXT OPPONENT IS THE REAL PROBLEM...
BLOC B
URUHA-RAI
ELEKIBRAN
URUHA-KURENAI
P.O.G.
D BLOC
BLOC A
HOKAGE
CIRCUS
URUHA-MA
KAIENTAI
B BLOC
WHOEVER WINS BLOC A IS SURE TO FACE STIFFER COMPETITION ON THE NEXT LEVEL.
...
TUP
HUH?
DON'T WORRY...
THEY'RE NOT IN MY SIGHTS.
To Be Continued!!

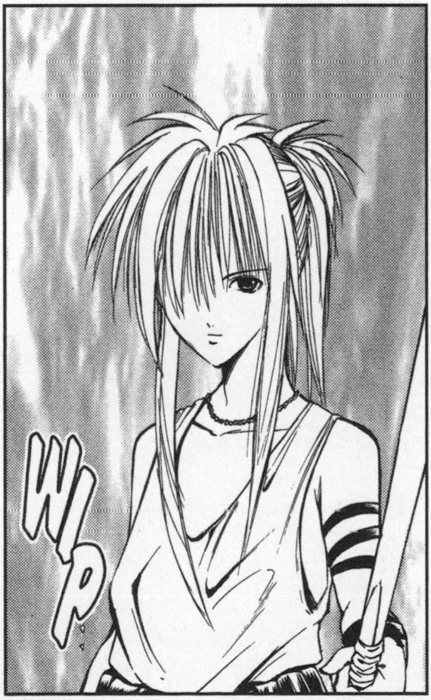
WIP

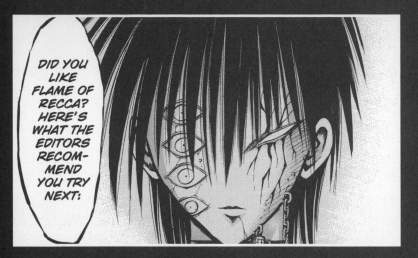

DID YOU LIKE FLAME OF RECCA? HERE'S WHAT THE EDITORS RECOMMEND YOU TRY NEXT:

Editor's Recommendations

© 1998, 1999, 2001, 2003 I.T. Planning, Inc.

© 1997 Rumiko Takahashi/Shogakukan, Inc.

© 2000 Shin Takahashi/Shogakukan, Inc.

Vagabond: The continuing saga of a young samurai on a spiritual quest to become the greatest swordsman of Japan. Easily, one of the most beautiful illustrated comics in the world.

InuYasha: Historical action with a dash of romance. A teenage girl and her friends fight off demons in their search for the shards of the powerful Shikon Jewel.

Saikano: What do you do if the girl you love turns out to be a weapon of mass destruction? Love was never this complicated.

COMPLETE OUR SURVEY AND LET US KNOW WHAT YOU THINK!

☐ Please do NOT send me information about VIZ products, news and events, special offers, or other information.

☐ Please do NOT send me information from VIZ's trusted business partners.

Name: _____

Address: _____

City: _____ **State:** _____ **Zip:** _____

E-mail: _____

☐ Male ☐ Female   Date of Birth (mm/dd/yyyy): ____ / ____ / ____   (Under 13? Parental consent required)

What race/ethnicity do you consider yourself? (please check one)

☐ Asian/Pacific Islander   ☐ Black/African American   ☐ Hispanic/Latino

☐ Native American/Alaskan Native ☐ White/Caucasian   ☐ Other: _____

What VIZ product did you purchase? (check all that apply and indicate title purchased)

☐ DVD/VHS _____

☐ Graphic Novel _____

☐ Magazines _____

☐ Merchandise _____

Reason for purchase: (check all that apply)

☐ Special offer   ☐ Favorite title   ☐ Gift

☐ Recommendation   ☐ Other _____

Where did you make your purchase? (please check one)

☐ Comic store   ☐ Bookstore   ☐ Mass/Grocery Store

☐ Newsstand   ☐ Video/Video Game Store ☐ Other: _____

☐ Online (site: _____)

What other VIZ properties have you purchased/own? _____

_____

How many anime and/or manga titles have you purchased in the last year? How many were VIZ titles? (please check one from each column)

ANIME	MANGA	VIZ
☐ None	☐ None	☐ None
☐ 1-4	☐ 1-4	☐ 1-4
☐ 5-10	☐ 5-10	☐ 5-10
☐ 11+	☐ 11+	☐ 11+

I find the pricing of VIZ products to be: (please check one)

☐ Cheap ☐ Reasonable ☐ Expensive

What genre of manga and anime would you like to see from VIZ? (please check two)

☐ Adventure ☐ Comic Strip ☐ Science Fiction ☐ Fighting

☐ Horror ☐ Romance ☐ Fantasy ☐ Sports

What do you think of VIZ's new look?

☐ Love It ☐ It's OK ☐ Hate It ☐ Didn't Notice ☐ No Opinion

Which do you prefer? (please check one)

☐ Reading right-to-left

☐ Reading left-to-right

Which do you prefer? (please check one)

☐ Sound effects in English

☐ Sound effects in Japanese with English captions

☐ Sound effects in Japanese only with a glossary at the back

THANK YOU! Please send the completed form to:

VIZ Survey
42 Catharine St.
Poughkeepsie, NY 12601

All information provided will be used for internal purposes only. We promise not to sell or otherwise divulge your information.